W9-BWE-471

"This book synthesizes the teachings of many disciplines to illuminate the causes of major problems besetting college students and campuses, including declines in mental health, academic freedom, and collegiality. More important, the authors present evidence-based strategies for overcoming these challenges. An engrossing, thought-provoking, and ultimately inspiring read."

—**Nadine Strossen**, past president, ACLU; professor, New York Law School; and author of *HATE: Why We Should Resist It with Free Speech, Not Censorship*

"We can talk ourselves into believing that some kinds of speech will shatter us, or we can talk ourselves out of that belief. The authors know the science. We are not as fragile as our self-appointed protectors suppose. Read this deeply informed book to become a more resilient soul in a more resilient democracy."

—**Philip E. Tetlock**, professor, University of Pennsylvania, and author of *Superforecasting*

"This book is a much-needed guide for how to thrive in a pluralistic society. Lukianoff and Haidt demonstrate how ancient wisdom and modern psychology can encourage more dialogue across lines of difference, build stronger institutions, and make us happier. They provide an antidote to our seemingly intractable divisions, and not a moment too soon."

—**Kirsten Powers**, CNN political analyst, *USA Today* columnist, and author of *The Silencing*

"A compelling and timely argument against attitudes and practices that, however well-intended, are damaging our universities, harming our children, and leaving an entire generation intellectually and emotionally ill-prepared for an ever more fraught and complex world. A brave and necessary work."

—**Rabbi Lord Jonathan Sacks**, Emeritus Chief Rabbi of UK & Commonwealth; professor, New York University; and author of *Not in God's Name*

"Objectionable words and ideas, as defined by self-appointed guardians on university campuses, are often treated like violence from sticks and stones. Many students cringe at robust debate; maintaining their ideas of good and evil requires no less than the silencing of disagreeable speakers. Lukianoff and Haidt brilliantly explain how this drift to fragility occurred, how the distinction between words and actions was lost, and what needs to be done. Critical reading to understand the current campus conflicts."

—**Mark Yudof**, president emeritus, University of California; and professor emeritus, UC Berkeley School of Law

"I lament the title of this book, as it may alienate the very people who need to engage with its arguments and obscures its message of inclusion. Equal parts mental health manual, parenting guide, sociological study, and political manifesto, it points to a positive way forward of hope, health, and humanism. I only wish I had read it when I was still a professor and a much younger mother."

—**Anne-Marie Slaughter**, president and CEO, New America;
and author of *Unfinished Business*

The Coddling of
the American Mind

The Coddling of the American Mind

HOW GOOD INTENTIONS AND BAD IDEAS ARE SETTING UP A GENERATION FOR FAILURE

Greg Lukianoff and Jonathan Haidt

Penguin Press | New York | 2018

PENGUIN PRESS
An imprint of Penguin Random House LLC
375 Hudson Street
New York, New York 10014
penguinrandomhouse.com

ISBN 9780735224896 (hardcover)
ISBN 9780735224902 (ebook)

Printed in the United States of America
1   3   5   7   9   10   8   6   4   2

Designed by Gretchen Achilles

Prepare the child for the road, not the road for the child.

FOLK WISDOM, origin unknown

*Your worst enemy cannot harm you as much as your own thoughts,
unguarded. But once mastered, no one can help you as much,
not even your father or your mother.*

BUDDHA, *Dhammapada*[1]

*The line dividing good and evil cuts through
the heart of every human being.*

ALEKSANDR SOLZHENITSYN, *The Gulag Archipelago*[2]

For our mothers, who did their best to prepare us for the road.

JOANNA DALTON LUKIANOFF

ELAINE HAIDT (1931–2017)

CONTENTS

INTRODUCTION | The Search for Wisdom   1

PART I

Three Bad Ideas

CHAPTER 1 | The Untruth of Fragility:
           What Doesn't Kill You Makes You Weaker   19
CHAPTER 2 | The Untruth of Emotional Reasoning:
           Always Trust Your Feelings   33
CHAPTER 3 | The Untruth of Us Versus Them: Life Is a Battle
           Between Good People and Evil People   53

PART II

Bad Ideas in Action

CHAPTER 4 | Intimidation and Violence   81
CHAPTER 5 | Witch Hunts   99

PART III

How Did We Get Here?

CHAPTER 6 | The Polarization Cycle   125

CHAPTER 7 | Anxiety and Depression 143

CHAPTER 8 | Paranoid Parenting 163

CHAPTER 9 | The Decline of Play 181

CHAPTER 10 | The Bureaucracy of Safetyism 195

CHAPTER 11 | The Quest for Justice 213

PART IV

Wising Up

CHAPTER 12 | Wiser Kids 235

CHAPTER 13 | Wiser Universities 253

CONCLUSION | Wiser Societies 263

Acknowledgments 271

Appendix 1: How to Do CBT 275

Appendix 2: The Chicago Statement on Principles of Free Expression 279

Notes 283

References 321

Index 329

The Search for Wisdom

This is a book about wisdom and its opposite. The book grows out of a trip that we (Greg and Jon) took to Greece in August of 2016. We had been writing about some ideas spreading through universities that we thought were harming students and damaging their prospects for creating fulfilling lives. These ideas were, in essence, making students less wise. So we decided to write a book to warn people about these terrible ideas, and we thought we'd start by going on a quest for wisdom ourselves. We both work on college campuses; in recent years, we had heard repeated references to the wisdom of Misoponos, a modern-day oracle who lives in a cave on the north slope of Mount Olympus, where he continues the ancient rites of the cult of Koalemos.

We flew to Athens and took a five-hour train ride to Litochoro, a town at the foot of the mountain. At sunrise the next day, we set off on a trail that Greeks have used for thousands of years to seek communion with their gods. We hiked for six hours up a steep and winding path. At noon we came to a fork in the path where a sign said MISOPONOS, with an arrow pointing to the right. The main path, off to the left, looked forbidding: it went straight up a narrow ravine, with an ever-present danger of rockslides.

The path to Misoponos, in contrast, was smooth, level, and easy—a welcome change. It took us through a pleasant grove of pine and fir trees, across a strong wooden pedestrian bridge over a deep ravine, and right to the mouth of a large cave.

Inside the cave we saw a strange scene. Misoponos and his assistants had installed one of those take-a-number systems that you sometimes find in sandwich shops, and there was a line of other seekers ahead of us. We took a number, paid the 100 euro fee to have a private audience with the great man, performed the mandatory rituals of purification, and waited.

When our turn came, we were ushered into a dimly lit chamber at the back of the cave, where a small spring of water bubbled out from a rock wall and splashed down into a large white marble bowl somewhat reminiscent of a birdbath. Next to the bowl, Misoponos sat in a comfortable chair that appeared to be a Barcalounger recliner from the 1970s. We had heard that he spoke English, but we were taken aback when he greeted us in perfect American English with a hint of Long Island: "Come on in, guys. Tell me what you seek."

Jon spoke first: "O Wise Oracle, we have come seeking wisdom. What are the deepest and greatest of truths?"

Greg thought we should be more specific, so he added, "Actually, we're writing a book about wisdom for teenagers, young adults, parents, and educators, and we were kind of hoping that you could boil down your insights into some pithy axioms, ideally three of them, which, if followed, would lead young people to develop wisdom over the course of their lives."

Misoponos sat silently with his eyes closed for about two minutes. Finally, he opened his eyes and spoke.

"This fountain is the Spring of Koalemos. Koalemos was a Greek god of wisdom who is not as well-known today as Athena, who gets far too much press, in my opinion. But Koalemos has some really good stuff, too, if you ask me. Which you just did. So let me tell you. I will give you three cups of wisdom."

He filled a small alabaster cup from the water bowl and handed it to us. We both drank from it and handed it back.

"This is the first truth," he said: "*What doesn't kill you makes you weaker. So avoid pain, avoid discomfort, avoid all potentially bad experiences.*"

Jon was surprised. He had written a book called *The Happiness Hypothesis*, which examined ancient wisdom in light of modern psychology. The book devoted an entire chapter to testing the opposite of the oracle's claim, which was most famously stated by Friedrich Nietzsche: "What doesn't kill me makes me stronger."[1] Jon thought there must be some mistake. "Excuse me, Your Holiness," he said, "but did you really mean to say 'weaker'? Because I've got quotes from many wisdom traditions saying that pain, setbacks, and even traumatic experiences can make people *stronger.*"

"Did I say 'weaker'?" asked Misoponos. "Wait a minute . . . is it weaker or stronger?" He squeezed his eyes shut as he thought about it, and then opened his eyes and said, "Yes, I'm right, weaker is what I meant. Bad experiences are terrible, who would want one? Did you travel all this way to have a bad experience? Of course not. And pain? So many oracles in these mountains sit on the ground twelve hours a day, and what does it get them? Circulation problems and lower-back pain. How much wisdom can you dispense when you're thinking about your aches and pains all the time? That's why I got this chair twenty years ago. Why shouldn't I be comfortable?" With clear irritation in his voice, he added, "Can I finish?"

"I'm sorry," said Jon meekly.

Misoponos filled the cup again. We drank it. "Second," he continued: "*Always trust your feelings. Never question them.*"

Now it was Greg's turn to recoil. He had spent years practicing cognitive behavioral therapy, which is based on exactly the opposite advice: feelings so often mislead us that you can't achieve mental health *until* you learn to question them and free yourself from some common distortions of reality. But having learned to control his immediate negative reactions, he bit his tongue and said nothing.

Misoponos refilled the cup, and we drank again. "Third: *Life is a battle between good people and evil people.*"

We looked at each other in disbelief. Greg could no longer keep quiet: "O Great Oracle of Koalemos," he began, haltingly, "can you explain that one to us?"

"Some people are good," Misoponos said slowly and loudly, as if he thought we hadn't heard him, "and some people are bad." He looked at us pointedly and took a breath. "There is so much evil in the world. Where does it come from?" He paused as if expecting us to answer. We were speechless. "From evil people!" he said, clearly exasperated. "It is up to you and the rest of the good people in the world to fight them. You must be warriors for virtue and goodness. You can see how bad and wrong some people are. You must call them out! Assemble a coalition of the righteous, and shame the evil ones until they change their ways."

Jon asked, "But don't they think the same about us? How can we know that it is *we* who are right and *they* who are wrong?"

Misoponos responded tartly, "Have you learned nothing from me today? Trust your feelings. Do you *feel* that you are right? Or do you *feel* that you are wrong? *I* feel that this interview is over. Get out."

. . . . .

There is no Misoponos,[2] and we didn't really travel to Greece to discover these three terrible ideas. We didn't have to. You can find them on college campuses, in high schools, and in many homes. These untruths are rarely taught explicitly; rather, they are conveyed to young people by the rules, practices, and norms that are imposed on them, often with the best of intentions.

This is a book about three Great Untruths that seem to have spread widely in recent years:

1. The Untruth of Fragility: *What doesn't kill you makes you weaker.*
2. The Untruth of Emotional Reasoning: *Always trust your feelings.*
3. The Untruth of Us Versus Them: *Life is a battle between good people and evil people.*

While many propositions are untrue, in order to be classified as a Great Untruth, an idea must meet three criteria:

1. It contradicts ancient wisdom (ideas found widely in the wisdom literatures of many cultures).
2. It contradicts modern psychological research on well-being.
3. It harms the individuals and communities who embrace it.

We will show how these three Great Untruths—and the policies and political movements that draw on them—are causing problems for young people, universities, and, more generally, liberal democracies. To name just a few of these problems: Teen anxiety, depression, and suicide rates have risen sharply in the last few years. The culture on many college campuses has become more ideologically uniform, compromising the ability of scholars to seek truth, and of students to learn from a broad range of thinkers. Extremists have proliferated on the far right and the far left, provoking one another to ever deeper levels of hatred. Social media has channeled partisan passions into the creation of a "callout culture"; anyone can be publicly shamed for saying something well-intentioned that someone else interprets uncharitably. New-media platforms and outlets allow citizens to retreat into self-confirmatory bubbles, where their worst fears about the evils of the other side can be confirmed and amplified by extremists and cyber trolls intent on sowing discord and division.

The three Great Untruths have flowered on many college campuses, but they have their roots in earlier education and childhood experiences, and they now extend from the campus into the corporate world and the public square, including national politics. They are also spreading outward from American universities to universities throughout the English-speaking world.[3] These Great Untruths are bad for everyone. Anyone who cares about young people, education, or democracy should be concerned about these trends.

The Real Origins of This Book

In May of 2014, we (Greg and Jon) sat down for lunch together in New York City's Greenwich Village. We were there to talk about a puzzle that Greg had been trying to solve for the past year or two. Greg is a First Amendment lawyer. Since 2001, he has been fighting for academic freedom and freedom of speech on campus as the head of the Foundation for Individual Rights in Education (FIRE).[4] A nonpartisan, nonprofit organization, FIRE is dedicated to defending liberty, freedom of speech, due process, and academic freedom on the country's college campuses.

Throughout Greg's career, the calls for campus censorship had generally come from administrators. Students, on the other hand, had always been the one group that consistently supported free speech—in fact, demanded it. But now something was changing; on some campuses, words were increasingly seen as sources of danger. In the fall of 2013, Greg began hearing about students asking for "triggering" material to be removed from courses. By the spring of 2014, *The New Republic*[5] and *The New York Times*[6] were reporting on this trend. Greg also noticed an intensified push from students for school administrators to disinvite speakers whose ideas the students found offensive. When those speakers were not disinvited, students were increasingly using the "heckler's veto"—protesting in ways that prevented their fellow students from attending the talk or from hearing the speaker. Most concerning to Greg, however, and the reason he wanted to talk to Jon, was the shift in the *justifications* for these new reactions to course materials and speakers.

In years past, administrators were motivated to create campus speech codes in order to curtail what they deemed to be racist or sexist speech. Increasingly, however, the rationale for speech codes and speaker disinvitations was becoming medicalized: Students claimed that certain kinds of speech—and even the content of some books and courses—interfered with their *ability to function.* They wanted protection from material that they believed could jeopardize their mental health by "triggering" them, or making them "feel unsafe."

To give one example: Columbia University's "Core Curriculum" (part of the general education requirement for all undergraduates at Columbia College) features a course called Masterpieces of Western Literature and Philosophy.[7] At one point, this included works by Ovid, Homer, Dante, Augustine, Montaigne, and Woolf. According to the university, the course is supposed to tackle "the most difficult questions about human experience." However, in 2015, four Columbia undergraduates wrote an essay in the school newspaper arguing that students "need to feel safe in the classroom" but "many texts in the Western canon" are "wrought with histories and narratives of exclusion and oppression" and contain "triggering and offensive material that marginalizes student identities in the classroom." Some students said that these texts are so emotionally challenging to read and discuss that professors should issue "trigger warnings" and provide support for triggered students.[8] (Trigger warnings are verbal or written notifications provided by a professor to alert students that they are about to encounter potentially distressing material.) The essay was nuanced and made some important points about diversifying the literary canon, but is safety versus danger a helpful framework for discussing reactions to literature? Or might that framework itself alter a student's reactions to ancient texts, creating a feeling of threat and a stress response to what otherwise would have been experienced merely as discomfort or dislike?

Of course, student activism is nothing new; students have been actively trying to shape their learning environment for decades, such as when they joined professors during the "canon wars" of the 1990s (the effort to add more women and writers of color to the lists of "dead white males" that dominated reading lists).[9] Students in the 1960s and 1970s often tried to keep speakers off campus or prevent speakers from being heard. For example, students at several universities protested lectures by Harvard biologist E. O. Wilson because of his writings about how evolution shaped human behavior—which some students thought could be used to justify existing gender roles and inequalities. (A sign advertising one protest urged fellow students to "bring noisemakers."[10]) But those efforts were not driven by health concerns. Students wanted to block people they thought were espousing evil ideas (as they do today), but back then, they were not saying that members of the school community would be *harmed* by the speaker's visit or by exposure to ideas. And they were certainly not asking that professors and administrators take a more protective attitude toward them by shielding them from the presence of certain people.

What is new today is the premise that students are fragile. Even those who are not fragile themselves often believe that *others* are in danger and therefore need protection. There is no expectation that students will grow stronger from their encounters with speech or texts they label "triggering." (This is the Untruth of Fragility: *What doesn't kill you makes you weaker.*)

To Greg, who had suffered from bouts of depression throughout his life, this seemed like a terrible approach. In seeking treatment for his depression, he—along with millions of others around the world—had found that cognitive behavioral therapy (CBT) was the most effective solution. CBT teaches you to notice when you are engaging in various "cognitive distortions," such as "catastrophizing" (*If I fail this quiz, I'll fail the class and be kicked out of school, and then I'll never get a job . . .*) and "negative filtering" (only paying attention to negative feedback instead of noticing praise as well). These distorted and irrational thought patterns are hallmarks of depression and anxiety disorders. We are not saying that students are never in real physical danger, or that their claims about injustice are usually cognitive distortions. We are saying that even when students are reacting to real problems, they are more likely than previous generations to engage in thought patterns that make those problems seem more threatening, which makes them harder to solve. An important discovery by early CBT researchers was that if people learn to stop thinking this way, their depression and anxiety usually subside. For this reason, Greg was troubled when he noticed that some students' reactions to speech on college campuses exhibited *exactly the same distortions* that he had learned to rebut in his own therapy. Where had students learned these bad mental habits? Wouldn't these cognitive distortions make students *more* anxious and depressed?

Of course, many things have changed on campus since the 1970s. College students today are far more diverse. They arrive on campus having faced varying degrees of bigotry, poverty, trauma, and mental illness. Educators must account for those differences, reevaluate old assumptions, and strive to create an inclusive community. But what is the best way to do that? If we are especially concerned about the students who have faced the most serious obstacles, should our priority be protecting them from speakers, books, and ideas that might offend them? Or might such protective measures—however well-intentioned—backfire and harm those very students?

All students must be prepared for the world they will face after college, and those who are making the largest jump—the ones most in danger of feeling like strangers in a strange land—are the ones who must learn fastest and prepare hardest. The playing field is not level; life is not fair. But college is quite possibly the best environment on earth in which to come face-to-face with people and ideas that are potentially offensive or even downright hostile. It is the ultimate mental gymnasium, full of advanced equipment, skilled trainers, and therapists standing by, just in case.

Greg worried that if students came to see themselves as fragile, they would stay away from that gym. If students didn't build skills and accept friendly invitations to spar in the practice ring, and if they avoided these opportunities because well-meaning people convinced them that they'd be harmed by such training, well, it would be a tragedy for all concerned. Their beliefs about their own and others' fragility in the face of ideas they dislike would become self-fulfilling prophecies. Not only would students come to *believe* that they can't handle such things, but if they acted on that belief and avoided exposure, eventually they would *become* less able to do so. If students succeeded in creating bubbles of intellectual "safety" in college, they would set themselves up for even greater anxiety and conflict after graduation, when they will certainly encounter many more people with more extreme views.

Based on Greg's personal and professional experience, his theory was this: Students were beginning to demand protection from speech because they had unwittingly learned to employ the very cognitive distortions that CBT tries to correct. Stated simply: *Many university students are learning to think in distorted ways, and this increases their likelihood of becoming fragile, anxious, and easily hurt.*

Greg wanted to discuss this theory with Jon because Jon is a social psychologist who has written extensively[11] about the power of CBT and its close fit with ancient wisdom. Jon immediately saw the potential in Greg's idea. As a professor at New York University's Stern School of Business, he had just begun to see the first signs of this new "fragile student model." His main research area is moral psychology, and his second book, *The Righteous Mind: Why Good People Are Divided by Politics and Religion*, was an effort to help people understand different moral cultures, or moral "matrices," particularly the moral cultures of the political left and right.

The term "matrix," as Jon used it, comes from the 1984 science fiction novel *Neuromancer*, by William Gibson (which was the inspiration for the later movie *The Matrix*). Gibson imagined a futuristic, internet-like network linking everyone together. He called it "the matrix" and referred to it as "a consensual hallucination." Jon thought it was a great way to think about moral cultures. A group creates a consensual moral matrix as individuals interact with one another, and then they act in ways that may be unintelligible to outsiders. At the time, it seemed to both of us that a new moral matrix was forming in some pockets of universities and was destined to grow. (Social media, of course, is perfectly designed to help "consensual hallucinations" spread within connected communities at warp speed—on campus and off, on the left and on the right.)

Jon eagerly agreed to join Greg in his attempt to solve this mystery. We wrote an article together exploring Greg's idea and using it to explain a number of events and trends that had arisen on campus in the previous year or two. We submitted the article to *The Atlantic* with the title "Arguing Towards Misery: How Campuses Teach Cognitive Distortions." The editor, Don Peck, liked the article, helped us strengthen the argument, and then gave it a more succinct and provocative title: "The Coddling of the American Mind."

In that article, we argued that many parents, K-12 teachers, professors, and university administrators have been unknowingly teaching a generation of students to engage in the mental habits commonly seen in people who suffer from anxiety and depression. We suggested that students were beginning to react to words, books, and visiting speakers with fear and anger because they had been taught to exaggerate danger, use dichotomous (or binary) thinking, amplify their first emotional responses, and engage in a number of other cognitive distortions (which we will discuss further throughout this book). Such thought patterns directly harmed students' mental health and interfered with their intellectual development—and sometimes the development of those around them. At some schools, a culture of defensive self-censorship seemed to be emerging, partly in response to students who were quick to "call out" or shame others for small things that they deemed to be insensitive—either to the student doing the calling out or to members of a group that the student was standing up for. We called this pattern *vindictive protectiveness* and argued that such behavior made it more difficult for all students to have open discussions in which they could practice the essential skills of critical thinking and civil disagreement.

Our article was published on *The Atlantic*'s website on August 11, 2015, and the magazine issue that featured it hit newsstands about a week later. We were expecting a wave of criticism, but many people both on and off campus and from across the political spectrum had noticed the trends we described, and the initial reception of the essay was overwhelmingly positive. Our piece became one of the five most-viewed articles of all time on *The Atlantic*'s website, and President Obama even referred to it in a speech a few weeks later, when he praised the value of viewpoint diversity and said that students should not be "coddled and protected from different points of view."[12]

By October, we had finished our media appearances related to the article, and both of us were happy to return to our other work. Little did we know that the coming months and years were about to turn not only the academic world but the entire country upside down. Also, in 2016, it became clear that the Great Untruths and their associated practices were spreading to universities in the United Kingdom,[13] Canada, and Australia.[14] So in the fall of 2016, we decided to take another, harder look at the questions we had raised in the article, and write this book.

Tumultuous Years: 2015–2017

Looking back from early 2018, it's amazing how much has changed since we published that article in August of 2015. A powerful movement for racial justice had already been launched and was gaining strength with each horrific cell phone video of police killing unarmed black men.[15] That fall, protests over issues of racial justice erupted at dozens of campuses around the country, beginning at the University of Missouri and Yale. It was a level of activism not seen on campus in decades.

Meanwhile, during this period, mass killings filled the news. Terrorists carried out large-scale attacks across Europe and the Middle East.[16] In the United States, fourteen people were killed and more than twenty others injured in an ISIS-inspired shooting in San Bernardino, California;[17] another ISIS-inspired attack, on a gay nightclub in Orlando, Florida, became the deadliest mass shooting in U.S. history, with forty-nine people killed,[18] and that number was surpassed just sixteen months later in Las Vegas when a man with what was essentially a machine gun shot and killed fifty-eight people and wounded 851 others at an outdoor concert.[19]

And 2016 became one of the strangest years ever in U.S. presidential politics when Donald Trump—a candidate with no prior political experience who had been widely regarded as unelectable because of the many groups of people he had offended—not only won the Republican primary but won the election. Millions turned out across the country to protest his inauguration, cross-partisan hatred surged, and the news cycle came to revolve around the president's latest tweet or latest comment about nuclear war.

Attention returned to campus protests in the spring of 2017 as violence broke out at Middlebury College and—on a scale not seen in decades—at the University of California, Berkeley, where self-described "anti-fascists" caused hundreds of thousands of dollars of damage to the campus and the town, injuring students and others. Six months later, neo-Nazis and Ku Klux Klansmen marched with torches across the grounds of the University of Virginia one day before a white nationalist drove his car into a crowd of counterprotesters, killing one of them and injuring others. The year ended with the #MeToo movement, as many women began to publicly share their stories of sexual misconduct and assault, stories that turned out to be common in professions dominated by powerful men.

In this environment, practically anyone of any age and at any point on the political spectrum could make the case for being anxious, depressed, or outraged. Isn't this a sufficient explanation for the unrest and new demands for "safety" on campus? Why return to the issues we raised in our original *Atlantic* article?

"Coddling" Means "Overprotecting"

We have always been ambivalent about the word "coddling." We didn't like the implication that children today are pampered, spoiled, and lazy, because that is not accurate. Young people today—at a minimum, those who are competing for places at selective colleges—are under enormous pressure to perform academically and to build up a long list of extracurricular accomplishments. Meanwhile, all teens face new forms of harassment, insult, and social competition from social media. Their economic prospects are uncertain in an economy being reshaped by globalization, automation, and artificial intelligence, and characterized by wage stagnation for most workers. So most kids don't have easy, pampered childhoods. But as we'll show in this book, *adults* are doing far more these days to protect children, and their overreach might be having some negative effects. Dictionary definitions of "coddle" emphasize this overprotection; for example, "to treat with extreme or excessive care or kindness."[20] The fault lies with adults and with institutional practices, hence our subtitle: "How Good Intentions and Bad Ideas Are Setting Up a Generation for Failure." That is exactly what this book is about. We will show how well-intentioned overprotection—from peanut bans in elementary schools through speech codes on college campuses—may end up doing more harm than good.

But overprotection is just one part of a larger trend that we call *problems of progress.* This term refers to bad consequences produced by otherwise good social changes. It's great that our economic system produces an abundance of food at low prices, but the flip side is an epidemic of obesity. It's great that we can connect and communicate with people instantly and for free, but this hyperconnection may be damaging the mental health of young people. It's great that we have refrigerators, antidepressants, air conditioning, hot and cold running water, and the ability to escape from most of the physical hardships that were woven into the daily lives of our ancestors back to the dawn of our species. Comfort and physical safety are boons to humanity, but they bring some costs, too. We adapt to our new and improved circumstances and then lower the bar for what we count as intolerable levels of discomfort and risk. By the standards of our great-grandparents, nearly all of us are coddled. Each generation tends to see the one after it as weak, whiny, and lacking in resilience. Those older generations may have a point, even though these generational changes reflect real and positive progress.

To repeat, we are *not* saying that the problems facing students, and young people more generally, are minor or "all in their heads." We are saying that what people choose to *do* in their heads will determine how those real problems affect them. Our argument is ultimately pragmatic, not moralistic: Whatever your identity, background, or political ideology, you will be happier, healthier, stronger, and more likely to succeed in pursuing your own goals if you do the *opposite* of what Misoponos advised. That means *seeking out challenges* (rather than eliminating or avoiding everything that "feels unsafe"), *freeing yourself from cognitive distortions* (rather than always trusting your initial feelings), and *taking a generous view of other people, and looking for nuance* (rather than assuming the worst about people within a simplistic us-versus-them morality).

What We Will Do in This Book

The story we tell is not simple, and while there are some heroes, there are no clear villains. Our tale is, rather, a social science detective story in which the "crime" was committed by a confluence of social trends and forces. Surprising events began happening on college campuses around 2013 and 2014, and they became stranger and more frequent between 2015 and 2017. In Part I of the book, we set the stage. We give you the intellectual tools you'll need to make sense of the new culture of "safety" that has swept across many college campuses since 2013. Those tools include learning to recognize the three Great Untruths. Along the way, we'll explain some of the key concepts of cognitive behavioral therapy, and we'll show how CBT improves critical thinking skills while counteracting the effects of the Great Untruths.

In Part II, we show the Great Untruths in action. We examine the "shout-downs," intimidation, and occasional violence that are making it more difficult for universities to fulfill their core missions of education and research. We explore the newly popular idea that speech is violence, and we show why thinking this way is bad for students' mental health. We explore the sociology of witch hunts and moral panics, including the conditions that can cause a college to descend into chaos.

In Part III, we try to solve the mystery. Why did things change so rapidly on many campuses between 2013 and 2017? We identify six explanatory threads: the rising political polarization and cross-party animosity of U.S. politics, which has led to rising hate crimes and harassment on campus; rising levels of teen anxiety and depression, which have made many students more desirous of protection and more receptive to the Great Untruths; changes in parenting practices, which have amplified children's fears even as childhood becomes increasingly safe; the loss of free play and unsupervised risk-taking, both of which kids need to become self-governing adults; the growth of campus bureaucracy and expansion of its protective mission; and an increasing passion for justice, combined with changing ideas about what justice requires. These six trends did not influence everyone equally, but they have all begun to intersect and interact on college campuses in the United States in the last few years.

Finally, in Part IV, we offer advice. We suggest specific actions that will help parents and teachers to raise wiser, stronger, more independent children, and we suggest ways in which professors, administrators, and college students can improve their universities and adapt them for life in our age of technology-enhanced outrage.

In 2014, we set out to understand what was happening on U.S. college campuses, but the story we tell in this book is about far more than that. It's the story of our strange and unsettling time, when many institutions are malfunctioning, trust is declining, and a new generation—the one after the Millennials—is just beginning to graduate from college and enter the workforce. Our story ends on a hopeful note. The problems we describe may be temporary. We believe they are fixable. The arc of history bends toward progress on most measures of health, prosperity, and freedom,[21] but if we can understand the six explanatory threads and free ourselves from the three Great Untruths, it may bend a little faster.

PART I

Three Bad Ideas

CHAPTER 1

The Untruth of Fragility: What Doesn't Kill You Makes You Weaker

When heaven is about to confer a great responsibility on any man,
it will exercise his mind with suffering, subject his sinews and
bones to hard work, expose his body to hunger, put him to poverty,
place obstacles in the paths of his deeds, so as to stimulate his mind,
harden his nature, and improve wherever he is incompetent.

MENG TZU (MENCIUS), *fourth century BCE*[1]

In August 2009, Max Haidt, age three, had his first day of preschool in Charlottesville, Virginia. But before he was allowed to take the first step on his eighteen-year journey to a college degree, his parents, Jon and Jayne, had to attend a mandatory orientation session where the rules and procedures were explained by Max's teacher. The most important rule, judging by the time spent discussing it, was: no nuts. Because of the risk to children with peanut allergies, there was an absolute prohibition on bringing anything containing nuts into the building. Of course, peanuts are legumes, not nuts, but some kids have allergies to tree nuts, too, so along with peanuts and peanut butter, all nuts and nut products were banned. And to be extra safe, the school also banned anything produced in a factory that processes nuts, so many kinds of dried fruits and other snacks were prohibited, too.

As the list of prohibited substances grew, and as the clock ticked on, Jon asked the assembled group of parents what he thought was a helpful question: "Does anyone here have a child with any kind of nut allergy? If we know about the kids' actual allergies, I'm sure we'll all do everything we can to avoid risk. But if there's no kid in the class with such an allergy, then maybe we can lighten up a bit and instead of banning all those things, just ban peanuts?"

The teacher was visibly annoyed by Jon's question, and she moved rapidly to stop any parent from responding. *Don't put anyone on the spot,* she said. *Don't make any parent feel uncomfortable. Regardless of whether anyone in the class is affected, these are the school's rules.*

You can't blame the school for being so cautious. Peanut allergies were rare among American children up until the mid-1990s, when one study found that only four out of a thousand children under the age of eight had such an allergy (meaning probably nobody in Max's entire preschool of about one hundred kids).[2] But by 2008, according to the same survey, using the same measures, the rate had more than tripled, to fourteen out of a thousand (meaning probably one or two kids in Max's school). Nobody knew why American children were suddenly becoming more allergic to peanuts, but the logical and compassionate response was obvious: Kids are vulnerable. Protect them from peanuts, peanut products, and anything that has been in contact with nuts of any kind. Why not? What's the harm, other than some inconvenience to parents preparing lunches?

But it turns out that the harm was severe.[3] It was later discovered that peanut allergies were surging precisely *because* parents and teachers had started protecting children from exposure to peanuts back in the 1990s.[4] In February 2015, an authoritative study[5] was published. The LEAP (Learning Early About Peanut Allergy) study was based on the hypothesis that "regular eating of peanut-containing products, when started during infancy, will elicit a protective immune response instead of an allergic immune reaction."[6] The researchers recruited the parents of 640 infants (four to eleven months old) who were at high risk of developing a peanut allergy because they had severe eczema or had tested positive for another allergy. The researchers told half the parents to follow the standard advice for high-risk kids, which was to avoid all exposure to peanuts and peanut products. The other half were given a supply of a snack made from peanut butter and puffed corn and were told to give some to their child at least three times a week. The researchers followed all the families carefully, and when the children turned five years old, they were tested for an allergic reaction to peanuts.

The results were stunning. Among the children who had been "protected" from peanuts, 17% had developed a peanut allergy. In the group that had been deliberately exposed to peanut products, only 3% had developed an allergy. As one of the researchers said in an interview, "For decades allergists have been recommending that young infants avoid consuming allergenic foods such as peanut to prevent food allergies. Our findings suggest that this advice was incorrect and may have contributed to the rise in the peanut and other food allergies."[7]

It makes perfect sense. The immune system is a miracle of evolutionary engineering. It can't possibly anticipate all the pathogens and parasites a child will encounter—especially in a mobile and omnivorous species such as ours—so it is "designed" (by natural selection) to learn rapidly from early experience. The immune system is a complex adaptive system, which can be defined as a dynamic system that is able to adapt in and evolve with a changing environment.[8] It *requires* exposure to a range of foods, bacteria, and even parasitic worms in order to develop its ability to mount an immune response to real threats (such as the bacterium that causes strep throat) while ignoring nonthreats (such as peanut proteins). Vaccination uses the same logic. Childhood vaccines make us healthier not by reducing threats in the world ("Ban germs in schools!") but by exposing children to those threats in small doses, thereby giving children's immune systems the opportunity to learn how to fend off similar threats in the future.

This is the underlying rationale for what is called the *hygiene hypothesis*,[9] the leading explanation for why allergy rates generally go up as countries get wealthier and cleaner—another example of a problem of progress. Developmental psychologist Alison Gopnik explains the hypothesis succinctly and does us the favor of linking it to our mission in this book:

Thanks to hygiene, antibiotics and too little outdoor play, children don't get exposed to microbes as they once did. This may lead them to develop immune systems that overreact to substances that aren't actually threatening—causing allergies. In the same way, *by shielding children from every possible risk, we may lead them to react with exaggerated fear to situations that aren't risky at all and isolate them from the adult skills that they will one day have to master [emphasis added].*[10]

This brings us to the oracle's first Great Untruth, the Untruth of Fragility: *What doesn't kill you makes you weaker.* Of course, Nietzsche's original aphorism—"What doesn't kill me makes me stronger"—is not entirely correct if taken literally; some things that don't kill you can still leave you permanently damaged and diminished. But teaching kids that failures, insults, and painful experiences will do lasting damage is harmful in and of itself. Human beings *need* physical and mental challenges and stressors or we deteriorate. For example, muscles and joints need stressors to develop properly. Too much rest causes muscles to atrophy, joints to lose range of motion, heart and lung function to decline, and blood clots to form. Without the challenges imposed by gravity, astronauts develop muscle weakness and joint degeneration.

Antifragility

No one has done a better job of explaining the harm of avoiding stressors, risks, and small doses of pain than Nassim Nicholas Taleb, the Lebanese-born statistician, stock trader, and polymath who is now a professor of risk engineering at New York University. In his 2007 best seller, *The Black Swan*, Taleb argued that most of us think about risk in the wrong way. In complex systems, it is virtually inevitable that unforeseen problems will arise, yet we persist in trying to calculate risk based on past experiences. Life has a way of creating completely unexpected events—events Taleb likens to the appearance of a black swan when, based on your past experience, you assumed that all swans were white. (Taleb was one of the few who predicted the global financial crisis of 2008, based on the financial system's vulnerability to "black swan" events.)

In his later book *Antifragile*, Taleb explains how systems and people can survive the inevitable black swans of life and, like the immune system, grow *stronger* in response. Taleb asks us to distinguish three kinds of things. Some, like china teacups, are *fragile*: they break easily and cannot heal themselves, so you must handle them gently and keep them away from toddlers. Other things are *resilient*: they can withstand shocks. Parents usually give their toddlers plastic cups precisely because plastic can survive repeated falls to the floor, although the cups do not benefit from such falls. But Taleb asks us to look beyond the overused word "resilience" and recognize that some things are *antifragile*. Many of the important systems in our economic and political life are like our immune systems: they *require* stressors and challenges in order to learn, adapt, and grow. Systems that are antifragile become rigid, weak, and inefficient when nothing challenges them or pushes them to respond vigorously. He notes that muscles, bones, and children are antifragile:

> Just as spending a month in bed . . . leads to muscle atrophy, complex systems are weakened, even killed, when deprived of stressors. Much of our modern, structured, world has been harming us with top-down policies and contraptions . . . which do precisely this: an insult to the antifragility of systems. This is the tragedy of modernity: *as with neurotically overprotective parents, those trying to help are often hurting us the most* [emphasis added].[11]

Taleb opens the book with a poetic image that should speak to all parents. He notes that wind extinguishes a candle but energizes a fire. He advises us not to be like candles and not to turn our children into candles: "You want to be the fire and wish for the wind."[12]

The foolishness of overprotection is apparent as soon as you understand the concept of antifragility. Given that risks and stressors are natural, unavoidable parts of life, parents and teachers should be helping kids develop their innate abilities to grow and learn from such experiences. There's an old saying: "Prepare the child for the road, not the road for the child." But these days, we seem to be doing precisely the opposite: we're trying to clear away anything that might upset children, not realizing that in doing so, we're repeating the peanut-allergy mistake. If we protect children from various classes of potentially upsetting experiences, we make it far more likely that those children will be unable to cope with such events when they leave our protective umbrella. The modern obsession with protecting young people from "feeling unsafe" is, we believe, one of the (several) causes of the rapid rise in rates of adolescent depression, anxiety, and suicide, which we'll explore in chapter 7.

The Rise of Safetyism

In the twentieth century, the word "safety" generally meant physical safety. A great triumph of the late part of that century was that the United States became physically safer for children. As a result of class action lawsuits, efforts by investigative journalists and consumer advocates (such as Ralph Nader and his exposé of the auto industry, *Unsafe at Any Speed*), and common sense, dangerous products and practices became less prevalent. Between 1978 and 1985, all fifty states passed laws making the use of car seats mandatory for children. Homes and day care centers were childproofed; choking hazards and sharp objects were removed. As a result, death rates for children have plummeted.[13] This is, of course, a very good thing, although in some other ways, the focus on physical safety may have gone too far. (The Alison Gopnik essay quoted above was titled "Should We Let Toddlers Play With Saws and Knives?"[14] Her answer was: maybe.)

But gradually, in the twenty-first century, on some college campuses, the meaning of "safety" underwent a process of "concept creep" and expanded to include "*emotional* safety." As an example, in 2014, Oberlin College posted guidelines for faculty, urging them to use trigger warnings to "show students that you care about their safety."[15] The rest of the memo makes it clear that what the college was really telling its faculty was: show students that you care about their *feelings*. You can see the conflation of safety and feelings in another part of the memo, which urged faculty to use each student's preferred gender pronoun (for example, "zhe" or "they" for students who don't want to be referred to as "he" or "she"), not because this was respectful or appropriately sensitive but because a professor who uses an incorrect pronoun "prevents or impairs their safety in a classroom." If students have been told that they can request gender-neutral pronouns and then a professor fails to use one, students may be disappointed or upset. But are these students *unsafe*? Are students in any *danger* in the classroom if a professor uses the wrong pronoun? Professors should indeed be mindful of their students' feelings, but how might it change Oberlin students—and the nature of class discussions—when the community is told repeatedly that they should judge the speech of others in terms of safety and danger?

To understand how an Oberlin administrator could have used the word "safety," we turn to an article published in 2016 by the Australian psychologist Nick Haslam, titled "Concept Creep: Psychology's Expanding Concepts of Harm and Pathology."[16] Haslam examined a variety of key concepts in clinical and social psychology—including abuse, bullying, trauma, and prejudice—to determine how their usage had changed since the 1980s. He found that their scope had expanded in two directions: the concepts had crept "downward," to apply to less severe situations, and "outward," to encompass new but conceptually related phenomena.

Take the word "trauma." In the early versions of the primary manual of psychiatry, the *Diagnostic and Statistical Manual of Mental Disorders* (DSM),[17] psychiatrists used the word "trauma" only to describe a physical agent causing physical damage, as in the case of what we now call *traumatic brain injury*. In the 1980 revision, however, the manual (DSM III) recognized "post-traumatic stress disorder" as a mental disorder—the first type of traumatic injury that isn't physical. PTSD is caused by an extraordinary and terrifying experience, and the criteria for a traumatic event that warrants a diagnosis of PTSD were (and are) strict: to qualify, an event would have to "evoke significant symptoms of distress in almost everyone" and be "outside the range of usual human experience."[18] The DSM III emphasized that the event was not based on a *subjective standard*. It had to be something that would cause most people to have a severe reaction. War, rape, and torture were included in this category. Divorce and simple bereavement (as in the death of a spouse due to natural causes), on the other hand, were not, because they are normal parts of life, even if unexpected. These experiences are sad and painful, but pain is not the same thing as trauma. People in these situations that don't fall into the "trauma" category might benefit from counseling, but they generally recover from such losses without any therapeutic interventions.[19] In fact, even most people who do have traumatic experiences recover completely without intervention.[20]

By the early 2000s, however, the concept of "trauma" within parts of the therapeutic community had crept down so far that it included anything "experienced by an individual as physically or emotionally harmful . . . with lasting adverse effects on the individual's functioning and mental, physical, social, emotional, or spiritual well-being."[21] The *subjective experience* of "harm" became definitional in assessing trauma. As a result, the word "trauma" became much more widely used, not just by mental health professionals but by their clients and patients—including an increasing number of college students.

As with trauma, a key change for most of the concepts Haslam examined was the shift to a *subjective standard*.[22] It was not for anyone else to decide what counted as trauma, bullying, or abuse; if it felt like that to you, trust your feelings. If a person reported that an event was traumatic (or bullying or abusive), his or her subjective assessment was increasingly taken as sufficient evidence. And if a rapidly growing number of students have been diagnosed with a mental disorder (as we'll see in chapter 7), then there is a rapidly growing need for the campus community to protect them.

Safe Spaces

Few Americans had ever heard of a "safe space" in an academic sense until March of 2015, when *The New York Times* published an essay by Judith Shulevitz about a safe space created by students at Brown University.[23] The students were preparing for an upcoming debate between two feminist authors, Wendy McElroy and Jessica Valenti, on "rape culture," the concept that "prevailing social attitudes have the effect of normalizing or trivializing sexual assault and abuse."[24] Proponents of the idea, like Valenti, argue that misogyny is endemic to American culture, and in such a world, sexual assault is considered a lesser crime. We can all see, especially in the #MeToo era, that sexual abuse is far too common. But does that make for a rape culture? It seems an idea worthy of debate.

McElroy disputes the claim that America is a rape culture, and to illustrate her argument, she contrasts the United States with countries in which rape is endemic and tolerated. (For example, in parts of Afghanistan, "women are married against their will, they are murdered for men's honor, they are raped. And when they are raped they are arrested for it, and they are shunned by their family afterward," she says. "Now that's a rape culture."[25]) McElroy has firsthand experience of sexual violence: she told the audience at Brown that she was brutally raped as a teenager, and as an adult she was so badly beaten by a boyfriend that it left her blind in one eye. She believes it is untrue and unhelpful to tell American women that they live in a rape culture.

But what if some Brown students *believe* that America is a rape culture? Should McElroy be allowed to challenge their belief, or would that challenge put them in danger? A Brown student explained to Shulevitz: "Bringing in a speaker like that could serve to invalidate people's experiences." It could be "damaging," she said.[26] The logic seems to be that some Brown students believe that America is a rape culture, and for some of them, this belief is based in part on their own lived experience of sexual assault. If, during the debate, McElroy were to tell them that America is *not* a rape culture, she could be taken to be saying that their personal experiences are "invalid" as grounds for the assertion that America is a rape culture. That could be painful to hear, but should college students interpret emotional pain as a sign that they are in danger?

Illustrating concept creep and the expansion of "safety" to include emotional comfort, the student quoted above, along with other Brown students, attempted to get McElroy disinvited from the debate in order to protect her peers from such "damage."[27] That effort failed, but in response, the president of Brown, Christina Paxson, announced that she disagreed with McElroy, and that during the debate, the college would hold a competing talk about rape culture—without debate—so students could hear about how America is a rape culture without being confronted by different views.[28]

The competing talk didn't entirely solve the problem, however. Any student who chose to attend the main debate could still be "triggered" by the presence of McElroy on campus and (on the assumption that students are fragile rather than antifragile) retraumatized. So the student quoted above worked with other Brown students to create a "safe space" where anyone who felt triggered could recuperate and get help. The room was equipped with cookies, coloring books, bubbles, Play-Doh, calming music, pillows, blankets, and a video of frolicking puppies, as well as students and staff members purportedly trained to deal with trauma. But the threat wasn't just the reactivation of painful personal memories; it was also the threat to students' beliefs. One student who sought out the safe space put it this way: "I was feeling bombarded by a lot of viewpoints that really go against my dearly and closely held beliefs."[29]

The general reaction to Shulevitz's article was incredulity. Many Americans (and surely many Brown students) could not understand why college students needed to keep themselves "safe" from ideas. Couldn't they do that by simply not going to the talk? But if you understand the fragile-student model—the belief that many college students are fragile in Taleb's sense of the word—then it makes sense that all members of a community should work together to protect those students from reminders of past trauma. All members of the Brown community should come together to demand that the president (or somebody) prevent the threatening speaker from setting foot on campus. If you see yourself or your fellow students as candles, you'll want to make your campus a wind-free zone. If the president won't protect the students, then the students must come together to care for one another, which seems to have been the positive motivation for creating the safe space.

But young adults are not flickering candle flames. They are antifragile, and that is true even of victims of violence and those who suffer from PTSD. Research on "post-traumatic growth" shows that *most people* report becoming stronger, or better in some way, after suffering through a traumatic experience.[30] That doesn't mean we should stop protecting young people from potential trauma, but it does mean that the culture of safetyism is based on a fundamental misunderstanding of human nature and of the dynamics of trauma and recovery. It is vital that people who have survived violence become habituated to ordinary cues and reminders woven into the fabric of daily life.[31] Avoiding triggers is a *symptom* of PTSD, not a treatment for it. According to Richard McNally, the director of clinical training in Harvard's Department of Psychology:

> Trigger warnings are counter-therapeutic because they encourage avoidance of reminders of trauma, and avoidance maintains PTSD. Severe emotional reactions triggered by course material are a signal that students need to prioritize their mental health and obtain evidence-based, cognitive-behavioral therapies that will help them overcome PTSD. These therapies involve gradual, systematic exposure to traumatic memories until their capacity to trigger distress diminishes.[32]

Cognitive behavioral therapists treat trauma patients by exposing them to the things they find upsetting (at first in small ways, such as imagining them or looking at pictures), activating their fear, and helping them habituate (grow accustomed) to the stimuli. In fact, the reactivation of anxiety is so important to recovery that some therapists advise their patients to avoid using antianxiety medication while undertaking exposure therapy.[33]

For a student who truly suffers from PTSD, appropriate treatment is necessary. But well-meaning friends and professors who work together to hide potential reminders of painful experiences, or who repeatedly warn the student about the possible reminders he or she might encounter, could be impeding the person's recovery. A culture that allows the concept of "safety" to creep so far that it equates emotional discomfort with physical danger is a culture that encourages people to systematically protect one another from the very experiences embedded in daily life that they need in order to become strong and healthy.

This is what we mean when we talk about *safetyism*. Safety is good, of course, and keeping others safe from harm is virtuous, but virtues can become vices when carried to extremes.[34] "Safetyism" refers to a culture or belief system in which safety has become a sacred value, which means that people become unwilling to make trade-offs demanded by other practical and moral concerns. "Safety" trumps everything else, no matter how unlikely or trivial the potential danger. When children are raised in a culture of safetyism, which teaches them to stay "emotionally safe" while protecting them from every imaginable danger, it may set up a feedback loop: kids become more fragile and less resilient, which signals to adults that they need more protection, which then makes them even more fragile and less resilient. The end result may be similar to what happened when we tried to keep kids safe from exposure to peanuts: a widespread backfiring effect in which the "cure" turns out to be a primary cause of the disease.

iGen and Safetyism

The preoccupation with safetyism is clearest in the generation that began to enter college around 2013. For many years, sociologists and marketers assumed that the "Millennial generation" encompassed everyone born between (roughly) 1982 and 1998 or 2000. But Jean Twenge, a psychologist at San Diego State University and an authority on intergenerational differences, has found a surprisingly sharp discontinuity that begins around birth-year 1995. She calls those born in and after 1995 "iGen," short for "internet Generation." (Others use the term "Generation Z.") Twenge shows that iGen suffers from far higher rates of anxiety and depression than did Millennials at the same age—and higher rates of suicide. Something is going on; something has changed the childhood experience of kids born in the late 1990s. Twenge focuses on the rapid growth of social media in the years after the iPhone was introduced, in 2007. By 2011 or so, most teens could check in on their social media status every few minutes, and many did.

We'll explore Twenge's data and arguments in chapter 7. For now, we simply note two things. First, members of iGen are "obsessed with safety," as Twenge puts it, and define safety as including "emotional safety."[35] Their focus on "emotional safety" leads many of them to believe that, as Twenge describes, "one should be safe not just from car accidents and sexual assault but from people who disagree with you."[36]

The second point we want to note about iGen is that the campus trends that led us to write our original *Atlantic* article—particularly the requests for safe spaces and trigger warnings—started to spread only when iGen began arriving on campus, around 2013. The demands for safety and censorship accelerated rapidly over the next four years as the last of the Millennials graduated,[37] to be replaced by iGen. This is not a book about Millennials; indeed, Millennials are getting a bad rap these days, as many people erroneously attribute recent campus trends to them. This is a book about the very different attitudes toward speech and safety that spread across universities as the Millennials were leaving. We are not blaming iGen. Rather, we are proposing that today's college students were raised by parents and teachers who had children's best interests at heart but who often did not give them the freedom to develop their antifragility.

In Sum

- Children, like many other complex adaptive systems, are antifragile. Their brains require a wide range of inputs from their environments in order to configure themselves for those environments. Like the immune system, children must be exposed to challenges and stressors (within limits, and in age-appropriate ways), or they will fail to mature into strong and capable adults, able to engage productively with people and ideas that challenge their beliefs and moral convictions.

- Concepts sometimes creep. Concepts like trauma and safety have expanded so far since the 1980s that they are often employed in ways that are no longer grounded in legitimate psychological research. Grossly expanded conceptions of trauma and safety are now used to justify the overprotection of children of all ages—even college students, who are sometimes said to need safe spaces and trigger warnings lest words and ideas put them in danger.

- Safetyism is the cult of safety—an obsession with eliminating threats (both real and imagined) to the point at which people become unwilling to make reasonable trade-offs demanded by other practical and moral concerns. Safetyism deprives young people of the experiences that their antifragile minds need, thereby making them more fragile, anxious, and prone to seeing themselves as victims.

CHAPTER 2

The Untruth of Emotional Reasoning: Always Trust Your Feelings

What really frightens and dismays us is not external events
themselves, but the way in which we think about them. It is not
things that disturb us, but our interpretation of their significance.

EPICTETUS, *1st–2nd century*[1]

Imagine that you are a sophomore in college. It's midwinter, and you've been feeling blue and anxious. You attach no stigma to seeing a psycho-therapist, so you take advantage of the campus counseling services to see if talking through your issues will help.

You sit down with your new therapist and tell him how you've been feeling lately. He responds, "Oh, wow. People feel very anxious when they're in great danger. Do you feel *very* anxious sometimes?"

This realization that experiencing anxiety means you are in great danger is making you very anxious *right now*. You say yes. The therapist answers, "Oh, no! Then you must be in *very* great danger."

You sit in silence for a moment, confused. In your past experience, ther-apists have helped you question your fears, not amplify them. The therapist adds, "Have you experienced anything really nasty or difficult in your life? Because I should also warn you that experiencing trauma makes you kind of broken, and you may be that way for the rest of your life."

He briefly looks up from his notepad. "Now, since we know you are in grave danger, let's discuss how you can hide." As your anxiety mounts, you realize that you have made a terrible mistake coming to see this therapist.

. . . . .

"Always trust your feelings," said Misoponos, and that dictum may sound wise and familiar. You've heard versions of it from a variety of sappy novels and pop psychology gurus. But the second Great Untruth—the Untruth of Emotional Reasoning—is a direct contradiction of much ancient wisdom. We opened this chapter with a quotation from the Greek Stoic philosopher Epictetus, but we could just as easily have quoted Buddha ("Our life is the creation of our mind")[2] or Shakespeare ("There is nothing either good or bad, but thinking makes it so")[3] or Milton ("The mind is its own place, and in itself can make a heaven of hell, a hell of heaven").[4]

Or we could have told you the story of Boethius, awaiting execution in the year 524. Boethius reached the pinnacle of success in the late Roman world—he had been a senator and scholar who held many high offices—but he crossed the Ostrogoth king, Theodoric. In *The Consolation of Philosophy*, written in his jail cell, he describes his (imaginary) encounter with "Lady Philosophy," who visits him one night and conducts what is essentially a session of cognitive behavioral therapy (CBT). She chides him gently for his moping, fearfulness, and bitterness at his reversal of fortune, and then she helps him to reframe his thinking and shut off his negative emotions. She helps him see that fortune is fickle and he should be grateful that he enjoyed it for so long. She guides him to reflect on the fact that his wife, children, and father are all still alive and well, and each one is dearer to him than his own life. Each exercise helps him see his situation in a new light; each one weakens the grip of his emotions and prepares him to accept Lady Philosophy's ultimate lesson: *"Nothing is miserable unless you think it so; and on the other hand, nothing brings happiness unless you are content with it."*[5]

Sages in many societies have converged on the insight that feelings are always compelling, but not always reliable. Often they distort reality, deprive us of insight, and needlessly damage our relationships. Happiness, maturity, and even enlightenment require rejecting the Untruth of Emotional Reasoning and learning instead to *question* our feelings. The feelings themselves are real, and sometimes they alert us to truths that our conscious mind has not noticed, but sometimes they lead us astray.

In *The Happiness Hypothesis*, Jon drew on Buddha and other sages to offer the metaphor that the mind is divided into parts that sometimes conflict, like a small rider sitting on top of a large elephant. The rider represents conscious or "controlled" processes—the language-based thinking that fills our conscious minds and that we can control to some degree. The elephant represents everything else that goes on in our minds, the vast majority of which is outside of our conscious awareness. These processes can be called intuitive, unconscious, or "automatic," referring to the fact that nearly all of what goes on in our minds is outside of our direct control, although the results of automatic processes sometimes make their way into consciousness.[6] The rider-and-elephant metaphor captures the fact that the rider often believes he is in control, yet the elephant is vastly stronger, and tends to win any conflict that arises between the two. Jon reviewed psychological research to show that the rider generally functions more like the elephant's servant than its master, in that the rider is extremely skilled at producing post-hoc justifications for whatever the elephant does or believes.

Emotional reasoning is the cognitive distortion that occurs whenever the rider interprets what is happening in ways that are consistent with the elephant's reactive emotional state, without investigating what is true. The rider then acts like a lawyer or press secretary whose job is to rationalize and justify the elephant's pre-ordained conclusions, rather than to inquire into—or even be curious about—what is really true.

Typically, the rider does his job without objection, but the rider has some ability to talk back to the elephant, particularly if he can learn to speak the elephant's language, which is a language of intuition rather than logic. If the rider can reframe a situation so that the elephant sees it in a new way, then the elephant will feel new feelings, too, which will then motivate the elephant to move in a new direction. Boethius illustrated this "talking back" process by creating "Lady Philosophy" and having her ask the sorts of questions one learns to ask oneself in CBT. As he answers her questions, Boethius sees his life in new ways. He feels flashes of love for his family, and gratitude that they are safe. He changes the ways in which he interprets things, which causes his emotions to change, which then causes his thinking to change even further.

If you engage in this "talking back" process on a regular basis, it becomes easier and easier to do. Over time, the rider becomes a more skillful trainer, and the elephant becomes better trained. The two work together in harmony. That is the power and promise of CBT.

What Is CBT?

Cognitive behavioral therapy was developed in the 1960s by Aaron Beck, a psychiatrist at the University of Pennsylvania. At the time, Freudian ideas dominated psychiatry. Clinicians assumed that depression and the distorted thinking it produces were just the surface manifestation of deeper problems, usually stretching back to unresolved childhood conflict. To treat depression, you had to fix the underlying problem, and that could take many years of therapy. But Beck saw a close connection between the thoughts a person had and the feelings that came with them. He noticed that his patients tended to get themselves caught in a feedback loop in which irrational negative beliefs caused powerful negative feelings, which in turn seemed to drive patients' reasoning, motivating them to find evidence to support their negative beliefs. Beck noticed a common pattern of beliefs, which he called the "cognitive triad" of depression: "I'm no good," "My world is bleak," and "My future is hopeless."

Many people experience one or two of these thoughts fleetingly, but depressed people tend to hold all three beliefs in a stable and enduring psychological structure. Psychologists call such structures *schemas*. Schemas refer to the patterns of thoughts and behaviors, built up over time, that people use to process information quickly and effortlessly as they interact with the world. Schemas are deep down in the elephant; they are one of the ways in which the elephant guides the rider. Depressed people have schemas about themselves and their paths through life that are thoroughly disempowering.

Beck's great discovery was that it is possible to break the disempowering feedback cycle between negative beliefs and negative emotions. If you can get people to examine these beliefs and consider counterevidence, it gives them at least some moments of relief from negative emotions, and if you release them from negative emotions, they become more open to questioning their negative beliefs. It takes some skill to do this—depressed people are very good at finding evidence for the beliefs in the triad. And it takes time—a disempowering schema can't be disassembled in a single moment of great insight (which is why insights gained from moments of enlightenment often fade quickly). But it is possible to train people to learn Beck's method so they can question their automatic thoughts on their own, every day. With repetition, over a period of weeks or months, people can change their schemas and create different, more helpful habitual beliefs (such as "I can handle most challenges" or "I have friends I can trust"). With CBT, there is no need to spend years talking about one's childhood.

The evidence that CBT works is overwhelming.[7] A common finding is that CBT works about as well as Prozac and similar drugs for relieving the symptoms of anxiety disorders and mild to moderate depression,[8] and it does so with longer-lasting benefits and without any negative side effects. But CBT is effective for more than anxiety and depression, including anorexia, bulimia, obsessive compulsive disorder, anger, marital discord, and stress-related disorders.[9] CBT is easy to do, has been widely used, has been demonstrated to be effective, and is the best-studied form of psychotherapy.[10] It is therefore the therapy with the strongest evidence that it is both safe and effective.

The list below shows nine of the most common cognitive distortions that people learn to recognize in CBT. It is these distorted thought patterns that Greg began to notice on campus, which led him to invite Jon out to lunch, which led us to write our *Atlantic* article and, eventually, this book. (Different CBT experts and practitioners use different lists of cognitive distortions. The nine in our list are based on a longer list in Robert Leahy, Stephen Holland, and Lata McGinn's book, *Treatment Plans and Interventions for Depression and Anxiety Disorders*. For more on CBT—how it works, and how to practice it—please see Appendix 1.)

EMOTIONAL REASONING: Letting your feelings guide your interpretation of reality. "I feel depressed; therefore, my marriage is not working out."

CATASTROPHIZING: Focusing on the worst possible outcome and seeing it as most likely. "It would be terrible if I failed."

OVERGENERALIZING: Perceiving a global pattern of negatives on the basis of a single incident. "This generally happens to me. I seem to fail at a lot of things."

DICHOTOMOUS THINKING (also known variously as "black-and-white thinking," "all-or-nothing thinking," and "binary thinking"): Viewing events or people in all-or-nothing terms. "I get rejected by everyone," or "It was a complete waste of time."

MIND READING: Assuming that you know what people think without having sufficient evidence of their thoughts. "He thinks I'm a loser."

LABELING: Assigning global negative traits to yourself or others (often in the service of dichotomous thinking). "I'm undesirable," or "He's a rotten person."

NEGATIVE FILTERING: You focus almost exclusively on the negatives and seldom notice the positives. "Look at all of the people who don't like me."

DISCOUNTING POSITIVES: Claiming that the positive things you or others do are trivial, so that you can maintain a negative judgment. "That's what wives are supposed to do—so it doesn't count when she's nice to me," or "Those successes were easy, so they don't matter."

BLAMING: Focusing on the other person as the *source* of your negative feelings; you refuse to take responsibility for changing yourself. "She's to blame for the way I feel now," or "My parents caused all my problems."[11]

As you read through that list of distortions, it's easy to see how somebody who habitually thinks in such ways would develop schemas that revolve around maladaptive core beliefs, which interfere with realistic and adaptive interpretations of social situations.

Everyone engages in these distortions from time to time, so CBT is useful for everyone. Wouldn't our relationships be better if we all did a little less blaming and dichotomous thinking, and recognized that we usually share responsibility for conflicts? Wouldn't our political debates be more productive if we all did less overgeneralizing and labeling, both of which make it harder to compromise? We are not suggesting that everybody needs to find a therapist and start treatment with CBT. Greg's original realization about cognitive distortions was that just learning how to recognize them and rein them in is a good intellectual habit for all of us to cultivate.

Learning about cognitive distortions is especially important on a college campus. Imagine being in a seminar class in which several of the students habitually engage in emotional reasoning, overgeneralization, dichotomous thinking, and simplistic labeling. The task of the professor in this situation is to gently correct such distortions, all of which interfere with learning—both for the students engaging in the distortions and for the other students in the class. For example, if a student is offended by a passage in a novel and makes a sweeping generalization about the bad motives of authors who share the demographic characteristics of the offending author, other students might disagree but be reluctant to say so publicly. In such a case, the professor could ask a series of questions encouraging the student to ground assertions in textual evidence and consider alternative interpretations. Over time, a good college education should improve the critical thinking skills of all students.

There is no universally accepted definition of "critical thinking," but most treatments of the concept[12] include a commitment to connect one's claims to reliable evidence in a proper way—which is the basis of scholarship and is also the essence of CBT. (Critical thinking is also needed to recognize and defeat "fake news.") It is not acceptable for a scholar to say, "You have shown me convincing evidence that my claim is wrong, but I still *feel* that my claim is right, so I'm sticking with it." When scholars cannot rebut or reconcile disconfirming evidence, they must drop their claims or else lose the respect of their colleagues. As scholars challenge one another within a community that shares norms of evidence and argumentation and that holds one another accountable for good reasoning, claims get refined, theories gain nuance, and our understanding of truth advances.

But what would happen if some professors *encouraged* students to use the distortions in our list above?

Microaggressions: The Triumph of Impact Over Intent

A prime example of how some professors (and some administrators) encourage mental habits similar to the cognitive distortions is their promotion of the concept of "microaggressions," popularized in a 2007 article[13] by Derald Wing Sue, a professor at Columbia University's Teachers College. Sue and several colleagues defined microaggressions as "brief and commonplace daily verbal, behavioral, or environmental indignities, whether intentional or unintentional, that communicate hostile, derogatory, or negative racial slights and insults toward people of color." (The term was first applied to people of color but is now applied much more broadly.)

Many people from historically marginalized groups continue to face frequent acts of bias and prejudice. Sometimes people make thinly veiled bigoted remarks, and in cases where the speaker is expressing hostility or contempt, it seems appropriate to call it aggression. If the aggressive act is minor or subtle, then the term "microaggression" seems well suited for the situation. But *aggression* is not unintentional or accidental. If you bump into someone by accident and never meant them any harm, it is not an act of aggression, although the other person may *misperceive* it as one.

Unfortunately, when Sue included "unintentional" slights, and when he defined the slights *entirely in terms of the listener's interpretation*, he encouraged people to make such misperceptions. He encouraged them to engage in emotional reasoning—to start with their feelings and then justify those feelings by drawing the conclusion that someone has committed an act of *aggression* against them. Those feelings do sometimes point to a correct inference, and it is important to find out whether an acquaintance feels hostility or contempt toward you. But it is not a good idea to start by *assuming the worst about people* and reading their actions as uncharitably as possible. This is the distortion known as mind reading; if done habitually and negatively, it is likely to lead to despair, anxiety, and a network of damaged relationships.

Sue's original essay included a number of examples of microaggressions, some of which imply that a person holds negative stereotypes toward various groups—for example, a white woman clutching her purse when a black person passes by; a taxi driver passing by a person of color to pick up a white passenger; a white person praising a black person for being "articulate." A person who has experienced these things repeatedly might be justified in suspecting that bigotry or negative stereotypes motivated the behaviors.[14]

However, many of the examples offered by Sue do *not* necessarily suggest that the speaker feels hostility or holds negative stereotypes toward any group. His list of microaggressions includes a white person asking an Asian American to teach her words in the Asian American's "native language," a white person saying that "America is a melting pot," and a white person saying, "I believe the most qualified person should get the job." These all hinge on the fact that listeners could *choose* to interpret the statement or question in a way that makes them feel insulted or marginalized. Sue explains that an Asian American could take the language question as an assertion that "you are a foreigner"; a Latino student could take the "melting pot" comment as an injunction to "assimilate/acculturate to the dominant culture"; a black student could interpret the "most qualified person" comment as an implicit statement that "people of color are given extra unfair advantages because of their race."

Yes, one certainly *could* interpret these everyday questions and comments in this way, as tiny acts of aggression, rebuke, or exclusion—and sometimes that is exactly what they are. But there are other ways to interpret these statements, too. More to the point, should we *teach* students to interpret these kinds of things as acts of aggression? If a student feels a flash of offense as the recipient of such statements, is he better off *embracing* that feeling and labeling himself a victim of a microaggression, or is he better off asking himself if a more charitable interpretation might be warranted by the facts? A charitable interpretation does not mean that the recipient of the comment must do nothing; rather, it opens up a range of constructive responses. A charitable approach might be to say, "I'm guessing you didn't mean any harm when you said that, but you should know that some people might interpret that to mean . . ." This approach would make it easier for students to respond when they feel hurt, it would transform a victimization story into a story about one's own agency, and it would make it far more likely that the interpersonal exchange would have a positive outcome. We all can be more thoughtful about our own speech, but it is unjust to treat people as if they are bigots when they harbor no ill will. Doing so can discourage them from being receptive to valuable feedback. It may also make them less interested in engaging with people across lines of difference.[15]

By Sue's logic, however, *CBT itself* can be a microaggression, because it requires questioning the premises and assumptions that give rise to feelings. Sue gives the example of a therapist asking a client, "Do you really think your problem stems from racism?" Depending on the therapist's intention, such a question could indeed be improperly dismissive. But if the intention of the therapist is to help the client talk back to his emotions, search for evidence to justify interpretations, and find the realistic appraisal of events that will lead to the most effective functioning in a world full of ambiguities, then the question may very well be appropriate and constructive. Teaching people to see *more* aggression in ambiguous interactions, take *more* offense, feel *more* negative emotions, and avoid questioning their initial interpretations strikes us as unwise, to say the least. It is also contrary to the usual goals of good psychotherapy.

Shadi Hamid, a scholar at The Brookings Institution, describes his approach to dealing with potential microaggressions in an article in *The Atlantic*: "As an Arab and a Muslim, I get the questions 'Where are you from?'—by which people usually mean 'Where are you *really* from?'—and 'Were you born here?' quite often. It doesn't usually occur to me to get offended."[16] As Hamid notes, "In our identitarian age, the bar for offense has been lowered considerably, which makes democratic debate more difficult—citizens are more likely to withhold their true opinions if they fear being labeled as bigoted or insensitive."

Hamid's point has important implications for the challenge of building a community on a college campus, where we want students to freely engage with one another rather than keeping their thoughts hidden. Imagine that you are in charge of new-student orientation at an American university that is very diverse—there are students from a wide variety of racial groups, ethnic groups, religions, and socioeconomic backgrounds. There are international students from Asia, Africa, Europe, and Latin America, some of whom don't speak English well; many don't understand the nuances of English words and American customs, and as a result, they often choose the wrong word to express themselves. There are also students on the autism spectrum who have difficulty picking up on subtle social cues.[17]

With all this diversity, there will be hundreds of misunderstandings on your campus each day. The potential for offense-taking is almost unlimited. How should you prepare these students to engage with one another in the most productive and beneficial way? Would you give them a day of microaggression training and encourage them to report microaggressions whenever they see them? To go along with that training, would you set up a Bias Response Team—a group of administrators charged with investigating reports of bias, including microaggressions?[18] Or would you rather give all students advice on how to be polite and avoid giving accidental or thoughtless offense in a diverse community, along with a day of training in giving one another the benefit of the doubt and interpreting everyone's actions in ways that elicit the least amount of emotional reactivity?

More generally, the microaggression concept[19] reveals a crucial moral change on campus: the shift from "intent" to "impact." In moral judgment as it has long been studied by psychologists, intent is essential for assessing guilt.[20] We generally hold people morally responsible for acts that they *intended* to commit. If Bob tries to poison Maria and he fails, he has committed a very serious crime, even though he has made no impact on Maria. (Bob is still guilty of attempted murder.) Conversely, if Maria accidentally kills Bob by (consensually) kissing him after eating a peanut butter sandwich, she has committed no offense if she had no idea he was deathly allergic to peanuts.

Most people understand concepts related to racism, sexism, homophobia, and other forms of bigotry in this way—they focus on intent. If, on the basis of group membership, you dislike people, wish them ill, or intend to do them harm, you are a bigot, even if you say or do something that inadvertently or unintentionally helps members of that group. Conversely, if you accidentally say or do something that a member of a group finds offensive, but harbor no dislike or ill will on the basis of group membership, then you are not a bigot, even if you have said something clumsy or insensitive for which an apology is appropriate. A faux pas does not make someone an evil person or an aggressor.

However, some activists say that bigotry is only about impact (as they define impact); intent is not even necessary. If a member of an identity group *feels* offended or oppressed by the action of another person, then according to the impact-versus-intent paradigm, that other person is guilty of an act of bigotry. As explained in an essay at EverydayFeminism.com, "In the end, what does the intent of our action really matter if our actions have the impact of furthering the marginalization or oppression of those around us?"[21]

It is undeniable that some members of various identity groups encounter repeated indignities because of their group membership. Even if none of the offenders harbored a trace of ill will, their clueless or ignorant questions could become burdensome and hard to tolerate. Comedian and diversity educator Karith Foster, a black woman who is married to a white man, had a particularly difficult experience when her husband was taken to the emergency room after a nearly fatal motorcycle accident. As hospital personnel asked him about his medical history, he slipped in and out of consciousness. Foster began to answer for him, but nobody seemed to be listening to her. "For the first time in my life I felt invisible," she said. She told us that a doctor glanced at her indifferently and finally asked—in a detached tone of voice—what her relationship was to the patient. Then, as they treated her husband, more members of the all-white staff asked her that same question with a similar intonation, until finally Foster was on the brink of tears. "It wasn't the question," she told us. "I understand that by law and hospital protocol it needed to be asked. What was so disconcerting was the tone I perceived." She remembers clearly thinking, "Am I seriously having to deal with this racist bullshit RIGHT NOW? As my husband's life is on the line?!" She described what happened next:

I wanted so badly to lose it and scream at the hospital staff: "We're living in the twenty-first century! It's called a mixed-race marriage!" But I knew my emotions were getting the best of me in this incredibly stressful moment and were leading me to label the doctors and nurses as racists. I was assuming that I knew what they were thinking. But that's not the way I normally think when I'm not under so much stress. It took everything I had, but I took a deep breath and practiced the C.A.R.E. model[22] that I teach: I reminded myself that everyone was doing their best to save my husband's life, that the stress of the situation might be influencing my interpretations, and that I needed to keep the lines of communication open. Doing that must have shifted how I was coming across, because although I don't remember acting any differently, it seemed like all of a sudden the doctors began showing me X-rays and explaining the procedures they were doing. One of the attendants even went out and bought me a cup of coffee and refused to let me pay for it. That's when I had the epiphany that what I had experienced wasn't racism. No one was being malicious because I was black and my spouse was white. But for them to fully comprehend our relationship, they had to change their default ideas of what a married couple looks like.[23]

Foster told us that in dealing with hospital personnel's insensitivity, "without taking a step back, I could have made an awful situation a lot worse." After the emergency—her husband is doing fine now—Foster made sure to speak with the hospital administration about the insensitivity and lack of awareness she and her husband experienced, and the administrative personnel were receptive and apologetic.

It is crucial to teach incoming students to be thoughtful in their interactions with one another. A portion of what is derided as "political correctness" is just an effort to promote polite and respectful interactions by discouraging the use of terms that are reasonably taken to be demeaning.[24] But if you teach students that intention doesn't matter, and you *also* encourage students to find more things offensive (leading them to experience more negative impacts), and you *also* tell them that whoever says or does the things they find offensive are "aggressors" who have committed acts of bigotry against them, then you are probably fostering feelings of victimization, anger, and hopelessness in your students. They will come to see the world—and even their university—as a hostile place where things never seem to get better.

If someone wanted to create an environment of perpetual anger and intergroup conflict, this would be an effective way to do it. Teaching students to use the least generous interpretations possible is likely to engender precisely the feelings of marginalization and oppression that almost everyone wants to eliminate. And, to add injury to insult, this sort of environment is likely to foster an external locus of control. The concept of "locus of control" goes back to behaviorist days, when psychologists noted that animals (including people) could be trained to expect that they could get what they wanted through their own behavior (that is, some control over outcomes was "internal" to themselves). Conversely, animals could be trained to expect that nothing they did mattered (that is, all control of outcomes was "external" to themselves).[25] A great deal of research shows that having an internal locus of control leads to greater health, happiness, effort expended, success in school, and success at work.[26] An internal locus of control has even been found to make many kinds of adversity less painful.[27]

Disinvitations and the Ideological Vetting of Speakers

Another way that emotional reasoning manifests itself on college campuses is through the "disinvitation" of guest speakers. The logic typically used is that if a speaker makes some students uncomfortable, upset, or angry, then that is enough to justify banning that speaker from campus entirely be- cause of the "danger" that the speaker poses to those students. In a typical case,[28] students pressure the organization that issued the invitation, or pe- tition the college president or relevant deans, demanding that someone re- scind the invitation. The threat is made (sometimes implicitly and sometimes explicitly) that if the speaker comes to campus, there will be loud, disruptive protests in an organized effort to stop the talk from taking place. Strategies include blocking entrances to the building; shouting exple- tives or "Shame! Shame! Shame!"[29] at anyone who tries to attend; banging loudly on doors and windows from outside the room; and filling up the auditorium with protesters, who eventually shout or chant for as long as it takes to prevent the speaker from speaking.

As the idea that the mere presence of a speaker on campus can be "dan- gerous" has spread more widely, efforts to disinvite speakers have become more common. Greg's organization, the Foundation for Individual Rights in Education (FIRE), has been tracking disinvitation attempts going back to 2000; the FIRE disinvitation database currently contains 379 such events. About 46% of the attempts were successful: the speaker was disinvited, or the event was otherwise canceled. Of the events that proceeded, about a third were disrupted by protesters to some degree. For most of the events, the disinvitation effort can be clearly categorized as coming from one side of the political spectrum or the other. As you can see in Figure 2.1, from 2000 through 2009, disinvitation efforts were just as likely to come from the right as from the left.[30] But after 2009, a gap opens up, and then widens beginning in 2013, right around the time that Greg began noticing things changing on campus.

Part of this change is because, on some campuses, conservative groups

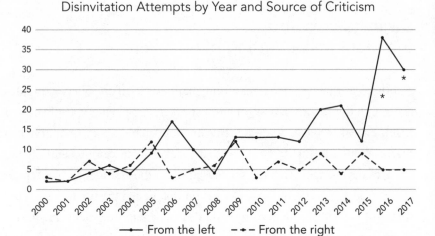

Disinvitation Attempts by Year and Source of Criticism

From the left   From the right

FIGURE 2.1. Disinvitation attempts each year since 2000. Solid line shows efforts initiated by people and groups on the political left; dashed line shows efforts from the right. Asterisks show where the solid line would have been had Milo Yiannopoulos been removed from the dataset. (Source: FIRE.)

began inviting more provocateurs, especially Milo Yiannopoulos, a master of the art of provoking what he calls "mild rage." Yiannopoulos describes himself as a "troll" and even named his 2017 speaking tour "Milo's Troll Academy Tour."[31] While trolls have, of course, been around for a long time, the dynamic of troll versus protesters became more common in 2016, and we have used asterisks in Figure 2.1 to show where the line for the left would have been had we not included the seventeen Yiannopoulos disinvitations.[32] Many of the speakers who faced disinvitation efforts from the left in 2013 and 2014 were serious thinkers and politicians, including conservative political journalist George Will, and managing director of the International Monetary Fund Christine Lagarde. Some of them were even clearly left leaning, such as former Secretary of State Madeleine Albright, comedian Bill Maher, and former U.S. Attorney General Eric Holder.

Something began changing on many campuses around 2013,[33] and the idea that college students should not be exposed to "offensive" ideas is now a majority position on campus. In 2017, 58% of college students said it is "important to be part of a campus community where I am not exposed to intolerant and offensive ideas."[34] This statement was endorsed by 63% of very liberal students, but it's a view that is not confined to the left; almost half of very conservative students (45%) endorsed that statement, too.

The notion that a university should protect all of its students from ideas that some of them find offensive is a repudiation of the legacy of Socrates, who described himself as the "gadfly" of the Athenian people. He thought it was his job to sting, to disturb, to question, and thereby to provoke his fellow Athenians to think through their current beliefs, and change the ones they could not defend.[35]

It was in this spirit that Zachary Wood, a left-leaning African American student at Williams College, in Massachusetts, led the "Uncomfortable Learning" series. Like Socrates, Wood wanted to expose students to ideas that they would otherwise not encounter, in order to spur them to better thinking. In October 2015, Wood invited Suzanne Venker,[36] a conservative critic of feminism and an advocate of traditional gender roles, to speak as part of the series. Wood's co-organizer, Matthew Hennessy, explained:

> We chose [Venker] because millions of Americans think her viewpoints carry weight, or even agree with her. We think it's important to get an understanding of why so many Americans do think these really interesting and difficult thoughts, so we can challenge them and better understand our own behaviors and our own thoughts.[37]

The response from Williams students was so ferocious that ultimately Wood and Hennessy decided they had to cancel the event. One student wrote on a Facebook page:

> When you bring a misogynistic, white supremacist men's rights activist to campus in the name of "dialogue" and "the other side," you are not only causing actual mental, social, psychological, and physical harm to students, but you are also—paying—for the continued dispersal of violent ideologies that kill our black and brown (trans) femme sisters. . . . Know, you are dipping your hands in their blood, Zach Wood.[38]

This response clearly illustrates the cognitive distortions of catastrophizing, labeling, overgeneralizing, and dichotomous thinking. It is also a textbook example of emotional reasoning, as Wood himself put it when explaining the decision to cancel the lecture:

> When an individual goes so far as to describe someone as having blood on their hands for supporting the idea of bringing a highly controversial speaker to Williams, they are advancing the belief that what offends them should not be allowed on this campus precisely because it offends them and people who agree with them.[39]

Should a student saying "I am offended" be sufficient reason to cancel a lecture? What if it's many students? What if members of the faculty are offended, too?

It depends on what you think is the purpose of education. Hanna Holborn Gray, the president of the University of Chicago from 1978 to 1993, once offered this principle: "Education should not be intended to make people comfortable; it is meant to make them think."[40] This, of course, was Zach Wood's belief, too, and Gray's principle allows us to distinguish the provocations of Wood and Socrates from the provocations of Yiannopoulos. Unfortunately, the president of Williams College had a different philosophy, and personally intervened to cancel a later invitation made to another controversial speaker.[41] In doing so, he implicitly endorsed Misoponos's dictum that "uncomfortable learning" is an oxymoron. He might as well have posted a sign on the entry gates to the college: EDUCATION SHOULD NOT BE INTENDED TO MAKE PEOPLE THINK; IT IS MEANT TO MAKE THEM COMFORTABLE.

In Sum

- Among the most universal psychological insights in the world's wisdom traditions is that *what really frightens and dismays us is not external events themselves but the way in which we think about them*, as Epictetus put it.

- CBT is a method anyone can learn for identifying common cognitive distortions and then changing their habitual patterns of thinking. CBT helps the rider (controlled processing) to train the elephant (automatic processing), resulting in better critical thinking and mental health.

- Emotional reasoning is among the most common of all cognitive distortions; most people would be happier and more effective if they did less of it.

- The term "microaggressions" refers to a way of thinking about brief and commonplace indignities and slights communicated to people of color (and others). Small acts of aggression are real, so the term could be useful, but because the definition includes accidental and *unintentional* offenses, the word "aggression" is misleading. Using the lens of microaggressions may amplify the pain experienced and the conflict that ensues. (On the other hand, there is nothing "micro" about intentional acts of aggression and bigotry.)

- By encouraging students to interpret the actions of others in the least generous way possible, schools that teach students about microaggressions may be encouraging students to engage in emotional reasoning and other distortions while setting themselves up for higher levels of distrust and conflict.

- Karith Foster offers an example of using empathy to reappraise actions that could be interpreted as microaggressions. When she interpreted those actions as innocent (albeit insensitive) misunderstandings, it led to a better outcome for everyone.

- The number of efforts to "disinvite" speakers from giving talks on campus has increased in the last few years; such efforts are often justified by the claim that the speaker in question will cause harm to students. But discomfort is not danger. Students, professors, and administrators should understand the concept of antifragility and keep in mind Hanna Holborn Gray's principle: "Education should not be intended to make people comfortable; it is meant to make them think."

The Untruth of Us Versus Them: Life Is a Battle Between Good People and Evil People

> *There is the moral dualism that sees good and evil as instincts within us between which we must choose. But there is also what I will call pathological dualism that sees humanity itself as radically . . . divided into the unimpeachably good and the irredeemably bad. You are either one or the other.*
>
> RABBI LORD JONATHAN SACKS, *Not in God's Name*[1]

Aprotest is always a claim that injustice is being done. When a group forms to protest together, they jointly construct a narrative about what is wrong, who is to blame, and what must be done to make things right. Reality is always more complicated than the narrative, however, and as a result, people are demonized or lionized—often unfairly. One such case happened in October 2015 at Claremont McKenna College, near Los Angeles.

A student named Olivia, whose parents emigrated from Mexico to California before she was born, wrote an essay in a student publication about her feelings of marginalization and exclusion.[2] Olivia noticed that Latinos were better represented on the blue-collar staff at CMC (including janitors and gardeners) than among its administrative and professional staff, and she found this realization painful. She wrote that she felt like she had been admitted to fill a racial quota. She suggested that there is a standard or typical person at CMC, and she is not it: "Our campus climate and institutional culture are primarily grounded in western, white, cisheteronormative upper to upper-middle class values." ("Cisheteronormative" describes a society in which people assume that other people are not transgender and not gay, unless there is information to the contrary.)[3]

In response to this essay, which Olivia sent in an email to "CMC Staff," Mary Spellman, the dean of students at CMC, sent her a private email two days later. Here is the entire email:

> Olivia—
>
> Thank you for writing and sharing this article with me. We have a lot to do as a college and community. Would you be willing to talk with me sometime about these issues? They are important to me and the [dean of students] staff and we are working on how we can better serve students, especially those who don't fit our CMC mold.
>
> I would love to talk with you more.
>
> Best,
> Dean Spellman[4]

What do you think about Dean Spellman's email? Cruel or kind? Most readers can probably see that she was showing concern and reaching out with an offer to listen and help. But Olivia was offended by the dean's use of the word "mold." She seemed to interpret it in the least generous way possible: that Spellman was implying that Olivia (and other students of color) do not fit the mold and therefore do not belong at CMC. This was clearly not Spellman's intent; Olivia herself had asserted that at CMC, there is a prototype or pattern of identities that she does not match, and, as Spellman later explained,[5] she used the word "mold" to express her empathy with Olivia, because it's a word that *other* CMC students use in conversations with her to describe their sense of not fitting in.

Any student who was already feeling like an outsider might well feel a flash of negativity upon reading the word "mold." But what should one do with that flash? There is a principle in philosophy and rhetoric called the principle of charity, which says that one should interpret other people's statements in their best, most reasonable form, not in the worst or most offensive way possible. Had Olivia been taught to judge people primarily on their intentions, she could have used the principle of charity in this situation, as Karith Foster did in the situation described in the previous chapter. If a student in Olivia's position was in the habit of questioning her initial reactions, looking for evidence, and giving people the benefit of the doubt, that student might get past her initial flash of emotion and avail herself of an invitation from a dean who wanted to know what she could do to address the student's concerns.

That is not what happened. Instead, Olivia posted Spellman's email on her Facebook page (about two weeks after receiving it) with the comment, "I just don't fit that wonderful CMC mold! Feel free to share." Her friends did share the email, and the campus erupted in protest.[6] There were marches, demonstrations, demands given to the president for mandatory diversity training, and demands that Spellman resign. Two students went on a hunger strike, vowing that they would not eat until Spellman was gone.[7] In one scene, which you can watch on YouTube, students formed a circle and spent over an hour airing their grievances—through bullhorns—against Spellman and other administrators who were there in the circle to listen.[8] Spellman apologized for her email being "poorly worded" and told the crowd that her "intention was to affirm the feelings and experiences expressed in the article and to provide support."[9] But the students did not accept her apology. At one point a woman berated the dean (to cheers from the students) for "falling asleep"[10] during the proceedings, which the woman interpreted as an act of disrespect. But it is clear from the video of the confrontation that Spellman was not falling asleep; she was trying to hold back her tears.

The university did not fire Spellman, but neither did its leaders publicly express any support for her.[11] Faced with the escalating anger of students—amplified by social media and then by national news coverage—Spellman resigned.[12]

As this was happening, another conflict over an email was unfolding at

Yale.[13] Erika Christakis, a lecturer at the Yale Child Study Center and associate master of Silliman College (one of Yale's residential colleges), wrote an email questioning whether it was appropriate for Yale administrators to give guidance to students about appropriate and inappropriate Halloween costumes, as the college dean's office had done.[14] Christakis praised their "spirit of avoiding hurt and offense," but she worried that "the growing tendency to cultivate vulnerability in students carries unacknowledged costs."[15] She expressed concern about the institutional "exercise of implied control over college students," and invited the community to reflect on whether, as adults, they could set norms for themselves and handle disagreements interpersonally. "Talk to each other," she wrote. "Free speech and the ability to tolerate offense are the hallmarks of a free and open society."

The email sparked an angry response from some students, who interpreted it as an indication that Christakis was in favor of racist costumes.[16] A few days later, a group of roughly 150 students appeared in the courtyard outside Christakis's home (within Silliman College), writing statements in chalk, including "We know where you live." Erika's husband, Nicholas Christakis, was the master of Silliman (a title that has since been changed to "head of college"). When he came out to the courtyard, students demanded that he apologize for—and renounce—his wife's email.[17] Nicholas listened, engaged in dialogue with them, and apologized several times for causing them pain, but he refused to renounce his wife's email or the ideas it espoused.[18] Students accused him and Erika of being "racist" and "offensive," "stripping people of their humanity," "creating an unsafe space," and enabling "violence." They swore at him, criticized him for "not listening" and for not remembering students' names. They told him not to smile, lean down, or gesticulate. And they told him they wanted him to lose his job. Eventually, in a scene that went viral,[19] one student screamed at him: "Who the fuck hired you? You should step down! It is not about creating an intellectual space! It is not! It's about creating a home here. . . . You should not sleep at night! You are disgusting!"[20]

The next day, the president of the university sent out an email acknowledging students' pain and committing to "take actions that will make us better."[21] He did not mention any support for the Christakises until weeks after the courtyard incident, by which time attitudes against the couple were entrenched. Amid ongoing demands that they be fired,[22] Erika resigned from her teaching position,[23] Nicholas took a sabbatical from teaching for the rest of the year, and at the end of the school year, the pair resigned from their positions in the residential college. Erika later revealed that many professors were very supportive privately, but were unwilling to defend or support the Christakises publicly because they thought it was "too risky" and they feared retribution.[24]

Why did students react so strongly to the emails from Dean Spellman and Erika Christakis, both of which were clearly intended to be helpful to students? Of course, there was a backstory at each school; there were incidents of racism or other reasons why some students were frustrated with the administration.[25] The protests were not *just* about the emails. But as far as we can tell, those backstories don't involve Spellman or Christakis. So why did students interpret the emails as offenses so grave that they justified calls for their authors to be fired? It's as though some of the students had their own mental prototype, a schema with two boxes to fill: *victim* and *oppressor*. Everyone is placed into one box or the other.

Groups and Tribes

There's a famous series of experiments in social psychology called the *minimal group paradigm*, pioneered by Polish psychologist Henri Tajfel, who served in the French Army during World War II and became a prisoner of war in Germany. Profoundly affected by his experiences as a Jew during that period in Europe, including having his entire family in Poland murdered by the Nazis, Tajfel wanted to understand the conditions under which people would discriminate against members of an outgroup. So in the 1960s he conducted a series of experiments, each of which began by dividing people into two groups based on trivial and arbitrary criteria, such as flipping a coin. For example, in one study, each person first estimated the number of dots on a page. Irrespective of their estimations, half were told that they had overestimated the number of dots and were put into a group of "overestimators." The other half were sent to the "underestimators" group. Next, subjects were asked to distribute points or money to all the other subjects, who were identified only by their group membership. Tajfel found that no matter how trivial or "minimal" he made the distinctions between the groups, people tended to distribute whatever was offered in favor of their in-group members.[26]

Later studies have used a variety of techniques to reach the same conclusion.[27] Neuroscientist David Eagleman used functional magnetic resonance imaging (fMRI) to examine the brains of people who were watching videos of other people's hands getting pricked by a needle or touched by a Q-tip. When the hand being pricked by a needle was labeled with the participant's own religion, the area of the participant's brain that handles pain showed a larger spike of activity than when the hand was labeled with a different religion. When arbitrary groups were created (such as by flipping a coin) immediately before the subject entered the MRI machine, and the hand being pricked was labeled as belonging to the same *arbitrary* group as the participant, even though the group hadn't even existed just moments earlier, the participant's brain still showed a larger spike.[28] We just don't feel as much empathy for those we see as "other."

The bottom line is that the human mind is prepared for tribalism. Human evolution is not just the story of individuals competing with other individuals within each group; it's also the story of groups competing with other groups—sometimes violently. We are all descended from people who belonged to groups that were consistently better at winning that competition. Tribalism is our evolutionary endowment for banding together to prepare for intergroup conflict.[29] When the "tribe switch"[30] is activated, we bind ourselves more tightly to the group, we embrace and defend the group's moral matrix, and we stop thinking for ourselves. A basic principle of moral psychology is that "morality binds and blinds,"[31] which is a useful trick for a group gearing up for a battle between "us" and "them." In tribal mode, we seem to go blind to arguments and information that challenge our team's narrative. Merging with the group in this way is deeply pleasurable—as you can see from the pseudotribal antics that accompany college football games.

But being *prepared* for tribalism doesn't mean we have to *live* in tribal ways. The human mind contains many evolved cognitive "tools." We don't use all of them all the time; we draw on our toolbox as needed. Local conditions can turn the tribalism up, down, or off. Any kind of intergroup conflict (real or perceived) immediately turns tribalism up, making people highly attentive to signs that reveal which team another person is on. Traitors are punished, and fraternizing with the enemy is, too. Conditions of peace and prosperity, in contrast, generally turn down the tribalism.[32] People don't need to track group membership as vigilantly; they don't feel pressured to conform to group expectations as closely. When a community succeeds in turning down everyone's tribal circuits, there is more room for individuals to construct lives of their own choosing; there is more freedom for a creative mixing of people and ideas.

So what happens to a community such as a college (or, increasingly, a high school[33]) when distinctions between groups are not trivial and arbitrary, and when they are emphasized rather than downplayed? What happens when you train students to see others—and themselves—as members of distinct groups defined by race, gender, and other socially significant factors, and you tell them that those groups are eternally engaged in a zero-sum conflict over status and resources?

Two Kinds of Identity Politics

"Identity politics" is a contentious term, but its basic meaning is simple. Jonathan Rauch, a scholar at The Brookings Institution, defines it as "political mobilization organized around group characteristics such as race, gender, and sexuality, as opposed to party, ideology, or pecuniary interest." He notes that "in America, this sort of mobilization is not new, unusual, un-American, illegitimate, nefarious, or particularly leftwing."[34] Politics is all about groups forming coalitions to achieve their goals. If cattle ranchers, wine enthusiasts, or libertarians banding together to promote their interests is normal politics, then women, African Americans, or gay people banding together is normal politics, too.

But *how* identity is mobilized makes an enormous difference—for the group's odds of success, for the welfare of the people who join the movement, and for the country. Identity can be mobilized in ways that emphasize an overarching common humanity while making the case that some *fellow human beings* are denied dignity and rights because they belong to a particular group, or it can be mobilized in ways that amplify our ancient tribalism and bind people together in shared hatred of a *group* that serves as the unifying common enemy.

COMMON-HUMANITY IDENTITY POLITICS

The Reverend Dr. Martin Luther King, Jr., epitomized what we'll call *common-humanity identity politics.* He was trying to fix a gaping wound— centuries of racism that had been codified into law in southern states and into customs, habits, and institutions across the country. It wasn't enough to be patient and wait for things to change gradually. The civil rights movement was a political movement led by African Americans and joined by others. Together, they engaged in nonviolent protests and civil disobedience, boycotts, and sophisticated public relations strategies to apply political pressure on intransigent lawmakers while working to change minds and hearts in the country at large.

Part of Dr. King's genius was that he appealed to the shared morals and identities of Americans by using the unifying languages of religion and patriotism. He repeatedly used the metaphor of family, referring to people of all races and religions as "brothers" and "sisters." He spoke often of the need for love and forgiveness, hearkening back to the words of Jesus and echoing ancient wisdom from many cultures: "Love is the only force capable of transforming an enemy into a friend"[35] and "Darkness cannot drive out darkness; only light can do that. Hate cannot drive out hate; only love can do that."[36] (Compare King's words to these from Buddha: "For hate is not conquered by hate; hate is conquered by love. This is a law eternal.")[37]

King's most famous speech drew on the language and iconography of what sociologists call the American civil religion.[38] Some Americans use quasi-religious language, frameworks, and narratives to speak about the country's founding documents and founding fathers, and King did, too. "When the architects of our republic wrote the magnificent words of the Constitution and the Declaration of Independence," he proclaimed on the steps of the Lincoln Memorial, "they were signing a promissory note."[39] King turned the full moral force of the American civil religion toward the goals of the civil rights movement:

> Even though we face the difficulties of today and tomorrow, I still have a dream. It is a dream deeply rooted in the American dream. I have a dream that one day this nation will rise up and live out the true meaning of its creed: "We hold these truths to be self-evident, that all men are created equal."[40]

King's approach made it clear that his movement would not destroy America; it would repair and reunite it.[41] This inclusive, common-humanity approach was also explicit in the words of Pauli Murray, a black and queer Episcopal priest and civil rights activist who, in 1965, at the age of fifty-five, earned a degree from Yale Law School. Today a residential college at Yale is named after her.[42] In 1945, she wrote:

> I intend to destroy segregation by positive and embracing methods. . . . When my brothers try to draw a circle to exclude me, I shall draw a larger circle to include them. Where they speak out for the privileges of a puny group, I shall shout for the rights of all mankind.[43]

A variant of this ennobling common-humanity approach played a major role in the movement that won marriage equality for gay people in several statewide elections in 2012, paving the way for the Supreme Court to rule that gay marriage would become the law of the land. Some of the most powerful advertisements of those 2012 campaigns used King's technique of appealing to love and shared moral values. If you want to experience the emotion of moral elevation, just go to YouTube and search for "Mainers United for Marriage." You'll find short clips showing firefighters,

Republicans, and Christians, all appealing to powerful moral principles, including religion and patriotism, to explain why they want their son/ daughter/coworker to be able to marry the person he or she loves. Here's the transcript from one such ad, featuring an Episcopal priest and his wife:[44]

> HUSBAND: Our son Hal led a platoon in Iraq.
>
> WIFE: When he got back he sat us down and said: "Mom, Dad, I'm gay."
>
> HUSBAND: That took some getting used to, but we love him and we're proud of him.
>
> WIFE: Our marriage has been the foundation of our lives for forty-six years.
>
> HUSBAND: We used to think civil unions were enough for gay couples.
>
> WIFE: But marriage is a commitment from the heart. A civil union is no substitute.
>
> HUSBAND: Our son fought for our freedoms. He should have the freedom to marry.

This is the way to win hearts, minds, and votes: you must appeal to the elephant (intuitive and emotional processes) as well as the rider (reasoning).[45] King and Murray understood this. Instead of shaming or demonizing their opponents, they *humanized* them and then relentlessly appealed to their humanity.

COMMON-ENEMY IDENTITY POLITICS

The common-humanity form of identity politics can still be found on many college campuses, but in recent years we've seen the rapid rise of a very different form that is based on an effort to unite and mobilize multiple groups to fight against a common enemy. It activates a powerful social-psychological mechanism embodied in an old Bedouin proverb: "I against my brothers. I and my brothers against my cousins. I and my brothers and my cousins against the world."[46] Identifying a common enemy is an effective way to enlarge and motivate your tribe.

Because we are trying to understand what is happening on campus, in what follows in this chapter, we'll be focusing on the identity politics of the campus left. We note, however, that developments on campus are often influenced by provocations from the right, which we will discuss in chapter 6. Provocations from the right mostly come from off campus (where the right is just as committed to identity politics as is the left).

There has never been a more dramatic demonstration of the horrors of common-enemy identity politics than Adolf Hitler's use of Jews to unify and expand his Third Reich. And it is among the most shocking aspects of our current age that some Americans (and Europeans), mostly young white men, have openly embraced neo-Nazi ideas and symbols. They and other white nationalist groups rally around a shared hatred not just of Jews, but also of blacks, feminists, and "SJWs" (social justice warriors). These right-wing extremist groups seem not to have played significant roles in campus politics before 2016, but by 2017 many of them had developed methods of trolling and online harassment that began to have an influence on campus events, as we'll discuss further in chapter 6.

As for the identity politics originating from left-leaning on-campus sources, here's a recent example that drew a great deal of attention. In December 2017, a Latino student at Texas State University wrote an opinion essay in his school's student-run, independent newspaper under the headline YOUR DNA IS AN ABOMINATION.[47] The essay began like this:

When I think of all the white people I have ever encountered—whether they've been professors, peers, lovers, friends, police officers, et cetera—there is perhaps only a dozen I would consider "decent."

The student then argued that "whiteness" is "a construct used to perpetuate a system of racist power," and asserted that "through a constant ideological struggle in which we aim to deconstruct 'whiteness' and everything attached to it, we will win." The essay ended with this:

Ontologically speaking, white death will mean liberation for all. . . .
Until then, remember this: I hate you because you shouldn't exist.
You are both the dominant apparatus on the planet and the void in
which all other cultures, upon meeting you, die.

Right-wing sites interpreted the essay as a call for actual genocide
against white people. The author seems, rather, to have been calling for
cultural genocide: the end of white dominance and the culture of "whiteness" in the United States. In any case, the backlash was swift and severe
and came from both on campus and off.[48] From off campus, the paper received hate mail, calls for resignations, and even death threats. More than
two thousand people signed a petition to defund the student paper.[49] (FIRE
defended the newspaper's First Amendment rights.) The student editors
quickly apologized,[50] retracted the article, and fired the writer. The president of the university called the essay a "racist opinion column" and said
she expected the student editors to "exercise good judgment in determining
the content that they print."[51]

In calling for the dismantling of power structures, the author was using
a set of terms and concepts that are common in some academic departments; the main line of argumentation fell squarely within the large family
of Marxist approaches to social and political analysis. It's a set of approaches
in which things are analyzed primarily in terms of power. Groups struggle
for power. Within this paradigm, when power is perceived to be held by one
group over others, there is a moral polarity: the groups seen as powerful are
bad, while the groups seen as oppressed are good. It's a variant of the patho-
logical dualism that Rabbi Sacks described in the quotation at the start of
this chapter.

Writing during the nineteenth-century Industrial Revolution, Karl
Marx focused on conflict between economic classes, such as the proletariat
(the working class) and the capitalists (those who own the means of production). But a Marxist approach can be used to interpret any struggle
between groups. One of the most important Marxist thinkers for understanding developments on campus today is Herbert Marcuse, a German
philosopher and sociologist who fled the Nazis and became a professor at

several American universities. His writings were influential in the 1960s and 1970s as the American left was transitioning away from its prior focus on workers versus capital to become the "New Left," which focused on civil rights, women's rights, and other social movements promoting equality and justice. These movements often had a left-right dimension to them—progressives wanted progress and conservatives wanted to conserve the existing order. Marcuse therefore analyzed the conflict between the left and the right in Marxist terms.

In a 1965 essay titled "Repressive Tolerance," Marcuse argued that tolerance and free speech confer benefits on society only under special conditions that almost never exist: absolute equality. He believed that when power differentials between groups exist, tolerance only empowers the already powerful and makes it easier for them to dominate institutions like education, the media, and most channels of communication. Indiscriminate tolerance is "repressive," he argued; it blocks the political agenda and suppresses the voices of the less powerful.

If indiscriminate tolerance is unfair, then what is needed is a form of tolerance that *discriminates*. A truly "liberating tolerance," claimed Marcuse, is one that favors the weak and restrains the strong. Who are the weak and the strong? For Marcuse, writing in 1965, the weak was the political left and the strong was the political right. Even though the Democrats controlled Washington at that time, Marcuse associated the right with the business community, the military, and other vested interests that he saw as wielding power, hoarding wealth, and working to block social change.[52] The left referred to students, intellectuals, and minorities of all kinds. For Marcuse, there was no moral equivalence between the two sides. In his view, the right pushed for war; the left stood for peace; the right was the party of "hate," the left the party of "humanity."[53]

Someone who accepts this framing—that the right is powerful (and therefore oppressive) while the left is weak (and therefore oppressed)—might be receptive to the argument that indiscriminate tolerance is bad. In its place, *liberating tolerance*, Marcuse explained, "would mean intolerance against movements from the Right, and toleration of movements from the Left."[54]

Marcuse recognized that what he was advocating seemed to violate both the spirit of democracy and the liberal tradition of nondiscrimination, but he argued that when the majority of a society is being repressed, it is justifiable to use "repression and indoctrination" to allow the "subversive majority" to achieve the power that it deserves. In a chilling passage that foreshadows events on some campuses today, Marcuse argued that true democracy might require denying basic rights to people who advocate for conservative causes, or for policies he viewed as aggressive or discriminatory, and that true freedom of thought might require professors to indoctrinate their students:

> The ways should not be blocked [by] which a subversive majority could develop, and if they are blocked by organized repression and indoctrination, their reopening may require apparently undemocratic means. They would include the withdrawal of toleration of speech and assembly from groups and movements which promote aggressive policies, armament, chauvinism, discrimination on the grounds of race and religion, or which oppose the extension of public services, social security, medical care, etc. Moreover, the restoration of freedom of thought may necessitate new and rigid restrictions on teachings and practices in the educational institutions which, by their very methods and concepts, serve to enclose the mind within the established universe of discourse and behavior.[55]

The end goal of a Marcusean revolution is not equality but a reversal of power. Marcuse offered this vision in 1965:

> It should be evident by now that the exercise of civil rights by those who don't have them presupposes the withdrawal of civil rights from those who prevent their exercise, and that liberation of the Damned of the Earth presupposes suppression not only of their old but also of their new masters.[56]

The student who wrote that essay at Texas State University may not have read Marcuse directly, yet somehow he ended up with a Marcusean view of the world. Marcuse was known as the "father" of the New Left; his ideas were taken up by the generation of students in the 1960s and 1970s who are the older professors of today, so a Marcusean view is still widely available. But why does this vision continue to flourish fifty years after the publication of "Repressive Tolerance," in a country that has made enormous progress on extending civil rights to groups that did not have them in 1965, and in an educational system that cannot be said to be controlled by the right? Even if Marcuse's arguments made sense to many people in 1965, can his ideas be justified on campus today?

Modern Marcuseanism

In the decades after "Repressive Tolerance" was published, a variety of theories and approaches flourished on campus in humanities and social science departments that offered ways of analyzing society through the lens of power relationships among groups. (Examples include deconstructionism, poststructuralism, postmodernism, and critical theory.) One such theory deserves special mention, because its ideas and terminology are widely found in the discourse of today's campus activists. The approach known as *intersectionality* was advanced by Kimberlé Williams Crenshaw, a law professor at UCLA (and now at Columbia, where she directs the Center on Intersectionality and Social Policy Studies).[57] In a 1989 essay, Crenshaw noted that a black woman's experience in America is not captured by the summation of the black experience and the female experience.[58] She made her point vividly by analyzing a legal case in which black women were victims of discrimination at General Motors even when the company could show that it hired plenty of black people (in factory jobs dominated by men) and plenty of women (in clerical jobs dominated by white people).[59] So even though GM was found not to have discriminated against black people or women, it ended up hiring hardly any black women. Crenshaw's important insight was that you can't just look at a few big "main effects" of discrimination; you have to look at interactions, or "intersections." More generally, as explained in a recent book by Patricia Hill Collins and Sirma Bilge:

> Intersectionality as an analytic tool examines how power relations are intertwined and mutually constructing. Race, class, gender, sexuality, dis/ability, ethnicity, nation, religion, and age are categories of analysis, terms that reference important social divisions. But they are also categories that gain meaning from power relations of racism, sexism, heterosexism, and class exploitation.[60]

Intersectionality is a theory based on several insights that we believe are valid and useful: power matters, members of groups sometimes act cruelly or unjustly to preserve their power, and people who are members of multiple identity groups can face various forms of disadvantage in ways that are often invisible to others. The point of using the terminology of "intersectionalism," as Crenshaw said in her 2016 TED Talk, is that "where there's no name for a problem, you can't see a problem, and when you can't see a problem, you pretty much can't solve it."[61]

Our purpose here is not to critique the theory itself; it is, rather, to explore the effects that certain *interpretations* of intersectionality may now be having on college campuses. The human mind is prepared for tribalism, and these interpretations of intersectionality have the potential to turn tribalism way up.

These interpretations of intersectionality teach people to see bipolar dimensions of privilege and oppression as ubiquitous in social interactions. It's not just about employment or other opportunities, and it's not just about race and gender. Figure 3.1 shows the sort of diagram that is sometimes used to teach intersectionality. We modeled ours on a figure[62] by Kathryn Pauly Morgan, a professor of philosophy at the University of Toronto. (For simplicity, we show only seven of her fourteen intersecting axes.) In an essay describing her approach, Morgan explains that the center point represents a particular individual living at the "intersection" of many dimensions of power and privilege; the person might be high or low on any of the axes. She defines her terms like this: "Privilege involves the power to dominate in systematic ways. . . . Oppression involves the lived, systematic experience of being dominated by virtue of one's position on various particular axes."[63]

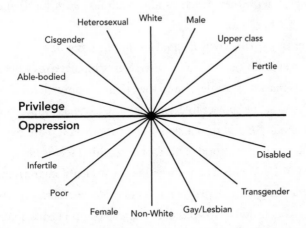

FIGURE 3.1. *Seven intersecting axes of privilege and oppression. According to intersectionality, each person's lived experience is shaped by his or her position on these (and many other) dimensions. (We created this figure as a simpler version of a figure found in Morgan [1996], p. 107. We left out her axes of gender-typical vs. deviant, young vs. old, European vs. non-European, credentialed vs. non-literate, Anglophone vs. English as second language, light vs. dark, and gentile vs. Jew.)*

Morgan draws on the writings of French philosopher Michel Foucault to argue that each of us occupies a point "on each of these axes (at a minimum) and that this point is simultaneously a locus of our agency, power, disempowerment, oppression, and resistance. The [endpoints] represent maximum privilege or extreme oppression with respect to a particular axis."[64] She analyzes how two of those axes, race and gender, interact to structure schools in ways that privilege the ideas and perspectives of white males. Girls and women, she claims, are effectively a "colonized population." They make up a majority of all students but are forced to live and learn within ideas and institutions structured by white men.

Morgan is certainly right that it was mostly white males who set up the educational system and founded nearly all the universities in the United

States. Most of those schools once excluded women and people of color. But does that mean that women and people of color should think of themselves as "colonized populations" today? Would doing so empower them, or would it encourage an external locus of control? Would it make them more or less likely to engage with their teachers and readings, work hard, and benefit from their time in school?

More generally, what will happen to the thinking of students who are trained to see everything in terms of intersecting bipolar axes where one end of each axis is marked "privilege" and the other is "oppression"? Since "privilege" is defined as the "power to dominate" and to cause "oppression," these axes are inherently *moral* dimensions. The people on top are bad, and the people below the line are good. This sort of teaching seems likely to encode the Untruth of Us Versus Them directly into students' cognitive schemas: *Life is a battle between good people and evil people.* Furthermore, there is no escaping the conclusion as to who the evil people are. The main axes of oppression usually point to one intersectional address: straight white males.

An illustration of this way of thinking happened at Brown University in November of 2015, when students stormed the president's office and presented their list of demands to her and the provost (the chief academic officer, generally considered the second-highest post).[65] At one point in the video of the confrontation, the provost, a white man, says, "Can we just have a conversation about—?" but he is interrupted by shouts of "No!" and students' finger snaps. One protester offers this explanation for cutting him off: "The problem they are having is that heterosexual white males have always dominated the space." The provost then points out that he himself is gay. The student stutters a bit but continues on, undeterred by the fact that Brown University was led by a woman and a gay man: "Well, homosexual . . . it doesn't matter . . . white males are at the top of the hierarchy."

In short, as a result of our long evolution for tribal competition, the human mind readily does dichotomous, us-versus-them thinking. If we want to create welcoming, inclusive communities, we should be doing everything we can to turn down the tribalism and turn up the sense of common humanity. Instead, some theoretical approaches used in universities today may be hyperactivating our ancient tribal tendencies, even if that was not the intention of the professor. Of course, some individuals truly are racist, sexist, or homophobic, and some institutions are, too, even when the people who run them mean well, if they end up being less welcoming to members of some groups. We favor teaching students to recognize a variety of kinds of bigotry and bias as an essential step toward reducing them. Intersectionality can be taught skillfully, as Crenshaw does in her TED Talk.[66] It can be used to promote compassion and reveal injustices not previously seen. Yet somehow, many college students today seem to be adopting a different version of intersectional thinking and are embracing the Untruth of Us Versus Them.

Why Common-Enemy Identity Politics Is Bad for Students

Imagine an entire entering class of college freshmen whose orientation program includes training in the kind of intersectional thinking described above, along with training in spotting microaggressions. By the end of their first week on campus, students have learned to score their own and others' levels of privilege, identify more distinct identity groups, and see more differences between people.[67] They have learned to interpret more words and social behaviors as acts of aggression. They have learned to associate aggression, domination, and oppression with privileged groups. They have learned to focus only on perceived impact and to ignore intent. How might students at such a school react to the sorts of emails sent by Dean Spellman and Erika Christakis?[68]

The combination of common-enemy identity politics and microaggression training creates an environment highly conducive to the development of a "call-out culture," in which students gain prestige for identifying small offenses committed by members of their community, and then publicly "calling out" the offenders.[69] One gets no points, no credit, for speaking privately and gently with an offender—in fact, that could be interpreted as colluding with the enemy. Call-out culture requires an easy way to reach an audience that can award status to people who shame or punish alleged offenders. This is one reason social media has been so transformative: there is always an audience eager to watch people being shamed, particularly when it is so easy for spectators to join in and pile on.

Life in a call-out culture requires constant vigilance, fear, and self-censorship. Many in the audience may feel sympathy for the person being shamed but are afraid to speak up, yielding the false impression that the audience is unanimous in its condemnation. Here is how a student at Smith College describes her induction into its call-out culture in the fall of 2014:

> During my first days at Smith, I witnessed countless conversations that consisted of one person telling the other that their opinion was wrong. The word "offensive" was almost always included in the reasoning. Within a few short weeks, members of my freshman class had quickly assimilated to this new way of non-thinking. They could soon detect a politically incorrect view and call the person out on their "mistake." I began to voice my opinion less often to avoid being berated and judged by a community that claims to represent the free expression of ideas. I learned, along with every other student, to walk on eggshells for fear that I may say something "offensive." That is the social norm here.[70]

Reports from around the country are remarkably similar: students at many colleges today are walking on eggshells, afraid of saying the wrong thing, liking the wrong post, or coming to the defense of someone whom they know to be innocent, out of fear that they themselves will be called out by a mob on social media.[71] Conor Friedersdorf, who writes about higher education at *The Atlantic*, looked into the matter in response to our original "Coddling" article in 2015. Students told him things like this: "Students get worked up over the smallest of issues . . . which has led to the disintegration of school spirit and the fracture of campus." And this, from another student:

> I probably hold back 90 percent of the things that I want to say due to fear of being called out. . . . People won't call you out because your opinion is wrong. People will call you out for literally anything.

On Twitter today I came across someone making fun of a girl who made a video talking about how much she loved God and how she was praying for everyone. There were hundreds of comments, rude comments, below the video. It was to the point that they weren't even making fun of what she was standing for. They were picking apart everything. Her eyebrows, the way her mouth moves, her voice, the way her hair was parted. Ridiculous.[72]

In this comment, we can begin to see the way that social media amplifies the cruelty and "virtue signaling" that are recurrent features of call-out culture. (Virtue signaling refers to the things people say and do to advertise that they are virtuous. This helps them stay within the good graces of their team.) Mobs can rob good people of their conscience, particularly when participants wear masks (in a real mob) or are hiding behind an alias or avatar (in an online mob). Anonymity fosters deindividuation—the loss of an individual sense of self—which lessens self-restraint and increases one's willingness to go along with the mob.[73]

The intellectual devastation wrought by this way of thinking can be seen in a report from Trent Eady, a young Canadian queer activist who escaped from this mindset in 2014. He then wrote an essay titled "'Everything Is Problematic': My Journey Into the Centre of a Dark Political World, and How I Escaped." Eady identifies four features of the culture: dogmatism, groupthink, a crusader mentality, and anti-intellectualism. Of greatest relevance to the Untruth of Us Versus Them, he wrote:

Thinking this way quickly divides the world into an ingroup and an outgroup—believers and heathens, the righteous and the wrongteous. . . . Every minor heresy inches you further away from the group. When I was part of groups like this, everyone was on exactly the same page about a suspiciously large range of issues. Internal disagreement was rare.[74]

It is difficult to imagine a culture that is more antithetical to the mission of a university.[75]

The Power of Common Humanity Today

Michelle Alexander, in her best-selling book, *The New Jim Crow: Mass Incarceration in the Age of Colorblindness*,[76] illustrates what happens to the millions of black men dragged into the criminal justice system—often for possession or use of small amounts of marijuana. They are released into a society where they struggle to find jobs, are disqualified from state benefits, and sometimes face the loss of the right to vote, leading to an "undercaste" in American society that is in some ways reminiscent of the Jim Crow South.

The book has had a powerful impact on the political left, but the issues it raises resonate across the political spectrum. In books like Radley Balko's *Rise of the Warrior Cop: The Militarization of America's Police Forces*[77] and FIRE cofounder Harvey Silverglate's *Three Felonies a Day: How the Feds Target the Innocent*,[78] libertarians have expressed opposition to both overpolicing and the excesses of the war on drugs. The conservative group Right on Crime opposes overcriminalization, mass incarceration, and the drug war.[79] There are opportunities for real cooperation on serious but potentially solvable issues.[80]

For activists seeking reform, the lesson is to find common ground. Marches and rallies are good for energizing your "team," but as Columbia University professor of humanities Mark Lilla points out in his book *The Once and Future Liberal: After Identity Politics*, they are not enough to bring about lasting change. You have to win elections to do that, and to win elections, you have to draw in very large numbers of people from diverse groups. Lilla argues that the left did that successfully from the presidency of Franklin D. Roosevelt through the Great Society era of the 1960s, but then it took a wrong turn into a new, more divisive, and less successful kind of politics:

> Instead they threw themselves into the movement politics of identity, losing a sense of what we share as citizens and what binds us as a nation. An image for Roosevelt liberalism and the unions that

supported it was that of two hands shaking. A recurring image of identity liberalism is that of a prism refracting a single beam of light into its constituent colors, producing a rainbow. This says it all.[81]

Yet appeals to common humanity still work just as well today as when Dr. King made them. On September 16, 2017, on the National Mall in Washington, DC, a group of Trump supporters organized a rally they called "the Mother of All Rallies Patriot Unification Gathering."[82] Counterprotesters from Black Lives Matter (BLM) showed up and shouted at the Trump supporters. The Trump supporters shouted back. Someone onstage told the Trump supporters to pay no attention to the counterprotesters: "They don't exist," he said. Hawk Newsome, the leader of the BLM counterprotesters, later said that he expected to "stand there with [his] fist in the air in a very militant way and to exchange insults." Tensions mounted, and onlookers recorded video of the potentially explosive situation. Then the Trump rally organizer, who goes by the name Tommy Gunn, took the stage. "It's about freedom of speech," he said. And in an unexpected move, he invited Newsome and other BLM supporters onto the stage. "We're going to give you two minutes of our platform to put your message out," Gunn told Newsome. "Now, whether they disagree or agree with your message is irrelevant. It's the fact that you have the right to have the message."

Newsome took the stage. "I am an American," he began, and the crowd cheered. "And the beauty of America is that when you see something broke in your country, you can mobilize to fix it." But then, as he spoke about a black man being killed by police, the crowd began to turn on him. They booed. "Shut up! That was a criminal!" a woman shouted. Newsome explained, "We are not anti-cop!" "Yes, you are!" people shouted. "We're anti–*bad* cop!" Newsome insisted. He still seemed to be losing them. "We don't want handouts," he told the crowd. "We don't want anything that is yours. We want our God-given right to freedom, liberty, and the pursuit of happiness." Now they were coming back around. People cheered. Someone in the crowd shouted, "All lives matter!" which is usually intended as a rebuke to those who say that "black lives matter." But Newsome responded in the tradition of Pauli Murray, by drawing a larger circle around everyone in the crowd: "You're right, my brother, you're right. You are so right. All lives matter, right? But when a black life is lost, we get no justice. That is why we say 'black lives matter.' . . . If we really want to make America great, we do it together."

The crowd cheered and chanted "USA-USA . . ." In an instant, the two groups were no longer "us" and "them." Their ideological differences remained, but within that larger circle around them, their enmity melted away. And, at least for a short while, they interacted as fellow human beings and fellow Americans. "It kind of restored my faith," Newsome said when interviewed afterward. "Two sides that never listen to each other actually made progress today."[83] One of the leaders of Bikers for Trump came up to Newsome afterward and shook his hand. The two men talked and then posed for a photo together, with Newsome holding the other man's young son cradled in his arm.

In Sum

- The human mind evolved for living in tribes that engaged in frequent (and often violent) conflict; our modern-day minds readily divide the world into "us" and "them," even on trivial or arbitrary criteria, as Henri Tajfel's psychological experiments demonstrated.
- Identity politics takes many forms. Some forms, such as that practiced by Martin Luther King, Jr., and Pauli Murray, can be called *common-humanity identity politics*, because its practitioners humanize their opponents and appeal to their humanity while also applying political pressure in other ways.
- *Common-enemy identity politics*, on the other hand, tries to unite a coalition using the psychology embedded in the Bedouin proverb "I against my brothers. I and my brothers against my cousins. I and my brothers and my cousins against the world." It is used on the far right as well as the far left.
- Intersectionality is a popular intellectual framework on campuses today; certain versions of it teach students to see multiple axes of privilege

and oppression that intersect. While there are merits to the theory, the way it is interpreted and practiced on campus can sometimes amplify tribal thinking and encourage students to endorse the Untruth of Us Versus Them: *Life is a battle between good people and evil people.*

• Common-enemy identity politics, when combined with microaggression theory, produces a call-out culture in which almost anything one says or does could result in a public shaming. This can engender a sense of "walking on eggshells," and it teaches students habits of self-censorship. Call-out cultures are detrimental to students' education and bad for their mental health. Call-out cultures and us-versus-them thinking are incompatible with the educational and research missions of universities, which require free inquiry, dissent, evidence-based argument, and intellectual honesty.

This concludes Part I of this book. In these three chapters, we presented three really bad ideas and showed how each one meets the three criteria for being called a Great Untruth, which we laid out in the introductory chapter: it contradicts ancient wisdom, it contradicts modern psychological research on flourishing, and it harms the individuals and communities that embrace it. In Part II, we'll examine some dramatic recent events on campus that have been incomprehensible to many outside observers. We'll show that these events become much more intelligible once you understand the three Great Untruths and their effects on individuals and on groups.

PART II

Bad Ideas in Action

CHAPTER 4

Intimidation and Violence

*When we dehumanise and demonise our opponents, we abandon
the possibility of peacefully resolving our differences, and seek to
justify violence against them.*

NELSON MANDELA[1]

On the night of February 1, 2017, the University of California's
Berkeley campus exploded into violence. An estimated 1,500
protesters surrounded the building where Milo Yiannopoulos, a
young, British, gay Trump supporter, was scheduled to speak. Yiannopoulos was formerly an editor at Breitbart News, a principal outlet of the "alt-
right" movement that had come to national prominence during the previous
year's presidential campaign. He had been banned from Twitter the summer before when Twitter concluded that he had violated its policy regarding
"inciting or engaging in the targeted abuse or harassment of others."[2] Yiannopoulos was a skilled provocateur—a master of the art of triggering outrage and then using that outrage to embarrass his opponents and advance
his goals.[3]

The protesters' goal was to prevent the speech from happening. Many of
them came from local radical anarchist groups that call themselves "anti-
fascists," or "Antifa."[4] UC Berkeley officials claimed[5] that only about 150 of the
protesters were responsible for the vandalism and violence that ensued—
knocking down a light generator;[6] shooting commercial-grade fireworks[7] into
buildings[8] and at police officers;[9] smashing ATMs;[10] setting fires;[11] dismantling barricades[12] and using them (as well as bats)[13] to break windows; throwing rocks at police officers;[14] and even hurling Molotov cocktails.[15] The
property damage (exceeding $500,000 for the university and town combined)[16]

was less chilling, however, than the physical attacks on students and others who attempted to attend the speech.

One man carrying a sign saying "The First Amendment is for everyone" was hit in the face, leaving him bloody.[17] Others also suffered bloodying blows to the face and head as protesters attacked with fists, pipes, sticks, and poles.[18] Recorded on video, a young woman sporting a red MAKE BITCOIN GREAT AGAIN baseball cap told a reporter, "I'm looking to make a statement by just being here, and I think the protesters are doing the same. Props to the ones who are doing it non-violently, but I think that's a very rare thing indeed." As she turned, the camera caught a black-gloved hand pepper-spraying her in the face.[19]

Masked Antifa protesters clad in black used flagpoles to batter a woman and her husband as they were pinned against metal barriers, unable to get away. The woman, Katrina Redelsheimer, was clubbed on the head, and her husband, John Jennings, was struck in the temple and began to bleed. Immediately afterward, other protesters blinded the couple and three of their friends by spraying them in the eyes with mace. As the friends cried for help, protesters punched them and hit them in the head with sticks, until onlookers pulled the victims over the barricades. Meanwhile, five or six protesters dragged Jennings a few feet away, where they kicked and beat him until bystanders pulled attackers off him as he lost consciousness.[20] The police, according to Redelsheimer, had by this point barricaded themselves inside a building, refusing people entrance—which she learned when someone tried to help her get into the building to rinse her eyes and the police turned them away.[21] Meanwhile, Pranav Jandhyala, a UC Berkeley student journalist and self-described "moderate liberal," who used his cell phone to record events as they unfolded, was attacked by protesters, who tried to take his phone.[22] When he fled, they chased him, punching him in the head, beating him with sticks, and calling him a "neo-Nazi."[23]

The mob got its way. The speech was canceled. Police issued a "shelter-in-place" campus lockdown order[24] and escorted Yiannopoulos to an undisclosed location.[25]

This all happened just ten days after Donald Trump's inauguration as president. Tensions across the country were high, and the president's inaugural address and first executive orders (among them, to close the borders to people from seven Muslim-majority countries)[26] did little to calm them. The fact that some Berkeley students and residents reacted strongly to an anticipated speech by a pro-Trump provocateur does not prove that they are closed-minded or fearful of every idea they don't like. But it's important to take a close look at the February 1 riots at UC Berkeley, because they marked a turning point—an escalation of conflicts over campus speakers. Berkeley and its aftermath were the start of a new and more dangerous era. Since then, many students on the left have become increasingly receptive to the idea that violence is sometimes justified as a response to speech they believe is "hateful." At the same time, many students on the right have become increasingly eager to invite speakers that are likely to provoke a reaction from the left.

Some early reports claimed that the violent, mask-wearing "black bloc" protesters were outside agitators, not students from UC Berkeley.[27] It is impossible to know how many Berkeley students took part, because the university never undertook a public investigation into the riots to determine precisely who the black bloc protesters were. One UC Berkeley employee bragged on social media about beating Jennings—even posting a photo of Jennings unconscious on the ground—and several Berkeley students admitted that they had participated.[28] One student who wrote about having joined Antifa explained in an op-ed that "black bloc tactics" (dressing in black, wearing black gloves, and masking faces) were used that night "to protect the identities of the individuals in the bloc," and asserted that "behind those bandanas and black T-shirts were the faces of your fellow UC Berkeley [students]."

The failure of UC Berkeley to openly discipline *any* of the students who engaged in violence or vandalism during the mayhem[29]—even those who publicly admitted participating—and the fact that the police arrested just one person that night (for failure to disperse)[30] seems to have taught the protesters an important lesson: Violence works. Unsurprisingly, the Antifa activists built on their success by threatening more violence in response to campus invitations to conservatives David Horowitz, Ann Coulter, and Ben Shapiro.[31]

The "Milo riot" at UC Berkeley caught the attention of the national and international media, not only because of its scale but because of its symbolism. This was, after all, the very place where the campus free speech movement started. In 1964, when left-leaning students demanded the right to advocate for political causes and hear controversial political speakers, Berkeley student Mario Savio, the leader of the movement, famously spoke of freedom of speech as "something that represents the very dignity of what a human being is."[32] Savio had marched with the civil rights movement in Mississippi the summer before, and, inspired by the power of their peaceful tactics, he began working for the Student Nonviolent Coordinating Committee when he returned to campus. It was that activity that first brought him into conflict with university authorities, leading up to his impassioned activism for free speech.[33] The fact that in 2017, Berkeley students were protesting to *shut down* a speech—and even using vandalism and violence to do it—seemed ironic to many observers. Particularly troubling were the ways in which some Berkeley students justified the violence.

Words Are Violence; Violence Is Safety

A few days after the riot, *The Daily Californian*, UC Berkeley's leading student newspaper, ran five op-eds under the headline VIOLENCE AS SELF-DEFENSE,[34] all of which offer examples of the Great Untruths and illustrate the cognitive distortions we described in chapter 2.

Here's one excerpt from an essay titled "Condemning Protesters Same as Condoning Hate Speech":

> If you condemn the actions that shut down Yiannopoulos' literal hate speech, you condone his presence, his actions and his ideas; you care more about broken windows than broken bodies. I can't impeach Trump, and I can't stop the alt-right from recruiting nationwide. I can only fight tooth and nail for the right to exist in my hometown. So it's time for those waiting in the center to pick a side.[35]

Taken at face value, the author seems to be engaging in a number of cognitive distortions. The most evident is catastrophizing: If Milo Yiannopoulos is allowed to speak, there will be "broken bodies" on our side. I might lose my "right to exist." Therefore, violence is justified, because it is self-defense. The author also engages in dichotomous thinking: If you condemn my side's *violence*, that means you condone Yiannopoulos's *ideas*. You must "pick a side." You're either with us or against us. Life is a battle between good people and evil people, and if you disagree with us, you're one of the evil people.

The other essays are similar in appearing to employ multiple cognitive distortions to justify physical violence as a reasonable way to prevent a speech. Some of the essays offer Orwellian inversions of common English words. For example, from another essay: "Asking people to maintain peaceful dialogue with those who legitimately do not think their lives matter is a violent act."[36]

A bit of background is needed here. Weeks earlier, at another college, Yiannopoulos had displayed the name and photo of a trans woman in order to mock her.[37] In advance of the Berkeley event, rumors had circulated that Yiannopoulos planned to identify Berkeley students who were undocumented immigrants. He denied the allegation, the protesters offered no evidence for it, and it's not clear how shutting down his talk on campus would have stopped him from revealing those names if that had been his intention. (He could have easily disseminated the information on the internet.) Nonetheless, you can see why people might think that calls for peaceful dialogue with Yiannopoulos are misguided or counterproductive. It is not irrational, in our nasty political climate, to worry that some of the things he might say could lead to online harassment or even physical harm to innocent people.

But if *asking* for peaceful dialogue is *violent*, then it seems that the word "violence" is taking on new meanings for some students. This is another example of *concept creep*. In just the last few years, the word "violence" has expanded on campus and in some radical political communities beyond campus to cover a multitude of nonviolent actions, including speech that this political faction claims will have a negative impact on members of protected identity groups.

Outside of cultures of safetyism, the word "violence" refers to *physical* violence. The word is sometimes used metaphorically (as in "I violently disagree"), but few of us, including those who claim that speech is violence, have any difficulty understanding the statement "We should reduce incarceration for *nonviolent* offenses." However, now that some students, professors, and activists are labeling their opponents' *words* as violence, they give themselves permission to engage in ideologically motivated *physical* violence. The rationale, as an essay in the Berkeley op-ed series argued, is that physically violent actions, if used to shut down speech that is deemed hateful, are "not acts of violence" but, rather, "acts of self defense."[38]

This is not an uncommon view on many campuses. Almost one in five students surveyed in a 2017 Brookings Institution study agreed that using violence to prevent a speaker from speaking was sometimes "acceptable."[39] While some critics challenged the sampling used in that study, findings in a second study by McLaughlin and Associates were similar; 30% of undergraduate students surveyed agreed with this statement: "If someone is using hate speech or making racially charged comments, physical violence can be justified to prevent this person from espousing their hateful views."[40]

If that sounds reasonable to you, just think about what the statement implies after concept creep and emotional reasoning expand the meaning of "hate speech" and "racially charged." In a call-out culture, almost anything that is interpreted by anyone as having a negative impact on vulnerable members of the community—regardless of intent—can be called hate speech. The Columbia University linguist John McWhorter describes how the term "white supremacist" is now used in an "utterly athletic, recreational" way, as a "battering ram" to attack anyone who departs from the party line.[41] McWhorter himself (who is African American) has been called a white supremacist for questioning received wisdom on matters related to race.[42] But if some students now think it's OK to punch a fascist or white supremacist,[43] and if anyone who disagrees with them can be labeled a fascist or white supremacist, well, you can see how this rhetorical move might make people hesitant to voice dissenting views on campus.[44]

Violence and Intimidation After Berkeley

It's hard to know whether the events at Berkeley played a causal role in later instances of violence on campus, but the spring semester of 2017 saw an increase in politically motivated violence, vandalism, and intimidation, all of which was justified by moral arguments about violence and safety, with the goal of shutting down speakers on campus. One of the most widely covered events occurred on March 2 in Vermont, at Middlebury College. Charles Murray, a libertarian scholar affiliated with the conservative think tank the American Enterprise Institute, was invited by a student group to speak about his 2012 book, *Coming Apart*. The college's Political Science Department cosponsored the talk. The book is about one of the most important and widely discussed topics of 2017: the social and economic dysfunction of the white working class, which (according to many commentators) made voters in that group respond more enthusiastically to the anti-immigrant and protectionist messages of Donald Trump.[45] But in a previous book, published in 1994 (*The Bell Curve*), Murray and his coauthor, Richard Herrnstein, proposed that differences in average IQ scores found across racial groups may not be caused entirely by environmental factors; genetic differences may play a role, too.[46] Some Middlebury students and professors maintained that anyone who makes such a claim is a white supremacist, and they came together to demand that Murray's talk about his later book be canceled.[47]

When the disinvitation effort failed, a large number of students attended Murray's talk just to shut it down by chanting in unison and shouting over his attempts to speak. College administrators had anticipated this possibility, so Murray and Allison Stanger, a political science professor who had agreed to question Murray after his talk, were moved to a different room so he could deliver his talk via livestream, behind a locked door. But students soon discovered where they were and continued to try to stop Murray from speaking by pounding on the walls and pulling fire alarms in the building. When the livestream ended, as Murray and Professor Stanger left the building, they were swarmed by protesters. One shoved Stanger; another grabbed her hair and pulled with such force that she suffered a concussion and a whiplash injury.[48] As Murray and Stanger attempted to flee campus by car, protesters, some of them masked, pounded on the car, rocked it back and forth, and jumped onto the hood.[49] Someone threw a large traffic sign in front of their car to prevent them from leaving, but public safety officials cleared a path, and the car eventually drove off to a dinner with selected students and faculty.[50] The protesters, however, somehow discovered where the group had gathered for dinner, so the Middlebury administrators quickly moved the group to yet another location, this time miles from campus.[51]

After dinner, Professor Stanger went to the hospital, where her injuries were diagnosed. She required physical therapy for the next six months.[52] Stanger later described her experience in a New York Times essay. "What alarmed me most," she wrote, "was what I saw in the eyes of the crowd. Those who wanted the event to take place made eye contact with me. Those intent on disrupting it steadfastly refused to do so. They couldn't look at me directly, because if they had, they would have seen another human being."[53]

Just one month later, at Claremont McKenna College, near Los Angeles, about 250 students[54] prevented fellow students from attending a speech by journalist, attorney, and social commentator Heather Mac Donald.[55] In her 2016 book, The War on Cops, Mac Donald argued that Black Lives Matter protests made the police more hesitant to enter and actively engage in minority neighborhoods, thereby leaving the people in those neighborhoods less protected and more vulnerable to crime. Her theory had been the subject of lively national debate. As Neil Gross, a left-leaning sociologist, wrote in The New York Times: "There is now some evidence that when all eyes are on police misconduct, crime may edge up. Progressives should acknowledge that this idea isn't far-fetched."[56] But for some students, allowing Mac Donald to present her thesis would be allowing "violence" on campus, so she had to be stopped. These students mobilized with a call on Facebook to "show up wearing black" and "bring your comrades, because we're shutting this down."[57] Protesting students prevented anyone from entering the building to hear the talk, which Mac Donald gave via livestream as protesters pounded on the clear glass wall of the nearly empty ground-level lecture hall. Mac Donald was later evacuated from the building through a kitchen door and into a waiting police car.

After the event, the president of Pomona College[58] (part of the Claremont consortium of five colleges) wrote a statement in defense of academic freedom and Mac Donald's right to speak on campus. In response to his letter, three Pomona students wrote a letter, signed by twenty-four other students, explaining why Mac Donald should not be allowed to speak. As at Berkeley, the students asserted that the speech itself was a form of violence: "Engaging with her, a white supremacist fascist supporter of the police state, is a form of violence."

The letter exemplified the dichotomous thinking of the Untruth of Us Versus Them:

> Either you support students of marginalized identities, particularly Black students, or leave us to protect and organize for our communities without the impositions of your patronization, without your binary respectability politics, and without your monolithic perceptions of protest and organizing.[59]

The students continued: "If engaged, Heather Mac Donald would not be debating on mere difference of opinion, but the right of Black people to exist." This sentence includes *fortune-telling*, as the students predict what Mac Donald would say. It also includes a rhetorical flourish that became common in 2017: the assertion that a speaker will "deny" people from certain identity groups "the right to exist."[60] This thinking is a form of *catastrophizing*, in that it inflates the horrors of a speaker's words far beyond what the speaker might actually say. The students also called Mac Donald "a fascist, a white supremacist, a warhawk, a transphobe, a queerphobe, [and] a classist." This is *labeling* running wild—a list of serious accusations made without supporting evidence.[61]

Where did college students learn to think this way? We don't know what courses they took at Pomona, or whether they thought this way before they arrived on campus, but the letter overall shows the influence of the common-enemy identity politics we described in chapter 3, and it makes extensive use of the language of intersectionality. For example, the students end their letter with a demand that the president must send an email

> to the entire student body, faculty, and staff by Thursday, April 20, 2017, apologizing for the previous patronizing statement [his defense of academic freedom], enforcing that Pomona College does not tolerate hate speech and speech that projects violence onto the bodies of its marginalized students and oppressed peoples, especially Black students who straddle the intersection of marginalized identities.

As we saw in chapter 3, this kind of identity politics amplifies the human proclivity for us-versus-them thinking. It prepares students for battle, not for learning.

Violence in Charlottesville

The events at Berkeley, Middlebury, and Claremont McKenna were, in a sense, shocks from the left, which angered and radicalized some conservatives on and off campus. But there was also a continuing series of shocks from the right, which angered and radicalized the left, giving us a year of rapidly escalating mutual outrage. The most shocking event of all occurred in Charlottesville, Virginia. On the night of August 11, 2017, members of the self-described alt-right, including many neo-Nazis and Ku Klux Klansmen, marched across the fabled grounds of the University of Virginia, carrying Tiki torches and chanting neo-Nazi and white supremacist slogans, including "Jews will not replace us." If you are looking for examples of common-enemy identity politics, it doesn't get any clearer than this.

The next day, the racist mob marched through downtown Charlottesville, carrying swastika flags while making a pilgrimage to a statue of Robert E. Lee, the commander of the Confederate Army in the American Civil War. During the march, six of the alt-right marchers beat a black man with metal pipes and poles, causing broken bones, lacerations, internal injuries, and a concussion.[62] The marchers also violently clashed with Antifa counter-protesters.[63] And a white supremacist who idolized Adolf Hitler[64] stopped his car in front of a group of counterprotesters, backed up, and then sped forward, slamming into them, sending people into the air, badly injuring at least nineteen peaceful counterprotesters, and killing thirty-two-year-old Heather Heyer, a paralegal described by friends as "a passionate advocate for the disenfranchised who was often moved to tears by the world's injustices."[65] Her mother said that she began receiving threats in the aftermath of Heyer's death, and as a result, her grave is in a secret location to protect it from being desecrated by neo-Nazis.[66]

The sight of Nazi flags and the murder of Heyer profoundly shook an already divided nation. It was a moment that brought together many Republicans and Democrats in leadership positions in a forceful denunciation of the white supremacists and neo-Nazis. Yet one voice was conspicuously absent from the conversation: President Trump's. The president had by that time demonstrated a willingness to condemn many people harshly and promptly, yet he was restrained and slow in his criticism of the white supremacist marchers in Charlottesville. On the day of Heyer's death, when most Americans were looking to the president to clearly and unambiguously condemn neo-Nazis and the Ku Klux Klan, he condemned hatred, bigotry, and violence "on many sides." Two days later, he read aloud a written statement that offered condemnation, but the very next day, in unscripted remarks, he said that there were "very fine people on both sides."[67] With those three words—"very fine people"[68]—the president showed that he was sympathetic to the men who staged the most highly publicized march for racism and antisemitism in the United States in many decades.

The Autumn of 2017

Charlottesville was a tragedy that presented an opportunity. With many Republicans, conservatives, and leaders from both business and the military distancing themselves from the president and his remarks,[69] it would have been a good time to draw larger circles and change the landscape of American politics.[70] On campus, however, where levels of fear and anger were understandably elevated in the wake of the events in Charlottesville, the more common response seemed to be an increase in us-versus-them thinking, including hostility aimed at people and groups (including many on the left) who otherwise could have become allies. The autumn of 2017 saw more episodes of students using the heckler's veto to shut down classes and speeches than in any previous semester on record.[71] For example, students at William & Mary shut down a speech by Claire Guthrie Gastañaga, the executive director of the Virginia affiliate of the American Civil Liberties Union (ACLU), because the ACLU had defended the constitutional rights of the Charlottesville alt-right march organizers.[72] The ACLU has consistently defended the rights of the poor, minority populations, LGBTQ individuals, and others whom progressives reliably defend. For example, it defended the right of a pregnant, undocumented teen to get an abortion,[73] the rights of English translators of radical Islamic texts that call for jihad,[74] and the rights of the Black Panthers.[75] The ACLU defends *rights*, not ideologies. But William & Mary students chanted, among other things, "The revolution will not uphold the Constitution!" and "Liberalism is white supremacy!"[76]

A few weeks later, the president of the University of Oregon's "State of the University" speech was shut down by close to fifty students who seized the stage, chanting "Nothing about us without us." A student with a megaphone insisted, "We will not be ignored" and "Expect resistance to anyone who opposes us." A student protester complained about the oppression of minority students, tuition increases, and indigenous rights, and described "fascism and neo-Nazis" as the reason for the protest.[77] (The president, Michael Schill, whose extended family members were murdered by actual fascists during World War II, responded with a *New York Times* op-ed piece titled "The Misguided Student Crusade Against 'Fascism.'"[78]) The following week, at the question-and-answer session of an event at UCLA titled "What Is Civil Discourse? Challenging Hate Speech in a Free Society," sponsored by the United States Holocaust Memorial Museum, protesters from a group called "Refuse Fascism" disrupted the event.[79]

And then there's Reed College, in Portland, Oregon. For *thirteen months*, beginning in September of 2016, campus activists tried to shut down the freshman humanities course because it focused on the thinkers of ancient Greece and the eastern Mediterranean world (who would be considered white today).[80] These tactics often work against the protesters' own goals, as they alienate many people who might otherwise support them. For example, one of the lecturers in the course was Lucía Martínez Valdivia, who tried to teach the work of Sappho, an ancient Greek poet from the island of Lesbos and an icon of both feminism and lesbian liberation.[81] Martínez Valdivia found it hard to lecture while students were waving signs with aggressive and vulgar statements *right next to her* at the front of the classroom. She shared with students the fact that she has PTSD and asked them, out of concern for her health, not to protest in her classroom. They complained in an open letter[82] that her request "creates a hierarchy [of traumas] where your traumas matter more" and accused her of being "anti-black," "ableist," and engaging in "gaslighting," that is, manipulating victims by making them question their perceptions or their sanity. She was shocked that the college allowed these intimidating in-class protests to go on, and decided she had to speak out. In October 2017, she wrote a powerful essay in *The Washington Post* titled "Professors Like Me Can't Stay Silent About This Extremist Moment on Campuses." Here is an excerpt:

No one should have to pass someone else's ideological purity test to be allowed to speak. University life—along with civic life—dies without the free exchange of ideas. In the face of intimidation, educators must speak up, not shut down. Ours is a position of unique responsibility: We teach people not what to think, but how to think. Realizing and accepting this has made me—an eminently replaceable, untenured, gay, mixed-race woman with PTSD—realize that no matter the precariousness of my situation, I have a responsibility to model the appreciation of difference and care of thought I try to foster in my students. If I, like so many colleagues nationwide, am afraid to say what I think, am I not complicit in the problem?[83]

. . . . .

Charlottesville was a national tragedy that sent shock waves through many American institutions, particularly universities. It occurred in the middle of the tumultuous first year of Donald Trump's presidency. In the months afterward, there was a big increase in efforts by off-campus white suprem-acist organizations to provoke students and recruit members by putting up racist posters, flyers, and stickers on hundreds of campuses.[84] We under-stand why so many students embraced more active and confrontational forms of protest. But because their activism is often based on an embrace of the Great Untruths and a tendency to attack potential allies, and because aggressive protests are often exactly what right-wing provocateurs are hop-ing to provoke, we believe that many student activists are harming them-selves as well as their causes.

Why It Is Such a Bad Idea to Tell Students That Words Are Violence

Most students oppose the use of violence. When asked in a poll conducted by FIRE whether they themselves would use violence to stop someone from speaking, only 1% said yes.[85] But there is a much larger group—roughly 20% to 30%, according to the two surveys we described earlier—that is will-ing to support *other* students who use violence, drawing on the sorts of justifications offered by the Berkeley students. The most common justifica-tion is that hate speech is violence, and some students believe it is therefore legitimate to use violence to shut down hate speech. Setting aside the ques-tions of moral and constitutional legitimacy, what are the psychological consequences of thinking this way?

Members of some identity groups surely face more frequent insults to their dignity than do straight white males, on average. A free-for-all attitude toward speech that allows people to say whatever they want with no fear of consequences can therefore affect people with different social identities dif-ferently. As we noted in chapter 2, some portion of what is commonly called political correctness is just being thoughtful or polite—using words in a way that is considerate to others.[86] But students make a serious mistake when they interpret words—even words spoken with hatred—as violence.

In a widely circulated essay in *The New York Times* in July 2017, the argument that words can be violence was made by Lisa Feldman Barrett, a well-respected professor of psychology and emotion researcher at Northeastern University.[87] Barrett offered this syllogism: "If words can cause stress, and if prolonged stress can cause physical harm, then it seems that speech—at least certain types of speech—can be a form of violence."

We responded in an essay in *The Atlantic,* in which we noted that it is a logical error to accept the claim that harm—even physical harm—is the same as violence.[88] Barrett's syllogism takes the form that if A can cause B and B can cause C, then A can cause C. Therefore, if words can cause stress and stress can cause harm, then words can cause *harm*, but that does not establish that words are *violence*. It only establishes that words can result in harm—even physical harm—which we don't doubt. To see the difference, just rerun the syllogism by swapping in "breaking up with your girlfriend" or "giving students a lot of homework." Both of these can provoke stress in someone else (including elevated levels of cortisol), and stress can cause harm, so both can cause harm. That doesn't mean that they are violent acts.

Interpreting a campus lecture as violence is a choice, and it is a choice that increases your pain with respect to the lecture while reducing your options for how to respond. If you interpret a speech by Milo Yiannopoulos as a violent attack on your fellow students, then you have a moral obligation to do something about it, perhaps even something violent. That is precisely how trolls manipulate their victims.

But if you keep the distinction between speech and violence clear in your mind, then many more options are available to you. First, you can take the Stoic response and develop your ability to remain unmoved. As Marcus Aurelius advised, "Choose not to be harmed—and you won't feel harmed. Don't feel harmed—and you haven't been."[89] The more ways your identity can be threatened by casual daily interactions, the more valuable it will be to cultivate the Stoic (and Buddhist, and CBT) ability to *not be emotionally reactive*, to not let others control your mind and your cortisol levels. The Stoics understood that words don't cause stress directly; they can only provoke stress and suffering in a person who has interpreted those words as posing a threat. You can choose whether to interpret a visiting speaker as harmful. You can pick your battles, devote your efforts to changing policies that matter to you, and make yourself immune to trolls. The internet will always be there; extremists will always be posting potentially offensive images and statements; some groups will be targeted more than others. It's not fair, but even as we work to lessen hatred and heal divisions, all of us must learn to ignore some of the things we see and just carry on with our day.

A second and more radical response opens up when you reject the "speech is violence" view: you can use your opponents' ideas and arguments to make yourself stronger. The progressive activist Van Jones (who was President Barack Obama's green jobs advisor) endorsed this view in February of 2017 in a conversation at the University of Chicago's Institute for Politics. When Democratic strategist David Axelrod asked Jones about how progressive students should react when people they find ideologically offensive (such as someone associated with the Trump administration) are invited to speak on campus, Jones began by noting the distinction we described in chapter 1 between physical and emotional "safety":

> There are two ideas about safe spaces: One is a very good idea and one is a terrible idea. The idea of being physically safe on a campus—not being subjected to sexual harassment and physical abuse, or being targeted specifically, personally, for some kind of hate speech—"you are an n-word," or whatever—I am perfectly fine with that. But there's another view that is now I think ascendant, which I think is just a horrible view, which is that "I need to be safe ideologically. I need to be safe emotionally. I just need to feel good all the time, and if someone says something that I don't like, that's a problem for everybody else, including the [university] administration."[90]

Jones then delivered some of the best advice for college students we have ever heard. He rejected the Untruth of Fragility and turned safetyism on its head:

I don't want you to be safe *ideologically*. I don't want you to be safe *emotionally*. I want you to be *strong*. That's different. I'm not going to pave the jungle for you. Put on some boots, and learn how to deal with adversity. I'm not going to take all the weights out of the gym; that's the whole point of the gym. This is the gym.

Jones understands antifragility. Jones wants progressive college students to see themselves not as fragile candles but as fires, welcoming the wind by seeking out ideologically different speakers and ideas.

In Sum

- The "Milo Riot" at UC Berkeley on February 1, 2017, marked a major shift in campus protests. Violence was used successfully to stop a speaker; people were injured, and there were (as far as we can tell) no costs to those who were violent. Some students later justified the violence as a legitimate form of "self-defense" to prevent speech that they said was violent.
- Hardly any students say that they themselves would use violence to shut down a speech, but two surveys conducted in late 2017 found that substantial minorities of students (20% in one survey and 30% in the other) said it was sometimes "acceptable" for *other* students to use violence to prevent a speaker from speaking on campus.
- The "Unite the Right" rally in Charlottesville, Virginia, in which a white nationalist killed a peaceful counterprotester and injured others, further raised tensions on campus, especially as provocations from far-right groups increased in the months afterward.
- In the fall of 2017, the number of efforts to shut down speakers reached a record level.
- In 2017, the idea that speech can be violence (even when it does not involve threats, harassment, or calls for violence) seemed to spread, assisted by the tendency in some circles to focus only on perceived impact, not on intent. Words that give rise to stress or fear for members of some groups are now often regarded as a form of violence.

- Speech is not violence. Treating it as such is an interpretive choice, and it is a choice that increases pain and suffering while preventing other, more effective responses, including the Stoic response (cultivating nonreactivity) and the antifragile response suggested by Van Jones: "Put on some boots, and learn how to deal with adversity."

In the quotation that opened this chapter, Nelson Mandela warned us against the danger of demonizing opponents and using violence against them. Like Mahatma Gandhi, Martin Luther King, Jr., and other advocates of nonviolent resistance, Mandela noted that violent and dehumanizing tactics are self-defeating, closing off the possibility of peaceful resolution. But what if the goal of a movement isn't entirely peaceful resolution but, rather—at least in part—group cohesion? What might we see if we take a sociological approach to the new culture of safetyism?

CHAPTER 5

Witch Hunts

*Mass movements can rise and spread without belief in a God, but
never without belief in a devil.*

ERIC HOFFER, *The True Believer*[1]

aoist," "McCarthyite," "Jacobin," and above all, "witch hunt."
These terms are sometimes applied to the sorts of events we described in the last chapter. Those who apply such terms are
claiming that what we are witnessing on campus exemplifies a situation
long studied by sociologists in which a community becomes obsessed with
religious or ideological purity and believes it needs to find and punish enemies within its own ranks in order to hold itself together.

From the fifteenth through the seventeenth century, Europe experienced multiple waves of witch hunts, driven primarily by religious wars and
conflicts in the wake of the Reformation, and also by fears brought on by
recurring plague outbreaks.[2] Tens of thousands of innocent people—and
possibly hundreds of thousands—were put to death, often after being "put
to the question" (that is, tortured) with the aid of boiling oil, red-hot iron
bars, or thumbscrews.[3]

The most famous witch hunt in U.S. history occurred in Salem, Massachusetts. In January of 1692, two young girls began to suffer from fits and
tremors, which their elders attributed to witchcraft. In the following
months, dozens of people claimed that they were tormented by witches or
that they or their animals had been bewitched. Legal action was taken
against at least 144 people (38 of them male) who were accused of practicing witchcraft. Nineteen were executed by hanging; one was crushed by
heavy stones.[4]

Historical and sociological analyses of witch trials have generally explained these outbreaks as responses to a group experiencing either a sense of threat from outside, or division and loss of cohesion within. In Salem, a terrifying border war had broken out a few years earlier against the French and their Native American allies in what is now Maine (but was at that time part of Massachusetts). The townspeople were still anxious about attacks.[5] Do the campus events making national headlines since the fall of 2015 fit into this sociological framework?

One of Jon's favorite thinkers of all time is Emile Durkheim, the nineteenth- to early twentieth-century French sociologist. Durkheim saw groups and communities as being in some ways like organisms—social entities that have a chronic need to enhance their internal cohesion and their shared sense of moral order. Durkheim described human beings as "homo duplex," or "two-level man."[6] We are very good at being individuals pursuing our everyday goals (which Durkheim called the level of the "profane," or ordinary). But we also have the capacity to transition, temporarily, to a higher collective plane, which Durkheim called the level of the "sacred." He said that we have access to a set of emotions that we experience only when we are part of a collective—feelings like "collective effervescence," which Durkheim described as social "electricity" generated when a group gathers and achieves a state of union. (You've probably felt this while doing things like playing a team sport or singing in a choir, or during religious worship.) People can move back and forth between these two levels throughout a single day, and it is the function of religious rituals to pull people up to the higher collective level, bind them to the group, and then return them to daily life with their group identity and loyalty strengthened. Rituals in which people sing or dance together or chant in unison are particularly powerful.

A Durkheimian approach is particularly helpful when applied to sudden outbreaks of moralistic violence that are mystifying to outsiders. In 1978, the sociologist Albert Bergesen wrote an essay titled "A Durkheimian Theory of 'Witch-Hunts' With the Chinese Cultural Revolution of 1966–1969 as an Example."[7] Bergesen used Durkheim to illuminate the madness that erupted in Beijing in May 1966, when Mao Zedong began warning about the rising threat of infiltration by pro-capitalist enemies. Zealous college students responded by forming the Red Guards to find and punish enemies of the revolution. Universities across the country were shut down for several years. During those years, the Red Guards rooted out any trace they could find—or imagine—of capitalism, foreign influence, or bourgeois values. In practice, this meant that anyone who was successful or accomplished was suspect, and many professors, intellectuals, and campus administrators were imprisoned or murdered.[8]

Among the many cruel features of the Cultural Revolution were the "struggle sessions," in which those accused of ideological impurity were surrounded by their accusers, taunted, humiliated, and sometimes beaten as they confessed to their crimes, offered abject apologies, and vowed to do better. Students sometimes turned on their own teachers. Over the next few years, tens of millions were persecuted, and hundreds of thousands were murdered.[9]

How could such an orgy of self-destruction have happened? Bergesen notes that there are three features common to most political witch hunts: they arise very quickly, they involve charges of crimes against the collective, and the offenses that lead to charges are often trivial or fabricated. Here's how Bergesen puts it:

1. *They arise quickly:* "Witch-hunts seem to appear in dramatic outbursts; they are not a regular feature of social life. A community seems to suddenly find itself infested with all sorts of subversive elements which pose a threat to the collectivity as a whole. Whether one thinks of the Reign of Terror during the French Revolution, the Stalinist Show Trials, or the McCarthy period in the United States, the phenomenon is the same: a community becomes intensely mobilized to rid itself of internal enemies."[10]

2. *Crimes against the collective:* "The various charges that appear during one of these witch-hunts involve accusations of crimes committed against the nation as a corporate whole. It is the whole of collective existence that is at stake; it is The Nation, The People, The Revolution, or The State which is being undermined and subverted."[11]

3. *Charges are often trivial or fabricated:* "These crimes and deviations seem to involve the most petty and insignificant behavioral acts which are somehow understood as crimes against the nation as a whole. In fact, one of the principal reasons we term these events 'witch-hunts' is that innocent people are so often involved and falsely accused."[12]

To Bergesen's list we'll add a fourth feature, which necessarily follows from the first three:

4. *Fear of defending the accused:* When a public accusation is made, many friends and bystanders know that the victim is innocent, but they are afraid to say anything. Anyone who comes to the defense of the accused is obstructing the enactment of a collective ritual. Siding with the accused is *truly* an offense against the group, and it will be treated as such. If passions and fears are intense enough, people will even testify against their friends and family members.

Does Bergesen's Durkheimian analysis of the Cultural Revolution help to explain the dramatic events that have been happening on campus since 2015, some of which we described in the previous chapter? As historical events, the two movements are radically different, most notably in that the Red Guards were supported by a totalitarian dictator who encouraged them to use violence, while American college students have been self-organized and almost entirely nonviolent. Yet there are similarities, too. For example, both movements were initiated by idealistic students fighting for what seemed to them a noble ideal: the remaking of society along egalitarian lines. Bergesen's analysis captures the fact that both movements began with "dramatic outbursts," which were followed by intense and rapid mobilization on college campuses across the country.[13] It also captures the fact that large reactions are often launched in response to small acts, such as Erika Christakis's email about Halloween costumes at Yale[14] and Mary Spellman's use of the word "mold" when reaching out to a student at

Claremont McKenna College.[15] Outside observers were often unable to comprehend how these two emails could have triggered mass movements demanding that the two women be denounced and fired.

Bergesen's approach also works well when applied to the violence at Middlebury College. The videos of the main shout-down show students chanting, singing, and at times swaying in unison to prevent Charles Murray from speaking.[16] It's a striking demonstration of Durkheim's "collective effervescence" building up a charge of social electricity that prepares the group for action. Research shows that synchronous movements like singing and swaying make groups more cooperative and make people who participate physically stronger in challenges they undertake right afterward.[17] Perhaps the violent attack on Professor Stanger would not have taken place if Murray had been moved out immediately and the students had not had so much time to sway and chant in unison.

We call a campaign a witch hunt when we believe that the targets of the attacks (such as Erika Christakis and Mary Spellman) are innocent, but even if we are right, that does not mean that the people doing the hunting lack any valid reason for their anger and fear. By 2015, most people had seen videos of police officers shooting or choking unarmed black men. It is understandable that many black students were on edge, felt a generalized sense of threat, and became increasingly active in movements to oppose systemic racism, particularly in the criminal justice system. But why did college students direct so much of their passion and effort toward changing their universities and to finding enemies *within* their own communities? And here's a related puzzle: Why were the protests strongest and most common at schools known for progressive politics in the most progressive parts of the United States (New England and the West Coast)?[18] Are these not the schools that are already the most devoted to enacting progressive and inclusive social policies?

To advance in our inquiry, let's switch our focus away from students for a moment. We will examine a trend among *professors* that seems to fit the Durkheimian framework quite well: the use of open letters of denunciation. Professors try to round up hundreds of other professors to condemn a fellow professor or to demand that an academic article be retracted (rather than simply rebutting it). Something has been changing among the faculty, as well as among the students. (We'll examine these changes in the broader national context of rising political polarization in the next chapter, when we'll examine the role that provocation from the right from off campus plays in these unusual events on campus.)

A Provocative Idea

On March 29, 2017, *Hypatia: A Journal of Feminist Philosophy* posted to its website an article titled "In Defense of Transracialism."[19] In the essay, Rebecca Tuvel, an assistant professor of philosophy at Rhodes College in Memphis, Tennessee, juxtaposed the largely positive public reaction to news of Caitlyn Jenner's gender transition (from man to woman) with the "ridicule and condemnation" that accompanied the revelation that Rachel Dolezal, a former chapter president of the NAACP, a civil rights organization, was not black but, rather, a white woman who claimed that she "identif[ies] as black."[20] Tuvel, noting that her concerns were not with the particulars of the Dolezal case but "with the arguments for and against transracialism," argued that while society is hostile to transracialism and more open to transgenderism, the two kinds of identity transformation raise many of the same considerations.

In the article, Tuvel stressed that she is a strong advocate of transgender rights and that she was "not suggesting that race and sex are equivalent." She had explored similar ideas before without controversy; her Rhodes College web page states that her research "lies at the intersection of feminist philosophy, philosophy of race and animal ethics." In much of her work, she considers the ways in which the oppression of "animals, women and racially subordinated groups" overlap to "maintain erroneous and harmful conceptions of humanity."[21] This is a scholar who knows her way around contemporary debates, and surely meant no harm to transgender people.

But in today's culture of safetyism, intent no longer matters; only perceived impact does, and thanks to concept creep, just about anything can be perceived as having a harmful—even violent—impact on vulnerable groups. According to Bergesen, anything that can be construed as an attack on a group can serve as an opportunity for collective punishment and the enhancement of group solidarity.

Within a few weeks of its publication, the article had generated such an uproar that an open letter was published, addressed to an editor of *Hypatia* and the "broader *Hypatia* community."[22] The letter demanded that the article be retracted—not *rebutted* but *retracted*. The signers were not asking for a chance to respond to Tuvel and correct her alleged mistakes (a common practice in academia); they were demanding that the article vanish from the scholarly record (a very rare occurrence, usually reserved for cases of fraud or plagiarism). They contended that the "continued availability" of the article caused "harm" to women of color and the transgender community. Yet, although the letter's authors asserted that "many harms" were "committed by [the article's] publishing," the alleged "harm" was not described. In fact, by claiming that the letter "is not an exhaustive summary of the many harms caused by this article," they sidestepped their lack of evidence that the article had caused (or could cause) any harm at all.[23]

Individual critics were quick to chime in, calling the article "transphobic," "violent," and an expression of "all that is wrong with white feminism." Nora Berenstain, an assistant professor of philosophy at the University of Tennessee, took to Facebook to expound on the article's "discursive transmisogynistic violence." She asserted that Tuvel "enacts violence and perpetuates harm in numerous ways throughout her essay," because she "deadnames a trans woman" (that is, Tuvel mentioned that Jenner's former male, or "dead," name, was Bruce),[24] she "uses the term 'transgenderism,'" she "talks about 'biological sex,'" and she "uses phrases like 'male genitalia.'" It is striking how many of the critics' complaints refer not to Tuvel's *arguments* but to her *word choices*. In fact, one of the arguments for retraction given in the open letter was that Tuvel used "vocabulary and frameworks not recognized, accepted, or adopted by the conventions of the relevant subfields." As when Dean Spellman used the word "mold" in her email, "petty and insignificant behavioral acts" (to use Bergesen's phrase) can be considered "crimes against the [group] as a whole."[25]

Jesse Singal, a left-leaning social science journalist, read the list of charges in the open letter and then read Tuvel's original essay. As he put it in an online article for *New York* magazine, "Each and every one of the falsifiable points [that the open letter] makes is, based on a plain reading of Tuvel's article, simply false or misleading." He concluded:

> All in all, it's remarkable how many basic facts this letter gets wrong about Tuvel's paper. Either the authors simply lied about the article's contents, or they didn't read it at all. Every single one of the hundreds of signatories on the open letter now has their name on a document that severely (and arguably maliciously) mischaracterizes the work of one of their colleagues. This is not the sort of thing that usually happens in academia—it's a really strange, disturbing instance of mass groupthink, perhaps fueled by the dynamics of online shaming and piling-on.[26]

The reaction to Tuvel's article fits well into a Durkheimian framework: it is a surprising, "out of nowhere" eruption of "mass groupthink" in which trivial things (such as using the phrase "male genitalia") are taken as grave attacks on a vulnerable community. These attacks then warrant a collective, solidarity-boosting response: an open letter that recruits hundreds of people to publicly sign their names and collectively point their fingers at the accused witch. Singal even titled his essay "This Is What a Modern-Day Witch Hunt Looks Like."

The Tuvel affair also shows the fourth criterion of a witch hunt: fear of defending the accused.[27] Tuvel's Ph.D. advisor, Kelly Oliver, wrote an essay defending her former student, in which she lamented the cowardice of so many of her colleagues:

> In private messages [to Oliver, and to Tuvel], some people commiserated, expressed support, and apologized for what was happening and for not going public with their support. As one academic

wrote to me in a private message, "sorry I'm not saying this publicly (I have no interest in battling the mean girls on Facebook) but FWIW [for what it's worth] it's totally obvious to me that you haven't been committing acts of violence against marginalized scholars."

Oliver noted that some scholars went beyond cowardice, privately supporting Tuvel while publicly attacking her:

In private messages, these people apologized for what she must be going through, while in public they fanned the flames of hatred and bile on social media. The question is, why did so many scholars, especially feminists, express one sentiment behind closed doors and another out in the open? Why were so many others afraid to say anything in public?[28]

Durkheim and Bergesen give us a direct answer to Oliver's question.[29] This is precisely what people do during a witch hunt.

Retraction Is the New Rebuttal

Other open letters condemning professors and demanding retraction of their work soon followed.[30] In August 2017, two law professors, Amy Wax from the University of Pennsylvania and Larry Alexander from the University of San Diego, wrote a short opinion essay in a Philadelphia newspaper titled "Paying the Price for Breakdown of the Country's Bourgeois Culture."[31] They argued that many of today's social problems, including unemployment, crime, drug use, and the intergenerational transmission of poverty, are partially caused by the fading away of the "bourgeois cultural script" that used to compel Americans to "get married before you have children and strive to stay married for their sake. Get the education you need for gainful employment, work hard, and avoid idleness." The authors included one particular line that caused a firestorm: "All cultures are not equal. Or at least they are not equal in preparing people to be productive in an advanced economy." The line is provocative because it violates a widespread taboo in the academic world: One is not supposed to say that a dominant culture is superior to a nondominant one in any way. But anthropologists generally agree that cultures and subcultures instill different goals, skills, and virtues in their members,[32] and it can't possibly be true that all cultures prepare children equally well for success in all other cultures. If we want to improve outcomes for immigrants and the poor in a free-market, service-oriented capitalist economy such as ours, Wax and Alexander argued, it would be useful to talk about bourgeois culture.

A week later, fifty-four graduate students and alumni of the University of Pennsylvania published a statement that condemned the essay and its authors for exemplifying the "malignant logic of hetero-patriarchal, class-based, white supremacy." In good Durkheimian fashion, the open letter issued a strong call for solidarity among "all members of the University of Pennsylvania community who claim to fight systemic inequality," and it included a demand that the president of the university confront the racism of Wax and Alexander and "push for an investigation into Wax's advocacy for white supremacy."[33] The call for denunciation was taken up by thirty-three of Wax's colleagues in the law school (nearly half the faculty), who wrote their own open letter of denunciation. They did not do what scholars are supposed to do: use their scholarly abilities to show where Wax and Alexander were wrong. They simply "condemned" and "categorically rejected" Wax's claims.[34]

Solidarity or Diversity?

Solidarity is great for a group that needs to work in unison or march into battle. Solidarity engenders trust, teamwork, and mutual aid. But it can also foster groupthink, orthodoxy, and a paralyzing fear of challenging the collective. Solidarity can interfere with a group's efforts to find the truth, and the search for truth can interfere with a group's solidarity. The Greek historian Thucydides saw this principle in action over two thousand years ago.

Writing about a time of wars and revolutions in the fifth century BCE, he noted that "the ability to understand a question from all sides meant that one was totally unfitted for action."[35]

This is why viewpoint diversity is so essential in any group of scholars. Each professor is—like all human beings—a flawed thinker with a strong preference for believing that his or her own ideas are right. Each scholar suffers from the confirmation bias—the tendency to search vigorously for evidence that confirms what one already believes.[36] One of the most brilliant features of universities is that, when they are working properly, they are communities of scholars who cancel out one another's confirmation biases. Even if professors often cannot see the flaws in their own arguments, other professors and students do them the favor of finding such flaws. The community of scholars then judges which ideas survive the debate. We can call this process *institutionalized disconfirmation*. The institution (the academy as a whole, or a discipline, such as political science) guarantees that every statement offered as a research finding—and certainly every peer-reviewed article—has survived a process of challenge and vetting. That is no guarantee that it is true, but it *is* a reason to think that the statement is likely to be more reliable than alternative statements made by partisan think tanks, corporate marketers, or your opinionated uncle. It is only because of institutionalized disconfirmation that universities and groups of scholars can claim some authority to be arbiters of factual questions, such as whether certain vaccines caused the rise in autism (they didn't)[37] or whether social programs designed to help poor children close achievement gaps with wealthier kids actually work (some do, some don't).[38]

But what would happen to a university, or an academic field, if everyone were on the same team and everyone shared the same confirmation bias? The disconfirmation process would break down. Research shows that reviewers go easy on articles and grant proposals that support their political team, and they are more critical of articles and proposals that contradict their team's values or beliefs.[39] This, to some extent, is what has happened in many academic fields since the 1990s, with enormous ramifications for university culture today.

It is no surprise that, on the whole, professors lean left. So do artists, poets, and people who love to watch foreign movies. One of the strongest personality correlates of left-wing politics is the trait of *openness to experience*, a trait that describes people who crave new ideas and experiences and who tend to be interested in changing traditional arrangements.[40] On the other hand, members of the military, law enforcement personnel, and students who have well-organized dorm rooms tend to lean right. (Seriously. You can guess people's political leanings at better-than-chance levels just from photographs of their desks.)[41] Social conservatives tend to be lower on openness to experience and higher on *conscientiousness*—they prefer things to be orderly and predictable, they are more likely to show up on time for meetings, and they are more likely to see the value of traditional arrangements.

In a free society, therefore, it will simply *never* be the case that every occupation is evenly balanced, politically, and it will generally be the case that professors lean left, especially in the humanities and social sciences. This is not a problem as long as there are enough professors who don't lean left to guarantee institutionalized disconfirmation in any field that addresses politicized topics. A left-to-right ratio of two or three to one should be enough to sustain institutionalized disconfirmation. And that's about what the ratio was for most of the twentieth century.

Figure 5.1 shows the percentage of professors (across all fields) who self-identified on a survey as being on the left (in the top line), the right (bottom line) or "middle of the road" (middle line). The left-to-right ratio in the early 1990s was around two to one. The few studies we have that go back to the mid-twentieth century generally also show that professors leaned to the left, or voted for Democrats, but not by a very lopsided margin.[42] Things began to change rapidly, however, in the late 1990s. That's when the professors from the Greatest Generation began to retire, to be replaced by members of the Baby Boom generation. By 2011, the ratio had reached five to one. The Greatest Generation professors were predominantly white men who had fought in World War II, and then got a boost into higher education from legislation designed to help them in the postwar period. That wave of scholars included many Republicans and many conservatives.

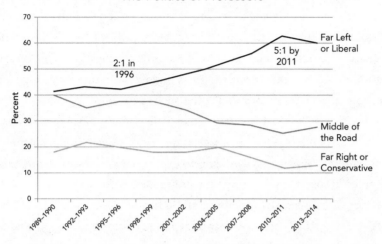

FIGURE 5.1. *How professors described their own politics. The left-right ratio has increased rapidly since the mid-1990s. (Source: Higher Education Research Institute.[43] Data is from nationally representative surveys of professors in the United States. Graphed by Sam Abrams.)*

The Baby Boom professors, in contrast, were more diverse by race and gender but less diverse in their politics. Many of them were influenced by the great wave of social protests in the 1960s; many went into academic careers in the social sciences and education in order to continue to fight for social justice and progressive social causes.

This is why the ratio changes so much more dramatically when we look at fields that are associated with addressing social justice concerns. In Jon's field, academic psychology, the left-to-right ratio was between two to one and four to one from the 1930s through the mid-1990s, but then it began to shoot upward, reaching seventeen to one by 2016.[44] The ratios in other core fields in the humanities and social sciences are nearly all above ten to one. The imbalance is larger at more prestigious universities and in New England.[45] The only field among all of the humanities and social sciences that is known to have enough political diversity to allow for institutionalized disconfirmation is economics, where the left-to-right ratio found in a study of the voter registrations of professors was a comparatively low four to one.[46]

The loss of political diversity among professors, particularly in fields that deal with politicized content, can undermine the quality and rigor of scholarly research. Six social scientists (including Jon) wrote an academic article in 2015 that explains how.[47] For example, when a field lacks political diversity, researchers tend to congregate around questions and research methods that generally confirm their shared narrative, while ignoring questions and methods that don't offer such support.

The loss of political diversity among the faculty has negative consequences for students, too, in three ways. First, there's the problem that many college students have little or no exposure to professors from half of the political spectrum.[48] Many students graduate with an inaccurate understanding of conservatives, politics, and much of the United States. Three days after Donald Trump's widely unexpected electoral victory, the editors of Harvard's main student newspaper made exactly this case in an editorial invoking Harvard's motto, *Veritas*—the Latin word for "truth"—calling on the administration to give them more political diversity:

> The pursuit of "Veritas" which undergirds our intellectual life demands not only that each member of our community be able to debate politics freely, but also that we attend to the multitude of political views that exist in our nation. Stifling this discussion on campus is a disservice to our peers in the campus political minority, and to our own educational growth.[49]

Second, the loss of viewpoint diversity among the faculty means that what students learn about politically controversial topics will often be "left shifted" from the truth. There is a range of reasonable opinions on many factual questions. (For example: How much does raising the minimum wage cause employers to hire fewer low-skilled workers? How much of an influence do prenatal hormones have on the differing toy and play preferences of boys versus girls?) But students in politically homogeneous departments will mostly be exposed to books and research studies drawn from the left half of the range, so they are likely to come down to the "left" of the truth, on average. (For example, they are likely to underestimate the elasticity of labor demand, especially if they attended prestigious universities in New England.) Sometimes the left-leaning view turns out to be correct, sometimes it's the right-leaning view, but on average, students will get closer to the truth if they are exposed to debates among credentialed scholars who approach difficult problems from differing perspectives.

To compound this second problem, during the same period in which the faculty were becoming more politically homogeneous, so were the students. Surveys of incoming freshmen conducted by the Higher Education Research Institute show that roughly 20% of incoming students identify as conservative, and that figure has held steady since the early 1980s. Self-described "moderates" made up roughly half of all incoming students in the 1980s and 1990s, but that figure has been dropping since the early 2000s—it's now in the low forties—as the percentage of progressives (self-described "liberals") rises into the high 30s.[50] The shift has accelerated since 2012.[51]

We are not saying there is anything inherently wrong with the increasing number of left-leaning students on campus. But we *are* saying that viewpoint diversity is necessary for the development of critical thinking, while viewpoint homogeneity (whether on the left or the right) leaves a community vulnerable to groupthink and orthodoxy. If both the faculty and the students have been losing moderates and gaining progressives since the 1990s, and if this shift among students has accelerated since 2012, then we would expect to see some changes in the culture and social dynamics of American universities, especially after 2012.[52]

This is the third problem. It is the Durkheimian problem. It is the risk that *some* academic communities—particularly those in the most progressive parts of the country—may attain such high levels of political homogeneity and solidarity that they undergo a phase change, taking on properties of a collective entity that are antithetical to the normal aims of a university. A collective entity mobilized for action is more likely to enforce political orthodoxy and less likely to tolerate challenges to its key ideological beliefs. Politically homogeneous communities are more susceptible to witch hunts, particularly when they feel threatened from outside.

Welcome to Evergreen

The Evergreen State College, a small public college an hour's drive south of Seattle, has long had a reputation for quirky progressivism. The college is located on a nature reserve and has its own organic farm. Instead of grades, students receive narrative reports. It has been listed as one of the ten most liberal colleges in the country.[53] In 2011, the college changed its mission statement to include this: "Evergreen supports and benefits from local and global commitment to social justice, diversity, environmental stewardship and service in the public interest."[54] In May of 2017, Evergreen slipped into a state of anarchy that is difficult to explain without the help of Durkheim.

Campus tensions had already been rising when, on March 15, Bret Weinstein, a politically progressive biology professor, emailed a faculty list-serv[55] to express his concern about plans for that year's "Day of Absence,"[56] which was scheduled to take place the following month. Inspired by a Douglas Turner Ward play of the same name,[57] staff and faculty members of color (and later students, too) had been spending one day off campus each year since the 1970s in order to make their absence—and thus the impor-tance of their contributions—felt. In the wake of Donald Trump's election, however, the organizers of the 2017 event decided to make a change: instead of the day being an opportunity for people of color to voluntarily absent themselves, this year, white students and faculty were asked to stay away from campus.[58]

Professor Weinstein thought this was wrong.[59] He wrote, "There is a huge difference between a group or coalition deciding to voluntarily absent themselves from a shared space in order to highlight their vital and under-appreciated roles" and "encouraging another group to go away."[60] In a shared space, "one's right to speak—or to be," he said, "must never be based on skin color." He also feared that white students and faculty who did not support the *structure* of the Day of Absence and chose to come to campus that day would be viewed negatively; their very presence might be interpreted to mean they did not support the *goals* of the event.[61] Weinstein had expressed other concerns about the direction the college was taking when, a year earlier, the college president, administrators, and select faculty committed to a campuswide "equity" agenda, including a proposed policy that would require all new employees to have an "equity" justification. The president of Evergreen, George Bridges, had begun using the phrase "education-solidarity-inclusion" in his memos and mailings. He and his "equity council" had also undertaken various solidarity-building exercises, one of which included an event during which faculty were publicly pressured by name to get into an imaginary canoe, in which the faculty and administration then symbolically journeyed toward equity together (to the sounds of crashing waves and a Native American drumbeat).[62] These rituals and talk of campuswide "solidarity" make sense from a Durkheimian perspective. They are ways to prepare a community for collective action.

The Day of Absence came and went "almost without incident," according to Weinstein,[63] although not all white members of the community complied. But more than a month later, on May 23, after other instances of campus unrest, a multiethnic group of angry students marched to Weinstein's classroom door, cornered him in the hallway, and berated him.[64] They swore at him, calling him a "piece of shit" and telling him to "get the fuck out." They claimed that he made racist statements in his email,[65] and they demanded that he not only apologize but also resign. Weinstein disagreed with their assessment of his email as "harmful" and "racist," and he refused to apologize. But he did try to engage the students in discussion or, as he called it, "dialectic, which does mean I listen to you and you listen to me." The response was not positive: "We don't care what terms you want to speak on . . . we are not speaking on terms of white privilege."[66]

The students continued to blast the professor, and tensions mounted. Concerned for Weinstein's safety, his students contacted the police, but protesters physically prevented the police from reaching him.[67] Campus police requested backup from other police departments.[68]

Protesters, claiming to be "fearful for their lives," marched on to the administration building, where they found and confronted President Bridges outside his office. Videos of the event show protesters saying, "Fuck you, George, we don't want to hear a Goddamn thing you have to say. . . . You shut the fuck up."[69] The president agreed to meet with protesters along with the staff and administrators who supported them, and then assured them that, with respect to errant faculty in the sciences (such as Weinstein), "they're going to say some things we don't like, and our job is to bring them all in or get 'em out. And what I hear us stating that we are working toward is: bring 'em in, train 'em, and if they don't get it, sanction 'em."[70] (Yes, that is the president of a U.S. public college, which is bound by the First Amendment to protect academic freedom, proposing to fire or punish professors who do not accept the teachings of a mandatory political reeducation program.)

Some of the protesters insisted that campus police chief Stacy Brown join the meeting—unarmed. Brown, who would not disarm in uniform, changed into civilian clothes and arrived to find students shouting expletives and slurs, some directed at her.[71] Certain protesters were assigned to her and followed her to another meeting later in the day, attended by hundreds of others. At this larger gathering, protesters attached themselves to Brown, Weinstein, and a few other noncompliant faculty and students. At all times, the protesters controlled the exits.[72] When Weinstein's students overheard protesters say they had mace and planned to prevent Weinstein from leaving the building, they texted him to alert him. Weinstein texted his wife, Heather Heying, a fellow biology professor: "I am told I will not be allowed to leave," and then, "Not sure what to do."[73]

Video of that meeting is startling.[74] Student protesters can be heard insisting that Weinstein be fired in order to prevent him from what one white protester later described as "spread[ing] this problematic rhetoric."[75] Students of color who spoke supportively of Weinstein, or who even asked to hear from people not in the protesters' camp, were shouted down and called "race traitors."[76] (White students who were not protesting were told to stand in the back and were not allowed to speak.[77])

Students repeatedly and publicly ridiculed the college president, even berating him for smiling. One student yelled at President Bridges (who often gesticulates with his hands), "Put your hand down!" while another student mockingly imitated his hand gestures, adding, "That's *my* problem [with you], George, you keep making these little hand movements." The president immediately put his hands behind his back as the student walked

around him to laughter and applause, announcing that she was "decoloniz-
ing the space." Bridges responded, "My hands are down."[78]

The next day, May 24, protesters searched cars looking for Weinstein.[79]
They interrupted a faculty meeting and took the cake meant to celebrate
retiring faculty, while asking, "Didn't you educate us on how to do shit like
this?"[80] Then, according to the student newspaper, student protesters barricaded the main entrance to the administration building,[81] and for several
hours, having occupied the building and gathered together the leadership
of the college, including President Bridges,[82] they held them in an office.
With the leadership team sequestered, the students prepared and later presented their demands. These included mandatory bias training for faculty,
and permission for protesters to not turn in their homework on time.[83]

Outside the office, students video-recorded themselves making sure
that the room had no escape routes and that there was enough student
"presence" to prevent administrators from leaving. Bridges ordered the
campus police not to intervene. One organizer of the protest told students
there was a room for them to "rest" and advised protesters to "make sure
you're all taking care of yourselves in these moments." Immediately after
giving those instructions, the same organizer entered the president's office
and asked the administrators if they needed anything. Bridges is seen on
video saying, "I need to pee." The organizer replies, "Hold it," as several
people laugh. (Protesters later escorted Bridges to the bathroom.)[84]

Inside the president's office, one student protester asked captive administrators, "Don't you think it's continuing white supremacy when the leadership is only white people?" Several administrators nodded and said yes,
thereby validating the students' grossly expanded definition of white supremacy.[85] Outside the office, students chanted, "Hey hey/ho ho/these racist faculty have got to go." That night, in an email to the campus community,
an Evergreen media studies professor wrote approvingly that the protesting
students were "doing exactly what we've taught them."

The following day, May 25, the police received information that protesters intended to target the campus police department building. Ordered to
stand down,[86] the police evacuated, setting up a post off campus and monitoring the highly charged situation using campus security cameras and a

local law enforcement helicopter.[87] Students who defended Weinstein were stalked, and were targeted by protesters in thinly veiled online threats. The campus police chief informed Weinstein that, out of concern for his safety, she thought it would be best if he left campus.[88] He held all but one of his remaining classes that quarter off campus.[89]

Aside from his wife, Heather Heying, only one professor on the entire faculty,[90] Mike Paros, a professor of veterinary science, publicly supported Weinstein.[91] Weinstein later learned that several other professors were supportive but afraid to say so in public.[92] With so little support, with the police urging him to stay off campus, and with no national media covering the story of Evergreen's descent into anarchy and intimidation, on May 26, Weinstein accepted an invitation to be interviewed on the Fox News TV show *Tucker Carlson Tonight*.[93]

Once the story went public, it attracted attention from the political right and harassment from the alt-right, which we will discuss further in the next chapter. On Thursday, June 1, a man in New Jersey called the Thurston County emergency line and told the dispatcher he was on his way to Evergreen to "execute as many people on campus as I can get ahold of."[94] Law enforcement informed the school that there was no active threat, but as a precautionary measure, the campus was shut down until Saturday, June 3.[95] On June 3 and 4, bands of students began to roam the campus armed with baseball bats and tasers, searching for "white supremacists." They vandalized buildings and assaulted several students.[96] The New Jersey man was arrested a month later.

How did this mess end? Who was held accountable? On June 2, roughly a quarter of the college's faculty signed a letter calling for Weinstein to be investigated, blaming him for provoking "white supremacist backlash," and claiming that by speaking about what was happening on Fox News TV, he "endangered" students.[97] Weinstein and Heying rejected the assertion that he was to blame. As employees of Evergreen, they filed a tort claim against the college for tolerating, and even endorsing, egregious violations of the student conduct code—including criminal behavior—and for fostering a racially hostile work environment. In September 2017, the couple and Evergreen agreed on a settlement, and the professors resigned.[98] Police chief

Stacy Brown later made similar charges, claiming that "the hostile environment left her with no choice but to resign from the College."[99]

President Bridges, who at the beginning of the school year had criticized the University of Chicago for its policy protecting free speech and academic freedom,[100] agreed to many of the protesters' demands.[101] He announced that he was "grateful" for the "passion and courage" the protesters displayed,[102] and later, he hired one of the leaders of the protests to join his Presidential Equity Advisors.[103] One of their primary tasks was to rewrite the student code of conduct.

Great Untruth U

The events at Evergreen illustrate just about everything we've talked about in this book so far. The early stages illustrate Bergesen's three features of political witch hunts: the movement seemed to come out of nowhere, it was in response to a trivial provocation (a polite email sent to a faculty listserv), and the provocation was interpreted as an attack on the entire Evergreen community. As the drama unfolded, it illustrated our fourth criterion: faculty and administrators who wanted to defend Weinstein were afraid to do so.

The protesting Evergreen students—and the faculty and administrators who encouraged them—repeatedly displayed all three of the Great Untruths. For example, one professor who supported the protesters addressed some of her faculty colleagues in an angry monologue that included a line similar to the Untruth of Fragility (*What doesn't kill you makes you weaker*): "I am too tired. This shit is literally going to kill me."[104]

A student illustrated the Untruth of Emotional Reasoning (*Always trust your feelings*) at the large town-hall meeting when she used her own anxiety as evidence that something was very wrong at Evergreen: "I want to cry, I can't tell you how fast my heart is beating. I am shaking in my boots."[105]

And of course, the entire episode was an illustration of the Untruth of Us Versus Them (*Life is a battle between good people and evil people*). The protesting students and their faculty supporters engaged in a giant game of common-enemy identity politics by interpreting a politically progressive college and its politically progressive leadership and faculty as exemplars of white supremacy in action. As one student who refused to join the protesters later put it while testifying before the college trustees, "If you offer any kind of alternative viewpoint, you're 'the enemy.'"[106]

Evergreen State College is not typical. With the exception of the "Milo riot" at UC Berkeley, its meltdown into anarchy in the spring of 2017 is more extreme than anything else that has happened in recent decades on an American college campus, as far as we know. We have presented its story in detail because it is a warning to everyone who cares about students or universities. The Evergreen story shows what is possible when political diversity is reduced to very low levels, when the school's leadership is weak and easily intimidated, and when professors and administrators allow or even encourage the propagation of the three Great Untruths.

In Sum

- Humans are tribal creatures who readily form groups to compete with other groups (as we saw in chapter 3). Sociologist Emile Durkheim's work illuminates the way those groups engage in rituals—including the collective punishment of deviance—to enhance their cohesion and solidarity.

- Cohesive and morally homogeneous groups are prone to witch hunts, particularly when they experience a threat, whether from outside or from within.

- Witch hunts generally have four properties: they seem to come out of nowhere; they involve charges of crimes against the collective; the offenses that lead to those charges are often trivial or fabricated; and people who know that the accused is innocent keep quiet, or in extreme cases, they join the mob.

- Some of the most puzzling campus events and trends since 2015 match the profile of a witch hunt. The campus protests at Yale, Claremont McKenna, and Evergreen all began as reactions to politely worded emails, and all led to demands that the authors of the emails be fired. (We repeat that the concerns that provide the context for a witch hunt may be valid, but in a witch hunt, the attendant fears are channeled in unjust and destructive ways.)

- The new trend in 2017 for professors to join open letters denouncing their colleagues and demanding the retraction or condemnation of their work (as happened to Rebecca Tuvel, Amy Wax, and others) also fits this pattern. In all of these cases, colleagues of the accused were afraid to publicly stand up and defend them.

- Viewpoint diversity reduces a community's susceptibility to witch hunts. One of the most important kinds of viewpoint diversity, diversity of political thought, has declined substantially among both professors and students at American universities since the 1990s. These declines, combined with the rapidly escalating political polarization of the United States (which is our focus in the next chapter), may be part of the reason why the new culture of safetyism has spread so rapidly since its emergence around 2013.

This concludes Part II of this book. In these two chapters, we examined some dramatic events that occurred on American college campuses in the two years after we published our article in *The Atlantic*, laying out our concerns about cognitive distortions on campus. The new campus trends make a lot more sense once you understand the three Great Untruths and can spot them in action. In Part III, we'll ask: Why, and why now? Where did the three Great Untruths and the culture of safetyism come from, and why did they spread so quickly in the last few years?

How Did We Get Here?

CHAPTER 6

The Polarization Cycle

For every action, there is an equal and opposite reaction.

Isaac Newton's third law of motion

We began this book with a presentation of three Great Untruths—ideas so out of tune with human flourishing that they harm anyone who embraces them. In Part II, we narrated a variety of campus events that have attracted national and sometimes global attention, and we showed how some students and professors involved in these events seem to have embraced the Great Untruths. Now, in Part III, we widen the lens and look at how we got here. Why did a set of interrelated ideas—which we have called a culture of *safetyism*—sweep through many universities between 2013 and 2017? Students who graduated from college in 2012 generally tell us that they saw little evidence of these trends. Students who began college at some elite universities in 2013 or 2014 tell us they saw the new culture arrive over the course of their four years. What is going on?

There is no simple answer. In Part III, we present six interacting explanatory threads: rising political polarization and cross-party animosity; rising levels of teen anxiety and depression; changes in parenting practices; the decline of free play; the growth of campus bureaucracy; and a rising passion for justice in response to major national events, combined with changing ideas about what justice requires. We believe that it is impossible to understand the state of higher education today without understanding all six. Before we present these threads, however, we must make two points explicitly and emphatically.

The first point is that there are different threads for different people. Part of the complexity of our story is that not all of the threads have influenced each person and group on campus equally. The rising political polarization in the United States, in which universities are increasingly seen as bastions of the left, has led to an increase in hostility and harassment from some off-campus right-wing individuals and groups. Some of these events qualify as hate crimes and are targeted especially at Jews and people of color. We discuss that thread in this chapter. Rising rates of teen depression and anxiety affect both boys and girls but have hit young women particularly hard (as you'll see in chapter 7). The rise in overprotective or "helicopter" parenting and the decline of free play (chapters 8 and 9) have negatively affected kids from wealthier families (mostly white and Asian)[1] more than kids from working class or poor families. The increase in the number of campus administrators, along with the scope of their duties, may be having an effect at all schools (chapter 10), but new ideas and stronger passions about social justice may matter most on campuses where students are more engaged politically (chapter 11).

The second point is that this is a book about good intentions gone awry. In all of the six chapters in this part of the book, you'll read about people primarily acting from good or noble motivations. In most cases, the motive is to help or protect children or people seen as vulnerable or victimized. But as we all know, the road to hell can be paved with good intentions. Our goal in Part III is not to blame; it is to understand. Only by identifying and analyzing all six explanatory threads can we begin to talk about possible solutions, which we do in Part IV.

The Boiling Point

In the last two chapters, we told many stories about students and faculty reacting to words in ways that seemed inappropriate, over-the-top, and in some cases, aggressive. Whether about a response to an email, an effort to shout a speaker down, or a petition to denounce a colleague, the stories in this book have mostly presented problems on campus that arise from a part of the political left. Sometimes the targets were on the right (such as Heather Mac Donald and Amy Wax), but more often the targets were themselves on the left (such as Nicholas and Erika Christakis, Rebecca Tuvel, Bret Weinstein, and the professors who taught the humanities course at Reed College). If we were to limit our analysis to events on campus, this would be most of the story. A set of new ideas about speech, violence, and safety has emerged on the far left in recent years, and the debate on campus is largely a debate *within* the left, pitting (mostly) older progressives, who generally have an expansive notion of free speech, against (mostly) younger progressives, who are more likely to support some limitations on speech in the name of inclusion.[2]

But if we step back and look at American universities as complex institutions nested within a larger society that has been growing steadily more divided, angry, and polarized, we begin to see the left and the right locked into a game of mutual provocation and reciprocal outrage that is an essential piece of the puzzle we are trying to solve in this book. Allison Stanger, the Middlebury professor who suffered a concussion at the hands of protesters, said exactly this in a *New York Times* essay titled "Understanding the Angry Mob at Middlebury That Gave Me a Concussion."[3] In it, she wrote:

In the days after the violence, some have spun this story as one about what's wrong with elite colleges and universities, our coddled youth or intolerant liberalism. Those analyses are incomplete. Political life and discourse in the United States is at a boiling point, and nowhere is the reaction to that more heightened than on college campuses.

She next listed several of the ways in which President Trump had insulted or offended members of marginalized groups while inspiring hateful speech among many of his followers, and added: "That is the context into which Dr. Murray walked [where he] was so profoundly misunderstood."

We agree with Stanger that the national political context is an essential part of any story about what has been happening on college campuses in recent years. Things are indeed at a "boiling point" in the United States. You can see the temperature rising in the next two figures.

Figure 6.1 comes from the Pew Research Center, which in 1994 began asking a nationally representative sample of Americans about their level of agreement with a set of ten policy statements, and repeated the survey every few years. The policy statements include "Government regulation of business usually does more harm than good," "Immigrants today are a burden on our country because they take our jobs, housing, and healthcare," and "The best way to ensure peace is through military strength."[4] Pew computes how far apart members of different groups are on each issue, then takes the average of the absolute values of those differences across all ten statements. As you can see in the line near the bottom marked "Gender," men and women are just about the same distance apart in 2017 (7 points) as they were in 1994 (9 points). Only two of the lines show a clear increase. People who attend religious services regularly are now 11 points away from those who never attend, compared to just 5 points apart in 1994. But that 6-point increase is dwarfed by the *21-point increase* in the distance between Republicans and Democrats over the same time period, nearly all of it occurring since 2004.

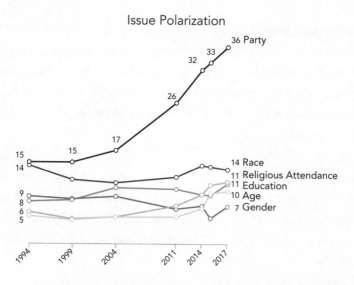

FIGURE 6.1. *The distance between Republicans and Democrats, on a set of 10 policy questions, has grown very large since 2004. Differences by race, gender, education, and age have not changed much since 1994. (Source: Pew Research Center.)*

If the people on the "other side" are moving farther and farther away from you on a broad set of moral and political issues, it stands to reason that you would feel more and more negatively toward them. Figure 6.2 shows that this has been happening. Every two years, the American National Election Study measures Americans' attitudes on a variety of topics. In part of the survey, the researchers use a "feeling thermometer," which is a set of questions asking respondents to rate a variety of groups and institutions on a scale where 0 is defined as "very cold or unfavorable" and 100 is defined as "very warm or favorable." The top two lines in the graph show that when Republicans and Democrats are asked to rate their own party, the lines are in positive territory and haven't moved much since the 1970s.[5] The bottom two lines show what they think about the other party. These lines have always been in negative territory, but many will be surprised to see that the cross-party ratings weren't all that negative from the 1970s until 1990—they hovered in the 40s. It's only in the 1990s that the lines begin to drop, with a plunge between 2008 and 2012 (the years of the Tea Party and Occupy Wall Street).

Why is this happening? There are many reasons, but in order to make

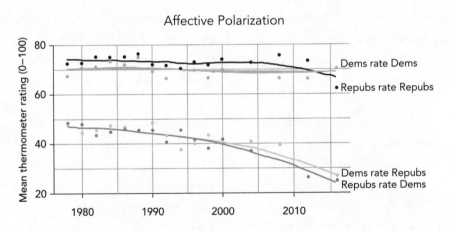

FIGURE 6.2. *Affective partisan polarization. Americans' feelings toward their own party have barely changed since the 1970s, but Americans have become increasingly "cold" or hostile toward the other party since the 1990s. (Source: American National Election Study,[6] plotted by Iyengar and Krupenkin, 2018.)*

sense of America's current predicament, you have to start by recognizing that the mid-twentieth century was a historical anomaly—a period of unusually low political polarization and cross-party animosity[7] combined with generally high levels of social trust and trust in government.[8] From the 1940s to around 1980, American politics was about as centrist and bipartisan as it has ever been. One reason is that, during and prior to this period, the country faced a series of common challenges and enemies, including the Great Depression, the Axis Powers during World War II, and the Soviets during the Cold War. Given the psychology of tribalism that we described in chapter 3, the loss of a common enemy after the collapse of the Soviet Union can be expected to lead to more intratribal conflict.

A second major reason is that, since the 1970s, Americans have been increasingly self-segregating into politically homogeneous communities, as Bill Bishop showed in his influential 2008 book, *The Big Sort: Why the Clustering of Like-Minded America Is Tearing Us Apart.* Subsequent research has shown that we live in increasingly economically and politically segregated communities right down to the city block.[9] The two major political parties have sorted themselves along similar lines: as the Republican Party becomes disproportionately older, white, rural, male, and Christian, the Democratic Party is increasingly young, nonwhite, urban, female, and nonreligious.[10] As political scientists Shanto Iyengar and Masha Krupenkin put it, "The result is that today, differences in party affiliation go hand in glove with differences in world view and individuals' sense of social and cultural identity."[11]

A third major reason is the media environment, which has changed in ways that foster division. Long gone is the time when everybody watched one of three national television networks. By the 1990s, there was a cable news channel for most points on the political spectrum, and by the early 2000s there was a website or discussion group for every conceivable interest group and grievance. By the 2010s, most Americans were using social media sites like Facebook and Twitter, which make it easy to encase oneself within an echo chamber. And then there's the "filter bubble," in which search engines and YouTube algorithms are designed to give you more of what you seem to be interested in, leading conservatives and progressives into disconnected moral matrices backed up by mutually contradictory informational worlds.[12] Both the physical and the electronic isolation from people we disagree with allow the forces of confirmation bias, groupthink, and tribalism to push us still further apart.

A fourth reason is the increasingly bitter hostility in Congress. The Democrats controlled the House of Representatives for about sixty years, with only brief interruptions in the mid- to late twentieth century, but their dominance ended in 1994, when the Republicans swept to victory under Newt Gingrich, who became Speaker of the House. Gingrich then imposed a set of reforms intended to discourage his many new members from forging the sort of personal relationships across party lines that had been normal in previous decades.[13] For example, Gingrich changed the work schedule to ensure that all business was done midweek, and then he encouraged his members not to move their families from their home districts, and instead fly to Washington for a few days each week. Gingrich wanted a more cohesive and combative Republican team, and he got it. The more combative norms then filtered up to the Senate as well (though in weaker form). With control shifting back and forth several times since 1995, and with so much at stake with each shift, norms of civility and possibilities for bipartisanship have nearly disappeared. As political scientists Steven Levitsky and Daniel Ziblatt put it, "Parties [have] come to view each other not as legitimate rivals but as dangerous enemies. Losing ceases to be an accepted part of the political process and instead becomes a catastrophe."[14]

These four trends, plus many more,[15] have combined to produce a very unfortunate change in the dynamics of American politics, which political scientists call *negative partisanship*. In a recent review of data on "affective polarization" (the degree to which members of each party feel negatively toward the other party), Iyengar and Krupenkin summarize the change like this:

Prior to the era of polarization, ingroup favoritism, that is, partisans' enthusiasm for their party or candidate, was the driving force behind political participation. More recently, however, it is hostility toward the out-party that makes people more inclined to participate.[16]

In other words, Americans are now motivated to leave their couches to take part in political action not by love for their party's candidate but by hatred of the other party's candidate. Negative partisanship means that American politics is driven less by hope and more by the Untruth of Us Versus Them. "They" must be stopped, at all costs.

This is an essential part of our story. Americans now bear such animosity toward one another that it's almost as if many are holding up signs saying, "Please tell me something horrible about the other side, I'll believe anything!" Americans are now easily exploitable, and a large network of profit-driven media sites, political entrepreneurs, and foreign intelligence agencies are taking advantage of this vulnerability.

The vulnerability comes with an unfortunate asymmetry: the faculty and students at universities have shifted to the left since the 1990s, as we showed in the last chapter, while the "outrage industry" of talk radio, cable news networks, and conspiracy websites is more developed and effective on the right.[17] (The mainstream media overall leans left,[18] but the left simply never found a format or formula that could match the influence of Rush Limbaugh, Glenn Beck, and Sean Hannity.) Right-wing media has long loved to make fun of professors and stir up anger over "politically correct" practices spotted on university campuses. But as campus activism increased in 2015 and offered up an unending stream of dramatic cell phone videos (including students cursing at professors and shouting down speakers), right-wing media outlets began to devote far more attention to campus events, which they portrayed gleefully, usually stripped of any explanatory context. The rising expressions of anger from the left on campus, sometimes directed against conservative speakers, led to rising expressions of anger from the right, off campus, sometimes directed in threatening ways at left-leaning professors and students, which in turn triggered more anger from the left on campus . . . and the cycle repeats.

Outrage From the Off-Campus Right

In the last two chapters, we examined protests, shout-downs, open letters, and witch hunts originating from the left, because the left is the dominant force on most college campuses (leaving aside religious and military academies). But if we step back from campus, we see that some people and groups on the right engage in moralistic, aggressive, and intimidating actions aimed at campus, too.

We told the story of Evergreen State College, but we left some of its aftermath for this chapter. As we noted, three days after the Evergreen implosion began at Professor Weinstein's door, when no national news outlets were covering the chaos, Weinstein agreed to appear on the Fox News show *Tucker Carlson Tonight*. After the show aired, the backlash began. Three days after Weinstein's appearance, a student protester posted an essay on the website Medium reporting that a spray-painted swastika appeared on the side of a seminar building, and that she and other protesters had been subjected to "doxxing" by the alt-right: "The faces, names and phone numbers of student organizers were published online on subreddits dedicated to harassing leftists and people of color," she wrote.[19] In a *New York Times* essay published weeks later, the student described protesters being harassed "with hundreds of phone calls, anonymous texts and terrifyingly specific threats of violence that show they know where we live and work." She also recounted finding rape threats directed at her on online message boards.[20] Sandra Kaiser, Evergreen's vice president for college relations, said the college received "the most stunning wave of social-media harassment you can possibly imagine."[21] But the mob wasn't just "phoning it in" from far away. Although it was quickly determined that the New Jersey man's phone threat was not credible, right-wing extremist groups did visit campus. For example, the neo-Nazi group Atomwaffen Division placed posters on campus buildings reading BLACK LIVES DON'T MATTER and JOIN YOUR LOCAL NAZIS. Then they posted a video depicting their members, dressed in black, with faces obscured, walking across campus at night, taping up those posters.[22]

In physics, as Newton's law tells us, every action produces an equal and opposite reaction. In a polarization spiral, however, for every action there is a disproportionate reaction. Many critics of campus protesters in 2015 accused them of overreacting to small things (such as Dean Spellman's email at Claremont McKenna). But beginning in late 2016, we began to see more examples of off-campus overreaction from the right in response to speech by professors on the left.

Lisa Durden, an adjunct professor at Essex County College in Newark, New Jersey, was hired in the spring of 2017 to teach Mass Communication and Popular Culture, as well as essay writing. Before coming to Essex, Durden was a motivational speaker, hosted her own talk show, appeared on various networks as a pop culture expert, and worked as a TV and movie producer. Then, on June 6, 2017, she appeared on Tucker Carlson's show to defend a Black Lives Matter "all-black" Memorial Day party (at which she was not present) in Brooklyn, New York. At one point, in response to Carlson's antagonistic questioning, she responded: "Boo-hoo-hoo. You white people are angry because you couldn't use your 'white privilege' card to get invited."[23]

Admittedly, what she said was provocative. But the "all-black" event was not at the college, so Durden wasn't defending the exclusion of white students—in fact, no one has ever alleged that Durden discriminated against students. Nonetheless, Durden's television appearance was met by wrath from the right; she received hate mail and anonymous threats, which included "I will come to your house and kill you dumb black bitch" and "Talk to me like you did that guy on Fox News, and I would beat you to a broken pulp and kick your throat in you racist devil." Durden showed us many more, which we will not reprint here, but suffice it to say, they were horrifically racist, sexist, and threatening.

The barrage of vitriol and the threats of violence have had a lasting effect on Durden. "I still get knots in my stomach whenever I think about it or talk about it," she told us in an email. "People say that things will get better because that's the politically correct thing to say to someone in my position. But things don't always get better, they sometimes get worse. And that's how I am feeling."[24] To make matters worse, the college suspended Durden and launched an investigation, claiming they had been "immediately inundated" with complaints.[25] FIRE filed records requests to see those alleged complaints, which Essex County College ignored until FIRE filed a lawsuit. As it turned out, the supposed deluge of complaints before the suspension amounted to a single email.[26] Nonetheless, on June 23, the college president announced that Durden had been fired.[27] Despite all of this, Durden tells us unequivocally that she doesn't regret speaking out.

Professor Durden's story is not unique. On Christmas Eve 2016, George Ciccariello-Maher, a professor at Drexel University in Philadelphia, posted the provocative tweet "All I want for Christmas is White Genocide." The tweet went viral, amplified by a Russia-linked Twitter account pretending to be based in Tennessee.[28] Taken at face value, the tweet sounds horrifying, but its meaning changes once you learn that "white genocide" is a term used by white nationalist groups to express their fear that mass immigration and racial intermarriage will eventually lead to the extinction of white people. As Ciccariello-Maher later explained: "'White genocide' is an idea invented by white supremacists and used to denounce everything from interracial relationships to multicultural policies. . . . It is a figment of the racist imagination, it should be mocked, and I'm glad to have mocked it."[29] Despite initially promising Ciccariello-Maher that he would not face punishment for the tweet, Drexel quietly initiated an investigation in February 2017 and later barred him from campus, citing "safety concerns." The investigation ended only because he resigned at the end of December 2017, one year after the initial tweet.[30] Ciccariello-Maher said he was subjected to "nearly a year of harassment by right-wing, white-supremacist media outlets and internet mobs, after death threats and threats of violence" were directed against him and his family.[31]

On May 20, 2017, Princeton professor Keeanga-Yamahtta Taylor, author of *From #BlackLivesMatter to Black Liberation*, gave a commencement speech at Hampshire College in which she called President Trump "a racist and sexist megalomaniac" who poses a threat to students' futures. The next week, Fox News publicized excerpts from her speech, which they called an "anti-POTUS tirade."[32] By May 31, Taylor reported having received "more than fifty hate-filled and threatening emails," some containing "specific threats of violence, including murder," as well as "lynching and having the bullet from a .44 Magnum put in [her] head."[33] Out of concern for her safety and that of her family, Taylor canceled her future scheduled speeches.

Conservative readers may dismiss the three cases we just presented on the grounds that the professors said things that were aggressive or deliberately provocative, so what did they expect the reaction to be? Progressives may see the humor in "white genocide," but if you make genocide jokes on Twitter, you've got to expect some people to take you literally. Therefore, one might conclude that if the three professors had spoken in a more deliberative style, befitting a professor, they would have had no trouble. But speaking in a scholarly way is not necessarily enough. In June 2017, Sarah Bond, an assistant professor of classics at the University of Iowa, published an article in an online arts magazine, *Hyperallergic*, titled "Why We Need to Start Seeing the Classical World in Color."[34] The title refers to the little-known fact that ancient Greek and Roman statues were usually painted with skin tones and bright colors, but when these buried and weathered statues were rediscovered during the Renaissance, the paint had worn off. Renaissance artists and their patrons believed that the unadorned white marble was part of the intended aesthetic, and these artists created new statues (such as Michelangelo's David) using what they mistakenly believed was the Greco-Roman ideal.[35] As a result, the white marble statues of the Renaissance have shaped our current image of what the ancient world must have looked like: white marble statues everywhere.

According to Bond, the erroneous idea that the Romans viewed white marble as depicting the idealized human form led to the idea among scholars in the nineteenth century that Romans were "white" (although there was no concept of a "white" race in ancient times). Bond wrote in her essay that the misunderstanding about white statues "provides further ammunition for white supremacists today, including groups like Identity Evropa, who use classical statuary as a symbol of white male superiority."[36] This strikes us as a novel and interesting idea, which Bond illustrates with compelling photographs and links to academic articles. Regardless of her thoughtful and academic presentation, the outrage machine went into action.

UNIVERSITY PROF: USING WHITE MARBLE IN SCULPTURES IS RACIST AND

CREATES "WHITE SUPREMACY," read one headline.[37] IOWA UNIVERSITY PRO-FESSOR SAYS "WHITE MARBLE" ACTUALLY INFLUENCES "WHITE SUPREMA-CIST" IDEAS, read another.[38] On Twitter, Bond was called an "SJW moron" and people tweeted that they hoped she would be fired or die.[39] She received death threats, calls for her firing, and a deluge of other online abuse.[40] One headline captured how the polarization spiral looks from the right: LIB-ERAL PROFESSORS SAY BIZARRE THINGS—AND THEN BLAME THE CONSER-VATIVE MEDIA FOR REPORTING ON THEM.[41] (The view from the left might very well be LIBERAL PROFESSORS SAY THINGS—AND THEN CONSERVATIVE MEDIA REPORT THEM AS IF PROFESSORS ARE CRAZY.)

The polarization cycle influencing university life since 2017 typically proceeds in this sequence:[42]

1. A left-wing professor says or writes something provocative or in-flammatory on social media, in mainstream media, in a lecture, or (less often) in an academic publication. The statement is often a re-action to perceived injustices committed by right-wing groups or politicians off campus. A video clip or screen shot is then shared on social media.

2. Right-wing media outlets pick up the story and then retell it in ways that amplify the outrage, often taking it out of context and some-times distorting the facts.[43]

3. Dozens or even hundreds of people who hear about it write angry posts or comments on social media, or send emails to the professor, often including racist or sexist slurs, sometimes including threats of rape or death. Some people publicly call for the university to fire the professor.

4. Meanwhile, the college administration fails to defend the professor. Sometimes an investigation follows, and sometimes the professor is put on leave. Professors who are untenured are at high risk of being fired or of not having their contracts renewed.

5. Most partisans who hear any part of the story find that it confirms their worst beliefs about the other side. The right focuses on what the professor said or wrote. The left focuses on the racist/sexist

reaction to it. With their anger fortified, people on both sides are primed to repeat the cycle.

This pattern is different from the pattern when professors arouse the ire of students on campus, and calling someone racist or demanding that they be disinvited is in no way equivalent to making rape threats or death threats. That distinction is recognized in law; the First Amendment does not protect credible rape or death threats. Those are criminal. But whether the reaction comes from the off-campus right or the on-campus left, the response from university leadership is usually weak and often doesn't support the professor. Things spiral rapidly out of control, and observers on the left and the right draw the same conclusion: the other side is evil.

Many professors say they now teach and speak more cautiously, because one slip or one simple misunderstanding could lead to vilification and even threats from any number of sources.[44] Add to that an insidious new problem: professors are being closely watched because of their politics. The conservative campus group Turning Point USA (TPUSA) even created a "Professor Watchlist" in order to "expose and document" faculty members "who discriminate against conservative students, promote anti-American values and advance leftist propaganda in the classroom."[45] Many free-speech advocates watched the unveiling of TPUSA's watchlist with concern—after all, the keeping of lists of disfavored ideas and the people who hold them has a distinct and ugly history in the United States.[46] These lists are meant as a warning for those on them to watch what they say. Provoking uncomfortable thoughts is an essential part of a professor's role, but professors now have reason to worry that provocative educational exercises and lines of questioning could spell the end of their reputations and even careers.

Threat Comes to Campus

After declining for twenty-five years, reported incidents of hate crimes increased in 2015.[47] In 2016, those numbers, tracked by the FBI, rose a further 5%.[48] One study of major U.S. cities from January to August 2017 suggests a

20% rise in reported hate crimes compared to the first eight months of 2016.[49] It is extremely difficult to obtain accurate statistics on hate crimes, and some widely publicized events have turned out to be hoaxes.[50] Nonetheless, there is a widespread perception on campus that hate crimes are increasing in the Trump era, and as far as we can tell from our review of the available research, there is some truth to that perception.

On campus, threats take concrete and sometimes terrifying forms. In 2015, a white student at Missouri University of Science and Technology was arrested for posting on social media that he was going to the Mizzou campus (the main campus of the University of Missouri), where black students were protesting, and would "shoot every black person" he saw.[51] This happened five months after Dylann Roof murdered nine black parishioners in a church in Charleston, South Carolina. In October 2017, a white University of Maryland student was charged with murder and a hate crime after stabbing to death Richard Collins III, a visiting Bowie State student, who was apparently targeted for being black.[52]

In the aftermath of the murder of Heather Heyer and the violence at the white supremacists' march through Charlottesville, the physical threat posed by the alt-right and neo-Nazis became far more real for many observers who might have previously thought the alt-right was limited to internet trolls. In October 2017, only two months after the Charlottesville march, avowed white nationalist Richard Spencer spoke at the University of Florida. An hour and a half after Spencer's speech ended, three men proclaiming to be white nationalists drove their car over to a group of protesters at a bus stop and began to yell neo-Nazi chants at them. After one of the protesters hit the rear window of the vehicle with a baton, the three men jumped out of the car, reportedly yelling, "I'm going to fucking kill you!" and "Shoot them!" One of the white nationalists, Tyler Tenbrink, was carrying a gun. He fired one shot, missing the protesters, and then the men fled. All three were later caught and charged with attempted homicide.[53] Months later, at Wayne State University in Michigan, a student pulled a knife during a dispute with a group that was handing out pamphlets in favor of immigrants' rights. He said he wanted to "kill all illegals that don't belong in our country."[54]

Students of color facing ongoing threats to their safety, and seeing frequent reports of threats elsewhere, are not new phenomena; the history of race in America is a history of discrimination and intimidation, intertwined with a history of progress. And yet, this new wave of racial intimidation may be particularly upsetting *because* of recent progress. In 2008, with the election of Barack Obama, many Americans had the sense that the country had turned a corner in its struggle with racism.[55] In late 2016, college students in the United States had spent the previous eight years in a country with a black president, and most experts and pundits were telling them to expect a transition to the country's first female president. The shock of Trump's victory must have been particularly disillusioning for many black students and left-leaning women. Between the president's repeated racial provocations and the increased visibility of neo-Nazis and their ilk, it became much more plausible than it had been in a long time that "white supremacy," even using a narrow definition, was not just a relic of the distant past.

We close this chapter by repeating Allison Stanger's assessment: "Political life and discourse in the United States is at a boiling point, and nowhere is the reaction to that more heightened than on college campuses." This is the context in which today's college students are trying to make sense of major national events and are reacting to seemingly small local incidents. We have suggested throughout this book that some interpretations of events are more constructive than others, but our point in this chapter is that there are reasons why students are doing what they are doing. There is a backstory. There is a national context. The polarization spiral and the growth of negative partisanship are influencing political activity all across the country, driving many Americans to embrace the Untruth of Us Versus Them.

In the next three chapters, we'll show that it is not just the college campuses that have been changing; it is also the young people coming into them. Changes in adolescent mental health and in the nature of American childhood may have rendered many current students more easily burned by the "boiling" that they find once they arrive on campus.

In Sum

- The United States has experienced a steady increase in at least one form of polarization since the 1980s: affective (or emotional) polarization, which means that people who identify with either of the two main political parties increasingly hate and fear the other party and the people in it. This is our first of six explanatory threads that will help us understand what has been changing on campus.

- Affective polarization in the United States is roughly symmetrical, but as university students and faculty have shifted leftward during a time of rising cross-party hatred, universities have begun to receive less trust and more hostility from some conservatives and right-leaning organizations.[56]

- Beginning in 2016, the number of high-profile cases of professors being hounded or harassed from the right for something they said in an interview or on social media began to increase.

- Rising political polarization, accompanied by increases in racial and political provocation from the right, usually directed from off-campus to on-campus targets, is an essential part of the story of why behavior is changing on campus, particularly since 2016.

CHAPTER 7

Anxiety and Depression

Depressed people often stick pins into their own life rafts.
The conscious mind can intervene. One is not helpless.

ANDREW SOLOMON, *The Noonday Demon: An Atlas of Depression*[1]

The second of our six explanatory threads is the rise in rates of depression and anxiety among American adolescents in the 2010s. These mood disorders have many close relationships with the three Great Untruths.

Here is a first-person account of depression. It is not from an adolescent, but it illustrates Andrew Solomon's statement above, about how the conscious mind can intervene:

I had spent the day scouring websites for ways to kill myself. At almost every turn, I found stories about how a method could fail, leaving you still alive but permanently injured. This even applied to shooting yourself. I could not risk that, so I went to the hardware store across the street, looking for strong plastic bags and metal wire. The idea was to crush up all the sleep meds, tranquilizers, and anti-anxiety meds I had, take them all at once, and then wrap my head so that even if the pills did not kill me, suffocation would. But it had to be strong enough that I could not claw my way out of the bag if I had a change of heart.

I needed to go through with it *now*, as quickly as possible. Because . . . why? Because it was the right thing to do, and if I waited, I might not go through with it, and I needed to go through with it while I had the will. If I felt better later, it would somehow be a lie. I had a powerful sense that I was in touch with some dark, larger truth: that I needed to die.

I don't know if it was briefly sensing how strange this thought was that gave me that tiny flash of sanity that caused me to call 911. First, I started to explain what I had planned in a detached way, but soon I was crying. The voice on the other side of the line told me to get myself to a hospital right away. I listened.

I spent the next three days of December 2007 at a psychiatric facility in North Philadelphia. I was already scheduled to move from Philadelphia, where I felt utterly isolated, back to New York City, where I had friends and family. I found a doctor who was the first person in years to reduce—rather than increase—my meds. And I started cognitive behavioral therapy as soon as I moved to New York.

At first, it seemed to make little difference. The doctor showed me time and time again how I used every bit of brain power to support a view of myself—a schema—that said I was a hopeless, broken person. I did my CBT exercises twice a day, and I gradually came to recognize my angry, flailing, defensive mind trying to protect that nasty vision of myself.

There was no "eureka" moment. My rational mind could understand that my thoughts were distorted, but nothing changed until it simply became a habit to hear the cruelest, craziest, and most destructive voices in my head without believing I had to act on them. When I stopped letting those voices win, they got quieter. Thanks to CBT, my mind is now in the habit of hearing my worst thoughts as if they are speaking in silly cartoon voices. While I still get depressed, the frequency and severity of those bouts are nowhere near as powerful as they used to be.

The author of this account is Greg. He believes that CBT saved his life. In a matter of just a few months, he began to learn how to catch his own distortions. And once he learned to spot them in himself, he started to hear them coming from other people, too. Once you are accustomed to looking for them, it's not very hard to identify catastrophizing, dichotomous think-ing, labeling, and all the rest.

Almost as soon as he started practicing CBT, in 2008, Greg noticed, in his work as the president of FIRE, that administrators on campus were sometimes modeling cognitive distortions for students. Administrators of-ten acted in ways that gave the impression that students were in constant danger and in need of protection from a variety of risks and discomforts (as we'll discuss in chapter 10). But back then, Millennial students mostly rolled their eyes at administrative overreaction. It was only when the first members of iGen started entering college, around 2013, that Greg began to notice this more fearful attitude about speech coming from the students themselves. In the new discussions about safe spaces, trigger warnings, mi-croaggressions, and speech as violence, students often employed arguments and justifications that seemed to come right out of the CBT training man-ual. That's why Greg invited Jon to lunch in 2014, and that's why we wrote our *Atlantic* article in 2015.

In that essay, we briefly discussed changes in childhood in the United States, such as the decline in unsupervised time and the recent rise of social media, but we focused our attention on what was happening after students arrived at college. At the time, we had just begun to hear the first alarms being raised by college mental health professionals, who said they were be-ing overwhelmed by rising demand.[2] We suggested that perhaps some of the very things colleges were doing to protect students from words and ideas ended up increasing the demand for mental health services by inad-vertently increasing the use of cognitive distortions.

By 2017, however, it was clear we had misunderstood what was going on. Colleges were not the primary cause of the wave of mental illness among their students; rather, the students seeking help were part of a much larger national wave of adolescent anxiety and depression unlike anything seen in modern times. Colleges were struggling to cope with rapidly rising num-bers of students who were suffering from mental illness—primarily mood disorders.[3] The new culture of safetyism can be understood in part as an effort by some students, faculty, and administrators to remake the campus in response to this new trend. If more students say they feel threatened by certain kinds of speech, then more protections should be offered. Our basic message in this book is that this way of thinking may be wrong; college students are antifragile, not fragile. Some well-intended protections may backfire and make things worse in the long run for the very students we are trying to help.

In this chapter, we explore recent findings on the declining mental health of American adolescents. There is some evidence that similar trends may be happening in Canada[4] and the United Kingdom,[5] although the evidence in those countries is not as clear and consistent as it is in the United States.[6] In all three countries, girls seem to be more affected than boys. How is mental health changing, on campus and off, and why did the new culture of safetyism emerge only after 2013?

iGen

In the 2017 book *iGen* (which we discussed briefly in chapter 1), Jean Twenge, a social psychologist at San Diego State University, gives us the most detailed picture yet of the behavior, values, and mental state of today's teenagers and college students. Twenge is an expert on how generations differ psychologically and why. She calls the generation after the Millennials iGen (like iPhone), which is short for "internet generation," because they are the first generation to grow up with the internet in their pockets. (Some people use the term Generation Z.) Sure, the oldest Millennials, born in 1982, searched for music and MapQuest directions using Netscape and AltaVista on their Compaq home computers in the late 1990s, but search engines don't change social relationships. Social media does.

Marking the line between generations is always difficult, but based on their psychological profiles, Twenge suggests that 1994 is the last birth year for Millennials, and 1995 is the first birth year for iGen. One possible reason for the discontinuity in self-reported traits and attitudes between Millennials and iGen is that in 2006, when iGen's oldest were turning eleven, Facebook changed its membership requirement. No longer did you have to prove enrollment in a college; now any thirteen-year-old—or any younger child willing to claim to be thirteen—could join.

But Facebook and other social media platforms didn't really draw many middle school students until after the iPhone was introduced (in 2007) and was widely adopted over the next few years. It's best, then, to think about the entire period from 2007 to roughly 2012 as a brief span in which the social life of the average American teen changed substantially. Social media platforms proliferated, and adolescents began using Twitter (founded in 2006), Tumblr (2007), Instagram (2010), Snapchat (2011), and a variety of others. Over time, these companies became ever more skilled at grabbing and holding "eyeballs," as they say in the industry. Social media grew more and more addictive. In a chilling 2017 interview, Sean Parker, the first president of Facebook, explained those early years like this:

> The thought process that went into building these applications, Facebook being the first of them . . . was all about: "How do we consume as much of your time and conscious attention as possible?" . . . And that means that we need to sort of give you a little dopamine hit every once in a while, because someone liked or commented on a photo or a post or whatever. And that's going to get you to contribute more content, and that's going to get you . . . more likes and comments. . . . It's a social-validation feedback loop . . . exactly the kind of thing that a hacker like myself would come up with, because you're exploiting a vulnerability in human psychology.[7]

Earlier in the interview, he said, "God only knows what it's doing to our children's brains."

In short, iGen is the first generation that spent (and is now spending) its formative teen years immersed in the giant social and commercial experiment of social media. What could go wrong?

Twenge's book is based on her deep dives into four surveys that stretch back several decades. One survey focuses on college students, two of them focus on teenagers more generally, and one samples the entire U.S. adult population. Her book contains dozens of graphs she created from these four datasets, showing changes in teen behavior and attitudes since the 1980s or 1990s. The lines mostly amble along horizontally until some point between 2005 and 2012, at which point they arc upward or plunge downward. Some of the trends are quite positive: members of iGen drink less and smoke less; they are safer drivers and are waiting longer to have sex. But other trends are less positive, and some are quite distressing. The subtitle of the book summarizes her findings: *Why Today's Super-Connected Kids Are Growing Up Less Rebellious, More Tolerant, Less Happy—and Completely Unprepared for Adulthood—and What That Means for the Rest of Us.*

Twenge's analyses suggest that there are two major generational changes that may be driving the rise of safetyism on campus since 2013. The first is that kids now grow up much more slowly. Activities that are commonly thought to mark the transition from childhood to adulthood are happening later—for example, having a job, driving a car, drinking alcohol, going out on a date, and having sex. Members of iGen wait longer to do these things—and then do less of them—than did members of previous generations. Instead of engaging in these activities (which usually involve interacting with other people face-to-face), teens today are spending much more time alone, interacting with screens.[8] Of special importance, the combination of helicopter parenting, fears for children's safety, and the allure of screens means that members of iGen spend much less time than previous generations did going out with friends while unsupervised by an adult.

The bottom line is that when members of iGen arrived on campus, beginning in the fall of 2013, they had accumulated less unsupervised time and fewer offline life experiences than had any previous generation. As Twenge puts it, "18-year-olds now act like 15-year-olds used to, and 13-year-olds like 10-year-olds. Teens are physically safer than ever, yet they are more mentally vulnerable."[9] Most of these trends are showing up across social classes, races, and ethnicities.[10] Members of iGen, therefore, may not (on average) be as ready for college as were eighteen-year-olds of previous generations. This might explain why college students are suddenly asking for more protection and adult intervention in their affairs and interpersonal conflicts.

The second major generational change is a rapid rise in rates of anxiety and depression.[11] We created three graphs below using the same data that Twenge reports in *iGen*. The graphs are straightforward and tell a shocking story.

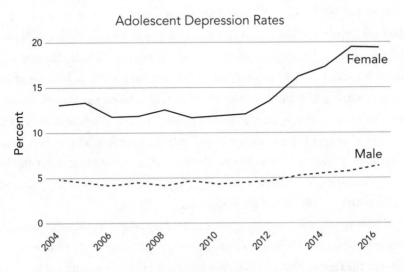

FIGURE 7.1. *Percent of adolescents aged 12–17 who had at least one major depressive episode in the past year. Rates have been rising since 2011, especially for girls. (Source: Data from National Survey on Drug Use and Health.)*

Studies of mental illness have long shown that girls have higher rates of depression and anxiety than boys do.[12] The differences are small or nonexistent before puberty, but they increase at the start of puberty. The gap between adolescent girls and boys was fairly steady in the early 2000s, but beginning around 2011, it widened as the rate for girls grew rapidly. By 2016, as you can see in Figure 7.1, roughly *one out of every five girls* reported symptoms that met the criteria for having experienced a major depressive episode in the previous year.[13] The rate for boys went up, too, but more slowly (from 4.5% in 2011 to 6.4% in 2016).

Have things really changed so much for teenagers just in the last seven years? Maybe Figure 7.1 merely reflects changes in diagnostic criteria? Perhaps the bar has been lowered for giving out diagnoses of depression, and maybe that's a good thing, if more people now get help?

Perhaps, but lowering the bar for diagnosis and encouraging more people to use the language of therapy and mental illness are likely to have some negative effects, too. Applying labels to people can create what is called a looping effect: it can change the behavior of the person being labeled and become a self-fulfilling prophecy.[14] This is part of why labeling is such a powerful cognitive distortion. If depression becomes part of your identity, then over time you'll develop corresponding schemas about yourself and your prospects (*I'm no good and my future is hopeless*). These schemas will make it harder for you to marshal the energy and focus to take on challenges that, if you were to master them, would weaken the grip of depression. We are not denying the reality of depression. We would never tell depressed people to just "toughen up" and get over it—Greg knows firsthand how unhelpful that would be. Rather, we are saying that lowering the bar (or encouraging "concept creep") in applying mental health labels may increase the number of people who suffer.

There is, tragically, strong evidence that the rising prevalence of teen depression illustrated in Figure 7.1 is not just a result of changes in diagnostic criteria: the teen suicide rate has been increasing in tandem with the increase in depression. Figure 7.2 shows the annual rate of suicide for each 100,000 teens (ages fifteen to nineteen) in the U.S. population. Suicide and attempted suicide rates vary by sex; girls make more attempts, but boys die more often by their own hand, because they tend to use irreversible methods (such as guns or tall buildings) more often than girls do. The boys' suicide rate has moved around in recent decades, surging in the 1980s during the gigantic wave of crime and violence that receded suddenly in the 1990s. The rate of boys' suicide reached its highest point in 1991. While the rise since 2007 does not bring it back up to its highest level, it is still disturbingly high. The rate for girls, on the other hand, had been fairly constant all the way back to 1981, when the dataset begins, and although their rate of suicide is still substantially lower than that of boys, the steady rise since 2010 brings their rate up to the highest levels recorded for girls since 1981. Compared to the early 2000s, *nearly twice as many teenage girls now end their own lives*. In Canada, too, the suicide rate for teen girls is rising, though not as sharply, while the rate for teen boys has

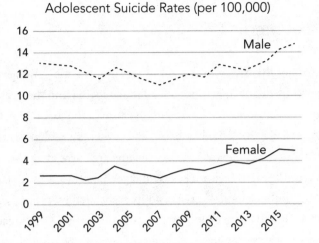

Adolescent Suicide Rates (per 100,000)

FIGURE 7.2. *Suicide rate per 100,000 population, ages 15–19, by sex. (Source: CDC, Fatal Injury Reports, 1999–2016.[15])*

fallen.[16] (In the United Kingdom, there is no apparent trend for either gender in recent years.[17])

Confirming this increase in mental illness with a different dataset, a recent study looked at "nonfatal self-inflicted injuries."[18] These are cases in which adolescents were admitted to emergency rooms because they had physically harmed themselves by doing such things as cutting themselves with a razor blade, banging their heads into walls, or drinking poison. The researchers examined data from sixty-six U.S. hospitals going back to 2001 and were able to estimate self-harm rates for the entire country. They found that the rate for boys held steady at roughly 200 per hundred thousand boys in the age range of fifteen to nineteen. The rate for girls in that age range was much higher, but had also been relatively steady from 2001 to 2009, at around 420 per hundred thousand girls. Beginning in 2010, however, the girls' rate began to rise steadily, reaching 630 per hundred thousand in 2015. The rate for younger girls (ages ten to fourteen) rose even more quickly, nearly tripling from roughly 110 per hundred thousand in 2009 to 318 per hundred thousand in 2015. (The corresponding rate for boys in that age range was around 40 throughout the period studied.) The years since 2010 have been very hard on girls.

Antisocial Media?

What is driving this surge in mental illness and suicide? Twenge believes that the rapid spread of smartphones and social media into the lives of teenagers, beginning around 2007, is the main cause of the mental health crisis that began around 2011. In her book, she presents graphs showing that digital media use and mental health problems are correlated: they rose together in recent years. That makes digital media a more likely candidate than, say, the global financial crisis and its associated recession, which began in 2008. By 2011, the economy and the job market were steadily improving in the United States, so economic factors are unlikely to be the cause of deteriorating adolescent mental health in the following years.[19]

Simple correlations are suggestive, but they can't tell us what caused what. Lots of things were changing during that time period, so there are many opportunities for what are called *spurious correlations*. For example, the annual per capita consumption of cheese in the United States correlates almost perfectly with the number of people who die each year from becoming entangled in their bedsheets, but that's not because eating cheese causes people to sleep differently.[20] That correlation is "spurious" because it's just a coincidence that both numbers rose steadily over the same period of time.

To avoid getting fooled by spurious correlations, we need to consider additional variables that would be expected to change if a particular causal explanation were true. Twenge does this by examining all the daily activities reported by individual students, in the two datasets that include such measures. Twenge finds that there are just two activities that are significantly correlated with depression and other suicide-related outcomes (such as considering suicide, making a plan, or making an actual attempt): electronic device use (such as a smartphone, tablet, or computer) and watching TV. On the other hand, there are five activities that have inverse relationships with depression (meaning that kids who spend *more* hours per week on these activities show *lower* rates of depression): sports and other forms of exercise, attending religious services, reading books and other print media, in-person social interactions, and doing homework.

Notice anything about the difference between the two lists? Screen versus nonscreen. When kids use screens for two hours of their leisure time per day or less, there is no elevated risk of depression.[21] But above two hours per day, the risks grow larger with each additional hour of screen time. Conversely, kids who spend more time off screens, especially if they are engaged in nonscreen social activities, are at lower risk for depression and suicidal thinking.[22] (Twenge addresses the possibility that the relationship runs the other way—that depression is what causes kids to spend more time with their screens—and she shows that this is unlikely to be the case.[23])

Part of what's going on may be that devices take us away from people. Human beings are an "ultrasocial" species. Chimpanzees and dogs have very active social lives, but as an *ultra*social species, human beings go beyond those "social" species.[24] Like bees, humans are able to work together in large groups, with a clear division of labor. Humans love teams, team sports, synchronized movements, and anything else that gives us the feeling of "one for all, and all for one." (Ultrasociality is related to the psychology of tribalism that we talked about in chapter 3. The trick is to satisfy people's needs to belong and interact without activating the more defensive and potentially violent aspects of tribalism.) Of course, social media makes it easier than ever to create large groups, but those "virtual" groups are not the same as in-person connections; they do not satisfy the need for belonging in the same way. As Twenge and her coauthors put it:

> It is worth remembering that humans' neural architecture evolved under conditions of close, mostly continuous face-to-face contact with others (including non-visual and non-auditory contact; i.e., touch, olfaction), and that a decrease in or removal of a system's key inputs may risk destabilization of the system.[25]

This idea is supported by Twenge's finding that time spent using electronic devices was not generally harmful for highly sociable kids—the ones who spent more time than the average kid in face-to-face social interactions.[26] In other words, the potentially negative impact of screens and social media might depend on the amount of time teens spend with other people.

But electronic devices are harmful not just because they take kids away from face-to-face interactions; there are more insidious effects, which are felt more strongly by girls.

Why Is It Mostly Girls Who Suffer?

The previous graphs show that mental health has deteriorated much further among iGen girls than among iGen boys. Furthermore, to the extent that social media seems to bear some of the blame, that may be true only for girls. For boys, Twenge found that total screen time is correlated with bad mental health outcomes, but time specifically using social media is not.[27] Why might social media be more harmful for girls than for boys?

There are at least two possible reasons. The first is that social media presents "curated" versions of lives, and girls may be more adversely affected than boys by the gap between appearance and reality. Many have observed that for girls, more than for boys, social life revolves around inclusion and exclusion.[28] Social media vastly increases the frequency with which teenagers see people they know having fun and doing things together—including things to which they themselves were not invited. While this can increase FOMO (fear of missing out), which affects both boys and girls, scrolling through hundreds of such photos, girls may be more pained than boys by what Georgetown University linguistics professor Deborah Tannen calls "FOBLO"—fear of *being left out*.[29] When a girl sees images of her friends doing something she was invited to do but couldn't attend (missed out), it produces a different psychological effect than when she is intentionally not invited (left out). And as Twenge reports, "Girls use social media more often, giving them additional opportunities to feel excluded and lonely when they see their friends or classmates getting together without them." The number of teens of all ages who feel left out, whether boys or girls, is at an all-time high, according to Twenge, but the increase has been larger for girls. From 2010 to 2015, the percentage of teen boys who said they often felt left out increased from 21 to 27. For girls, the percentage jumped from 27 to 40.[30]

Another consequence of social media curation is that girls are bombarded with images of girls and women whose beauty is artificially enhanced, making girls ever more insecure about their own appearance. It's not just fashion models whose images are altered nowadays; platforms such as Snapchat and Instagram provide "filters" that girls use to enhance the selfies they pose for and edit, so even their *friends* now seem to be more beautiful. These filters make noses smaller, lips bigger, and skin smoother.[31] This has led to a new phenomenon: some young women now want plastic surgery to make themselves look like they do in their enhanced selfies.[32]

The second reason that social media may be harder on girls is that girls and boys are aggressive in different ways. Research by psychologist Nicki Crick shows that boys are more physically aggressive—more likely to shove and hit one another, and they show a greater interest in stories and movies about physical aggression. Girls, in contrast, are more "relationally" aggressive; they try to hurt their rivals' relationships, reputations, and social status—for example, by using social media to make sure other girls know who is intentionally being left out.[33] When you add it all up, there's no overall sex difference in total aggression, but there's a large and consistent sex difference in the preferred *ways* of harming others. (At least, that was Crick's finding in the 1990s, before the birth of social media.) Plus, if boys' aggression is generally delivered in person, then the targets of boys' aggression can escape from it when they go home. On social media, girls can never escape.

Given the difference in preferred forms of aggression, what would happen if a malevolent demon put a loaded handgun into the pocket of every adolescent in the United States? Which sex would suffer more? Boys, most likely, because they would find gunplay more appealing and would use guns more often to settle conflicts. On the other hand, what would happen if, instead of guns, that same malevolent demon put a smartphone, loaded up with social media apps, into the pocket of every adolescent? Other than the demon part, that is more or less what happened between 2007 and 2012, and it's now clear that girls have suffered far more. Social media offers many benefits to many teens: it can help to strengthen relationships as well as damage them, and in some ways it is surely giving them valuable practice in the art of social relationships. But it is also the greatest enabler of relational aggression since the invention of language, and the evidence available today suggests that girls' mental health has suffered as a result.

iGen Goes to College

The first members of iGen started arriving on college campuses in September 2013; by May 2017, when the eldest members began graduating, the student body at U.S. colleges was almost entirely iGen (at least in selective four-year residential colleges). These are precisely the years in which the new culture of safetyism seemed to emerge from out of nowhere.

These are also the years in which college mental health clinics found themselves suddenly overwhelmed by new demand, according to many newspaper and magazine articles profiling the lengthening waiting lists for psychological counseling at universities across the United States.[34] At the time, these profiles of crises at individual universities seemed somewhat anecdotal. When we were writing our *Atlantic* article, there was no nationally representative survey documenting the trend. But now, three years later, there are several.

A 2016 report by the Center for Collegiate Mental Health, using data from 139 colleges, found that by the 2015–2016 school year, *half* of all students surveyed reported having attended counseling for mental health concerns.[35] The report notes that the only mental health concerns that were increasing in recent years were anxiety and depression. Confirming these upward trends with a different dataset,[36] Figure 7.3 shows the percentage of college students who describe themselves as having a mental disorder. That number increased from 2.7 to 6.1 for male college students between 2012 and 2016 (that's an increase of 126%). For female college students, it rose even more: from 5.8 to 14.5 (an increase of 150%). Regardless of whether all these students would meet rigorous diagnostic criteria, it is clear that iGen college students *think about themselves* very differently than did Millennials. The change is greatest for women: *One out of every seven women at U.S. universities now thinks of herself as having a psychological disorder*, up from just one in eighteen women in the last years of the Millennials.

Percentage of College Students Who Say That
They Have a Psychological Disorder

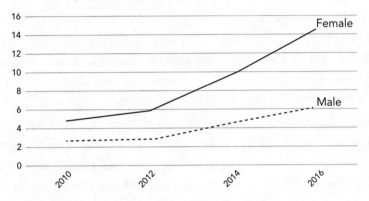

FIGURE 7.3. *Percentage of college students responding "yes" to the question "Do you have [a] psychological disorder (depression, etc.)." (Source: Higher Education Research Institute.)*

These years also saw a rise in self-reports of anxiety as the reason for seeking help. One large survey of university counseling centers found that only 37% of students who came through their doors in 2009 and prior years had complained about problems with anxiety—roughly on a par with the two other leading concerns, depression and relationships.[37] But beginning in 2010, the percentage of students with anxiety complaints began to increase. It reached 46% in 2013 and continued climbing to 51% in 2016. It is now by far the leading problem for which college students seek treatment. These years also saw substantial increases in rates of self-injury and suicide among college students,[38] so while part of the increase may be due to students being more willing to self-diagnose, once again, we know that the underlying rates of mental illness were increasing. Something was changing in the lives and minds of adolescents before they reached college, and when growing numbers of depressed and anxious students began arriving on campus, beginning around 2013, it was bound to have some effect on university culture and norms.

You can see why it was hard for us to make a strong case that universities were causing students to *become* anxious and depressed by teaching them disordered ways of thinking. Anxiety and depression rates were already rising for all teenagers before they arrived at college, and for those who never attended college as well. Clearly universities were not *causing* a national mental health crisis; they were *responding* to one, and this may explain why the practices and beliefs of safetyism spread so quickly after 2013. But safetyism does not help students who suffer from anxiety and depression. In fact, as we argue throughout this book, safetyism is likely to make things even worse for students who already struggle with mood disorders. Safetyism also inflicts collateral damage on the university's culture of free inquiry, because it teaches students to see words as violence and to interpret ideas and speakers as safe versus dangerous, rather than merely as true versus false. That way of thinking about words is likely to promote the intensification of a call-out culture, which, of course, gives students one more reason to be anxious.

Depression and anxiety tend to go together.[39] Both conditions create strong negative emotions, which feed emotional reasoning. Anxiety changes the brain in pervasive ways such that threats seem to jump out at the person, even in ambiguous or harmless circumstances.[40] Compared to their nonanxious peers, anxious students are therefore more likely to perceive danger in innocent questions (leading them to embrace the concept of microaggressions) or in a passage of a novel (leading them to ask for a trigger warning) or in a lecture given by a guest speaker (leading them to want the lecturer disinvited or for someone to create a safe space as an alternative to the lecture). Depression distorts cognition, too, and gives people much more negative views than are warranted about themselves, other people, the world, and the future.[41] Problems loom larger and seem more pervasive. One's resources for dealing with those problems seem smaller, and one's perceived locus of control becomes more external,[42] all of which discourages efforts to act vigorously to solve problems. Repeated failures to escape from what is perceived to be a bad situation can create a mental state that psychologist Martin Seligman called "learned helplessness," in which a person believes that escape is impossible and therefore stops trying, even in new situations where effort would be rewarded.[43] Furthermore, when people are depressed, or when their anxiety sets their threat-response system on high alert, they can succumb to a "hostile attribution bias," which means that they are more likely to see hostility in benign or even benevolent people, communications, and situations.[44] Misunderstandings are more likely, and more likely to escalate into large-scale conflicts.

Screen Time: A Caution About Caution

The rise in adolescent mental illness is very large and is found in multiple datasets, but the percentage of that rise that can be attributed to smartphones and screen time is small, and the evidence is more indirect. Twenge uses the data available, and those datasets report crude measures of what kids are doing—mostly the approximate number of hours per week spent on various activities, including using devices. Twenge finds relationships that are statistically significant yet still generally small in magnitude. That doesn't mean that the effects of smartphones are small; it just means that the amount of variance in mental illness that we can explain right now, using existing data, is small. If we had better measures of what kids are doing and what is happening to their mental health, we'd be able to explain a lot more of the variance. These problems are very new, and a lot more research is needed before we'll know why rates of mood disorders began rising so quickly in the 2010s.

One conclusion that future research is almost certain to reach is that the effects of smartphones and social media are complicated, involving mixtures of benefits and harms depending on which kinds of kids are doing which kinds of online activities instead of doing which kinds of offline activities. One factor that is already emerging as a central variable for study is the quality of a teenager's relationships and how technology is impacting it. In a recent review of research on the effects of social media, social psychologists Jenna Clark, Sara Algoe, and Melanie Green offer this principle: "Social network sites benefit their users when they are used to make meaningful social connections and harm their users through pitfalls such as isolation and social comparison when they are not."[45]

So we don't want to create a moral panic and frighten parents into banning all devices until their kids turn twenty-one. These are complicated issues, and much more research is needed. In the meantime, as we'll say in chapter 12, there is enough evidence to support placing time limits on device use (perhaps two hours a day for adolescents, less for younger kids) while limiting or prohibiting the use of platforms that amplify social comparison rather than social connection. There is also a strong case to be made for rethinking device use in the context of one's overall parenting philosophy, especially given everything we know about children's overarching need to play. We take up those topics in the next two chapters.

In Sum

- The national rise in adolescent anxiety and depression that began around 2011 is our second explanatory thread.
- The generation born between 1995 and 2012, called iGen (or sometimes Gen Z), is very different from the Millennials, the generation that preceded it. According to Jean Twenge, an expert in the study of generational differences, one difference is that iGen is growing up more slowly. On average, eighteen-year-olds today have spent less time unsupervised and have hit fewer developmental milestones on the path to autonomy (such as getting a job or a driver's license), compared with eighteen-year-olds in previous generations.
- A second difference is that iGen has far higher rates of anxiety and depression. The increases for girls and young women are generally much larger than for boys and young men. The increases do not just reflect changing definitions or standards; they show up in rising hospital admission rates of self-harm and in rising suicide rates. The suicide rate of adolescent boys is still higher than that of girls, but the suicide rate of adolescent girls has doubled since 2007.
- According to Twenge, the primary cause of the increase in mental illness is frequent use of smartphones and other electronic devices. Less than two hours a day seems to have no deleterious effects, but adolescents who spend several hours a day interacting with screens, particularly if they start in their early teen years or younger, have

worse mental health outcomes than do adolescents who use these devices less and who spend more time in face-to-face social interaction.

- Girls may be suffering more than boys because they are more adversely affected by social comparisons (especially based on digitally enhanced beauty), by signals that they are being left out, and by relational aggression, all of which became easier to enact and harder to escape when adolescents acquired smartphones and social media.

- iGen's arrival at college coincides exactly with the arrival and intensification of the culture of safetyism from 2013 to 2017. Members of iGen may be especially attracted to the overprotection offered by the culture of safetyism on many campuses because of students' higher levels of anxiety and depression. Both depression and anxiety cause changes in cognition, including a tendency to see the world as more dangerous and hostile than it really is.

CHAPTER 8

Paranoid Parenting

*So many teens have lost the ability to tolerate distress and
uncertainty, and a big reason for that is the way we parent them.*

KEVIN ASHWORTH, *clinical director,*
NW Anxiety Institute in Portland, Oregon[1]

A few days after Greg and his wife came home from the hospital
with their first child, they received an unusual gift in the mail: a
shiny red fire extinguisher. Not a toy fire truck. An actual fire
extinguisher. What made the gift especially meaningful was that the sender
was Lenore Skenazy, an author, journalist, and New York City mother of
two. You may know her as "America's Worst Mom."

Skenazy's journey to infamy began in 2008, when she permitted her
nine-year-old son, Izzy, to ride the New York City subway by himself. Izzy
had been begging her for weeks to take him someplace he'd never been before and let him find his own way home. So, one sunny Sunday, Skenazy
decided the time was right. She took him along on a trip to Bloomingdale's.
Confident that Izzy would find his way home and could ask a stranger for
help if he needed it, she armed him with a subway map, a MetroCard, a
twenty-dollar bill, and several quarters in case he needed to make a call,
and then sent him on his way. Forty-five minutes later (right on time), Izzy
arrived home (where his father was waiting for him) and was ecstatic about
his success—and eager to do it again.

Skenazy published a column about this little experiment in childhood
independence in *The New York Sun*,[2] describing both Izzy's joy and the
horrified reactions she received from other parents who heard what she had
allowed Izzy to do. Two days later, she was on the *Today* show, and then

MSNBC, Fox News, and NPR. Online message boards were flooded with posts, mostly condemning her decision, though some applauded it. Soon, Skenazy was decried as "America's Worst Mom."[3]

Most mothers would probably be mortified by that nickname, but Skenazy embraced the title. She had given her son the kind of independence that she (and most of today's parents) had enjoyed back in the 1970s, when the crime rate was much higher. So why had her choice generated so much outrage and condemnation? Skenazy realized that something was seriously wrong with modern parenting. In response, she created a blog to explain her philosophy and to call attention to the paranoia and overprotection that have become normal features of American parenting. She called it *Free-Range Kids*. Since then, *Free-Range Kids* has grown into a full-fledged movement, including a book of the same name, the reality TV show *World's Worst Mom*, and a nonprofit called Let Grow (see LetGrow.org).

The fire extinguisher was such an apt gift coming from Skenazy (who included a note that read, "See, I care about safety!"), because the gift represents her message in a nutshell: We should all take reasonable precautions to protect our children's physical safety—for example, by owning a fire extinguisher—but we should not submit to the pull of safetyism (overestimating danger, fetishizing safety, and not accepting *any* risk), which deprives kids of some of the most valuable experiences in childhood.

In chapter 1, we discussed Nassim Taleb's concept of antifragility. We explained how the well-intentioned project of keeping kids "safe" from peanuts had backfired; it prevented many kids' immune systems from learning that peanut proteins are harmless, which ultimately increased the number of kids who are allergic to peanuts and who could actually die from exposure to them. We suggested that this same dynamic might be partially responsible for the rise of safetyism on college campuses, beginning around 2013. In chapter 7, we discussed Jean Twenge's finding that members of iGen (born in 1995 and later) are having very different childhoods than kids in previous generations had, and are also suffering from much higher levels of anxiety and depression. In this chapter, we look more closely at how American childhood has changed in recent decades. We suggest that modern parenting practices may unwittingly teach children the Great

Untruths, and we examine how parents and elementary schools may un-knowingly work together to induct children into the culture of safetyism. The shift to this more fearful and overprotective way of treating children, which began in the 1980s and reached high levels in the 1990s—especially among more educated parents—is our third explanatory thread.

To learn more about parenting and childhood, we sought advice from three experts. In addition to Lenore Skenazy, we spoke with Julie Lythcott-Haims, the author of the best-selling book for parents *How to Raise an Adult*, and Erika Christakis, an expert in early-childhood development and author of *The Importance of Being Little*. (It was Christakis's professional concerns about the effects of oversupervision that led her to write the email about Halloween costumes at Yale, which we described in chapter 3.) These experts all came to the conclusion that modern parenting is preventing kids from growing strong and independent, but each arrived at this conclusion via a different path: Skenazy through the experiences we described above, Christakis through her work as a preschool teacher and her research on early childhood education, and Lythcott-Haims through her experience as the dean of freshmen at Stanford University for more than a decade. All three have also raised children of their own.

A Parent's Worst Fear

On May 25, 1979, a few blocks south of New York University, a six-year-old boy named Etan Patz persuaded his parents to let him walk the two blocks from their apartment to his school bus stop. He never came home, and his body was never found.[4] Anyone who lived in New York at the time probably remembers seeing signs all over the city and the distraught parents on the evening news, pleading for anyone with information to come forward.

But it was a second highly publicized murder, in 1981, that changed the course of American childhood by initiating a sustained movement to pro-tect children from strangers. Adam Walsh was six years old. His mother took him shopping at a Sears in Hollywood, Florida, and let him play at a kiosk promoting a new Atari video game system. The kiosk had attracted a gaggle of older boys, so Adam's mom let him stay there to watch while she went off to the lamp department for a few minutes. A scuffle broke out among the boys over whose turn was next, and the Sears security guards kicked all the boys out of the store. It seems that the other boys then left the scene, and Adam was too shy to speak up and say that his mother was inside. Standing alone outside the store, he was lured into a car by a drifter and serial murderer, who promised him toys and candy. Two weeks later, Adam's severed head was found in a canal 130 miles away.

Adam's father, John Walsh, has devoted his life to trying to save other children from suffering a similar fate. He created the Adam Walsh Child Resource Center, which advocated for legislative reform and succeeded in prodding the U.S. government to create the National Center for Missing & Exploited Children in 1984. He worked with producers to create the made-for-TV movie *Adam*, which was seen by 38 million viewers when it first aired. In 1988, Walsh launched a true-crime TV show, *America's Most Wanted*, which presented cases of unsolved crimes, including child abductions, and asked the public for help. Walsh was instrumental in a novel method of disseminating photographs of missing children: printing them on milk cartons, under the big all-caps word MISSING.[5] The first such cartons appeared in 1984, and one of the first photos was of Etan Patz. By the early 1990s, the program had spread, and photos of missing children were reproduced on grocery bags, billboards, pizza boxes, even utility bills. Norms changed, fears grew, and many parents came to believe that if they took their eyes off their children for an instant in any public venue, their kid might be snatched. It no longer felt safe to let kids roam around their neighborhoods unsupervised.

The abduction and murder of a child by a stranger is among the most horrific crimes one can imagine. It is also, thankfully, among the rarest. According to the FBI, almost 90% of children who go missing have either miscommunicated their plans, misunderstood directions, or run away from home or foster care,[6] and 99.8% of the time, missing children come home.[7] The vast majority of those who are abducted are taken by a biological parent who does not have custody; the number abducted by a stranger is a tiny fraction of 1% of children reported missing—roughly one hundred children per year in a nation with more than 70 million minors.[8] And since the 1990s, the rates of all crimes against children have gone down,[9] while the chances of a kidnapped child surviving the ordeal have gone up.[10]

Actual Versus Imagined Risk

The cities and towns in which the parents of iGen were raised were far more dangerous than they are today. Baby Boomers and Gen-Xers grew up with rising rates of crime and mayhem.[11] Muggings were a normal part of urban life, and city dwellers sometimes carried "muggers' money" in a cheap wallet so they would not have to hand over their real wallet.[12] Heroin syringes and later crack vials became common city sights. When you combine the giant crime wave that began in the 1960s with the rapid spread of cable TV in the 1980s, including news channels that offered round-the-clock coverage of missing-child cases,[13] you can see why American parents grew fearful and defensive by the 1990s.

The crime wave ended rather abruptly in the early 1990s, when rates of nearly all crimes began to plummet all over the United States.[14] In 2013, for example, the murder rate dropped to the same level it had been at *sixty years earlier.*[15] Nevertheless, the *fear* of crime did not diminish along with the crime rate, and the new habits of fearful parenting seem to have become new national norms. American parenting is now wildly out of sync with the actual risk that strangers pose to children.

To see how far into safetyism some parents have gone, consider the Missouri family that staged a kidnapping of their own six-year-old son in 2015. They wanted to "teach him a lesson" about how dangerous it is to be friendly to strangers. After getting off his school bus, the boy was lured into a pickup truck by his aunt's coworker. The man then told the little boy that he would never "see his mommy again," according to the sheriff's statement. The police also reported that the man covered the boy's face with a jacket so he couldn't tell he was being taken into his own basement. The boy was tied up, threatened with a gun, and told he would be sold into sex slavery.[16]

Of course, few parents would ever terrorize their children in this way, but less extreme forms of safetyism are taught in subtler ways. Lythcott-Haims and Skenazy both shared stories with us about parents who are afraid to let their *teenagers* ride their bikes to neighbors' houses. A psychologist who writes for HealthyChildren.org reported that "the National Center for Missing and Exploited Children feels that children *of any age* should not be permitted to use public restrooms alone."[17] While referencing her own nine-year-old son, the psychologist offered these tips:

- Never send a child into a public restroom alone.
- Instruct your child to use a private bathroom stall rather than a urinal.
- Avoid restrooms with more than one entrance.
- Stand in the door and talk to your child throughout their time in the bathroom.

We can understand a mother's fear that her son might encounter a pervert in a public restroom. But wouldn't it be better to teach the boy to recognize perverted or inappropriate bathroom behavior so he can get away from it on those very rare occasions when he might encounter it, rather than teaching him to fear for his life and maintain verbal contact with a parent every time he needs to use a public restroom?

The Dangers of Safetyism

If you spend time on Facebook, you've probably seen posts with titles like: "8 Reasons Children of the 1970s Should All Be Dead."[18] (Reason #1: Lawn darts. Reason #4: Tanning oil instead of sunscreen.) Such posts are shared widely by children of the 1970s (like us), because they allow our generation to laugh at the safety concerns of today's parents and to point out that when we grew up, nobody wore seat belts or bike helmets, most of the adults smoked (even around children), paint and gasoline were leaded, and children were encouraged to go—on their own—to parks and playgrounds, where anyone could kidnap them.

While the tone is frequently mocking and dismissive, these posts also highlight some important successes in the pursuit of child safety. Increased use of seat belts has saved many lives,[19] bicycle helmets lower the risk of traumatic brain injuries,[20] not smoking around children confers many health benefits on the kids,[21] and removing lead from paint and gasoline has prevented untold numbers of medical problems and deaths.[22] Putting it all together, from 1960 to 1990, there was a 48% reduction in deaths from unintended injuries and accidents among kids between five and fourteen years of age, and a 57% drop in deaths of younger kids (ages one to four).[23] The success of childhood safety campaigns helps explain why modern parents often take a concern about safety to the extreme of safetyism. After all, if focusing on big threats produces such dividends, why not go further and make childhood as close to perfectly safe as possible?

A problem with this kind of thinking is that when we attempt to produce perfectly safe systems, we almost inevitably create new and unforeseen problems. For example, efforts to prevent financial instability by bailing out companies can lead to larger and more destructive crashes later on;[24] efforts to protect forests by putting out small fires can allow dead wood to build up, eventually leading to catastrophic fires far worse than the sum of the smaller fires that were prevented.[25] Safety rules and programs—like most efforts to change complex systems—often have unintended consequences. Sometimes these consequences are so bad that the intended beneficiaries are worse off than if nothing had been done at all.

We believe that efforts to protect children from environmental hazards and vehicular accidents have been very good for children. Exposure to lead and cigarette smoke confer no benefits; being in a car crash without a seat belt does not make kids more resilient in future car crashes. But efforts to protect kids from risk by preventing them from gaining *experience*—such as walking to school, climbing a tree, or using sharp scissors—are different. Such protections come with costs, as kids miss out on opportunities to learn skills, independence, and risk assessment. (Keeping them indoors also raises their risk of obesity.) Skenazy puts the case succinctly: "The problem with this 'everything is dangerous' outlook is that over-protectiveness is a danger in and of itself."[26]

Lythcott-Haims concurs:

I've met parents who won't let their seventeen-year-old take the subway. And I said to them, "What's your long-term strategy for her?" . . . I see it all around me. I see kids afraid to be alone on the sidewalk. They don't like walking places alone. They don't like biking places alone. And it's probably because they've been basically made to feel that they can be abducted at any moment.[27]

As Taleb showed us in *Antifragile*, by placing a protective shield over our children, we inadvertently stunt their growth and deprive them of the experiences they need to become successful and functional adults. Journalist Hara Estroff Marano has been sounding the alarm about this trend for more than fifteen years. "Parents are going to ludicrous lengths to take the bumps out of life for their children," she says. "However, parental hyperconcern has the net effect of making kids more fragile."[28] Most parents know this on some level but still find themselves hovering and overprotecting. Even Lythcott-Haims has caught herself:

So here I was, highly critical of parents who couldn't let go of their college students. And then one day, when my kid was ten, I leaned over at dinner and began cutting his meat. And I realized in that moment: Holy cow! I'm cutting his meat and he's ten! I was babysitting other kids when I was ten, but my own kid needs to have his meat cut. What the hell is up with that?[29]

The blame for creating the culture of safetyism does not fall entirely on individual parents. At a fundamental level, overparenting and safetyism are "problems of progress," which we mentioned in the introductory chapter. Thankfully, gone are the days when families routinely had five or more children and expected one or more of them to die. When countries attain material prosperity and women gain educational equality, full political rights, and access to good healthcare and contraception, birth rates plunge and most couples have just one or two children. They invest more time in these fewer, healthier children.[30] In fact, even though mothers today have fewer children and spend far more time working outside the home than they did in 1965, they are spending more total time taking care of their children.[31] Fathers' time with kids has increased even more.

Parents spending time with their kids is generally a good thing, but too much close supervision and protection can morph into safetyism. Safety-ism takes children who are antifragile by nature and turns them into young adults who are more fragile and and anxious, and therefore more receptive to the Untruth of Fragility: *What doesn't kill you makes you weaker.*

Pressured Into Overprotection

When parents get together and talk about parenting, it is common to hear condemnations of helicopter parenting. Many parents want to do less hovering and give their kids more freedom, but it's not so easy; there are pressures from other parents, from schools, and even from laws that push parents to be more protective than they would like to be. Skenazy says that societal pressures often prompt parents to engage in "worst-first thinking."[32] Unless parents prepare for the worst possible outcomes, they are looked down on by other parents and by teachers for being bad parents (or even "America's Worst Mom"). Good parents are expected to believe that their children are in danger every moment they are unsupervised.

It gets worse. Parents who reject overparenting and give their kids more freedom can actually be *arrested.* In 2015, two Florida parents were charged with felony child neglect when they were delayed getting home.[33] Unable to get into his house, their eleven-year-old son played with a basketball in their yard for ninety minutes. A neighbor called the police. After being handcuffed, strip-searched, fingerprinted, and held overnight in jail, the parents were arrested for negligence, and the boy and his four-year-old brother (who had not been left alone) were put in foster care for a month. Even after being returned to their parents, the children were required to attend "play" therapy. The parents, who had no history of neglecting their children, were mandated to get therapy and take parenting classes.

In Bristol, Connecticut, in 2014, a woman left her daughter alone in her car while she went into a CVS pharmacy. This might sound bad to you, especially when you learn that it was summertime and the car windows were all closed. An alert passerby called the police, who were able to open the car door. The police reported that the child was "responsive" and not in distress. But here's the thing: the girl was eleven years old. She had told her mother that she preferred to wait in the car rather than come into the store.[34]

Before the rise of paranoid parenting, eleven-year-olds could earn money and learn responsibility by babysitting for neighbors, as Jon and his sisters did in the 1970s. Now, according to some police departments and local busybodies, eleven-year-olds need babysitters themselves. The mother was issued a misdemeanor summons and forced to appear in court.

When the police endorse safetyism, it forces parents to overprotect. The police chief of New Albany, Ohio, advises that children should not be allowed outside without supervision *until the age of 16.*[35] When you combine peer pressure, shaming, and the threat of arrest, it's no wonder that so many American parents simply don't let their kids out of their sight anymore, even though many of those same parents report that their fondest memories of childhood were unsupervised outdoor adventures with friends.

SAFE BOOKS FOR SAFE KIDS

Lenore Skenazy points out that most great children's books involve kids going off on adventures without adult supervision. For parents who don't want to put dangerous ideas in their kids' heads, she and her readers offer a set of classic titles updated for the age of safetyism:

Oh, the Places You Won't Go!

The Playdates of Huckleberry Finn

Harold and the Purple Sofa

Encyclopedia Brown Solves the Worksheet

Harry Potter and the Sit-Still Challenge

Dora in the Ford Explorer (But Not Without a Parent!)

Class Matters

Different explanatory threads matter more for different people, and perhaps the biggest differentiator of life experiences in the United States today is social class. To understand how social class influences parenting practices, we'll draw on two books that combine in-depth profiles of families with sociological theory and data: *Unequal Childhoods: Class, Race, and Family Life*, by University of Pennsylvania sociologist Annette Lareau, and *Our Kids: The American Dream in Crisis*, by Harvard political scientist Robert Putnam. Both scholars find that, with respect to parenting practices, social class matters far more than race, so we'll set race aside and focus on the ways that class differences in parenting may be relevant for understanding what is now happening on college campuses. For simplicity, we'll use Lareau's terms "middle class" and "working class," but "middle class" means middle class and above, including the upper class. The term "working class" is used for everyone below middle class, including poor families.

The big divide in parenting practices is best seen in the contrast between two kinds of families: those in which children are raised by two parents who each have four-year-college degrees and are married to each other throughout their children's childhood, and those in which children are raised by a single or divorced parent (or other relative) who does not have a four-year-college degree. The first kind of family is very common in the upper third of the socioeconomic spectrum, in which marriage rates are high and divorce rates are low. These families generally employ a parenting style that Lareau calls "concerted cultivation." Parents using this style see their task as cultivating their children's talents while stimulating the development of their cognitive and social skills. They fill their children's calendars with adult-guided activities, lessons, and experiences, and they closely monitor what happens in school. They talk with their children a great deal, using reasoning and persuasion, and they hardly ever use physical force or physical punishment. The second kind of family is very common in the bottom third of the socioeconomic spectrum, where most children are born to unmarried mothers. These families generally employ a parenting style that Lareau calls "natural growth parenting." Working-class parents tend to believe that children will reach maturity without needing much guidance or interference from adults. Children therefore experience "long stretches of leisure time, child-initiated play, clear boundaries between adults and children, and daily interactions with kin."[36] Parents spend less time talking with their children, and reason with them far less, compared with middle-class parents; they also give more orders and directives, and they sometimes use spanking or physical discipline.

From these descriptions, it would seem that working-class kids have one advantage: they get more unstructured and unsupervised play time, which, as we'll say in the next chapter, is very good for developing social skills and a sense of autonomy. In fact, Putnam points to this class difference as something relatively new and very important. He notes that the parents of Baby Boomers were strongly influenced by the writings of childrearing expert Dr. Benjamin Spock, who taught that "children should be permitted to develop at their own pace, not pushed to meet the schedules and rules of adult life."[37] Spock encouraged parents to relax and let children be children, and indeed, Baby Boomers and GenX children were generally given the freedom to roam around their neighborhoods and play without adult supervision. But Putnam notes that, beginning in the 1980s and accelerating in the 1990s, "the dominant ideas and social norms about good parenting [had] shifted from Spock's 'permissive parenting' to a new model of 'intensive parenting,'"[38] which essentially describes Lareau's *concerted cultivation*. This change happened primarily among middle-class parents, who were immersed in news reports about the importance of early stimulation (for example, the erroneous idea that babies who listen to Mozart will become smarter)[39] and who wanted to give their children every possible advantage in the increasingly competitive race to get into a good college. This shift did not happen among working-class parents. The change in middle-class parenting norms is crucial for our story. Putnam identifies the shift as kicking in just before iGen was born. To the extent that iGen college students are behaving differently from previous generations of college students, a contributing factor may be that, compared with previous generations, middle-class iGen (and late Millennial) students were overscheduled and overparented as children.

It would be a mistake, however, to think that working-class kids had an *overall* advantage. Putnam and Lareau both note a variety of factors that make it harder for working-class kids to succeed in general, and in college in particular, even if they are admitted to selective universities. One is that all those organized activities help to familiarize middle-class children with the ways of adults in professional settings and adult-run institutions. Parental modeling gives them a sense that institutions can be made to serve their needs if they can make the right argument to the right person at the right time. Working-class kids, in contrast, have generally had less exposure to adult institutions and have not seen their parents engage with these institutions with the same sense of strength, rights, or entitlement to good treatment. Working-class kids are therefore more likely to feel like "fish out of water" in college. (This may have contributed to the feelings of not belonging that Olivia wrote about, from the Claremont McKenna College story we presented in chapter 3.)

Compared with middle-class kids, the second major disadvantage plaguing working-class kids is that they are more likely to have been affected by chronic and severe adversity. In the 1990s, a group of researchers developed a survey to standardize the assessment of "Adverse Childhood Experiences" (ACE).[40] The survey asked people to report which items, from a list of ten, they had been exposed to in childhood; things like "Parents separated/divorced," "You lacked food or clothes or your parents were too drunk or high to care for you," "Felt no one in family loved or supported you," "Adult sexually abused you." As the number of yes responses increases beyond two, measures of health and success in adulthood tend to decline, and this introduces an important complication to our story about antifragility: Severe adversity that hits kids early, especially in the absence of secure and loving attachment relationships with adults, does not make them stronger; it makes them weaker. Chronic, severe adversity creates "toxic stress." It resets children's stress responses to kick in more readily and for longer periods in the future. Putnam summarizes the findings like this:

Moderate stress buffered by supportive adults is not necessarily harmful, and may even be helpful, in that it can promote the development of coping skills. On the other hand, severe and chronic stress, especially if unbuffered by supportive adults, can disrupt the basic executive functions that govern how various parts of the brain work together to address challenges and solve problems. Consequently, children who experience toxic stress have trouble concentrating, controlling impulsive behavior, and following directions.[41]

Kids raised in families below the middle class score much higher, on average, on the ACE survey. Their family situations tend to be more unstable; their economic lives are often precarious, and they are much more likely to witness violence or be victims of violence. This means that even if they make it to college, they may still be carrying scars and disadvantages with them, and in order to thrive in college, they may need different kinds of support than are appropriate for their wealthier peers, whose brains were shaped by concerted cultivation.

The lesson we draw from this brief review of research on social class and parenting is that although kids are naturally antifragile, there are two very different ways to damage their development. One is to neglect and underprotect them, exposing them early to severe and chronic adversity. This has happened to some of today's college students, particularly those from working-class or poor families. The other is to overmonitor and overprotect them, denying them the thousands of small challenges, risks, and adversities that they need to face on their own in order to become strong and resilient adults.

America's selective universities are dominated by children from the upper class and upper-middle class. A recent analysis found that at thirty-eight top schools, including most of the Ivy League, there are more undergraduate students from families in the top 1% of the income distribution than from the bottom 60%.[42] This means that overparenting is probably a much greater cause of fragility on such campuses than is underparenting.

Safe and Unwise

Paranoid parenting and the cult of safetyism teach kids some of the specific cognitive distortions that we discussed in chapter 1. We asked Skenazy which of the distortions she encounters most often in her work with parents. "Almost all of them," she said.[43]

Skenazy sees *discounting positives* when parents overmonitor. "Any upside to free, unsupervised time (joy, independence, problem-solving, resilience) is seen as trivial, compared to the infinite harm the child could suffer without you there. There is nothing positive but safety." Parents also use *negative filtering* frequently, Skenazy says. "Parents are saying, 'Look at all the foods/activities/words/people that could harm our kids!' rather than 'I'm so glad we've finally overcome diphtheria, polio, and famine!'" She also points out the ways that parents use *dichotomous thinking*: "If something isn't 100% safe, it's dangerous."

Paranoid parenting is a powerful way to teach kids all three of the Great Untruths. We convince children that the world is full of danger; evil lurks in the shadows, on the streets, and in public parks and restrooms. Kids raised in this way are emotionally prepared to embrace the Untruth of Us Versus Them: *Life is a battle between good people and evil people*—a worldview that makes them fear and suspect strangers. We teach children to monitor themselves for the degree to which they "feel unsafe" and then talk about how unsafe they feel. They may come to believe that *feeling* "unsafe" (the feeling of being uncomfortable or anxious) is a reliable sign that they *are* unsafe (the Untruth of Emotional Reasoning: *Always trust your feelings*). Finally, feeling these emotions is unpleasant; therefore, children may conclude, the feelings are dangerous in and of themselves—stress will harm them if it doesn't kill them (the Untruth of Fragility: *What doesn't kill you makes you weaker*).

If children develop the habit of thinking in these ways when they are young, they are likely to develop corresponding schemas that guide the way they interpret new situations in high school and college. They may see more danger in their environment and more hostile intent in the actions of others. They may be more likely than kids in previous generations to believe that they should flee or avoid anything that could be construed as even a minor threat. They may be more likely to interpret words, books, and ideas in terms of safety versus danger, or good versus evil, rather than using dimensions that would promote learning, such as true versus false, or fascinating versus uninteresting. While it is easy to see how this way of thinking, when brought to a college campus, could lead to requests for safe spaces, trigger warnings, microaggression training, and bias response teams, it is difficult to see how this way of thinking could produce well-educated, bold, and open-minded college graduates.

In Sum

- Paranoid parenting is our third explanatory thread.
- When we overprotect children, we harm them. Children are naturally antifragile, so overprotection makes them weaker and less resilient later on.
- Children today have far more restricted childhoods, on average, than those enjoyed by their parents, who grew up in far more dangerous times and yet had many more opportunities to develop their intrinsic antifragility. Compared with previous generations, younger Millennials and especially members of iGen (born in and after 1995) have been deprived of unsupervised time for play and exploration. They have missed out on many of the challenges, negative experiences, and minor risks that help children develop into strong, competent, and independent adults (as we'll show in the next chapter).
- Children in the United States and other prosperous countries are safer today than at any other point in history. Yet for a variety of historical reasons, fear of abduction is still very high among American parents, many of whom have come to believe that children should never be without adult supervision. When children are repeatedly led

to believe that the world is dangerous and that they cannot face it alone, we should not be surprised if many of them believe it.

- Helicopter parenting combined with laws and social norms that make it hard to give kids unsupervised time may be having a negative impact on the mental health and resilience of young people today.

- There are large social class differences in parenting styles. Families in the middle class (and above) tend to use a style that sociologist Annette Lareau calls "concerted cultivation," in contrast to the "natural growth parenting" used by families in the working class (and below). Some college students from wealthier families may have been rendered more fragile from overparenting and oversupervision. College students from poorer backgrounds are exposed to a very different set of risks, including potential exposure to chronic, severe adversity, which is especially detrimental to resilience when children lack caring relationships with adults who can buffer stress and help them turn adversity into growth.

- Paranoid parenting prepares today's children to embrace the three Great Untruths, which means that when they go to college, they are psychologically primed to join a culture of safetyism.

CHAPTER 9

The Decline of Play

All work and no play makes Jack a dull boy.

PROVERB, *seventeenth century*

hy don't kids like to be "it"? Why, at the start of a game of tag, do they each call out, "Not it!" and then point to the loser, the last one to reject the role?

A provocative answer can be found by looking at the play of other mammals, most of which have some version of chasing games. In species that are predators, such as wolves, their pups seem to prefer to be the chasers. In species that are prey, such as rats, the pups prefer to be chased.[1] Our primate ancestors were both prey and predator, but they were prey for much longer. That may be why human children particularly enjoy practicing their fleeing and hiding skills.[2]

When seen from a distance, child's play is a strange thing. Peter LaFreniere, a developmental psychologist at the University of Maine, notes that children's play "combines the expenditure of great energy with apparently pointless risk."[3] But if nearly all mammals do it, and if some of them get injured or eaten while doing it, it must offer some pretty powerful benefits to compensate for the risks.

It does. Play is essential for wiring a mammal's brain to create a functioning adult. Mammals that are deprived of play won't develop to their full capacity. In one experiment demonstrating this effect, rat pups were raised in one of three conditions: (1) totally alone in a cage; (2) alone except for one hour a day with a normal, playful young rat, during which time normal rough-and-tumble play occurred; and (3) same as condition 2, except that the visiting young rat was treated with a drug that knocked out rough-and-tumble play while leaving other social behaviors, such as sniffing and nuzzling. When the young rats were later put into new situations, those that had engaged in rough-and-tumble play showed fewer signs of fearfulness and engaged in more exploration of the new environment.[4]

A key concept from developmental biology is "experience-expectant development."[5] Human beings have only about 22,000 genes, but our brains have approximately 100 billion neurons, with hundreds of trillions of synaptic connections. Our genes could never offer a codebook or blueprint for building anything so complex. Even if a blueprint could be passed down in our genes, it would not be flexible enough to build children who were well adapted to the vast range of environments and problems that our wandering species has gotten itself into. Nature found a better way to wire our large brains, and it goes like this: Genes are essential for getting the various cell lines started in the embryo, and genes guide brain development toward a "first draft" in utero. But experience matters, too, even while the baby is in the uterus; and after birth, it matters enormously. Experience is so essential for wiring a large brain that the "first draft" of the brain includes a strong motivation to practice behaviors that will give the brain the right kind of feedback to optimize itself for success in the environment that happens to surround it. That's why young mammals are so keen to play, despite the risks.

It's easy to see how this works with language in humans: The genes get the ball rolling on the development of brain structures for language, but the child must actually encounter and practice a language to finish the process. The linguistic brain is "expecting" certain kinds of input, and children are therefore motivated to engage in back-and-forth reciprocal exchanges with others in order to get that input. It's fun for them to exchange sounds, and later, real words, with other people. A child who was deprived of these linguistic interactions until puberty would be unable to fully acquire a language or learn to speak normally, having missed the "critical period" for language learning that is part of the normal developmental process.[6]

It's the same logic for physical skills (such as fleeing from predators) and social skills (such as negotiating conflicts and cooperation). The genes get the ball rolling on the first draft of the brain, but the brain is "expecting" the child to engage in thousands of hours of play—including thousands of falls, scrapes, conflicts, insults, alliances, betrayals, status competitions, and acts of exclusion—in order to develop. Children who are deprived of play are less likely to develop into physically and socially competent teens and adults.[7]

Research on play has increased rapidly since 1980. Evidence for the benefits of play is now strong, and there's a growing body of scholarship—suggestive though not conclusive—linking play deprivation to later anxiety and depression.[8] As stated in one review of this literature:

> Research has shown that anxious children may elicit overprotective behavior from others, such as parents and caretakers, and that this reinforces the child's perception of threat and decreases their perception of controlling the danger. Overprotection might thus result in exaggerated levels of anxiety. Overprotection through governmental control of playgrounds and exaggerated fear of playground accidents might thus result in an increase of anxiety in society. *We might need to provide more stimulating environments for children, rather than hamper their development* [emphasis added].[9]

Given this research, and given the rising levels of adolescent anxiety, depression, and suicide, which we described in chapter 7, our educational system and parenting practices should offer kids more time for free play. But in fact, the opposite has happened.

In this chapter, we investigate why the most beneficial forms of play have declined sharply since the 1970s, and we ask what effects this change in childhood might have on teens and college students. The decline of unsupervised free play—including ample opportunities to take small risks—is our fourth explanatory thread.

The Decline of Free Play

Peter Gray, a leading researcher of play, defines "free play" as "activity that is freely chosen and directed by the participants and undertaken for its own sake, not consciously pursued to achieve ends that are distinct from the activity itself."[10] Piano lessons and soccer practice are not free play, but goofing around on a piano or organizing a pickup soccer game are. Gray and other researchers note that all play is not equal. Vigorous physical free play—outdoors, and with other kids—is a crucial kind of play, one that our evolved minds are "expecting." It also happens to be the kind of play that kids generally say they like the most.[11] (There is also a good case to be made for the importance of imaginative or pretend play,[12] which is found not only in less rambunctious kinds of indoor free play but often in rough-and-tumble outdoor free play as well.)

Gray notes the tendency of kids to introduce danger and risk into outdoor free play, such as when they climb walls and trees, or skateboard down staircases and railings:

> They seem to be dosing themselves with moderate degrees of fear, as if deliberately learning how to deal with both the physical and emotional challenges of the moderately dangerous conditions they generate. . . . All such activities are fun to the degree that they are moderately frightening. If too little fear is induced, the activity is boring; if too much is induced, it becomes no longer play but terror. Nobody but the child himself or herself knows the right dose.[13]

Unfortunately, outdoor physical play is the kind that has declined the most in the lives of American children. The study that offers the clearest picture of the relevant trends was carried out in 1981 by sociologists at the University of Michigan, who asked parents of children under thirteen to keep detailed records of how their kids spent their time on several randomly chosen days. They repeated the study in 1997, and found that time spent in any kind of play went down 16% overall, and much of the play had shifted to indoor activities, often involving a computer and no other children.[14] This kind of play does not build physical strength and is not as effective at building psychological resilience or social competence, so the drop in real, healthy, sociable free play was much greater than 16%. That study compared

Generation X (who were kids in 1981) to Millennials (who were kids in 1997). Twenge's analysis of iGen, the current generation of kids, shows that the drop in free play has accelerated. Compared with Millennials, iGen spends less time going out with friends, more time interacting with parents, and much more time interacting with screens (which can be a form of social interaction but can have some negative effects, as we discussed in chapter 7).[15]

Compared with previous generations, members of iGen have therefore had much less of the kind of unsupervised free play that Gray says is most valuable. They have been systematically deprived of opportunities to "dose themselves" with risk. Instead of enjoying a healthy amount of risk, this generation is more likely than earlier ones to avoid it. Twenge shows how responses have changed to the survey question "I get a real kick out of doing things that are a little dangerous." From 1994 through 2010, the percentage of adolescents who agreed with that question held steady, in the low 50s. But as iGen enters the dataset, agreement drops, dipping to 43% by 2015. If members of iGen have been risk-deprived and are therefore more risk averse, then it is likely that they have a lower bar for what they see as daunting or threatening. They will see more ordinary life tasks as beyond their ability to handle on their own without help from an adult. It should not surprise us that anxiety and depression rates began rising rapidly on campus as soon as iGen arrived.

In contrast to the decreased time spent in play between 1981 and 1997, that same time-use study found that time spent in school went up 18%, and time spent doing homework went up 145%.[16] Research by Duke University psychologist Harris Cooper indicates that while there are benefits to homework in middle school and high school, provided it's relevant and in the right amount, achievement benefits in elementary school are smaller, and homework that isn't realistic in length and difficulty can even decrease achievement.[17] Yet elementary school students have seen an increase in homework over the past twenty years.[18] Some schools even assign homework in kindergarten. (Lenore Skenazy told us that when she asked her son's teacher why homework was being assigned in kindergarten, the teacher responded, "So they will be ready for homework in first grade."[19])

Why is this happening? Why have we deprived kids of the healthiest forms of play and given them more homework and more supervision instead? One of the major reasons for the decline of all forms of unsupervised outdoor activity is, of course, the unrealistic media-amplified fear of abduction, which we described in the previous chapter. In one large survey, published in 2004, 85% of mothers said that their children played outdoors less frequently than they themselves had played when they were the same age. When asked to select reasons to explain why their children didn't spend more time on outdoor play, 82% of the mothers chose "safety concerns," including the fear of crime.[20]

But there's a second reason, a second fear that haunts American parents and children—particularly those in the middle class and above—far more than it did in the late twentieth century: the college admissions process.

Childhood as Test Prep

When the parents of Millennials and iGen were children, early education was very different than it is today. Take a look at a checklist from 1979[21] that helped parents decide whether their six-year-old was ready to start first grade. It has just twelve items, and almost all of them are about physical and emotional maturation and independence—including one item that could get parents arrested today (#8).

IS YOUR CHILD READY FOR FIRST GRADE: 1979 EDITION

1. Will your child be six years, six months or older when he begins first grade and starts receiving reading instruction?

2. Does your child have two to five permanent or second teeth?

3. Can your child tell, in such a way that his speech is understood by a school crossing guard or policeman, where he lives?

4. Can he draw and color and stay within the lines of the design being colored?
5. Can he stand on one foot with eyes closed for five to ten seconds?
6. Can he ride a small two-wheeled bicycle without helper wheels?
7. Can he tell left hand from right?
8. Can he travel alone in the neighborhood (four to eight blocks) to store, school, playground, or to a friend's home?
9. Can he be away from you all day without being upset?
10. Can he repeat an eight- to ten-word sentence, if you say it once, as "The boy ran all the way home from the store"?
11. Can he count eight to ten pennies correctly?
12. Does your child try to write or copy letters or numbers?[22]

Compare that to one from today. A checklist from a school in Austin, Texas, has thirty items on it, almost all of which are academic, including:

- Identify and write numbers to 100
- Count by 10's to 100, by 2's to 20, by 5's to 100
- Interpret and fill in data on a graph
- Read all kindergarten-level sight words
- Be able to read books with five to ten words per page
- Form complete sentences on paper using phonetic spelling (i.e., journal and story writing)[23]

Kindergarten in 1979 was devoted mostly to social interaction and self-directed play, with some instruction in art, music, numbers, and the alphabet thrown in. Erika Christakis notes that kindergarten classrooms would have been organized to build social relationships and facilitate hands-on exploration (such as with blocks or Lincoln Logs) and imaginative and symbolic play (such as a store or housekeeping corner with props and costumes). Back then, kindergarten, which for most children was a half day, probably looked more like what passes for a progressive preschool today, consisting of "open-ended free play, snack, singing songs with rhyming words for a little oral language exposure, a story, maybe an art project and some sorting games or block building for math awareness."[24] Today, kindergarten is much more structured and sedentary, with children spending more time sitting at their desks and receiving direct instruction in academic subjects—known as the "drill and skill" method of instruction, but that teachers not-so-affectionately call "drill and kill."[25] Such methods are sometimes effective ways to communicate academic information to older children, but they are not appropriate for use with young children. There is growing evidence that with young children, these methods can backfire and produce negative effects on creativity as well as on social and emotional development.[26]

Researchers at the University of Virginia compared kindergarten classes in 1998 (composed of some of the last members of the Millennial generation) to kindergarten in 2010 and found that by 2010, the use of standardized tests in kindergarten was much more common. Teaching methods and classroom organization had changed, and far more time was spent on advanced reading and math content. The study also found that teachers' academic expectations of kindergarteners in 2010 were far higher than they had been in 1998,[27] a trend that seems to continue. For example, today's Common Core kindergarten math standards include "construct viable arguments and critique the reasoning of others,"[28] and reading skills include "read emergent-reader texts with purpose and understanding."[29]

In response to things like the No Child Left Behind Act of 2001, state preschool standards, a general emphasis on testing, and then the introduction of Common Core standards, the preschool and kindergarten landscape has changed enormously.[30] Christakis laments that social time and play have been sacrificed in preschool to keep up with academic expectations for kindergarten readiness. As she reports, kindergarten teachers still claim that the most important skills for kindergarten are not academic but social and emotional (like listening and being able to take turns).[31]

Beginning in preschool and continuing throughout primary school, children's days are now more rigidly structured. Opportunities for self-direction, social exploration, and scientific discovery are increasingly lost to direct instruction in the core curriculum, which is often driven by the schools' focus on preparing students to meet state testing requirements. Meanwhile, especially for wealthier kids, instead of neighborhood children finding one another after school and engaging in free play, children have after-school activities like music lessons, team sports, tutoring, and other structured and supervised activities.[32] For younger children, parents schedule playdates,[33] which are likely to occur under the watchful eye of a parent.

For children of many educated parents with means, instead of afternoons and weekends spent hanging out with friends or resting, that nonschool time is increasingly used to cultivate skills that will allow those children to stand out later on in the college admissions game. It's no wonder that parents work so hard to plan their children's time. What eight-year-old has the foresight to play the tuba or girls' golf—activities that might make them more attractive to colleges?[34] What thirteen-year-old has the organizational skills and forward thinking (not to mention transportation plan) to follow the advice of The Princeton Review, which urges students to increase their appeal to colleges by picking one community-service activity early on and sticking with it year after year, volunteering two hours a week through senior year?[35]

The Resume Arms Race

It has become much more difficult to gain admission to the top U.S. universities. For example, in the 1980s and '90s, Yale's acceptance rate hovered around 20%. By 2003, the admission rate was down to 11% and in 2017 it was 7%.[36] So it makes sense that parents have increasingly teamed up with their children to help them pack their resumes with extracurricular activities. It's what former Yale English professor William Deresiewicz calls "the resume arms race," and any family that doesn't come together to play the game puts their child at a disadvantage. "The only point of having more," Deresiewicz explains in his book *Excellent Sheep*, "is having more than everybody else. Nobody needed 20,000 atomic warheads until the other side had 19,000. Nobody needs eleven extracurriculars, either—what purpose does having them actually serve?—unless the other guy has ten."[37]

Given the fierce competition, parents in some social circles convey a sense of panic about children's grades, even in middle school—as if not getting an A will determine the course of a child's life. This would normally be a clear example of catastrophizing, but in some highly competitive school districts, it may not be entirely unrealistic. Julie Lythcott-Haims puts it like this: "Let's say this is math. If they don't get an A in sixth-grade math, it means they might not be on track to be in the highest level of math in high school, which means they won't get into Stanford."[38] So it isn't surprising that so many parents are hovering and oversupervising, not just to ensure safety but to ensure that children do homework and prepare for tests.[39] Some of these parents may think that making sure their children do whatever it takes to succeed in advanced courses helps their children develop "grit." But "grit is often misunderstood as perseverance without passion, and that's tragic," psychology professor Angela Duckworth, author of the book *Grit*, told us. "Perseverance without passion is mere drudgery." She wants young people to "devote themselves to pursuits that are intrinsically fulfilling."[40]

The college admissions process nowadays makes it harder for high school students to enjoy school and pursue intrinsic fulfillment. The process "warps the values of students drawn into a competitive frenzy" and "jeopardizes their mental health,"[41] says Frank Bruni, a *New York Times* columnist and author of *Where You Go Is Not Who You Will Be: An Antidote to the College Admissions Mania*. Nowhere is that more apparent than in suicide clusters at highly competitive high schools, such as those in Palo Alto, California, and the suburbs of Boston, which have been profiled in *The Atlantic*[42] and *The New York Times*.[43] In a 2015 survey, 95% of students at Lexington High School in Massachusetts reported "a lot of stress" or "extreme stress" about their classes, and in a 2016 study, the Centers for Disease Control reported that the teen suicide rate in Palo Alto, California, was more than four times the national average.[44]

And it is precisely these elite, wealthy, and hypercompetitive school districts that provide the largest share of students at the top universities in the United States.[45] "Students are prepared academically, but they're not prepared to deal with day-to-day life," says Gray, "which comes from a lack of opportunity to deal with ordinary problems."[46] One paradox of upper-middle-class American life is that some of the things parents and schools do to help kids get admitted to college may make them less able to thrive once they're there.

Childhood as Democracy Prep

The effects of play deprivation and oversupervision may extend far beyond college. Steven Horwitz, an economist at Ball State University in Indiana, took the same research on play that we have reviewed in this chapter and worked out some possible consequences for the future of liberal democracies.[47] He drew on the work of political scientists Elinor Ostrom[48] and Vincent Ostrom,[49] both of whom studied how self-governing communities resolve conflicts peacefully. Successful democracies do this by developing a variety of institutions and norms that enable people with different goals and conflicting desires to resolve their problems while rarely appealing to the police or the state to coerce their fellow citizens. This is the "art of association" that so impressed Alexis de Tocqueville when he traveled through the United States in 1835.

Citizens of a democracy don't suddenly develop this art on their eighteenth birthday. It takes many years to cultivate these skills, which overlap with the ones that Peter Gray maintains are learned during free play. Of greatest importance in free play is that it is always voluntary; anyone can quit at any time and disrupt the activity, so children must pay close attention to the needs and concerns of others if they want to keep the game going. They must work out conflicts over fairness on their own; no adult can be called upon to side with one child against another.

Horwitz points out that when adult-supervised activities crowd out free play, children are less likely to develop the art of association:

Denying children the freedom to explore on their own takes away important learning opportunities that help them to develop not just independence and responsibility, but a whole variety of social skills that are central to living with others in a free society. If this argument is correct, parenting strategies and laws that make it harder for kids to play on their own pose a serious threat to liberal societies by flipping our default setting from "figure out how to solve this conflict on your own" to "invoke force and/or third parties whenever conflict arises." This is one of the "vulnerabilities of democracies" noted by Vincent Ostrom.[50]

The consequences for democracies could be dire, particularly for a democracy such as the United States, which is already suffering from ever-rising cross-party hostility[51] and declining trust in institutions.[52] Here is what Horwitz fears could be in store:

> A society that weakens children's ability to learn these skills denies them what they need to smooth social interaction. The coarsening of social interaction that will result will create a world of more conflict and violence, and one in which people's first instinct will be increasingly to invoke coercion by other parties to solve problems they ought to be able to solve themselves.[53]

This is what Greg began to see around 2013: increasing calls from students for administrators and professors to regulate who can say what, who gets to speak on campus, and how students should interact with one another, even in private settings. The calls for more regulation and the bureaucratic impulse to provide that regulation are the subject of our next chapter.

We end this chapter, however, on a more positive note. In contrast to all the unwisdom kids are exposed to in the form of the three Great Untruths, here is a better way to frame the experiences of childhood and adolescence. In June 2017, John Roberts, the chief justice of the United States, was invited to be the commencement speaker at his son's graduation from middle school. Like Van Jones (whom we quoted in chapter 4),

Roberts understands antifragility. He wishes for his son's classmates to have the sorts of painful experiences that will make them better people and better citizens.[54] Here is an excerpt from his speech:

From time to time in the years to come, I hope you will be treated unfairly, so that you will come to know the value of justice. I hope that you will suffer betrayal because that will teach you the importance of loyalty. Sorry to say, but I hope you will be lonely from time to time so that you don't take friends for granted. I wish you bad luck, again, from time to time so that you will be conscious of the role of chance in life and understand that your success is not completely deserved and that the failure of others is not completely deserved either. And when you lose, as you will from time to time, I hope every now and then, your opponent will gloat over your failure. It is a way for you to understand the importance of sportsmanship. I hope you'll be ignored so you know the importance of listening to others, and I hope you will have just enough pain to learn compassion. Whether I wish these things or not, they're going to happen. And whether you benefit from them or not will depend upon your ability to see the message in your misfortunes.[55]

In Sum

- The decline of unsupervised free play is our fourth explanatory thread. Children, like other mammals, need free play in order to finish the intricate wiring process of neural development. Children deprived of free play are likely to be less competent—physically and socially—as adults. They are likely to be less tolerant of risk, and more prone to anxiety disorders.
- Free play, according to Peter Gray, is "activity that is freely chosen and directed by the participants and undertaken for its own sake, not consciously pursued to achieve ends that are distinct from the activity

itself." This is the kind of play that play experts say is most valuable for children, yet it is also the kind of play that has declined most sharply in the lives of American children.

- The decline in free play was likely driven by several factors, including an unrealistic fear of strangers and kidnapping (since the 1980s); the rising competitiveness for admission to top universities (over many decades); a rising emphasis on testing, test preparation, and homework; and a corresponding deemphasis on physical and social skills (since the early 2000s).

- The rising availability of smartphones and social media interacted with these other trends, and the combination has greatly changed the way American children spend their time and the kinds of physical and social experiences that guide the intricate wiring process of neural development.

- Free play helps children develop the skills of cooperation and dispute resolution that are closely related to the "art of association" upon which democracies depend. When citizens are not skilled in this art, they are less able to work out the ordinary conflicts of daily life. They will more frequently call for authorities to apply coercive force to their opponents. They will be more likely to welcome the bureaucracy of safetyism.

CHAPTER 10

The Bureaucracy of Safetyism

> *The sovereign power [or soft despot] extends its arms over the entire society; it covers the surface of society with a network of small, complicated, minute, and uniform rules . . . it does not tyrannize, it hinders, it represses, it enervates, it extinguishes, it stupefies, and finally it reduces each nation to being nothing more than a flock of timid and industrious animals, of which the government is the shepherd.*
>
> ALEXIS DE TOCQUEVILLE, *Democracy in America*[1]

Remember the thought experiment in chapter 2, in which you visited your campus counseling center and the psychologist there made you more anxious rather than less?

Now, imagine it's a few days after your visit, and you receive an email from the associate dean of students with "Conduct Policy Reminder" in the subject line. You open it nervously, wondering why the associate dean would be reminding you about the conduct policy. You can't remember doing anything that might violate it. The note reads:

> I received a report that others are worried about your well-being. I'd like to meet with you to discuss your options for support and see what I can do to help. . . . Engaging in any discussion of suicidal or self-destructive thoughts or actions with other students interferes with, or can hinder, their pursuit of education and community. It is important that you refrain from discussing these issues with other students and use the appropriate resources listed below. If you involve other students in suicidal or self-destructive thoughts or

actions, you will face disciplinary action. My hope is that, knowing exactly what could result in discipline, you can avoid putting yourself in that position.[2]

You are confused. You didn't mention anything about "suicidal or self-destructive thoughts or actions" when you visited the counseling center, and you have no intention of hurting yourself. A thousand thoughts rush through your head: How did the associate dean of students find out about your visit to the center? Isn't therapy supposed to be confidential? Why is the dean sending you a warning and a threat? And can the dean really tell you what you can and can't say to your friends?

This scenario is not fiction. In 2015, a student at Northern Michigan University (NMU) visited the campus counseling center to get help in the aftermath of being sexually assaulted the year before. She did not mention anything about self-harm or suicidal thoughts during her session, yet the email she received from NMU's associate dean of students included the exact text we quoted above. And she was not alone; 25–30 NMU students *per semester* received a version of that letter—whether or not they had expressed thoughts about suicide or self-harm.[3] It was NMU's policy that students could be disciplined (and even expelled) for revealing these kinds of thoughts to other students. Given that the misguided policy was both stigmatizing and likely to put suicidal students at increased risk, mental health professionals roundly criticized the policy. Nevertheless, in an interview with a local newspaper, the dean defended the practice, claiming that "relying on your friends can be very disruptive to them."[4] Please read that quote again. The dean seemed to believe that if students talked about their suffering, it would harm their friends. It is an illustration of the Untruth of Fragility (*What doesn't kill you makes you weaker*) trumping common sense and basic humanity.

What could compel a university—and, in particular, its associate dean of students—to be so callous? This kind of administrative overkill was what first got Greg thinking about the ways in which universities teach cognitive distortions. When he started studying CBT in 2008, he saw administrators acting in ways that encouraged students to embrace a distorted sense that they lacked resilience—acting as if students could not handle uncomfortable conversations with, or relatively small slights from, their fellow students. In order to fully grasp the success of the three Great Untruths on campus, it's essential to understand how a growing campus bureaucracy has been unintentionally encouraging these bad intellectual habits for years, and how they still do today. This is our fifth explanatory thread.

The Corporatization of College

When the federal Office of Education began collecting data in 1869, there were only 63,000 students enrolled in higher education institutions throughout the United States; they represented just 1 percent of all eighteen- to twenty-four-year-olds.[5] Today, an estimated 20 million students are enrolled in American higher education, including roughly 40% of all eighteen- to twenty-four-year-olds.[6] In the 2015–2016 school year, the most recent year for which statistics are available, combined revenues at U.S. postsecondary institutions totaled about $548 billion.[7] (A country with that GDP, to give a sense of scale, would rank twenty-first, between Argentina and Saudi Arabia.)[8] At the end of the 2015 fiscal year, the U.S. universities with the 120 largest endowments held a total of $547 billion.[9] U.S. elite institutions draw substantial international enrollment,[10] and seventeen of the top twenty-five universities in the world are in the United States.[11] The enormous expansion of scope, scale, and wealth demands professionalization, specialization, and a lot of support staff.

In 1963, Clark Kerr, the president of the University of California system, called the resulting structure the "multiversity." In a multiversity, different departments and power structures within a university pursue different goals in parallel—for example, research, education, fundraising, branding, and legal compliance.[12] Kerr predicted that as faculty increasingly focused on their own departments, noninstructional employees would take over in leading the institution. As he anticipated, the number of administrators has climbed upward.[13] At the same time, their responsibilities have crept outward.[14]

Some administrative growth is necessary and sensible, but when the rate of that expansion is several times higher than the rate of faculty hiring,[15] there are significant downsides, most obviously the increase in the cost of a college degree.[16] A less immediately obvious downside is that goals other than academic excellence begin to take priority as universities come to resemble large corporations—a trend often bemoaned as "corporatization."[17] Political scientist Benjamin Ginsberg, author of the 2011 book *The Fall of the Faculty: The Rise of the All-Administrative University and Why It Matters*, argues that over the decades, as the administration has grown, the faculty, who used to play a major role in university governance, have ceded much of that power to nonfaculty administrators.[18] He notes that once the class of administrative specialists was established and became more distinct from the professor class, it was virtually certain to expand; administrators are more likely than professors to think that the way to solve a new campus problem is to create a new office to address the problem.[19] (Meanwhile, professors have generally been happy to be released from administrative duties, even as they complain about corporatization.)

The Customer Is Always Right

A hallmark of the campus protests that began in 2015 was irresolute and accommodating responses by university leadership. Few schools imposed any kind of penalty on students for shouting down speakers or disrupting classes, even though these actions usually violated their own codes of conduct. Like George Bridges at Evergreen, many university presidents accepted ultimatums from students and then tried to meet many of the demands, usually without a word of criticism of the students' tactics.[20] Critics of this approach have pointed out that this is the way organizations respond when their governing ethos is one of "customer service."

Eric Adler, a classics professor at the University of Maryland, distilled the argument in a 2018 *Washington Post* article. "The fundamental cause [of campus intolerance]," he suggests, "isn't students' extreme leftism or any other political ideology" but "a market-driven decision by universities, made decades ago, to treat students as consumers—who pay up to $60,000 per year for courses, excellent cuisine, comfortable accommodations and a lively campus life." On the subject of students preventing certain people from speaking on campus, he explains:

Even at public universities, 18-year-olds are purchasing what is essentially a luxury product. Is it any wonder they feel entitled to control the experience? . . . Students, accustomed to authoring every facet of their college experience, now want their institutions to mirror their views. If the customers can determine the curriculum and select all their desired amenities, it stands to reason that they should also determine which speakers ought to be invited to campus and what opinions can be articulated in their midst. For today's students, one might say, speakers *are* amenities.[21]

The consumerization theory fits with the trend toward greater spending on lifestyle amenities, which schools use when they compete with other schools to attract top students. From 2003 to 2013, public research universities increased spending on student services by 22.3%, which was far more than the increases for research (9.5%) or instruction (9.4%).[22] Many campuses have become less like scholarly monasteries and more like luxurious "country clubs."[23] The trend is exemplified by Louisiana State University's 536-foot-long "lazy river," paid for with $85 million in student fees. The slow-moving current gently pushes floating students through a winding pool in the shape of the school's initials, LSU.[24] At the ribbon cutting for the lazy river, LSU's president explained how his vision of education combines consumerism and safetyism: "Quite frankly, I don't want you to leave the campus ever. So whatever we need to do to keep you here, we'll keep you safe here. We're here to give you everything you need."[25]

How Campus Administrators Model Distorted Thinking

The shift toward seeing students as consumers explains a lot, but it cannot explain what happened at Northern Michigan University, or what administrators are thinking when they restrict the speech of their "customers." To comprehend those events, we need to understand other forces acting on administrators, including the fear of bad publicity and threats of litigation. Administrators are bombarded with directives (from in-house counsel, outside risk-management professionals, the school's public relations team, and the upper echelons of the administration) that they must limit the university's legal liability in everything from personal injury lawsuits to wrongful termination, and from intellectual property to wrongful-death actions. This is one reason they are so keen to regulate what students do and say.

In the first decade of the twenty-first century, FIRE was the only organization entirely focused on free speech, academic freedom, and due process on college campuses. The lack of public attention to free speech on campus during that decade is understandable given that the speech at the center of the debate was often rather unsympathetic—like what one professor said on September 11, 2001, when he joked, "anybody who can blow up the Pentagon has my vote." Eventually he lost his job. From a First Amendment standpoint, however, the cases were clear-cut. The amendment's bedrock principle is that offensiveness alone is no justification for banning or restricting speech—especially on campus.[26]

For most of Greg's career, students were consistently the most tolerant and pro–free speech constituency on campus—even more so than the faculty. Around 2013, however, Greg began to notice a change. More students seemed to be in agreement with administrators that *they were unsafe*, that many aspects of students' lives *needed to be carefully regulated by adults*, and that it was far better to *overreact to potential risks and threats* than to underreact. In this way, campus administrators—usually with the best of intentions—were modeling distorted thinking.[27]

Two categories of First Amendment cases on campus encourage this kind of thinking quite directly: overreaction and overregulation.

OVERREACTION CASES

We define overreaction cases exactly as the name suggests: they are disproportionate responses to perceived offenses. Almost all overreaction cases model the mental habit of catastrophizing, and communicate that disaster would result without the intervention of the administration.[28] Here are two examples:

- *Bergen Community College* (New Jersey, 2014): An art professor was placed on leave without pay and sent to psychological counseling for a social media post. The post showed a photograph of his young daughter wearing a T-shirt that depicted a dragon and the words I WILL TAKE WHAT IS MINE WITH FIRE & BLOOD, which the school claimed was "threatening." The professor explained that the shirt referenced the popular TV series *Game of Thrones*, but an administrator insisted that "fire" could refer to an AK-47.[29]
- *Oakton Community College* (Illinois, 2015): A professor received a cease-and-desist letter from his college based on a one-sentence email he had sent to a few colleagues. His email noted that May Day is a time "when workers across the world celebrate their struggle for union rights and remember the Haymarket riot in Chicago." The college alleged that the reference to the 1886 riot was threatening to the college president, because she was one of the recipients of the email. Why? Because the rally "resulted in 11 deaths and more than 70 people injured."[30] Of course, many major American holidays commemorate events that were far more costly in terms of lives lost. But when a reference is made to Memorial Day, Veterans Day, or even the Fourth of July, nobody assumes it is a threat.

OVERREGULATION CASES

Overregulation is less about policing actual offenses than it is about preventing potential offense. It is like a continuation of overprotective helicopter parenting: administrators tightly regulate students in order to keep them "safe." Speech remains a common target of overregulation, even though there have been more than seventy lawsuits against speech codes since the dawn of "politically correct" speech codes in the late 1980s. Almost all the codes challenged in court have been revised, abandoned, or ruled unconstitutional.

Here are two of the most absurd categories of speech regulation that keep popping up on American college campuses:

1. *Vague and Overbroad Speech Codes:* The code that epitomized the vagueness and breadth of the first wave of modern PC speech codes (roughly, the late 1980s to the mid-1990s) was the University of Connecticut's ban on "inappropriately directed laughter." The school was sued. It dropped the code as part of a settlement in 1990, but the same code, verbatim, was in effect at Drexel University in Philadelphia fifteen years later. That code was eventually repealed after being named one of FIRE's "Speech Codes of the Month."[31] Along similar lines, a speech code at Alabama's Jacksonville State University provided that "no student shall offend anyone on University property," and the University of West Alabama's code prohibited "harsh text messages or emails."[32] These codes teach students to use an overbroad and entirely subjective standard for determining wrongdoing. They also exemplify the Untruth of Emotional Reasoning: *Always trust your feelings.* If you feel offended, then a punishable offense must have occurred. Speech codes like these teach the Untruth of Fragility as well. They communicate that offensive speech or inappropriate laughter might be so damaging that administrators must step in to protect vulnerable and fragile students. And they empower college administrators to ensure that authority figures are always available to "resolve" verbal conflicts.

2. *Free Speech Zones:* Universities never seem to tire of creating "free speech zones," which restrict certain kinds of speech and expression to tiny and often remote parts of campus. FSZs seem to have first appeared in the 1960s and '70s as honored places where students

could always engage in free speech, like Speakers' Corner in London's Hyde Park. But in the 1990s, many campuses made them the *only* places students could engage in free speech on campus. Some FSZs were revised after coming under public scrutiny and criticism, such as at McNeese State University in Louisiana, where student groups' use of FSZs were limited to once per semester.[33] Some have been struck down by courts, such as the University of Cincinnati's FSZ, which covered 0.1% of campus and required speakers to register ten business days in advance.[34] And yet schools continue to maintain them.

If you look at a college student handbook today, you'll find policies affecting many other aspects of students' lives, including what they can post on social media, what they can say in the dormitories to one another, and what they can do off campus—including what organizations they can join.[35]

Overreaction and overregulation are usually the work of people within bureaucratic structures who have developed a mindset commonly known as CYA (Cover Your Ass). They know they can be held responsible for any problem that arises on their watch, especially if they took no action to prevent it, so they often adopt a defensive stance. In their minds, overreacting is better than underreacting, overregulating is better than underregulating, and caution is better than courage. This attitude reinforces the safetyism mindset that many students learn in childhood.

See Something, Say Something

It certainly did not help that today's college students were raised in the fearful years after the attacks of September 11, 2001. Ever since that awful day, the U.S. government has been telling us: "If you see something, say something." Even adults are told to follow their most anxious feelings, as you can see in Figure 10.1. It's a video sign at a New Jersey train station. New Jersey Transit urges its passengers to embrace the Untruth of Emotional Reasoning: *Always trust your feelings.* "If it doesn't feel right, it probably isn't," says the sign. But that can't really be true. In all likelihood, there are millions of moments each year when some American somewhere thinks that something "doesn't feel right" and worries about an attack. However, there are only a few terrorist attacks of any kind each year in the United States,[36] so in almost every case, the feeling is wrong. Of course, passengers on New Jersey Transit should alert someone if they see an abandoned backpack or suitcase, but that doesn't mean that their feelings are "probably" right.

FIGURE 10.1. *Video sign in the train station at Secaucus Junction, New Jersey. (Photo by Lenore Skenazy.)*

Young people have come to believe that danger lurks everywhere, even in the classroom, and even in private conversations. Everyone must be vigilant and report threats to the authorities. At New York University in 2016, for example, administrators placed signs in the restrooms urging everyone to take a "feel-something say-something" approach to speech. The signs outline for members of the NYU community how to report one another anonymously if they experience "bias, discrimination, or harassment," including by calling a "Bias Response Line."[37] NYU is not an outlier; a 2017 report by FIRE found that, of the 471 institutions cataloged in FIRE's Spotlight on Speech Codes database, 38.4% (181) maintain some form of bias reporting system.[38]

Of course, there should be an easy way to report cases of true harassment and employment discrimination; such actions are immoral and unlawful. But bias *alone* is not harassment or discrimination. The term is not defined on the NYU Bias Response website, but psychological experiments have consistently shown that to be human is to have biases. We are biased toward ourselves and our ingroups, toward attractive people, toward people who have done us favors, and even toward people who share our name or birthday.[39] Presumably the administrators running the Bias Response Line are most interested in negative biases based on identity categories, such as race, gender, and sexual orientation. But given the high levels of concept creep on university campuses and the widespread idea that microaggressions are ubiquitous and dangerous, there are sure to be some students who have a very low threshold for detecting bias in others and attributing ambiguous statements to prejudice.

It becomes more difficult to develop a sense of trust between professors and students in such an environment. The Bias Response Line allows students to report a professor for something said or shown even before the lecture has ended. Many professors now say that they are "teaching on tenterhooks" or "walking on eggshells,"[40] which means that fewer of them are willing to try anything provocative in the classroom—or cover important but difficult course material. For example, writing about her experience teaching sexual assault law, Professor Jeannie Suk Gersen of Harvard Law School observed in *The New Yorker* that "asking students to challenge each other in discussions of rape law has become so difficult that teachers are starting to give up on the subject. . . . If the topic of sexual assault were to leave the law-school classroom, it would be a tremendous loss—above all to victims of sexual assault."[41]

To show just one example of how bias response systems discourage risk-taking: University of Northern Colorado adjunct professor Mike Jensen was called to multiple meetings after a single student filed a "Bias Incident Report" following a discussion of controversial topics in a first-year writing class.[42] The first reading assigned in the class was our *Atlantic* article, "The Coddling of the American Mind." The professor asked the class to read the article and then engage in a discussion of a controversial topic, to be chosen by the class. The topic that the students chose was transgender issues. (One of the biggest stories that semester had been the revelation of

Caitlyn Jenner's identity as a trans woman.) Jensen suggested that students read an article about parents objecting to a transgender high school student using the girls' locker room. He explained that although most of the students might not agree with these skeptical views, in academia, grappling with difficult and controversial perspectives is expected, so it was important that even these viewpoints be discussed. Jensen later recalled the conversation as "a very nice discussion of seeing other perspectives."[43] He was surprised when he learned that a student had filed a Bias Incident Report against him.[44] He was advised to avoid the topic of transgender issues for the rest of the semester and was ultimately not rehired.[45]

The bureaucratic innovation of "bias response" tools may be well intended,[46] but they can have the unintended negative effect of creating an "us versus them" campus climate that results in hypervigilance and reduced trust. Some professors end up concluding that it isn't worth the risk of having to appear before a bureaucratic panel, so it's better to just eliminate any material from the syllabus or lecture that could lead to a complaint. Then, as more and more professors shy away from potentially provocative materials and discussion topics, their students miss out on opportunities to develop intellectual antifragility. As a result, they may come to find even more material offensive and require even more protection.

Harassment and Concept Creep

Universities have an important moral and legal duty to prevent harassment on campus. What counts as harassment, however, has changed quite a lot in recent years. Modern conceptions of discriminatory harassment have their origins in Titles VI and VII of the Civil Rights Act of 1964. Title IX of the Education Amendments of 1972 expanded these statutes, prohibiting colleges that receive federal funds from discriminating against women with respect to educational opportunity. This protection was overdue and includes discrimination via harassment.[47]

Under these statutes, the bar for what counts as harassment is high: a pattern of severe behavior that "effectively denies access to an educational opportunity or benefit."[48] The pattern of behavior must also be discriminatory—that is, directed at someone who belongs to a protected class named in the statute, such as gender, race, or religion.[49] In practice, however, the bar has been lowered; many universities use the concept of harassment to justify punishing one-time utterances that could be construed as offensive but don't really look anything like harassment—and some don't have anything to do with race or gender. For example, in 2005, at the University of Central Florida, a student was charged with harassment through "personal abuse" for creating a Facebook group that called a student government candidate a "Jerk and a Fool."[50] Perhaps you find that wrong or offensive, but should administrators be standing by, ready to step in whenever anyone feels offended?[51] Or consider the case in which a student who worked as a janitor at his college was sanctioned because he was seen reading a book called *Notre Dame vs. the Klan: How the Fighting Irish Defeated the Ku Klux Klan*, a book that celebrates *the defeat* of the Klan when they marched on Notre Dame in the 1920s. (The image on the cover was upsetting to the two people who reported him.)[52] Lowering the bar that far trivializes the real harm that true harassment can do—and frequently does—to students' education.[53] The purpose of these laws is to protect students from unlawful acts, not to empower censors.

Nonetheless, in the 1980s, colleges defended the earliest codes as anti-harassment codes. Courts had no trouble seeing through this kind of explanation and routinely struck down the codes of this era,[54] beginning in 1989 with the University of Michigan's speech code, which prohibited creating a "demeaning" environment through speech that "stigmatizes or victimizes an individual."[55] Yet even after numerous court defeats, universities claimed that the Department of Education required speech codes in order to comply with Title IX and other civil rights laws.[56]

In 2013, the Departments of Education and Justice issued a sweeping new definition of harassment: any "unwelcome conduct of a sexual nature," including "verbal, nonverbal, or physical conduct."[57] This definition was not limited to speech that would be offensive to a reasonable person, nor did it require that the alleged target actually be offended—both requirements of traditional harassment claims. By eliminating the reasonable-person standard, harassment was left to be defined by the self-reported subjective experience of every member of the university community. It was, in effect, emotional reasoning turned into a federal regulation.

The best example of how Title IX's expanded notions of harassment have come to threaten free speech and academic freedom comes from the case of Northwestern University professor Laura Kipnis. In a May 2015 *Chronicle of Higher Education* essay, Kipnis criticized what she saw as "sexual paranoia" on her campus, arising from changing attitudes toward sex, and new ideas in feminism that she found disempowering. She wrote:

> The feminism I identified with as a student stressed independence and resilience. In the intervening years, the climate of sanctimony about student vulnerability has grown too thick to penetrate; no one dares question it lest you're labeled antifeminist.[58]

Kipnis's essay criticized Northwestern's sexual misconduct policies—in particular, the prohibition on romantic relationships between adult students and faculty or staff. She also mentioned a graduate student's Title IX complaint against a professor. After her article was published, Kipnis was the target of protests from student activists, who carried mattresses across campus and demanded that the administration condemn the article. Then two graduate students filed a Title IX complaint against Kipnis, claiming that her article created a hostile environment. This resulted in a secret Title IX investigation of Kipnis that lasted seventy-two days.[59] (It ended after she published another article in the *Chronicle*, titled "My Title IX Inquisition.") When she wrote a book about her experience, she was subjected to yet *another* Title IX investigation, this time stemming from complaints by four Northwestern faculty members and six graduate students, who claimed that her book's discussion of both Title IX and false sexual misconduct accusations violated the university's policies on retaliation and sexual harassment.[60] This second investigation lasted a month. She was asked to respond to more than eighty written questions about her book and to turn over her source material.[61] While both of these investigations were eventually dropped, from beginning to end, the process took more than two years.[62]

Kipnis noted after her ordeal:

My sense was that all of these protections were not making people less vulnerable, they were making people more vulnerable. . . . [Students are] going to be impeded when they leave university and go out into the world, and nobody is going to protect them from the multitudes of injuries and slights and that kind of thing that we all have to deal with in the course of daily life.[63]

How to Foster Moral Dependency

In a prescient essay in 2014, two sociologists—Bradley Campbell and Jason Manning—explained where this new culture of vulnerability came from and how administrative actions helped it to grow.[64] They called it "victimhood culture," and they interpreted it as a new moral order that was in conflict with the older "dignity culture," which is still dominant in most parts of the United States and other Western democracies.

In an optimally functioning dignity culture, people are assumed to have dignity and worth regardless of what others think of them, so they are not expected to react too strongly to minor slights. Of course, full dignity was at one time accorded only to adult, white men; the rights revolutions of the twentieth and twenty-first centuries did essential work to expand dignity to all. This is in contrast to the older "honor cultures," in which men were so obsessed with guarding their reputations that they were expected to react violently to minor insults made against them or those close to them—perhaps with a challenge to a duel. In a dignity culture, however, dueling seems ridiculous. People are expected to have enough self-control to shrug off irritations, slights, and minor conflicts as they pursue their own projects. For larger conflicts or violations of one's rights, there are reliable legal or administrative remedies, but it would be undignified to call for such help for small matters, which one should be able to resolve on one's own. Perspective is a key element of a dignity culture; people don't view disagreements, unintentional slights, or even direct insults as threats to their dignity that must always be met with a response.

For example, one clear sign of a dignity culture is that children learn some version of "Sticks and stones will break my bones, but words will never harm me." That childhood saying is of course not literally true—people feel real pain as a result of words. (If no one felt hurt by words, the saying would never be needed.) But "sticks and stones" is a shield that children in a dignity culture use to dismiss an insult with contemptuous indifference, as if to say, "Go ahead and insult me. You cannot upset me. I really don't care what you think."

In 2013, Campbell and Manning began noticing the same changes on campus that Greg had been noticing—the interlocking set of new ideas about microaggressions, trigger warnings, and safe spaces. They noted that the emerging morality of victimhood culture was radically different from dignity culture. They defined a victimhood culture as having three distinct attributes: First, "individuals and groups display high sensitivity to slight"; second, they "have a tendency to handle conflicts through complaints to third parties"; and third, they "seek to cultivate an image of being victims who deserve assistance."[65]

Of special relevance to our concerns in this chapter is the second attribute. Campbell and Manning pointed out that the presence of administrators or legal authorities who can be persuaded to take one's side and intervene is a prerequisite for the emergence of victimhood culture. They noted that when administrative remedies are easily available and there is no shame in calling on them, it can lead to a condition known as "moral dependence." People come to rely on external authorities to resolve their problems, and, over time, "their willingness or ability to use other forms of conflict management may atrophy."[66]

This is the concern that Kipnis voiced when she said that overprotective policies make students more vulnerable instead of less, and that schools are creating a culture of vulnerability. This is the concern that Erika Christakis expressed when she wrote that "the growing tendency to cultivate vulnerability in students carries unacknowledged costs," and asked students to *talk to each other* rather than relying on administrative interventions.⁶⁷ And it's the same concern about overprotection that prompted Lenore Skenazy to start the Free-Range Kids movement.

It is also the concern that Steven Horwitz raised (and we discussed at the end of chapter 9) about oversupervision impeding the development of the art of association. A university that encourages moral dependence is a university that is likely to experience chronic conflict, which may then lead to more demands for administrative remedies and protections, which may then lead to more moral dependence.

In Sum

- The growth of campus bureaucracy and the expansion of its protective mission is our fifth explanatory thread.
- Administrators generally have good intentions; they are trying to protect the university and its students. But good intentions can sometimes lead to policies that are bad for students. At Northern Michigan University, a policy that we assume was designed to protect the university from liability led to inhumane treatment of students seeking therapy.
- In response to a variety of factors, including federal mandates and the risk of lawsuits, the number of campus administrators has grown more rapidly than the number of professors, and professors have gradually come to play a smaller role in the administration of universities. The result has been a trend toward "corporatization."
- At the same time, market pressures, along with an increasingly consumerist mentality about higher education, have encouraged universities to compete on the basis of the amenities they offer, leading them to think of students as customers whom they must please.
- Campus administrators must juggle many responsibilities and protect the university from many kinds of liabilities, so they tend to adopt a "better safe than sorry" (or "CYA") approach to issuing new regulations. The proliferation of regulations over time conveys a sense of

imminent danger even when there is little or no real threat. In this way, administrators model multiple cognitive distortions, promote the Untruth of Fragility, and contribute to the culture of safetyism.

• Some of the regulations promulgated by administrators restrict freedom of speech, often with highly subjective definitions of key concepts. These rules contribute to an attitude on campus that chills speech, in part by suggesting that freedom of speech can or should be restricted because of some students' emotional discomfort. This teaches catastrophizing and mind reading (among other cognitive distortions) and promotes the Untruth of Emotional Reasoning.

• One recent administrative innovation is the creation of "Bias Response Lines" and "Bias Response Teams," which make it easy for members of a campus community to report one another anonymously for "bias." This "feel something, say something" approach is likely to erode trust within a community. It may also make professors less willing to try innovative or provocative teaching methods; they, too, may develop a CYA approach.

• More generally, efforts to protect students by creating bureaucratic means of resolving problems and conflicts can have the unintended consequence of fostering moral dependence, which may reduce students' ability to resolve conflicts independently both during and after college.

CHAPTER 11

The Quest for Justice

Justice is the first virtue of social institutions, as truth is of systems of thought.

JOHN RAWLS, *A Theory of Justice*[1]

Here's a quirk about American politics: the majority of white Americans vote for Republicans for president, unless they were born after 1981 or between 1950 and 1954. Why those who were born after 1981 vote differently is easy to understand. They are Millennials or iGen; they lean left on most social issues and many economic ones (as Bernie Sanders discovered). They are less religious than previous generations, and the Republican Party turns them off in a variety of ways. But what's the story for those born from 1950 to 1954? They strongly favored Democrats through the 1980s and have been roughly evenly divided since then, with a slight lean overall toward the Democrats. (You can see this for yourself, and play with one of the best interactive political infographics ever, by searching the internet for "How Birth Year Influences Political Views."[2])

Why is there a little demographic island of Democrats among white Americans born in the early 1950s? Why do they vote differently in the twenty-first century than their siblings who were born a few years before or after them in the middle of the twentieth century?

The answer might be 1968. Or, rather, the period of emotionally intense national political events of 1968 and the years around it (roughly 1965–1972).[3] The political scientists Yair Ghitza and Andrew Gelman examined voting patterns of Americans to see whether political events or the political climate in childhood left some kind of mark on people's later political orientation.[4] They found that there is a window of higher impressionability running from about age fourteen to twenty-four, with its peak right around age eighteen. Political events—or perhaps the overall zeitgeist as people perceive it—are more likely to "stick" during that period than outside that age range.

For Americans born in the early 1950s, all you have to do to evoke visceral flashbacks to 1968 is say things like: MLK, RFK, Black Panthers, Tet offensive, My Lai, Chicago Democratic National Convention, Richard Nixon. If those words don't flood you with feelings, then do an internet search for "Chuck Braverman 1968." The five-minute video montage[5] will leave you speechless. Just imagine what it must have been like to be a young adult developing a political identity, perhaps newly arrived on a college campus, as momentous moral struggles, tragedies, and victories happened all around you.

We are in another such era today, and if Ghitza and Gelman are correct, then the events and the political climate of the last few years may influence the way today's college students vote for the rest of their lives. Suppose you were born in 1995, the first year of iGen. You entered your politically most impressionable period when you turned fourteen, in 2009, just as Barack Obama was being sworn in. You got your first iPhone a year or two later as smartphones became common among teenagers. If you went to college, you probably arrived on campus in 2013, the year you turned eighteen. What were the political events that you and your new friends were talking about, posting about, and protesting about? What were the issues on which you had to stake out your position with your tweets, posts, and "likes"? The government shutdown of October 2013? The long rise of the stock market?

Not likely. The interests and activism of teens have far more to do with social issues and injustices than with purely economic or political concerns, and the 2010s have been extraordinarily rich in such issues. The table below shows a small sampling of the major news stories related to what is commonly known as "social justice" in each year since the first members of iGen turned fourteen. In 2009 and 2010, some of the largest news stories in the United States were the ongoing financial crisis, health care reform, and the rise of the Tea Party. You can see that high-profile social justice stories become more numerous in subsequent years, just as the first members of iGen were preparing to go off to college.

YEAR	MAJOR NEWS STORIES RELATED TO SOCIAL JUSTICE
2009	Inauguration of Barack Obama
2010	Tyler Clementi suicide (raises awareness of bullying of LGBT youth)
2011	Occupy Wall Street (raises awareness of income inequality)
2012	Killing of Trayvon Martin; reelection of Barack Obama; Sandy Hook elementary school massacre (raises interest in gun control)
2013	George Zimmerman acquitted of murder in the death of Trayvon Martin; Black Lives Matter founded
2014	Police killing of Michael Brown in Ferguson, Missouri; police killing of Eric Garner in New York City (with video); Black Lives Matter protests spread across America; lead in drinking water in Flint, Michigan, raises awareness of "environmental justice"
2015	Supreme Court legalizes gay marriage; Caitlyn Jenner publicly identifies as a woman; white supremacist Dylann Roof massacres nine black worshipers in Charleston, South Carolina; Confederate flags removed from state capitol in South Carolina; police killing of Walter Scott (with video); universities erupt in protest over racism, beginning at Missouri and Yale, then spreading to dozens of others
2016	Terrorist Omar Mateen kills forty-nine in attack on gay nightclub in Orlando, Florida; police killing of Alton Sterling (with video); police killing of Philando Castile (with video); killing of five police officers in Dallas; quarterback Colin Kaepernick refuses to stand for national anthem; North Carolina requires transgender people to use bathrooms corresponding to the sex on their birth certificates; protest against Dakota Access Pipeline at Standing Rock Indian Reservation; nomination and election of Donald Trump
2017	Trump inauguration; Trump attempts to enact various "Muslim bans"; women's march in Washington; violent protests against campus speakers at UC Berkeley and Middlebury; Trump bans transgender people from military service; Trump praises "very fine people" in Charlottesville march, during which a neo-Nazi kills Heather Heyer and injures others by driving a car into a crowd; fifty-eight killed in largest mass shooting in U.S. history in Las Vegas; start of the #MeToo movement, to expose and stop sexual harassment and assault
2018 (through March)	Nikolas Cruz, expelled student with history of emotional and behavioral disorders, kills seventeen at high school in Parkland, Florida; students organize school walkouts and marches for gun control across the United States

Important, terrifying, thrilling, and shocking events happen every year, but the years from 2012 through 2018 seem like the closest we've come to the intensity of the stretch from 1968 to 1972. And if you are not convinced that the last few years are extraordinary by objective measures, then just add in the amplifying power of social media. Not since the Vietnam War and the civil rights struggles of the 1960s have so many Americans been exposed to a seemingly endless stream of videos showing innocent people— mostly people of color—being beaten, killed, or deported by armed representatives of the state. Today's college students have lived through extraordinary times, and, as a result, many of them have developed an extraordinary passion for social justice. That passion, which drives some of the changes we are seeing on college campuses in recent years, is our sixth explanatory thread.

This chapter is about social justice. We will explore the meaning of this term and embrace one version of it while criticizing another. The term is a lightning rod in the left-right culture war, so this is a good time for us to lay our cards on the table, politically speaking: Greg identifies as a liberal with some sympathy for libertarian perspectives. Before FIRE, he worked for an environmental justice group; he worked for an organization that advocates for refugee rights and protections in Central Europe; and he interned at the ACLU of Northern California. Jon considers himself a centrist who sides with the Democratic Party on the great majority of issues, but who has learned a lot from the writings of conservative intellectuals, from Edmund Burke through Thomas Sowell. Neither of us has ever voted for a Republican for Congress or the presidency. Both of us share most of the desired ends of social justice activism, including full racial equality, an end to sexual harassment and assault, comprehensive gun control, and responsible stewardship of the environment. We both believe that the way social justice is currently being conceptualized and pursued on campus is causing a variety of problems and engendering resistance and resentment for reasons that some of its advocates don't seem to recognize. In this chapter, we describe some of these conceptualizations. We also suggest a way to think about social justice that makes it more likely to be achieved and that harmonizes it with the traditional purpose of the university: the pursuit of truth.

What exactly is "social justice"? There is no widely shared definition. We'll try to draw out its meaning by starting with "justice" and then showing in what ways "social justice" differs, conceptually, and in what ways it is the same.

Intuitive Justice

Justice is arguably the most important moral concept in the history of Western philosophy. From Plato's *Republic* through John Rawls's *A Theory of Justice*, philosophers have tried to propose rules and principles that would underlie a fair or "just" society. Rather than review that history here in order to derive a philosophical definition of justice, we'll take a shortcut and tell you about two major areas of psychological research that, when combined, give us a working definition of people's everyday, ordinary, or "intuitive" notions of justice. Intuitive justice is the combination of *distributive justice* (the perception that people are getting what is deserved) and *procedural justice* (the perception that the process by which things are distributed and rules are enforced is fair and trustworthy). We'll show where claims about social justice fit well with intuitive justice and where they don't.

DISTRIBUTIVE JUSTICE

Sharing plays a big role in the moral lives of children, and they get a lot of practice dividing things equally. If there are four kids and twelve jelly beans, each kid should get three. Obviously. But what do kids do when the jelly beans are a reward for cleaning up the classroom, and one kid did most of the work while another kid did nothing? Even toddlers seem to recognize the importance of *proportionality*. In one experiment, two-year-olds showed signs of being surprised when two people were rewarded equally if only one of them did any work.[6] By the age of six, kids show a clear preference for rewarding the hard worker in a group, even if equal pay is an option.[7] At young ages, kids have trouble following this intuition when it means that they themselves get less reward, but by adolescence, they are much better at applying proportionality to themselves.[8] Developmental psychologists Christina Starmans, Mark Sheskin, and Paul Bloom reviewed the research on fairness in children and concluded that "humans naturally favour fair distributions, not equal ones," and "when fairness and equality clash, people prefer fair inequality over unfair equality."[9]

To be clear, sometimes distributive justice calls for equality. For example, Americans seem to have a common intuition that money inherited from a deceased parent should be divided equally among siblings, rather than trying to assess who did more for the parent or who needs the money more. And sometimes distributive justice calls for inequality; for example, when attending to need, particularly within a family or group that has some communal feeling and that thinks it fair and proper to route resources to whoever needs them most. But as the review by Starmans, Sheskin, and Bloom indicates, proportionality or merit is the most common and preferred principle children and adults use for allocating rewards outside a family.

Proportionality is the heart of "equity theory," the major theory of distributive justice in social psychology.[10] Its core assertion is that when the ratio of outcomes to inputs is equal for all participants, people perceive that to be equitable, or fair.[11] We can illustrate the theory with a simple equation, shown in Figure 11.1.

$$\frac{\text{Your outcomes}}{\text{Your inputs}} = \frac{\text{Mary's outcomes}}{\text{Mary's inputs}} = \frac{\text{Bob's outcomes}}{\text{Bob's inputs}} = \ldots$$

FIGURE 11.1. *Equity Theory. People keep close track of the ratio of everyone's outcomes to their inputs. When the ratios are equal, people perceive that things are fair.*

The consistent finding in equity theory research is that in most relationships, people keep close track of how much reward each person is reaping (their outcomes, such as pay and perks) in proportion to how much they are contributing (their inputs, such as hours worked and the skills or credentials they bring). They do this more in work relationships and less in intimate relationships, but even in marriages, people are not oblivious to these ratios, and because of the power of self-serving biases, they often have a sense that they are doing more than their "fair share" of some or all tasks.[12] When everyone perceives that all the proportions are equal, then everyone perceives that things are fair, and harmony is far more likely. When people believe that someone else's ratio is too high, they are likely to feel resentful toward that person, whose rewards are disproportionate to their contributions. They may also feel resentment toward the boss, company, or system that allows such inequities to persist. People are not just being greedy. An early study testing equity theory found that when people were led to believe that they were being *overpaid* for a job, they worked harder in order to deserve the pay—to get their ratio back into line.[13]

PROCEDURAL JUSTICE

Intuitive justice is not just about *how much* each person gets. It's also about the *process by which* decisions about distributions (and other matters) are made. The social psychologist Tom Tyler is one of the pioneers of research on "procedural justice."[14] His central finding is that people are much more willing to accept a decision or action, even one that goes against themselves, when they perceive that the process that led to the decision was fair.

There are two basic concerns that people bring to their judgments of procedural justice. The first is *how the decision is being made*. This includes whether the decision-makers are doing their best to be objective and neutral and are therefore trustworthy, or whether they have conflicts of interest, prejudices, or other factors that lead them to be biased in favor of a particular person or outcome. It also includes transparency—is it clear to all how the process works? The second basic concern is *how a person is being treated* along the way, which means primarily: Are people being treated with dignity, and do they have a voice—do they get to fully state their case, and are they taken seriously when they do?

Tyler's findings are especially important for understanding how people respond to the police. When people perceive that the police are following fair procedures and treating them and people like them with dignity, they are much more willing to support the police, help them to fight crime, and even accept occasionally being stopped and frisked by the police, whom they see as working to keep their neighborhood safe. But if people think that the way the police select people to frisk is racially biased and that people like them are treated disrespectfully, with hostility, or, even worse, with violence, they will understandably be angry and will see the police as the enemy. In a study published in 2002, Tyler and psychologist Yuen Huo found that white and nonwhite residents of two California cities had similar ideas about what procedural justice entails, but their experiences gave them very different perceptions of how the police treated people. It was this difference that explained racial differences in attitudes toward the police.[15]

Combining the two forms of justice, we can say this: Intuitive justice involves perceptions of distributive justice (as given by equity theory) *and* procedural justice. If you want to motivate people to support a new policy or join a movement in the name of justice, you need to activate in them a clear perception, or intuition, that someone didn't get what he or she deserved (distributive injustice) or that someone was a victim of an unfair process (procedural injustice). If you can't elicit at least one of those feelings, then people are much more likely to be content with the status quo, even if it is one in which some people or groups end up with more resources or more status than others.[16]

Proportional-Procedural Social Justice

Some conservatives and libertarians have argued that "social justice" is a useless term—there is only *justice*, and tacking on the word "social" adds nothing.[17] We don't agree. We think there are two forms of social justice identifiable in modern political debates across the Western world, one of which is a subset of intuitive justice and one of which is not.

Here's a definition of social justice that accords with intuitive notions of justice, from the National Association of Social Workers: "Social justice is the view that everyone deserves equal economic, political and social rights and opportunities. Social workers aim to open the doors of access and opportunity for everyone, particularly those in greatest need."[18] Most Americans would agree that everyone should have equal *rights* and *opportunities* and that *doors should be open* for everyone.[19] Much of the left-right divide on social policy involves how far the *government* should go to equalize opportunity for children who are born into unequal circumstances (and whether it is the federal government, state governments, or local governments that should be responsible for that equalization).

Using that definition of social justice, we'll define *proportional-procedural social justice* as *the effort to find and fix cases where distributive or procedural justice is denied to people because they were born into poverty or belong to a socially disadvantaged category*. Some of these cases are extremely obvious. The Jim Crow laws of the American South before 1965 were shockingly explicit violations of procedural justice: racist police, judges, and legislatures cruelly disregarded the dignity of black Americans and brutally violated their rights. These violations of procedural justice led directly to egregious violations of distributive justice in almost every area of life, including very unequal public expenditures on separate and vastly unequal schools.

The civil rights campaign was a long struggle for proportional-procedural social justice. Not everyone could see the injustice early on, and many white people were motivated to not see it.[20] This is why common-humanity identity politics—which emphasizes an overarching common humanity while calling attention to cases in which people are denied dignity and rights—was ultimately so effective. It did not try to force white Americans to accept a *new* conception of justice; it tried to help white Americans to see that their country was violating *its own* conceptions of justice, which had been so nobly expressed by the Founding Fathers but so imperfectly realized.

In our account, proportional-procedural social justice falls entirely within the larger domain of intuitive justice. That doesn't mean we should discard the term "social justice." Some injustices based on race, gender, or other factors (and their intersections) are obvious, but others are subtle, and people who do not experience them can be unaware of them (as Kimberlé Crenshaw noted).[21] It is useful to have specialists within the domain of justice research who focus on this subset of injustices. Furthermore, when such injustices are pointed out, members of the majority group are often motivated to ignore or deny them.[22] It is among the most important requirements of a democratic society that it provide a way for people and groups to make new claims about justice. An open democratic society considers such claims, debates them, and then acts on claims that combine compelling arguments with effective political pressure. If the outcome is new laws that are supported by widely shared new norms, as happened in the civil rights struggle of the 1960s, that's pretty much the definition of moral and social progress in a democracy.

To take just one example of a subtle injustice: Suppose there's a high school that is composed of 80% white students and 20% black students. The student committee planning the senior prom must decide what songs to play, and at this school, musical tastes tend to vary by race. The committee takes a vote on how to proceed, and the winning plan is to let students nominate a long list of songs, each of which will then be voted on by the entire student body. Democracy is all about voting, right? And the process itself was decided on democratically, so we have procedural fairness, right?

Harvard legal scholar Lani Guinier explored cases like this in her 1994 book, *The Tyranny of the Majority*.[23] She pointed out that seemingly fair processes can sometimes lead to a group that is in the minority getting entirely shut out at the end of the process. In the high school example above, it's quite possible that 100% of the songs chosen would be those nominated by the white students. If that example seems trivial to you, just imagine that you're choosing state legislators instead of songs. Guinier suggested some alternative ways that communities could run elections and divide electoral power, ways that would not exclude or disadvantage minorities.

Guinier's ideas elicited an angry reaction from some politicians on the right, particularly when she suggested methods that would change the basic system of "one person, one vote per seat." She was called a "quota queen" in *The Wall Street Journal*.[24] The controversy surrounding her ideas derailed her nomination to become Bill Clinton's assistant attorney general for civil rights.[25] But the *principle* she was elaborating is sound, even if her preferred methods are open to debate. This principle—the need for democracies to protect the rights of minorities—was one of the reasons that the U.S.

Constitution's first ten amendments (the Bill of Rights) were added so quickly. (You don't need a Bill of Rights to protect the rights of the majority in a democracy, because the vote already does that.)

When social justice is about searching for and ending violations of human or civil rights, particularly when those violations are related to membership in social identity groups, then it is about removing obstacles and creating equality of opportunity. It is exactly what those social workers called for when they defined social justice as the quest to "open the doors of access and opportunity for everyone, particularly those in greatest need." Proportional-procedural social justice is *justice*, and justice is never the enemy of truth. Justice *requires* truth and honesty, and justice is entirely compatible with the purpose, values, and daily life of a university. But what happens when social justice activists focus on a desired end-state and pursue that goal in ways that *violate* either distributive or procedural justice?

Equal-Outcomes Social Justice

When Jon taught at the University of Virginia (UVA), he sometimes hired members of the UVA men's crew team to do yard work for him. Each fall and spring, young men on the team put flyers in all faculty mailboxes, advertising their "rent-a-rower" service. At least, Jon *thought* he was hiring members of the UVA men's crew team. But after talking to the rowers, he learned that there is no such thing as the UVA men's crew team. There is only the Virginia Rowing Association. The men who row for the association are all students at the University of Virginia, but the university does not provide funding for their sport. They must each pay more than a thousand dollars a year to belong to the association, and they are also required to participate in the rent-a-rower program in order to raise money for their boats, coaching staff, travel to races, and other expenses. They share a boathouse on the Rivanna Reservoir with the UVA Women's Rowing Team—for which all expenses, including travel, coaching staff, and snacks at the boathouse, are fully funded by the university.

Why are UVA students who want to row treated so differently based on their gender? Because the implementation of Title IX was changed over the years. From its original goal of providing equal *access* to educational opportunities for women and men, the program morphed into one that pushes universities to obtain equal *outcomes* regardless of inputs.

On its face, Title IX is eminently fair and reasonable. It prohibits colleges that accept federal funds from discriminating against women with respect to "educational opportunity." In 1979, the Carter administration used an equal-opportunity interpretation of Title IX when applying it to college sports: scholarships were to be "available on a substantially proportional basis to the number of male and female participants in the institution's athletic program." Furthermore, "the governing principle in this area is that the athletic interests and abilities of male and female students must be equally effectively accommodated."[26] Outcomes (such as scholarships and slots on teams) had to be proportional to inputs (such as interest in participating). Men and women should find it equally easy to obtain a sports-related scholarship or a slot on a team.

But in 1996, the Clinton administration began to put pressure on schools to achieve equal *outcomes*.[27] The U.S. Department of Education's Office for Civil Rights issued a "Dear Colleague" letter (a general directive regarding Title IX compliance) to all schools receiving federal funding,[28] clarifying how schools could comply with Title IX's relevant obligations.[29] One compliance option was for schools to show that their sports programs (taken all together) mirrored the gender balance of the overall student body. The letter also offered two other ways to comply,[30] but in practice, if schools chose those options, they were in a compliance gray zone that invited monitoring and possible investigation by the Office for Civil Rights, so hardly any schools did. Furthermore, with the press and various organizations watching closely, schools would be judged by their overall numbers anyway.[31] Schools therefore began to strive for equal *outcomes*. Some schools cut men's sports teams as part of their effort to improve their gender balance, sometimes citing Title IX as the reason for the cuts.[32] More commonly, schools added women's teams, which is more consistent with the original spirit of Title IX, but that, too, sometimes created unequal treatment. That's what happened at UVA: before 1994, men's and women's crew had both been club sports—there was no varsity crew program. In its efforts to comply with Title IX, UVA elevated women's crew to a varsity sport, but did not do the same for the men's team.

Of course, if male and female students had equal levels of *interest* in participating in sports, then both versions of social justice would converge on the desired end-state of equal outcomes. Give everyone the same *access* to sports, and your teams will mirror the overall population. Note that "equal outcomes" in these cases doesn't necessarily mean fifty-fifty; it means representative of the overall student body, which is usually mostly female. "Equal outcomes" means that of all the students who participate in sports, the ratio of men to women will be the same as the ratio of men to women in the student body as a whole. More generally, equal-outcomes social justice activists seem to believe that all institutions and occupations should mirror the overall U.S. population: 50% female, roughly 15% African American, 15% Latino, and so on. Any departure from those numbers means that a group is "underrepresented," and underrepresentation is often taken to be direct evidence of systemic bias or injustice.

Yet men and women differ in their interests on many things, including sports. A review of the literature led by psychologist Robert Deaner, of Grand Valley State University (Michigan), finds that boys and men show greater interest in playing sports and watching sports than do girls and women, and this is true across cultures, eras, and age groups, whether one uses interview methods or observations of play behavior.[33] Of course, those differences could just reflect a pervasive cross-cultural tendency to steer girls away from sports and deprive them of opportunities, but if that were true—if girls were being discouraged from doing what they wanted to do—then sex differences would be smaller in informal settings, such as when kids are playing in a park, compared with school settings. But in fact, the opposite is true. The gender difference is relatively small in school—girls constitute about 42% of the athletes on high school teams—but it is much larger when adolescents are observed in public parks or when they are surveyed about how they use their leisure time.[34] The available research suggests that girls and women are often as interested as boys and men in getting physical exercise, but not in playing team sports.[35]

If this is true—if boys and men are more interested, on average, in playing team sports—then universities cannot achieve the equal-outcome target just by offering equal opportunity. They must work harder to recruit women and, perhaps, discourage men. In fact, in order to meet their equal-outcomes targets, many universities are resorting to ethically questionable techniques, known collectively as "roster management," which sometimes border on fraud. As reported in a 2011 *New York Times* exposé,[36] it is very common for schools to pad the rosters of their women's teams with women who never come to practice and sometimes don't even know they are signed up. Some schools invite men to practice with the women and then count the men on the women's team roster. The exposé gives the impression that U.S. universities are sneaky and dishonest institutions, but this is the predictable response of a bureaucracy, as we described in the previous chapter. When the federal government pressures universities to achieve equal outcomes in the face of unequal inputs, administrators do what they can to protect the institution. That might require them to violate procedural justice, distributive justice, and honesty along the way.

You can see the basic problem if you plug the terms into equity theory, as we do in Figure 11.2. At the University of Virginia, men who want to row must contribute much more than women ($1,000 or more per year, plus renting themselves out for labor). Yet their outcomes are less than those received by women (who have a much larger budget). The ratios are far from equal.

Of course, if we look at UVA sports as a whole, the picture looks different. The men's football program is gigantic and costly, and there is no women's football team. The university as a whole is still spending far more money on

$$\frac{\text{Men's outcomes}}{\text{Men's inputs}} \begin{array}{c} < \\ > \end{array} \frac{\text{Women's outcomes}}{\text{Women's inputs}}$$

FIGURE 11.2. *When male rowers must raise their own money, their ratio of outcomes to inputs is much lower than the ratio for female rowers, who are supported by the university.*

men's sports than on women's sports, and if you endorse equal-outcomes so-cial justice, you'll say that the unequal treatment of rowers is necessary in or-der to compensate for the money spent on male athletes elsewhere.

But when you leave campus, that argument is not going to convince many people; it's very hard to make it intuitively compelling by linking it to equity theory or procedural fairness. Most people want *individuals* to be treated well, and they recoil from cases where individuals are treated un-fairly in order to bring about some kind of group-level equality. This is why quotas generally produce such strong backlash: they mandate a violation of procedural justice (people are treated differently based on their race, sex, or some other factor) and distributive justice (rewards are not proportional to inputs) to achieve a specific end-state of equal outcomes.

To be clear: Departures from equality sometimes *do* indicate that some kind of bias or injustice is operating. Some institutions or companies make it harder for members of one group to succeed, as can be seen in recent books and articles about the toxic "bro culture" of Silicon Valley,[37] which violates the dignity and rights of women (procedural injustice) while deny-ing them the status, promotions, and pay that they deserve based on the quality of their work (distributive injustice). When you see a situation in which some groups are underrepresented, it is an invitation to investigate and find out whether there are obstacles, a hostile climate, or systemic fac-tors that have a disparate impact on members of those groups. But how can you know whether unequal outcomes truly reveal a violation of justice?

Correlation Does Not Imply Causation

All social scientists know that correlation does not imply causation. If A and B seem to be linked—that is, they change together over time or are found together in a population at levels higher than chance would predict—then it is certainly possible that A caused B. But it's also possible that B caused A (reverse causation) or that a third variable, C, caused both A and B and there is no direct relationship between A and B. (It's also possible, as we described in chapter 7, that it's a "spurious correlation"—that there is no link between A and B and the correlation is a coincidence.)

For example, a study of 7,500 German households found that people who had sex more than four times a week earned 3.2% more than people who had sex only once a week. Sexual frequency and paycheck are correlated (slightly), but why? What's the causal path? An article about the study that was published at Gawker.com featured this headline: MORE BUCK FOR YOUR BANG: PEOPLE WHO HAVE MORE SEX MAKE THE MOST MONEY.[38] The headline suggested that A (sex) causes B (money), which is surely the best causal path to choose if your goal is to entice people to click on your article. But any social scientist presented with that correlation would instantly wonder about reverse causation (does having more money cause people to have more sex?) and would then move on to a third-variable explanation, which in this case seems to be the correct one.[39] The Gawker story itself noted that people who are more extraverted have more sex and also make more money. In this case, a third variable, C (extraversion, or high sociability) may cause both A (more sex) and B (more money).

Social scientists analyze correlations like this constantly (to the great annoyance of friends and family). They are self-appointed conversation referees, throwing a yellow penalty flag when anyone tries to interpret a correlation as evidence of causation. But a funny thing has been happening in recent years on campus. Nowadays, when someone points to an outcome gap and makes the claim (implicitly or explicitly) that the gap itself is *evidence* of systemic injustice, social scientists often just nod along with everyone else in the room.

An outcome gap is a kind of correlation. But if someone quotes from a study or otherwise asserts that one group is overrepresented in a job category or that there is a gap in pay, often the implication is that being a member of one group *caused* members of that group to be preferentially hired or to be paid more. It would indeed be evidence of improper or illegal discrimination if there were no other reason for the outcome gap aside from group membership. For example, if someone notes that computer programmers at elite tech firms are mostly male, often the implication is that being male *caused* those employees to be more likely to be hired or promoted, which is obviously unjust if there are no other differences between male and female computer programmers.

But are there other differences? Are there other causal pathways? If you suggest an alternative explanation for the gap, others may take you to be saying that the problem is not as severe as the speaker believes it is— and if anyone in the room is displeased by that suggestion, then you may be accused of committing a microaggression (specifically a "micro-invalidation"[40]). If your alternative hypothesis includes the speculation that there could be differences in some underlying factor, some input that is relevant to the outcome (for example, a sex difference in how much men or women enjoy sports or computer programming),[41] then you may be violating a serious taboo.

In an article titled "The Psychology of the Unthinkable," social psychologist Philip Tetlock calls this the use of "forbidden base rates."[42] But if this kind of thinking is forbidden and social scientists don't work as hard to challenge the theories that are politically favored, then "institutionalized disconfirmation," the process of challenging and testing ideas, breaks down. If professors and students are hesitant to raise alternative explanations for outcome gaps, then theories about those gaps may harden into orthodoxy. Ideas may be accepted not because they are true but because the politically dominant group *wants* them to be true in order to promote its preferred narrative and preferred set of remedies.[43] At that point, backed by the passion and certainty of activists, flawed academic theories may get carried out of the academy and be applied in high schools, corporations, and other organizations. Unfortunately, when reformers try to intervene in complex institutions using theories that are based on a flawed or incomplete understanding of the causal forces at work, their reform efforts are unlikely to do any good—and might even make things worse.

* * * * *

College students today are living in an extraordinary time, and many have developed an extraordinary passion for social justice. They are identifying and challenging injustices that have been well documented and unsuccessfully addressed for too long. In the 1960s, students fought for many causes that, from the vantage point of today, were clearly noble causes, including ending the Vietnam War, extending full civil rights to African Americans and others, and protecting the natural environment. Students today are fighting for many causes that we believe are noble, too, including ending racial injustices in the legal system and in encounters with the police; providing equal educational and other opportunities for everyone, regardless of circumstances at birth; and extinguishing cultural habits that encourage or enable sexual harassment and gender inequalities. On these and many other issues, we think student protesters are on the "right side of history," and we support their goals. But if activists embrace the equal-outcomes form of social justice—if they interpret all deviations from population norms as *evidence* of systemic bias—then they will get drawn into endless and counterproductive campaigns, even against people who share their goals. Along the way, they will reinforce the bad mental habits that we have described throughout the book.

Instead, we urge students to treat deviations from population norms as invitations to investigate further. Is the deviation present in the pipeline or applicant pool for the job? If so, then look at the beginning of the pipeline more than at the end of it, and be willing to entertain the possibility that people of different genders and people from different cultures may have different preferences. Focus as much on procedural justice as on distributive: Are people in all identity groups treated with equal dignity? The answer to that question might be no in an organization that has achieved statistical equality, and it might be yes in an organization in which some groups are underrepresented. Be clear about what end states matter and why. As long as activists keep their eyes on the two components of intuitive justice that all of us carry in our minds—distributive and procedural—they will apply their efforts where they are likely to do the most good, and they will win more widespread support along the way.

In Sum

- Political events in the years from 2012 to 2018 have been as emotionally powerful as any since the late 1960s. Today's college students and student protesters are responding to these events with a powerful commitment to social justice activism. This is our sixth and final explanatory thread.

- People's ordinary, everyday, intuitive notions of justice include two major types: distributive justice (the perception that people are getting what is deserved) and procedural justice (the perception that the process by which things are distributed and rules are enforced is fair and trustworthy).

- The most common way that people think about distributive justice is captured by equity theory, which states that things are perceived to be fair when the ratio of outcomes to inputs is equal for all participants.

- Procedural justice is about how decisions are being made, and is also about how people are treated along the way, as procedures unfold.

- Social justice is a central concept in campus life today, and it takes a variety of forms. When social justice efforts are fully consistent with both distributive and procedural justice, we call it *proportional-procedural social justice*. Such efforts generally aim to remove barriers to equality of opportunity and also to ensure that everyone is treated with dignity. But when social justice efforts aim to achieve equality of *outcomes* by group, and when social justice activists are willing to violate distributive or procedural fairness for some individuals along the way, these efforts violate many people's sense of intuitive justice. We call this *equal-outcomes social justice*.

- Correlation does not imply causation. Yet in many discussions in universities these days, the correlation of a demographic trait or identity group membership with an outcome gap is taken as evidence that discrimination (structural or individual) *caused* the outcome gap. Sometimes it did, sometimes it didn't, but if people can't raise alternative possible causal explanations without eliciting negative consequences, then the community is unlikely to arrive at an accurate understanding of the problem. And without understanding the true nature of a problem, there is little chance of solving it.

This concludes Part III of this book. In these six chapters, we showed how the new culture of safetyism that we described in Part I and the dramatic events that we described in Part II are the result of many intersecting trends and explanatory threads that all came together in recent years. These threads reach back into history, down into childhood, and out into national politics. Having offered this explanation of how we got here, we now turn to the question of where to go next.

PART IV

Wising Up

CHAPTER 12

Wiser Kids

Something is going badly wrong for American teenagers, as we can see in the statistics on depression, anxiety, and suicide. Something is going very wrong on many college campuses, as we can see in the growth of call-out culture, in the rise in efforts to disinvite or shout down visiting speakers, and in changing norms about speech,[1] including a recent tendency to evaluate speech in terms of safety and danger. This new culture of safetyism and vindictive protectiveness is bad for students and bad for universities. What can we do to change course?

In the next chapter, we'll offer suggestions for improving universities, but first we must look at childhood. In chapters 8 and 9, we showed that there has been a shift, particularly in middle-class and wealthier families, to more intensive and overprotective parenting, and that this is, in part, a response to unrealistic fears of abduction, and to somewhat more realistic fears about admission to prestigious universities. We showed that the decline of free play may be part of the reason for children's increased fragility. In this chapter, we draw on earlier chapters to offer advice for raising children who are wiser, stronger, and antifragile; children who will thrive as they become more independent in college and beyond.

We are mindful that pathways through childhood vary by nation, decade, social class, and other factors. The suggestions we make here are tailored for American parents who use the "concerted cultivation" style of parenting that we described in chapter 8. That's the style that sociologist Annette Lareau found being used by middle-class parents of all races, and that political scientist Robert Putnam said had become the norm by the 1990s for families in the middle class and above. This time-intensive, labor-intensive strategy involves overprotecting, overscheduling, and overparenting children in hopes of giving them an edge in a competitive society that has forgotten the importance of play and the value of unsupervised experience.

But even though our advice grows out of our analysis of current trends in the United States, we expect that much of it will be relevant to parents and educators in other countries. South Korean parents, for example, are second to none in their fears about college admissions and their willingness to replace nearly all of their children's free play time with expensive and exhausting test preparation classes.[2] To take another example, British schools can hold their own in any competition with Americans to put safety ahead of common sense. Just as we were finishing this book, the head teacher of an elementary school in East London issued a rule that children must not even *touch* recently fallen snow, because touching could lead to *snowballs*. "The problem is it only takes one student, one piece of grit, one stone in a snowball in an eye with an injury and we change our view," he explained.[3] That is the epitome of safetyism: If we can prevent *one* child from getting hurt, we should deprive *all* children of slightly risky play.

We are also mindful that children are "complex adaptive systems," as we described in chapter 1. They are not simple machines. We have shown many examples in this book of well-intended reforms that backfired, beginning with our example of banning peanuts to protect kids from peanut allergies. We therefore offer these suggestions with the caveat that any effort to change one part of children's lives can produce unexpected effects in some other part. More research is needed, but we think these suggestions are likely to be helpful. We hope to start a conversation among parents, educators, and researchers, and we'll track that conversation on our website, TheCoddling.com.

We organize our advice under six general principles. The first three are the opposites of the Great Untruths.

1. Prepare the Child for the Road, Not the Road for the Child

The first of the three epigraphs that we used at the beginning of this book summarizes the book's most important single piece of advice: *Prepare the child for the road, not the road for the child.* That is eternally good advice, but it became even better once the internet came along and part of the road became virtual. It was foolish to think one could clear the road for one's child before the internet. Now it is delusional. To return to the example of peanut allergies: kids need to develop a normal immune response, rather than an allergic response, to the everyday irritations and provocations of life, including life on the internet.

You cannot teach antifragility directly, but you can give your children the gift of experience—the thousands of experiences they need to become resilient, autonomous adults. The gift begins with the recognition that kids need some unstructured, unsupervised time in order to learn how to judge risks for themselves and practice dealing with things like frustration, boredom, and interpersonal conflict. The most important thing they can do with that time is to play, especially in free play, outdoors, with other kids. In some situations, there may need to be an adult nearby for children's physical safety, but that adult should not intervene in general disputes and arguments.[4]

In that spirit, here are some specific suggestions for parents, teachers, and all who care for children:

A. *Assume that your kids are more capable this month than they were last month.* Each month, ask them what tasks or challenges they think they can do on their own—such as walking to a store a few blocks away, making their own breakfast, or starting a dog-walking business. Resist the urge to jump in and help them when they're struggling to do things and seem to be doing them the wrong way. Trial and error is a slower but usually better teacher than direct instruction.

B. *Let your kids take more small risks,* and let them learn from getting some bumps and bruises. Children need opportunities to "dose themselves" with risk, as Peter Gray noted. Jon's kids love the "junkyard playground"[5] on Governor's Island, in New York City. It lets children play with construction materials, including scrap lumber, hammers, and nails (after the parents sign a long liability waiver). On their first visit, Jon watched from outside the fence as two ten-year-old boys pounded nails into lumber. One of the boys accidentally hit his thumb with the hammer. The boy winced, shook his hand out, and went right back to pounding nails. This happened twice and did not deter the boy. He learned how to hammer nails.

C. *Learn about Lenore Skenazy's Free-Range Kids movement, and incorporate her lessons into your family's life.* Remember the first-grade readiness checklist from 1979 that asked whether your six-year-old can "travel alone in the neighborhood (four to eight blocks) to store, school, playground, or to a friend's home?" Start letting your kids walk places and play outside as soon as you think they are able. Send them out with siblings or friends. Tell them it's OK to talk to strangers and ask for help or directions, just never go off with a stranger. Remember that the crime rate is back down to where it was in the early 1960s.

D. *Visit LetGrow.org,* the website for an organization that Skenazy co-founded with Jon, Peter Gray, and investor/philanthropist Daniel Shuchman.[6] The site will keep you up to date on research, news, and ideas for giving your kids a childhood that will lead to resilience. One of our simplest ideas: Print out a "Let Grow License" like the one below,[7] then send your kids out into your neighborhood with less fear that they will be detained by busybodies who might call 911.[8] Learn what the laws in your state require by typing "state laws" into the site's search box.

I AM A "LET GROW" KID!

Hi! My name is _____:
I am not lost or neglected. I have been taught how to cross the street.
I know never to go off with strangers . . . but I can talk to them. (Including you!) The state allows parents to decide at what age their child can do some things independently. Mine believe it is safe, healthy and fun for me to explore my neighborhood. If you do not believe me, please call or text them at the numbers below. If you still think it is inappropriate or illegal for me to be on my own, please:

1) Read *Adventures of Huckleberry Finn*
2) Remember your own childhood! Were you under adult supervision at every moment? Today's crime rate is back to what it was in 1963, so it's safer to play outside NOW than when you were my age.
3) Visit the website LetGrow.org.

Parent's Name _____

Parent's Signature _____

Parent's Phone _____

Alternate Phone _____

E. *Encourage your children to walk or ride bicycles to and from school* at the earliest ages possible, consistent with local circumstances of distance, traffic, and crime. Ask your school to provide a way for kids to check in and check out, so parents can keep track of children who travel to school independently without having to give them a smartphone to track them directly.

F. *Help your kids find a community of kids in the neighborhood* who come from families that share your commitment to avoid overprotection. Find ways for kids to get together in nearby parks or in specific backyards. You'll need to work out boundaries and guidelines with other parents to be sure that the kids are safe from major physical risks, that they know to stick together and help one another, and that they know what to do when someone gets hurt. Kids are likely to develop more maturity and resilience in such groups than in supervised playdates or adult-organized activities.

G. *Send your children to an overnight summer camp in the woods* for a few weeks—without devices. "The old-fashioned generalist camps are where we see the most impact in terms of letting children develop their own interests," Erika Christakis says, "where kids can make choices about what they do and don't do."[9] YMCA overnight summer camps often fit this description, but even some narrower, interest-driven summer camps do, too—and many offer scholarships. The key, according to Christakis, is for children to be free of adult "guidance" or concerns about skill-building. Let them play and do things because they are interested, while practicing the "art of association" that de Tocqueville remarked on in 1835.

H. *Encourage your children to engage in a lot of "productive disagreement."* As psychologist Adam Grant notes, the most creative people grew up in homes full of arguments, yet few parents today teach their children how to argue productively; instead, "we stop siblings from quarreling and we have our own arguments behind closed doors." But learning how to give and take criticism without being hurt is an essential life skill. When serious thinkers respect someone, they are willing to engage them in a thoughtful argument. Grant offers the following four rules for productive disagreement:[10]

- Frame it as a debate, rather than a conflict.
- Argue as if you're right, but listen as if you're wrong (and be willing to change your mind).
- Make the most respectful interpretation of the other person's perspective.
- Acknowledge where you agree with your critics and what you've learned from them.

2. Your Worst Enemy Cannot Harm You as Much as Your Own Thoughts, Unguarded

Children (like adults) are prone to emotional reasoning. They need to learn cognitive and social skills that will temper emotional reasoning and guide them to respond more productively to life's provocations. Especially now that the internet guarantees that they will have to deal with trash all along the road of life, it is vital that they learn to notice and manage their emotional reactions and choose how to respond.

The second epigraph at the start of this book came from Buddha: "Your worst enemy cannot harm you as much as your own thoughts, unguarded. But once mastered, no one can help you as much, not even your father or your mother." Our advice is based on this insight.

A. *Teach children the basics of CBT.* CBT stands for "cognitive behavioral therapy," but in many ways it's really just "cognitive behavioral techniques," because the intellectual habits it teaches are good for everyone. Parents can teach children the basics of CBT at any age, starting with something as simple as getting in the habit of letting children watch parents talk back to their own exaggerated thoughts. A technique Greg learned involves practicing hearing his anxious and doomsaying automatic thoughts as if they are being said in funny voices, like Elmer Fudd's or Daffy Duck's. It may sound silly, but it can quickly turn an anxious or upsetting moment into a humorous one. Greg and his wife, Michelle, practice this with their two-year-old, as a way of calming everyone down during moments of stress.

Dr. Robert Leahy, the director of The American Institute for Cognitive Therapy,[11] suggests that when children are upset and may be subject to cognitive distortions, parents can walk their children through the following exercise:

Let's take this thought that you have and ask some questions about it. Sometimes we have a thought about someone and we think we are absolutely right. But then this way of thinking makes us upset and makes us angry or sad. Thoughts are not always true. I might be thinking it's raining outside, but then I go outside and it's not raining. We have to find out what the facts are, don't we? Sometimes we look at things like we are looking through a dark lens and everything seems dark. Let's try putting on different glasses.[12]

Parents can get an accessible overview of CBT from reading Dr. Leahy's book *The Worry Cure*. Also, *Freeing Your Child From Anxiety*, by Tamar Chansky,[13] is recommended by the Beck Institute,[14] which is another great resource for cognitive behavioral therapy. There are many books, blogs,[15] curricula, and even cell phone apps for practicing CBT. Two apps that are rated highly by the Anxiety and Depression Association of America are CPT Coach (for those who are in active treatment with a therapist)[16] and AnxietyCoach.[17]

B. *Teach children mindfulness.* According to Jon Kabat-Zinn, professor of medicine emeritus at the University of Massachusetts Medical School, "mindfulness" means "paying attention in a particular way: on purpose, in the present moment, and nonjudgmentally."[18] Research indicates that establishing a mindfulness practice reduces anxiety, diminishes stress reactivity, enhances coping, benefits attention, increases compassion (and self-compassion), and strengthens emotion regulation. Researchers see improvements in children's in-school behavior, test anxiety, perspective-taking, social skills, empathy, and even grades.[19] Children and teens who engage in mindfulness practices are better able to calm themselves and be more "present."[20] For more information and some easy mindfulness exercises for parents and children, see *The New York Times* "Mindfulness for Children" guide, by David Gelles,[21] and Cognitively-Based Compassion Training from the Emory-Tibet Partnership.[22]

3. The Line Dividing Good and Evil Cuts Through the Heart of Every Human Being

The third epigraph at the start of this book came from *The Gulag Archipelago*, the memoir of Aleksandr Solzhenitsyn, a Russian dissident of the Soviet era. In 1945, Solzhenitsyn criticized Joseph Stalin in private letters sent to a friend. He was arrested and sentenced to hard labor in the network of gulags (prison camps) spread out across Siberia, in which many inmates froze, starved, or were beaten to death. Solzhenitsyn was eventually released and exiled. In one moving passage, describing a time soon after his arrest, he is being marched for days with a few other men. He reflects upon his own virtue, his "unselfish dedication" to the motherland, when it occurs to him that he himself had nearly joined the security service (the NKVD, which evolved into the KGB). He realizes that he could just as easily have become the executioner, rather than the condemned man marching off to his possible execution. He then warns his readers to beware of the Untruth of Us Versus Them:

> If only it were so simple! If only there were evil people somewhere insidiously committing evil deeds, and it were necessary only to separate them from the rest of us and destroy them. But the line dividing good and evil cuts through the heart of every human being.[23]

How can we raise wiser children who will not fall prey to the Untruth of Us Versus Them and the self-righteous call-out culture it breeds? And how can teenagers and college students themselves create and foster a common-humanity way of thinking?

A. *Give people the benefit of the doubt.* Use the "principle of charity." This is the principle in philosophy and rhetoric of making an effort to interpret other people's statements in their best or most reasonable form, not in the worst or most offensive way possible. Parents can model the principle of charity by using it in family discussions and arguments.

B. *Practice the virtue of "intellectual humility."* Intellectual humility is the recognition that our reasoning is so flawed, so prone to bias, that we can rarely be certain that we are right. For kids in middle or high school, find the TED Talk titled "On Being Wrong."[24] The speaker, Kathryn Schulz, begins with the question "What does it feel like to be wrong?" She collects answers from the audience: "dreadful," "thumbs down," "embarrassing." Then she notes that her audience has actually described what it feels like the moment they *realize* they are wrong. Until that moment, the feeling of being *wrong* is indistinguishable from the feeling of being *right*. We are all wrong about many things at every moment, but until we know it, we are often quite certain that we are right. Having people around us who are willing to disagree with us is a gift. So when you realize you are wrong, admit that you are wrong, and thank your critics for helping you see it.[25]

C. *Look very carefully at how your school handles identity politics.* Does it look and sound like the common-humanity identity politics we described in chapter 3? Or is it more like common-enemy identity politics, which encourages kids to see one another not as individuals but as exemplars of groups, some of which are good, some bad? If the school is using a curriculum developed by an outside organization, find out which one, and look closely at the website of that organization to see whether they embrace a common-humanity or a common-enemy approach. If you are concerned that the school is leading students to embrace the Untruth of Us Versus Them, and you are a parent, express your concerns to the principal. If you are a high school student, see whether any of your peers have concerns about this, too. Brainstorm ways to bring a common-humanity perspective to your school.

4. Help Schools to Oppose the Great Untruths

Efforts made by parents have a greater chance of success if schools share parents' concerns about defeating the Great Untruths, and these efforts will be undercut if schools adhere to the Great Untruths. If you are in a position to influence policy at a school—as a teacher, as an administrator, or as a parent—you can have an enormous impact. Here are a few suggestions for educational changes related to the problems we covered in this book. We begin with ideas for elementary schools:

A. *Homework in the early grades should be minimal.* In the early grades, it's always good to encourage kids to read with their parents and on their own, but homework beyond that should not intrude on playtime or family time. Other than encouraging reading, minimize or eliminate all homework in kindergarten and first grade. In later elementary grades, homework should be simple and brief. As Duke University psychologist and homework expert Harris Cooper puts it:

> In elementary school, *short* and *simple* homework can help reinforce simple skills. Further, short and simple homework can help younger students begin to learn time management, organizational skills, and a sense of responsibility, and can help keep parents informed of their child's progress. But for elementary school children, the expectation of big improvements in achievement from long assignments is likely to be unmet.[26]

B. *Give more recess with less supervision.* Recess on school property generally provides an ideal and physically safe setting for free play. However, as we've noted, when adults are standing by to resolve disputes or stop children from taking small risks, this may breed moral dependency. To see an example of the positive effects that can come about when kids are entrusted with much greater autonomy at recess, search the internet for a video titled "No Rules School,"[27] about a New Zealand elementary school principal who gradually removed adult supervision from recess so kids could have "risky, unmanaged play." Kids there climb trees, make up their own games, and play with boards, scraps of wood, and *junk*. Kids get to calculate risks, take chances, and experience real-world consequences. Of course, there are (by intention) risks here. To implement this policy, much needs to be worked out regarding physical safety and preventing bullying. But if discussions about recess policies began with a screening of that video, the conclusions reached would likely be more aligned with the concept of antifragility. (In fact, the principal of the New Zealand school reports that bullying has gone *down* since instituting no-rules recess.) A simple way to give kids more unsupervised play time in a physically safe setting is to create an after-school play club by keeping the playground (or a gymnasium) open for a few hours after school each day.[28] Such free play, in a mixed-age setting, may be better for kids than many structured after-school activities. (It is surely better than sitting at home after school interacting with a screen.)

C. *Discourage the use of the word "safe" or "safety" for anything other than physical safety.* One of Jon's friends recently forwarded to him an email that a third-grade teacher sent to parents about recess and about children forming "clubs." (Kids who played together at recess were not allowing "nonmembers" to join in.) Reasonable minds can disagree about the wisdom of compelling kids to be inclusive at recess, but the last line of the email alarmed Jon: "We are thinking about how everyone at recess can *feel safe* and included." This is the seed of safetyism. It is painful to feel excluded, and it is good for the teacher to use kids' exclusion as a basis for discussion to help kids reflect on why inclusion is good. But the pain of occasional exclusion doesn't make kids *unsafe*. If we mandate inclusion in everything and teach kids that exclusion puts them in *danger*—that being excluded should make them *feel unsafe*—then we are making future experiences of exclusion more painful and giving kids the expectation that an act of exclusion warrants calling in an authority figure to make the exclusion stop.

D. *Have a "no devices" policy.* Some parents will want to give their kids smartphones to track them when they begin traveling to school with no adult, or to help with the complex logistics of pickup or after-school activities. The school policy should be that smartphones must be left in a locker or in some other way kept out of easy reach during the school day.[29]

Here are some ideas for middle schools and high schools:

E. *Protect or expand middle school recess.* In middle school the focus becomes more academic, so some middle schools have done away with recess. But the American Academy of Pediatrics notes in a 2013 statement that "cognitive processing and academic performance depend on regular breaks from concentrated classroom work. This applies equally to adolescents and to younger children."[30]

F. *Cultivate the intellectual virtues.* The intellectual virtues are the qualities necessary to be a critical thinker and an effective learner. They include curiosity, open-mindedness, and intellectual humility. The process of developing intellectual virtues must begin long before arriving on a university campus. The Intellectual Virtues Academy, a charter middle school in Long Beach, California, was created in 2013 to do just that.[31] The school operates on a foundation of three core values that are antithetical to the Untruth of Emotional Reasoning: a culture of thinking (ask questions, seek understanding, and practice the habits of good thinking), self-knowledge (practice ongoing self-reflection and self-awareness), and openness and respect (strive for a strong sense of community marked by collaboration, empowerment, and intentional openness and respect for the thinking of others; this is also an antidote to the Untruth of Us Versus Them). You can learn more about cultivating the intellectual virtues and about how to incorporate them in schools at intellectualvirtues.org and in the writings of Jason Baehr, a professor of philosophy at Loyola Marymount University and one of the founders of the Intellectual Virtues Academy.[32]

G. *Teach debate and offer debate club.* A great way for students to learn the skills of civil disagreement is by participating in structured, formal debates. It is especially important that students practice arguing for positions that oppose their own views. All students would benefit from learning debating techniques and participating in formal debates. In addition to the obvious benefits of learning how to make a well-supported case, debate helps students distinguish between a critique of ideas and a personal attack. The International Debate Education Association has suggestions for how to create a debate club.[33] Students (and their parents and teachers) can also watch Intelligence Squared debates to see skilled debaters in action.[34]

H. *Assign readings and coursework that promote reasoned discussion.* A schoolwide commitment to debate can be supplemented by readings and coursework that teach the habits of good thinking. We suggest that schools offer media literacy classes that teach students the difference between evidence and opinion, and how to evaluate the legitimacy of sources. In addition, Heterodox Academy (an association of professors that Jon co-founded to promote viewpoint diversity) has produced a free, illustrated PDF edition of chapter 2 of John Stuart Mill's classic work *On Liberty.*[35] Mill's book is perhaps the most compelling argument ever made for why we need to interact with people who see things differently from ourselves in order to find the truth. Heterodox Academy has also created OpenMind, a free interactive program that rapidly teaches basic social and moral psychology as a prelude to learning conversational skills for bridging divides.[36] Another suggestion is Annie Duke's 2018 book, *Thinking in Bets: Making Smarter Decisions When You Don't Have All the Facts.* Duke draws from her experience as a successful professional poker player and decision-strategy consultant. She delineates practices that can help students see why the habits of good thinking require rejecting the Untruth of Emotional Reasoning. By examining "tilt" (the term poker players use to describe when someone is too emotional to make good decisions), Duke makes it plain that we can't always trust our feelings. (Find more suggested resources at TheCoddling.com.)

5. Limit and Refine Device Time

Left to their own devices, as it were, many children would spend most of their free time staring into a screen. According to the nonprofit organization Common Sense Media, teens spend on average about *nine hours per day* on screens, and eight- to twelve-year-olds spend about *six hours;* that is *in addition* to whatever they are doing on screens for school.[37] A growing body of research indicates that such heavy use is associated with bad social and mental health outcomes. Because this topic is so complicated and the research base for making recommendations is still small, we offer just three general suggestions that we think will strike most parents and many teens as reasonable. (We'll say more on our website as more research comes in.)

A. *Place clear limits on device time.* Two hours a day seems to be a reasonable maximum, as there does not appear to be evidence of negative mental health effects at this level. For younger children, consider banning the use of devices during the school week entirely, in order to delay for as long as possible the incorporation of device-time into daily routines.

B. *Pay as much attention to what children are doing as you do to how much time they spend doing it.* In chapter 7, we presented the principle that social network sites and apps should be judged by whether they help or hinder adolescents in their efforts to build and maintain close relationships.[38] Talk with your children about the apps that they and their friends use and how they use them. Which ones are essential for their direct communication? Which ones do they experience as triggering FOMO ("fear of missing out"), social comparison, and unrealistically positive presentations of the lives of other kids? Read Twenge's book *iGen* (as a family, if you can) and then bring your teenager into the discussion of how to minimize the potential hazards of heavy device use. These devices and apps are extremely appealing and addictive, so it may be difficult for children to self-regulate. You may need to use a parental-restrictions app[39] or the parental-restrictions setting on your child's devices to manage and monitor usage.[40] And pay attention to what *you* are doing, too. Is your device use reducing the quality of your time with your child?[41]

C. *Protect your child's sleep.* Getting enough sleep will help your child succeed in school, avoid accidents, and stave off depression, among its many other benefits.[42] Yet most teens in America aren't getting enough sleep, and one reason is that so many are staying up late peering at their screens, experiencing painful social comparisons, and disrupting their sleep-wake cycles with light.[43] Electronic device use should be discontinued thirty to sixty minutes before bedtime, at which point all devices should be placed in a box or drawer in the kitchen (or somewhere away from the child's bedroom).

6. Support a New National Norm: Service or Work Before College

As we reported in chapter 7, kids grow up more slowly these days.[44] That trend—taking longer to reach adult milestones—has been going on for decades,[45] but it has been especially visible with iGen. There's nothing intrinsically wrong with delaying adulthood, but if that's happening, then shouldn't we consider delaying the start of college, too? Today's college students are suffering from much higher rates of anxiety and depression than did the Millennials or any other generation. They are cutting and killing themselves in higher numbers. Many are embracing safetyism and are objecting to books and ideas that gave Millennials little trouble. Whatever we are doing, it is not working.

We propose that Americans consider adopting a new national norm: taking a year off after high school—a "gap year"—as Malia Obama did in 2016. It's an idea that has been gaining support among high school counselors, experts in adolescent development, and college admissions officers.[46] High school graduates can spend a year working and learning away from their parents, exploring their interests, developing interpersonal skills, and generally maturing before arriving on campus. The year after high school is also an ideal time for teens to perform national service as a civic rite of passage.[47] Retired General Stanley McChrystal is the chair of Service Year Alliance, an organization that supports recent high school or college graduates in finding full-time, paid opportunities to spend a year working on projects to benefit American communities.[48] General McChrystal is at the forefront of an effort to create a national expectation that all Americans spend one year in some kind of service between the ages of eighteen and twenty-eight. "Through such service," he says, "young Americans from different income levels, races, ethnicities, political affiliations and religious beliefs could learn to work together to get things done."[49] We agree, and we believe that whether that year involves service or work, it would be good for America's polarized democracy if that year were spent in a part of the country very different from the one in which the young adult grew up.[50]

. . . . .

Robert Zimmer, the president of the University of Chicago, was interviewed in 2018 about the school's reputation for intellectual excellence and open inquiry. He noted that many students arrive on college campuses unprepared for a culture of free speech:

> High schools prepare students to take more advanced mathematics, and they prepare them to write history papers, and so on . . . [but] how are high schools doing in preparing students to be students in a college of open discourse and free argumentation?[51]

If parents and teachers can raise children who are antifragile; if middle schools and high schools can cultivate the intellectual virtues; if all high school graduates spend a year doing service or paid work away from home, before beginning college at age nineteen or later, we think most students will be ready for anything.

CHAPTER 13

Wiser Universities

Aristotle often evaluated a thing with respect to its "telos"—its purpose, end, or goal. The telos of a knife is to cut. A knife that does not cut well is not a good knife. The telos of a physician is health or healing. A physician who cannot heal is not a good physician. What is the telos of a university?

The most obvious answer is "truth"—the word appears on so many university crests. For example, *Veritas* ("truth") appears on Harvard's crest, and *Lux et Veritas* ("light and truth") appears on Yale's. If we allow the word "knowledge" as a close relative of truth, then we take in many more university mottos, such as the University of Chicago's, which, translated from Latin, is "Let knowledge grow from more to more; and so be human life enriched." (Even the fictional Faber College in the movie *Animal House* had the motto "Knowledge is good.")[1]

Of course, universities are now complex multiversities that have many departments, centers, stakeholders, and functions. The president's office has many goals besides pursuing the truth; so does the athletics department and the student health center. So do the students and the faculty. But why are all of these people and offices together in the first place? Why do people see universities as important and, until recently, as trusted institutions,[2] worthy of receiving billions of dollars of public subsidy? Because there is widespread public agreement that the discovery and transmission of truth is a noble goal and a public good.

If the telos of a university is truth, then a university that fails to add to humanity's growing body of knowledge, or that fails to transmit the best of that knowledge to its students, is not a good university. If scholars do not advance the frontiers of knowledge within their disciplines, or if they betray the truth to satisfy other goals (such as accumulating wealth or advancing an ideology), then they are not good scholars. If professors do not pass on to their students a richer understanding of the truth, as it has been discovered in their discipline, along with skills and habits that will make them better able to find the truth after they graduate, then they are not good professors.

There are alternative candidates one might propose for the telos of a university. Perhaps the most common alternative is something about progress, change, or making the world a better place. Karl Marx once critiqued the academy with these words: "The philosophers have only interpreted the world, in various ways; the point is to change it."[3] Some students and faculty today seem to think that the purpose of scholarship is to bring about social change, and the purpose of education is to train students to more effectively bring about such change.[4]

We disagree. The truth is powerful, yet the process by which we arrive at truth is easily corrupted by the desires of the seekers and the social dynamics of the community. If a university is united around a telos of change or social progress, scholars will be motivated to reach conclusions that are consistent with that vision, and the community will impose social costs on those who reach different conclusions—or who merely ask the wrong questions, as we saw in chapters 4 and 5. There will always be inconvenient facts for any political agenda, and you can judge a university, or an academic field, by how it handles its dissenters.

We agree with former Northwestern University professor Alice Dreger, who urges activist students and professors to "Carpe datum" ("Seize the data").[5] In her book *Galileo's Middle Finger*, she contends that good scholarship must "put the search for truth first and the quest for social justice second." She explains:

> Evidence really is an ethical issue, the most important ethical issue in a modern democracy. If you want justice, you must work for truth. And if you want to work for truth, you must do a little more than wish for justice.[6]

For those who want to attend, teach at, or lead universities of the sort Dreger imagines, where the telos is truth, we offer advice based on the ideas and research we covered earlier in this book. We organize our suggestions under four general principles that can help universities thrive, even in our age of outrage and polarization. High school students should consider these principles when applying to college, and college counselors should consider these principles when recommending schools to prospective applicants and their parents. We hope that students, professors, alumni, and trustees will discuss these suggestions with the leadership and administration of their schools.

1. Entwine Your Identity With Freedom of Inquiry

A. *Endorse the Chicago Statement.* Most colleges and universities, public and private, promise free speech, academic freedom, and freedom of inquiry in glowing language.[7] But these preexisting commitments to free speech, many of which were written in the early twentieth century, have not stopped professors and students from being punished for what they say. That is why we recommend that every college in the country renew its commitment to free speech by adopting a statement modeled after the one affirmed by the University of Chicago in 2015. That statement, written by a committee chaired by legal scholar Geoffrey Stone, comprises a commitment to free speech and academic freedom updated for our age of disinvitations, speaker shutdowns, and speech codes. Thus far, it has been adopted by administrations or faculty bodies at forty colleges and universities, including Amherst, Columbia, Johns Hopkins, Princeton, and Vanderbilt.[8]

FIRE has produced a modified version of the Chicago Statement that can serve as a template for other schools (see Appendix 2). Here is the key passage:

The [INSTITUTION]'s fundamental commitment is to the principle that debate or deliberation may not be suppressed because the ideas put forth are thought by some or even by most members of the [INSTITUTION] community to be offensive, unwise, immoral, or wrong-headed. It is for the individual members of the [INSTITUTION] community, not for the [INSTITUTION] as an institution, to make those judgments for themselves, and to act on those judgments not by seeking to suppress speech, but by openly and vigorously contesting the ideas that they oppose.

Colleges should also review their policies to ensure that they are consistent with the First Amendment. Public colleges are legally required to protect the expressive rights of students and faculty on campus, so making sure policies do not infringe on free speech is not only good for students, it also avoids the possibility of the college being on the losing side of a First Amendment lawsuit. As for the private colleges that promise freedom of speech, academic freedom, and free inquiry, revising (or eliminating) speech codes is a great sign that they are serious. Prospective applicants should take colleges' speech codes into account when deciding where to apply, and college students should be aware of their own school's policies.[9]

B. *Establish a practice of not responding to public outrage.* Strong and clear policies on free speech and academic freedom are useless if the people at the top aren't willing to stand by them when the going gets tough and the leadership faces a pressure campaign—whether from on or off campus. A university will find it easier to stand by these principles if the president publicly commits to them at the start of each year, before any controversies break out. Of course, if a student or faculty member's speech or behavior, whether online, in class, or in other campus settings, includes true threats, harassment, incitement to imminent lawless action, or any other kind of speech that is not protected by the First Amendment, the university should act. But even in these cases, university presidents should not act rashly; they should follow their own written policies and disciplinary procedures, which should be designed to ensure that any accused faculty member or student gets a fair hearing. The more reactive universities are to public outrage or illiberal demands for censorship and punishment, the more outrage and illiberal demands they will receive. In an age when outrage can be swift and intense but has a short half-life, universities should allow time for tempers to cool. This is particularly important for protecting junior and adjunct faculty, who can be fired far more easily than tenured faculty.

C. *Do not allow the "heckler's veto."* University presidents must make it clear that nobody has the right to prevent a fellow member of the community from attending or hearing a lecture. Protest that does not interfere with others' freedom of expression is protected speech and is a legitimate form of productive disagreement. Boisterous protests that *briefly* interfere with the rights of other audience members may even be allowed. But if the sum total of protesters' actions substantially interferes with the ability of audience members to listen, or the speaker to speak, then those who are responsible for the interference must face some punishment. Prospective students should avoid attending colleges that allow hecklers to disrupt events with no penalty.[10]

2. Pick the Best Mix of People for the Mission

A. *Admit more students who are older and can show evidence of their ability to live independently.* As we said in the previous chapter, adulthood is arriving later and later, and this trend has been going on for decades.[11] We believe there would be many benefits to students, to universities, and to the nation if a new national norm emerged of taking a gap year, or a year of national service, or a few years of military service, before attending college. Prestigious universities have enormous power to promote that new norm by announcing that they will give preference to students who take time off in ways that prepare them for independence. If universities stop admitting so many students whose childhoods were devoted to test prep and resume building and start admitting more students who can demonstrate a measure of autonomy, the culture on campus is likely to improve dramatically.

B. *Admit more students who have attended schools that teach the "intellectual virtues."* If prestigious universities draw heavily from schools that emphasize intellectual virtues, like the one we described in the previous chapter, and that give students practice in debate, then many more K–12 schools will adopt this approach. The next generation of college students will be better prepared to engage with challenging ideas and diverse fellow students.

C. *Include viewpoint diversity in diversity policies.* Diversity confers benefits on a community in large part because it brings together people who approach questions from different points of view. In recent decades, as we noted in chapter 5, the professoriate and the student body have become more diverse by race, gender, and other characteristics but less diverse in terms of political perspectives. We suggest that universities add "viewpoint diversity" to their diversity statements and strategies. This does not require equal or proportional representation of political views among the faculty or students, and it does not require that all viewpoints be represented, but it does commit the university to avoiding political uniformity and orthodoxy. [12]

3. Orient and Educate for Productive Disagreement

A. *Explicitly reject the Untruth of Fragility: What doesn't kill you makes you weaker.* A university devoted to the pursuit of truth must prepare its students for conflict, controversy, and argument. Many students will experience their most cherished beliefs being challenged, and they must learn that this is not harassment or a personal attack; it is part of the process by which people do each other the favor of counteracting each other's confirmation bias. Students must also learn to make well-reasoned arguments while avoiding ad hominem arguments, which criticize people rather than ideas. In summer reading suggestions and in orientation materials for new students, universities should clearly embrace the message of Ruth Simmons, former president of Brown University and the first black president of an Ivy League university: "One's voice grows stronger in encounters with opposing views. . . . The collision of views and ideologies is in the DNA of the academic enterprise. We do not need any collision avoidance technology here."[13] Explain that classrooms and public lectures at your university are not intellectual "safe spaces." (Of course, students have a right to freedom of association, and they are free to join and create those elsewhere, on their own time.[14]) Discourage the creep of the word "unsafe" to encompass "uncomfortable." Show students the short video clip we described in chapter 4 of Van Jones urging them to forswear emotional "safety" and instead treat college as "the gym."[15]

B. *Explicitly reject the Untruth of Emotional Reasoning: Always trust your feelings.* In orientations, colleges should emphasize the power of the confirmation bias and the prevalence of cognitive distortions. It is challenging to think well; we are easily led astray by feelings and by group loyalties. In the age of social media, cyber trolls, and fake news, it is a national and global crisis that people so readily follow their feelings to embrace outlandish stories about their enemies. A community in which members hold one another accountable for using evidence to substantiate their assertions is a community that can, collectively, pursue truth in the age of outrage. Emphasize the importance of critical thinking, and then give students the tools to engage in better critical thinking. One such tool is CBT. It is relatively easy to train students in CBT directly, or to offer free access to websites and apps that they can use on their own. (See Appendix 1.) Another tool is the OpenMind program, which equips students with the skills to navigate difficult conversations (see OpenMindPlatform.org).

C. *Explicitly reject the Untruth of Us Versus Them: Life is a battle between good people and evil people.* Look closely at how identity politics is introduced to first-year students, especially in summer readings and orientation materials. Draw on readings that take a non-moralistic, systems-level approach to understanding social problems. Given the diversity of the incoming class, including international students, it is a good idea to talk about the many ways that students may unwittingly offend or exclude one another, especially in this technologically supercharged age. Encourage politeness and empathy without framing issues as micro-*aggressions*. Try instead to use a more charitable frame, such as members of a family giving one another the benefit of the doubt; when problems arise, they try to resolve things privately and informally.

4. Draw a Larger Circle Around the Community

Throughout this book, we have emphasized a basic principle of social psychology: the more you separate people and point out differences among them, the more divided and less trusting they will become.[16] Conversely, the more you emphasize common goals or interests, shared fate, and common humanity, the more they will see one another as fellow human beings, treat one another well, and come to appreciate one another's contributions to the community. Pauli Murray expressed the power of this principle when she wrote, "When my brothers try to draw a circle to exclude me, I shall draw a larger circle to include them."[17] Students, professors, and administrators can all play an important role in widening that circle.

A. *Foster school spirit.* Some colleges work hard, in the opening weeks, to foster "school spirit" and forge a common identity. School spirit may sound trivial, but it can create a community of greater trust within which harder issues can be tackled later on.

B. *Protect physical safety.* We have argued throughout this book that emotional comfort should not be confused with physical safety. But as we showed in chapter 6, we live in a time when extremists increasingly use the internet and social media to threaten and harass students and professors, particularly those who are members of historically marginalized groups. Sometimes the threats leave the internet and come to campus. Universities must pay for adequate security; they must respond vigorously and work with campus police, local police, the FBI, and other authorities to investigate and punish threats and acts of violence, and they must do so consistently. Given frequent reports from students of color across the country regarding how they are sometimes treated by campus and local police, it is essential that police take extra care not to treat them like potential criminals. It is vital that students from all backgrounds are safe from physical attacks and know that their campus police are there to protect them.

C. *Host civil, cross-partisan events for students.* When a campus group invites speakers not for the quality of their ideas but for their ability to shock, offend, and provoke an overreaction, it exacerbates the mutual-outrage process we described in chapter 6. There are many organizations that can help bring interesting and ideologically diverse speakers to campus who can demonstrate the value of exposure to political diversity. If you are a student, try to enlist your school's College Republicans and College Democrats to cohost events. Whether or not you succeed, consider starting a chapter of BridgeUSA, a student-run network that hosts constructive political discussions.[18]

IDENTIFYING A WISE UNIVERSITY

Five questions alumni, parents, college counselors, and prospective students should ask universities:

1. What steps do you take (if any) to teach incoming students about academic freedom and free inquiry before they take their first classes?

2. How would you handle a demand that a professor be fired because of an opinion he or she expressed in an article or interview, which other people found deeply offensive?

3. What would your institution do if a controversial speaker were scheduled to speak, and large protests that included credible threats of violence were planned?

4. How is your institution responding to the increase in students who suffer from anxiety and depression?

5. What does your university do to foster a sense of shared identity?

Look for answers that indicate that the institution has a high tolerance for vigorous disagreement but no tolerance for violence or intimidation. Look for answers that indicate a presumption that students are antifragile, combined with the recognition that many students today need support as they work toward emotional growth. Look for answers that indicate that the institution tries to draw an encompassing circle around its members, within which differences can more productively be explored.

Many U.S. universities are having difficulties these days, but we believe the problems we discussed in this book are fixable. Combined with the changes we suggested in the previous chapter, the changes in this chapter can strengthen a university's ability to pursue the telos of truth. A school that makes freedom of inquiry an essential part of its identity, selects students who show special promise as seekers of truth, orients and prepares those students for productive disagreement, and then draws a larger circle around the whole community within which everyone knows that they are physically safe and that they belong—such a school would be inspiring to join, a joy to attend, and a blessing to society.

Wiser Societies

T his is a book about wisdom and its opposite. It is a book about three psychological principles and about what happens to young people when parents and educators—acting with the best of intentions— implement policies that are inconsistent with those principles. We can summarize the entire book by contrasting the three opening quotations and the three Great Untruths.

PSYCHOLOGICAL PRINCIPLE	WISDOM	GREAT UNTRUTH
Young people are antifragile.	*Prepare the child for the road, not the road for the child.*	*What doesn't kill you makes you weaker.*
We are all prone to emotional reasoning and the confirmation bias.	*Your worst enemy cannot harm you as much as your own thoughts, unguarded. But once mastered, no one can help you as much, not even your father or your mother.*	*Always trust your feelings.*
We are all prone to dichotomous thinking and tribalism.	*The line dividing good and evil cuts through the heart of every human being.*	*Life is a battle between good people and evil people.*

In Part I, we explained the three psychological principles and showed how some recent practices and policies on many campuses encourage students to embrace unwisdom rather than wisdom. In Part II, we showed what happens when students embrace all three untruths, within an institution that has low levels of viewpoint diversity, weak leadership, and a high sense of threat (caused in part by a real escalation of political polarization and provocations from off campus). In Part III, we showed that there is no simple explanation for what is happening. You have to look at six interacting trends: rising political polarization; rising rates of adolescent depression and anxiety; a shift to more fearful, protective, and intensive parenting in middle-class and wealthy families; widespread play deprivation and risk deprivation for members of iGen; an expanding campus bureaucracy taking an increasingly overprotective posture; and a rising passion for justice combined with a growing commitment to attaining "equal outcomes" in all areas. In Part IV, we offered suggestions based on the three psychological principles for improving childrearing, K–12 education, and universities.

We discussed some alarming trends in this book, particularly in the chapters on America's rising political polarization and rising rates of adolescent depression, anxiety, and suicide. These problems are serious, and we see no sign that either trend will be reversing in the next decade. And yet we are heartened and persuaded by cognitive psychologist Steven Pinker's argument, in *Enlightenment Now*, that in the long run most things are getting better, quickly and globally. Pinker notes that there are many psychological reasons why people are—and have always been—prone to catastrophizing about the future. For example, some of the problems we discuss in this book are examples of the "problems of progress" that we described in the Introduction. As we make progress in such areas as safety, comfort, and inclusion, we raise our expectations. The progress is real, but as we adapt to our improved conditions, we often fail to notice it.

We certainly don't want to fall prey to catastrophizing, so we should look for contrary evidence and contrary ways to appraise our present circumstances. Here's a powerful antidote to pessimism—a quote that was first brought to our attention by science writer Matt Ridley in his 2010 book, *The Rational Optimist*:

> We cannot absolutely prove that those are in error who tell us that
> society has reached a turning point, that we have seen our best
> days. But so said all who came before us, and with just as much

apparent reason. . . . On what principle is it that, when we see nothing but improvement behind us, we are to expect nothing but deterioration before us?[1]

Those words were written in 1830 by Thomas Babington Macaulay, a British historian and member of Parliament. Britain's best days were certainly not behind it.

Pinker and Ridley both base their optimism in part on a simple observation: The more serious a problem gets, the more inducements there are for people, companies, and governments to find innovative solutions, whether driven by personal commitment, market forces, or political pressures.

How might things change? Let us sketch out one possible vision, drawing on some "green shoots" that we already see. These are countertrends that *may already be under way* today, as this book goes to press in May 2018.

1. *Social media.* Social media is a major part of the problem, implicated both in rising rates of mental illness and in rising political polarization. But after two years of scandals, public outrage, and calls for government regulation, the major companies are finally responding; they are at least tweaking algorithms, verifying some identities, and taking steps to reduce harassment. In the wake of the Cambridge Analytica fiasco, there is likely to be far more pressure applied by governments. Parents, schools, and students will respond, too, gradually adopting better practices, just as we adapted (imperfectly) to life surrounded by junk food and cigarettes.

Green shoots: Facebook[2] and Twitter are both hiring social psychologists and putting out calls for research on how their platforms can change to "increase the collective health, openness, and civility of public conversation."[3] We hope to see some substantial changes in the next few years that will reduce the polarizing, depression-inducing, and harassment-supporting effects of social media. A partnership between Common Sense Media and the Center for Humane Technology (founded by a coalition of early employees at Facebook and Google) is working with the tech industry to lessen the negative effects of device use, especially for children. Their campaign, The Truth About Tech, informs students, parents, and teachers about the health effects of various technologies, and aims to reform the industry so that tech products are healthier for users.[4]

2. *Free play and freedom.* The adolescent mental health crisis has finally caught the attention of the public. As more parents and educators come to see that overprotection is harming children, and as we move further and further away from the crime wave of the 1970s and 1980s, more parents will try harder to let their kids play outside, with one another, and without adult supervision.

Green shoots: In March 2018, Utah became the first state to pass into law a "free-range parenting" bill—and with unanimous bipartisan support.[5] As we noted in chapter 8, parents in some localities currently run the risk of arrest for letting their children out without supervision. The Utah law affirms children's right to some unsupervised time, and parents' right to not be arrested when they give it to them. As more states pass laws like these, parents and schools will be more willing to try out policies and practices that give kids more autonomy and re-sponsibility.

3. *Better identity politics.* With the rise of the alt-right and white nation-alism since 2016, more scholars are writing about the ways in which emphasizing racial identity leads to bad outcomes in a multiracial soci-ety. It has become increasingly clear that identitarian extremists on both sides rely on the most outrageous acts of the other side to unite their group around its common enemy. This process is not unique to the United States, a fact that can be seen in Julia Ebner's new book, *The Rage: The Vicious Circle of Islamist and Far Right Extremism.* Ebner, an Austrian researcher at the London-based Institute for Strategic Dia-logue, did harrowing fieldwork befriending members of ISIS and

members of far-right groups, such as the English Defense League. In an interview, she summarized her conclusions:

> What we have is the far right depicting Islamist extremists as representative of the whole Muslim community, while Islamist extremists depict the far right as representative of the entire West. As the extremes [pull more people from] the political center, these ideas become mainstream, and the result is a clash-of-civilizations narrative turning into a self-fulfilling prophecy.[6]

Green shoots: More writers from many backgrounds are calling for a rethinking of identity politics. Turkish American political scientist Timur Kuran,[7] Chinese American law professor Amy Chua,[8] and gay author and activist Jonathan Rauch[9] (among many others) have been sounding the alarm about how the common-enemy identity politics of the far right and far left feed off one another. These authors are looking for ways to short-circuit the process and shift to a common-humanity perspective; they generally arrive at some version of the basic social psychology principles we've discussed in this book. Here is Rauch, reviewing and praising Chua's recent book, *Political Tribes: Group Instinct and the Fate of Nations:*

> Psychological research shows that tribalism can be countered and overcome by teamwork: by projects that join individuals in a common task on an equal footing. One such task, it turns out, can be to reduce tribalism. In other words, with conscious effort, humans can break the tribal spiral, and many are trying. "You'd never know it from cable news or social media," Chua writes, "but all over the country there are signs of people trying to cross divides and break out of their political tribes."[10]

The Dalai Lama has long urged such an approach, based on the same social psychology. In May 2018, he tweeted this:

> I'm Tibetan, I'm Buddhist and I'm the Dalai Lama, but if I emphasize these differences it sets me apart and raises barriers with other people. What we need to do is to pay more attention to the ways in which we are the same as other people.[11]

4. *Universities committing to truth as a process.* The University of Chicago has long been an outlier in the intensity of its academic culture. (It proudly embraces the unofficial motto "Where fun goes to die."[12]) When safetyism was sweeping through many other top American universities, it had less effect at Chicago. It is no coincidence that the best recent statement on freedom of expression was drafted there (see Appendix 2).

Green shoots: Many universities are adopting the Chicago Statement and are beginning to push back against the creep of safetyism. If that stance works out well for them and if those schools move up on various rankings and lists, then many more universities will follow suit.

Putting this all together: We predict that things will improve, and the change may happen quite suddenly at some point in the next few years. As far as we can tell from private conversations, most university presidents reject the culture of safetyism. They know it is bad for students and bad for free inquiry, but they find it politically difficult to say so publicly. From our conversations with students, we believe that most high school and college students despise call-out culture and would prefer to be at a school that had little of it. Most students are not fragile, they are not "snowflakes," and they are not afraid of ideas. So if a small group of universities is able to develop a different sort of academic culture—one that finds ways to make students from all identity groups feel welcome without using the divisive methods that seem to be backfiring on so many campuses—we think that market forces will take care of the rest. Applications and enrollment at those schools will surge. Alumni donations will increase. More high schools will prepare students to compete for slots at those schools, and more parents will prepare their kids to gain admission to those schools. This will mean less test prep, less overprotection, more free play, and more independence. Entire towns and school districts will organize themselves to enable and encourage more free-range parenting. They will do this not primarily to help their students get into college but to reverse the epidemic of depression, anxiety, self-injury, and suicide that is afflicting our children. There will be a growing recognition across the country that safetyism is dangerous and that it is stunting our children's development.

Some of the earliest colleges in Britain's American colonies were founded to train clergy. But as a more distinctively practical American culture developed, schools were increasingly founded to train young people in the skills and virtues that were essential for a self-governing civil society. In 1750, as he was founding the school that later became the University of Pennsylvania, Benjamin Franklin wrote this to Samuel Johnson:

> Nothing is of more importance to the public weal, than to form and train up youth in wisdom and virtue. Wise and good men are, in my opinion, the strength of a state: much more so than riches or arms, which, under the management of Ignorance and Wickedness, often draw on destruction, instead of providing for the safety of a people.[13]

This is a book about education and wisdom. If we can educate the next generation more wisely, they will be stronger, richer, more virtuous, and even safer.

ACKNOWLEDGMENTS

An unstated premise of this book is that thinking is social. As lone individuals, each of us is not terribly smart, for we are all prone to cognitive distortions and the confirmation bias. But if you put people into the right sorts of groups and networks, where ideas can be shared, criticized, and improved, something better and truer can emerge. We would like to thank the many people in our groups and networks who made this book better and truer.

First is Pamela Paresky, who joined us during the early stages of the project as Greg's chief research officer at FIRE. An accomplished writer with an interdisciplinary Ph.D. from the University of Chicago's Committee on Human Development, Pamela came to the project having written, taught, and spoken about themes similar to those in this book. A regular online contributor to *Psychology Today*, Pamela became our subject matter expert on many areas of research, and her extensive editing of the entire book helped us blend our two writing styles into one. We are extraordinarily grateful for the depth of her knowledge and expertise. She played devil's advocate, pressed us to sharpen our points, and contributed many of the important ideas in this book—including coining the term "safetyism."

Greg would like to thank many other people at FIRE, beginning with the board of directors for allowing him to undertake this project. In particular, Greg thanks FIRE's current chairman, Daniel Shuchman, who read multiple drafts of this book and offered advice throughout the process. Greg also wants to single out his remarkably unflappable executive assistant, Eli Feldman, and extraordinary former research assistant, Haley Hudler. Eli is a 2016 Yale graduate with a degree in psychology and was endlessly helpful from outline to completion, with keen insight about psychology and iGen, his own generation. Haley was with us as we wrote the original article for *The Atlantic* and the book proposal, and she performed several months of research for the book before she left FIRE to attend the University of Georgia School of Law. We would also like to thank FIRE attorney Adam Goldstein for his fast and thorough research in the last few months of the editing process, and FIRE's staff on the whole. Everyone from executive director Robert Shibley (and his wife, Araz Shibley, who helped us research several cases) and the most senior employees to our newest student "co-ops" (Alyssa Bennett, Kelli Kushner, and

Matthew Williams) helped along the way. While we can't list everyone at FIRE who pitched in, we must thank Sarah McLaughlin and Ryne Weiss for their incisive feedback and their insights about the climate on campus today, and Will Creeley, whose expert writing skills helped us fine-tune the manuscript. In addition, we are grateful for research support given by Laura Beltz and Cynthia Meyersburg, and for the feedback and advice from Peter Bonilla, Nico Perrino, Bonnie Snyder and FIRE attorney (and unofficial FIRE copy editor-in-chief) Samantha Harris, whose keen eye and unparalleled attention to detail during the final stages of production were invaluable.

Jon's acknowledgments begin with Caroline Mehl, a recent graduate of Yale and Oxford whom he hired as a research assistant well before this project began. Caroline contributed many ideas and most of the graphs. She pushed us to take multiple perspectives and, in a move that John Stuart Mill would have praised, she found us five readers who viewed campus events very differently from the way we did. We thank those readers, who were masters of constructive and nuanced criticism: Travis Gidado, Madeline High, Ittai Orr, Danielle Tomson, and one who wishes to remain anonymous. We also thank these readers who gave us detailed and very valuable comments on the entire manuscript, critiquing it from the left: Helen Kramer, Shuli Passow, and Khalil Smith; critiquing it from the right: Steve Messenger and William Modahl; and critiquing it from an unidentified location: Larry Amsel, Heather Heying, and Daniel Shuchman.

Jon owes special thanks to Valerie Purdie-Greenaway, whose deep critique of our first draft marked a turning point for the project. He is always grateful to the team at Heterodox Academy, particularly Raffi Grinberg, Nick Phillips, and Jeremy Willinger, who all read the whole manuscript; Sean Stevens, who helped with research; and Deb Mashek, who came aboard to lead the organization in a new direction that will make universities wiser.

Some of the scholars and experts whose work underlies the core arguments of the book helped us frequently along the way. We thank Erika Christakis, Peter Gray, Stephen Holland, Robert Leahy, Julie Lythcott-Haims, Hara Estroff Marano, Lenore Skenazy, and Jean Twenge.

We are grateful to the many friends, colleagues, and acquaintances who gave us valuable comments on one or more chapters, helped us analyze data, or provided their professional expertise: Jason Baehr, Andrew Becker, Caleb Bernard, Paul Bloom, Samantha Boardman, Bradley Campbell, Dennis Dalton, Clark Freshman, Brian Gallagher, Andrew Gates, Christopher Gates, Benjamin Ginsberg, Jesse Graham, Dan Griswold, Benjamin Haidt, Rebecca Haidt, Terry Hartle, Ravi Iyer, Robb Jones, Christina King, Susan Kresnicka, Calvin Lai, Marcella Larsen, Harry Lewis, Vanessa Lobue, Brian Lowe, Jason Manning, Ian McCready-Flora, John McWhorter, John Palfrey, Mike Paros, Nando Pelusi, Steven Pinker, Anne Rasmussen, Bradly Reed, Fabio Rojas, Kathleen Santora, Sally

Satel, Steve Schultz, Mark Shulman, Nadine Strossen, Joshua Sullivan, Marianne Toldalagi, John Tomasi, Tracy Tomasso, Rebecca Tuvel, Lee Tyner, Steve Vaisey, Robert Von Hallberg, Zach Wood, and Jared Zuker. We thank Omar Mahmood for volunteering to create our website, TheCoddling.com.

We thank Don Peck, at *The Atlantic,* for seeing the potential of this project back in 2014 and launching it, transformed, in 2015. We thank our agent, John Brockman, along with his team at Brockman, Inc., for guiding us to Penguin Press and to our brilliant editor, Virginia "Ginny" Smith. Ginny refined our ideas and our prose, working harder with each deadline we missed.

And last, we thank our families. Greg thanks his wife, Michelle LaBlanc, for her unending patience, flexibility, and support in this intense process—during which she gave birth to Maxwell (born November 2017) and continued to be an amazing mother to rambunctious two-year-old Benjamin while Daddy was kind of swamped.

Jon thanks his wife, Jayne Riew, who improves all that he writes, sees so many things that he misses—in writing and in life—and does the unpublished work in the shared adventure of raising Max and Francesca. Jon ends with an appreciation of his mother, Elaine Haidt, who passed away in May of 2017, while we were writing this book. She took parenting classes in the 1960s from the psychologist Haim Ginott, who taught her the maxim "Don't just do something, stand there." Jon and his sisters, Rebecca and Samantha, were so blessed to have a mother who knew what to do, and what not to do.

How to Do CBT

Sometimes people who wish to practice CBT find therapists who train them in techniques for diagnosing and then altering their distorted thought patterns. In other cases, they simply read books about how to practice CBT. A book that American mental health professionals frequently recommend for treating depression is David Burns's best-seller, *Feeling Good: The New Mood Therapy.* Several studies have found that reading the book—yes, just reading the book—is an effective treatment for depression.[1] We also recommend Dr. Robert Leahy's excellent book *The Worry Cure: Seven Steps to Stop Worry from Stopping You*, which is more focused on anxiety, and is updated with the latest CBT techniques.

The beauty of CBT is how easy it is to learn: All you need is pen and paper (or a laptop, or a device with an app that lets you take notes). The specific details for practicing CBT differ from book to book and therapist to therapist, but the basic process is something like this:

1. When you are feeling anxious, depressed, or otherwise distressed, take a moment to write down what you are feeling.
2. Write down your level of distress. (For example, you could score it on a scale of 1 to 100.)
3. Write down what happened and what your automatic thoughts were when you felt the pang of anxiety or despair. (For example, "Someone I was interested in canceled our date. I said to myself, 'This always happens. No one will ever want to go out with me. I'm a total loser.'")
4. Look at the categories of distorted automatic thoughts below, and ask yourself: Is this thought a cognitive distortion? Write down the

cognitive distortions you notice. (For example, looking at the automatic thoughts in number 3 above, you might write, "personalizing, overgeneralizing, labeling, and catastrophizing.")

5. Look at the evidence for and against your thought.
6. Ask yourself what someone might say who disagreed with you. Is there any merit in that opinion?
7. Consider again what happened, and reevaluate the situation without the cognitive distortions.
8. Write down your new thoughts and feelings. (For example, "I am sad and disappointed that a date I was excited about got canceled.")
9. Write down again, using the same scale as before, how anxious, depressed, or otherwise distressed you feel. Chances are the number will be lower—perhaps a lot lower.

CBT takes discipline, work, and commitment. Many therapists recommend doing this type of exercise at least once or twice a day. With time and practice, you are likely to find that your distorted negative thoughts no longer have the grip on you that they once did. (Note that in some cases, your initial automatic thoughts may not be distorted. Sometimes they turn out to be entirely reasonable.)

As we've argued in this book, the practice of CBT and its principles are useful even for people who do not experience depression or anxiety. We encourage all readers to learn more about CBT. If you are interested in working with a CBT therapist, you can find a list of doctors near you at the Association for Behavioral and Cognitive Therapies (http://www.findcbt.org) and the Academy of Cognitive Therapy (http://www.academyofct.org).

Of course, anyone who is suffering from severe psychological distress should seek professional help.

On the next pages we reprint the full list of cognitive distortions from *Treatment Plans and Interventions for Depression and Anxiety Disorders, Second Edition*, by Robert L. Leahy, Stephen J. F. Holland, and Lata K. McGinn (reprinted with permission).

Categories of Distorted Automatic Thoughts

1. MIND READING: You assume that you know what people think without having sufficient evidence of their thoughts. "He thinks I'm a loser."

2. FORTUNE-TELLING: You predict the future negatively: Things will get worse, or there is danger ahead. "I'll fail that exam," or "I won't get the job."

3. CATASTROPHIZING: You believe that what has happened or will happen will be so awful and unbearable that you won't be able to stand it. "It would be terrible if I failed."

4. LABELING: You assign global negative traits to yourself and others. "I'm undesirable," or "He's a rotten person."

5. DISCOUNTING POSITIVES: You claim that the positive things you or others do are trivial. "That's what wives are supposed to do—so it doesn't count when she's nice to me," or "Those successes were easy, so they don't matter."

6. NEGATIVE FILTERING: You focus almost exclusively on the negatives and seldom notice the positives. "Look at all of the people who don't like me."

7. OVERGENERALIZING: You perceive a global pattern of negatives on the basis of a single incident. "This generally happens to me. I seem to fail at a lot of things."

8. DICHOTOMOUS THINKING: You view events or people in all-or-nothing terms. "I get rejected by everyone," or "It was a complete waste of time."

9. SHOULDS: You interpret events in terms of how things should be, rather than simply focusing on what is. "I should do well. If I don't, then I'm a failure."

10. PERSONALIZING: You attribute a disproportionate amount of the blame to yourself for negative events, and you fail to see that certain events are also caused by others. "The marriage ended because I failed."

11. BLAMING: You focus on the other person as the source of your negative feelings, and you refuse to take responsibility for changing yourself. "She's to blame for the way I feel now," or "My parents caused all my problems."

12. UNFAIR COMPARISONS: You interpret events in terms of standards that are unrealistic—for example, you focus primarily on others who do better than you and find yourself inferior in the comparison. "She's more successful than I am," or "Others did better than I did on the test."

13. REGRET ORIENTATION: You focus on the idea that you could have done better in the past, rather than on what you can do better now. "I could have had a better job if I had tried," or "I shouldn't have said that."

14. WHAT IF?: You keep asking a series of questions about "what if" something happens, and you fail to be satisfied with any of the answers. "Yeah, but what if I get anxious?" or "What if I can't catch my breath?"

15. EMOTIONAL REASONING: You let your feelings guide your interpretation of reality. "I feel depressed; therefore, my marriage is not working out."

16. INABILITY TO DISCONFIRM: You reject any evidence or arguments that might contradict your negative thoughts. For example, when you have the thought "I'm unlovable," you reject as irrelevant any evidence that people like you. Consequently, your thought cannot be refuted. "That's not the real issue. There are deeper problems. There are other factors."

17. JUDGMENT FOCUS: You view yourself, others, and events in terms of evaluations as good–bad or superior–inferior, rather than simply describing, accepting, or understanding. You are continually measuring yourself and others according to arbitrary standards, and finding that you and others fall short. You are focused on the judgments of others as well as your own judgments of yourself. "I didn't perform well in college," or "If I take up tennis, I won't do well," or "Look how successful she is. I'm not successful."

The Chicago Statement on Principles of Free Expression

The Chicago Statement on Principles of Free Expression ("The Chicago Statement") was created in January of 2015 by a committee led by Geoffrey Stone, Edward H. Levi Distinguished Service Professor of Law. The committee was charged with crafting a statement "articulating the University's overarching commitment to free, robust, and uninhibited debate and deliberation among all members of the University's community."[1] Below is an abridged and adapted version of the statement FIRE has created in order to help schools tailor the concepts in the Chicago Statement to their own schools. By early 2018, over forty institutions had adopted it. One of the easiest things you can do to improve the situation on campus is to urge any school with which you have a relationship to adopt its own version of the Statement.

Because the [INSTITUTION] is committed to free and open inquiry in all matters, it guarantees all members of the [INSTITUTION] community the broadest possible latitude to speak, write, listen, challenge, and learn. Except insofar as limitations on that freedom are necessary to the functioning of the [INSTITUTION], the [INSTITUTION] fully respects and supports the freedom of all members of the [INSTITUTION] community "to discuss any problem that presents itself."

Of course, the ideas of different members of the [INSTITUTION] community will often and quite naturally conflict. But it is not the proper role of the [INSTITUTION] to attempt to shield individuals from ideas and opinions they find unwelcome, disagreeable, or even deeply offensive. Although the [INSTITUTION] greatly values civility, and although all members of the [INSTITUTION] community share in the responsibility for maintaining a climate of mutual respect, concerns about civility and mutual respect can never be used as a justification for closing off discussion of ideas, however offensive or disagreeable those ideas may be to some members of our community.

The freedom to debate and discuss the merits of competing ideas does not, of course, mean that individuals may say whatever they wish, wherever they wish. The [INSTITUTION] may restrict expression that violates the law, that falsely defames a specific individual, that constitutes a genuine threat or harassment, that unjustifiably invades substantial privacy or confidentiality interests, or that is otherwise directly incompatible with the functioning of the [INSTITUTION]. In addition, the [INSTITUTION] may reasonably regulate the time, place, and manner of expression to ensure that it does not disrupt the ordinary activities of the [INSTITUTION]. But these are narrow exceptions to the general principle of freedom of expression, and it is vitally important that these exceptions never be used in a manner that is inconsistent with the [INSTITUTION]'s commitment to a completely free and open discussion of ideas.

In a word, the [INSTITUTION]'s fundamental commitment is to the principle that debate or deliberation may not be suppressed because the ideas put forth are thought by some or even by most members of the [INSTITUTION] community to be offensive, unwise, immoral, or wrong-headed. It is for the individual members of the [INSTITUTION] community, not for the [INSTITUTION] as an institution, to make those judgments for themselves, and to act on those judgments not by seeking to suppress speech, but by openly and vigorously contesting the ideas that they oppose. Indeed, fostering the ability of members of the [INSTITUTION] community to engage in such debate and deliberation in an effective and responsible manner is an essential part of the [INSTITUTION]'s educational mission.

As a corollary to the [INSTITUTION]'s commitment to protect and promote free expression, members of the [INSTITUTION] community must also act in conformity with the principle of free expression. Although members of the [INSTITUTION] community are free to criticize and contest the views expressed on campus, and to criticize and contest speakers who are invited to express their views on campus, they may not obstruct or otherwise interfere with the freedom of others to express views they reject or even loathe. To this end, the [INSTITUTION] has a solemn responsibility not only to promote a lively and fearless freedom of debate and deliberation, but also to protect that freedom when others attempt to restrict it.

This resolution is adapted and excerpted from the 2015 University of Chicago Report of the Committee on Freedom of Expression. The full statement can be found at:

https://freeexpression.uchicago.edu/page/report-committee -freedom-expression

NOTES

For full information on books and academic journal articles, cited here by last name(s) and date only, see the References section. These notes are available at TheCoddling.com, to make it easy for readers to access the many online resources listed.

Epigraph

1. In Byrom (1993), chapter 3, verses 40–43. The more literal rendering in Mascaro (1973), chapter 3, verses 42–43, has the same meaning but is not as elegant: "An enemy can hurt an enemy, and a man who hates can harm another man, but a man's own mind, if wrongly directed, can do him a far greater harm. A father or a mother or a relative, can indeed do good to a man; but his own right-directed mind can do to him a far greater good."
2. Solzhenitsyn (1975), p. 168.

Introduction: The Search for Wisdom

1. Nietzsche (1889/1997). Maxim number 8.
2. Ponos was a minor Greek god of toil, pain, and hardship. *Miso* means "hatred" (as in "misogyny"), so the ancient Greek word *misoponos* means a hater of painful toil and hardship. We thank Professor Ian McCready-Flora, specialist in ancient Greek philosophy at the University of Virginia, for guiding us to this name. We cast Misoponos as the oracle of Koalemos. Koalemos is mentioned briefly in Aristophanes' play *The Birds* as the god of stupidity.
3. For readers outside the United States, let us take a moment here to clarify a few terms and Americanisms. We'll use the words "college" and "university" more or less interchangeably to refer to what in the United Kingdom and Canada is called "university." We'll often refer to "campus" to refer to the grounds, setting, and culture of universities. "High school" refers to grades nine through twelve, roughly ages fourteen to eighteen. We'll generally avoid using the word "liberal" to refer to the left, as is commonly done in the USA; we'll speak of left and right, progressive and conservative.
4. Find out more at http://www.theFIRE.org
5. Jarvie, J. (2014, March 3). Trigger happy. *The New Republic*. Retrieved from https://newrepublic.com/article/116842/trigger-warnings-have-spread-blogs-college-classes-thats-bad
6. Medina, J. (2014, May 17). Warning: The Literary Canon Could Make Students Squirm. *The New York Times*. Retrieved from https://www.nytimes.com/2014/05/18/us/warning-the-literary-canon-could-make-students-squirm.html
7. Columbia College. (n.d.). The Core curriculum: Literature Humanities. Retrieved from https://www.college.columbia.edu/core/lithum
8. Johnson, K., Lynch, T., Monroe, E., & Wang, T. (2015, April 30). Our identities matter in Core classrooms. *Columbia Daily Spectator*. Retrieved from http://spc.columbiaspectator.com/opinion/2015/04/30/our-identities-matter-core-classrooms
9. The "canon wars" that erupted after the publication of Allan Bloom's *The Closing of the American Mind* (1987) were mostly fought by faculty, but students often sided with the faculty favoring the inclusion of more women and people of color. For example, in a 1987 rally at Stanford celebrating such diversification, students chanted, "'Hey hey, ho ho, Western culture's got to go.'" See: Bernstein, R. (1988, January 19). In dispute on bias, Stanford is likely to alter Western culture program. *The New York Times*. Retrieved from

http://www.nytimes.com/1988/01/19/us/in-dispute-on-bias-stanford-is-likely-to-alter-western-culture-program.html

10. Pinker (2016), p. 110.

11. Haidt (2006).

12. Nelson, L. (2015, September 14). Obama on liberal college students who want to be "coddled": "That's not the way we learn." *Vox.* Retrieved from https://www.vox.com/2015/9/14/9326965/obama-political-correctness

13. There were hints in the United Kingdom as early as 2014; see O'Neill, B. (2014, November 22). Free speech is so last century. Today's students want the "right to be comfortable." *Spectator.* Retrieved from https://www.spectator.co.uk/2014/11/free-speech-is-so-last-century-todays-students-want-the-right-to-be-comfortable. But the number of news reports about "safe spaces" and related phenomena seemed to increase after the attention they got in the United States in the fall of 2015. See, for example: Gosden, E. (2016, April 3). Student accused of violating university "safe space" by raising her hand. *The Telegraph.* Retrieved from http://www.telegraph.co.uk/news/2016/04/03/student-accused-of-violating-university-safe-space-by-raising-he

14. See a summary of research and news reports from several countries at https://heterodoxacademy.org/international

15. There were dozens of cases, among them Eric Garner, Mike Brown, Tamir Rice, and Freddie Gray. It is less well-known that there were also several black women who were victims of police violence, including Michelle Cusseaux, Tanisha Anderson, Aura Rosser, and Meagan Hockaday. For more information on police shootings, see: Kelly, K., et al. (2016, December 30). Fatal shootings by police remain relatively unchanged after two years. *The Washington Post.* Retrieved from https://www.washingtonpost.com/investigations/fatal-shootings-by-police-remain-relatively-unchanged-after-two-years/2016/12/30/fc807596-c3ca-11e6-9578-0054287507db_story.html

16. Dorell, O. (2016, June 29). 2016 already marred by nearly daily terror attacks. *USA Today.* Retrieved from https://www.usatoday.com/story/news/world/2016/06/29/major-terrorist-attacks-year/86492692

17. Parvini, S., Branson-Potts, H., & Esquivel, P. (2017, February 1). For victims of San Bernardino terrorist attack, conflicting views about Trump policy in their name. *Los Angeles Times.* Retrieved from http://www.latimes.com/local/lanow/la-me-san-bernardino-trump-20170131-story.html

18. Ellis, R., Fantz, A., Karimi, F., & McLaughlin, E. (2016, June 13). Orlando shooting: 49 killed, shooter pledged ISIS allegiance. *CNN.* Retrieved from https://www.cnn.com/2016/06/12/us/orlando-nightclub-shooting/index.html

19. Branch, J., Kovaleski, S, & Tavernise, S. (2017, October 4). Stephen Paddock chased gambling's payouts and perks. *The New York Times.* Retrieved from https://www.nytimes.com/2017/10/04/us/stephen-paddock-gambling.html. See also: AP. (2018, January 19). The latest: Timeline offers look at Vegas shooter's moves. *U.S. News & World Report.* Retrieved from: https://www.usnews.com/news/us/articles/2018-01-19/the-latest-no-motive-uncovered-for-las-vegas-mass-shooting

20. Coddle [Def. 2]. (n.d.). *Merriam-Webster Dictionary* (11th ed.). Retrieved from https://www.merriam-webster.com/dictionary/coddling

21. You can find accessible, comprehensive data on these trends at the website humanprogress.org

Chapter 1: The Untruth of Fragility
What Doesn't Kill You Makes You Weaker

1. *The Book of Mencius,* in Chan (1963), p. 78.

2. Hendrick, B. (2010, May 14). Peanut allergies in kids on the rise. *WebMD.* Retrieved from http://www.webmd.com/allergies/news/20100514/peanut-allergies-in-kids-on-the-rise

3. Du Toit, Katz et al. (2008).

4. Christakis (2008).

5. Du Toit, Roberts et al. (2015).

6. LEAP Study Results. (2015). Retrieved from http://www.leapstudy.com/leap-study-results

7. LEAP Study Results. (2015); see n. 6.

8. Chan, S. (2001). Complex adaptive systems. Retrieved from http://web.mit.edu/esd.83/www/notebook/Complex%20Adaptive%20Systems.pdf. See also: Holland (1992).

9. Okada, Kuhn, Feillet, & Bach (2010).

10. Gopnik, A. (2016, August 31). Should we let toddlers play with saws and knives? *The Wall Street Journal.* Retrieved from http://www.wsj.com/articles/should-we-let-toddlers-play-with-saws-and-knives-1472654945

11. Taleb (2012), p. 5.

12. Taleb (2012), p. 3.
13. Child Trends Databank. (2016, November). Infant, child, and teen mortality. Retrieved from https://www .childtrends.org/indicators/infant-child-and-teen-mortality
14. Gopnik (2016); see n. 10.
15. Office of Equity Concerns. (2014). Support resources for faculty. *Oberlin College & Conservatory* [via Wayback Machine internet Archive]. Retrieved from http://web.archive.org/web/20131222174936
16. Haslam (2016).
17. American Psychiatric Association. (n.d.). DSM history. Retrieved from https://www.psychiatry.org/psy chiatrists/practice/dsm/history-of-the-dsm
18. Friedman, M. J. (2007, January 31). PTSD: National Center for PTSD. *U.S. Department of Veterans Affairs.* Retrieved from https://www.ptsd.va.gov/professional/ptsd-overview/ptsd-overview.asp. See also: Haslam (2016), p. 6.
19. Bonanno, Westphal, & Mancini (2011).
20. "Most trauma survivors are highly resilient and develop appropriate coping strategies, including the use of social supports, to deal with the aftermath and effects of trauma. Most recover with time, show minimal distress, and function effectively across major life areas and developmental stages." Center for Substance Abuse Treatment (U.S.). (2014). *Trauma-informed care in behavioral health services*, chapter 3, Understanding the impact of trauma. Rockville, MD: Substance Abuse and Mental Health Services Administration (U.S.). Retrieved from https://www.ncbi.nlm.nih.gov/books/NBK207191
21. Trauma. (n.d.). *SAMHSA-HRSA Center for Integrated Health Solutions.* Retrieved from https://www.inte gration.samhsa.gov/clinical-practice/trauma. Note: This tautological definition of "trauma" uses the reaction to the "experience" as the definition of whether trauma occurred.
22. This is particularly troubling, because if the effect is included in the definition of "trauma," when a person experiences what has come to be called "post-traumatic growth," whatever happened will no longer be defined as trauma, no matter how far outside the range of normal experience. This will eliminate the ability for people to experience post-traumatic growth, because if they are not suffering, the original events will not be defined as "traumatic." See: Collier (2016).
23. Shulevitz, J. (2015, March 21). In college and hiding from scary ideas. *The New York Times.* Retrieved from https://www.nytimes.com/2015/03/22/opinion/sunday/judith-shulevitz-hiding-from-scary-ideas.html
24. Rape culture. (n.d.). *Oxford Living Dictionaries.* Retrieved from https://en.oxforddictionaries.com/defini tion/rape_culture
25. McElroy, W. (2015, September 7). Debate with Jessica Valenti on "rape culture." Retrieved from https:// wendymcelroy.liberty.me/debate-with-jessica-valenti-on-rape-culture
26. Shulevitz (2015); see n. 23.
27. Around the same time, one student at Brown created a secret free speech Facebook group to engage in civil dialogue. See: Morey, A. (2015, December 28). FIRE Q&A: Reason@Brown's Christopher Robotham. *FIRE.* Retrieved from https://www.thefire.org/fire-qa-reasonbrowns-christopher-robotham. See also: Nordlinger, J. (2015, November 30). Underground at Brown. *National Review.* Retrieved from http://www.na tionalreview.com/article/427713/underground-brown-jay-nordlinger
28. This is a perfect example of what former Yale professor William Deresiewicz criticizes as the tendency for elite liberal arts colleges to avoid complex and challenging conversations about issues in favor of dogmatic conversations that create orthodox consensus. See: Deresiewicz, W. (2017, March 6). On political correctness. *The American Scholar.* Retrieved from https://theamericanscholar.org/on-political-correctness
29. Shulevitz (2015); see n. 23.
30. For a summary of this work, see: Haidt (2006), chapter 7. See also: work by Lawrence Calhoun & Richard Tedeschi. Posttraumatic Growth Research Group, UNC Charlotte. (n.d.). Retrieved from https://ptgi .uncc.edu
31. Foa & Kozak (1986).
32. McNally, R. (2016, September 13). If you need a trigger warning, you need PTSD. treatment. *The New York Times.* Retrieved from https://www.nytimes.com/roomfordebate/2016/09/13/do-trigger-warnings -work/if-you-need-a-trigger-warning-you-need-ptsd-treatment
33. R. Leahy (personal communication, December 29, 2017). See also: McNally (2016); see n. 32.
34. So said Aristotle in *The Nicomachean Ethics.* The only exception to this principle we can think of is wisdom.
35. Twenge (2017), p. 3.
36. Twenge (2017), p. 154.
37. For discussion and evidence about the changing dynamic around speech and censorship on college campuses, see Stevens, S., & Haidt, J. (2018, April 11). The skeptics are wrong part 2: Speech culture on campus is changing. Retrieved from https://heterodoxacademy.org/the-skeptics-are-wrong-part-2

Chapter 2: The Untruth of Emotional Reasoning
Always Trust Your Feelings

1. From the *Enchiridion*. Epictetus & Lebell (1st–2nd century/1995), p. 7.
2. Mascaro (1995), chapter 1, verse 1.
3. Shakespeare, W. *Hamlet*. II.ii, ll. 268–270.
4. Milton (1667/2017), bk. I, ll. 241–255.
5. Boethius (ca. 524 CE/2011). Note that the psychoanalyst Victor Frankl, reflecting on his years in a concentration camp, reached the same conclusion: "Everything can be taken from a man but one thing: the last of the human freedoms—to choose one's attitude in any given set of circumstances, to choose one's own way." See: Frankl (1959/2006), Part I, p. 66.
6. In his best-selling book *Thinking Fast and Slow* (Kahneman 2011), Nobel laureate psychologist Daniel Kahneman refers to automatic processes as System 1, which is fast, and controlled processes as System 2, which is slow.
7. Thousands of studies and hundreds of meta-analyses have now examined the effectiveness of CBT for treating depression and anxiety disorders. For a recent and accessible review of the literature, see: Hollon & DeRubeis (in press). We can summarize a common view with this sentence from the website of the United Kingdom's Royal College of Psychiatrists: CBT "is one of the most effective treatments for conditions where anxiety or depression is the main problem . . . [it is] the most effective psychological treatment for moderate and severe depression, [and] is as effective as antidepressants for many types of depression." Blenkiron, P. (2013, July). Cognitive behavioural therapy. *Royal College of Psychiatrists*. Retrieved from https://www.rcpsych.ac.uk/mentalhealthinformation/therapies/cognitivebehaviouraltherapy.aspx
8. "Cognitive therapy can be as efficacious as antidepressant medications . . . unlike medication, its benefits persist after treatment ceases . . . cognitive therapy is at least as efficacious and quite possibly longer lasting than alternative approaches [to Generalized Anxiety Disorder]." Hollon & DeRubeis (in press).
9. Blenkiron (2013); see n. 7. See also: CBT outcome studies. (2016, November 25). *Academy of Cognitive Therapy*. Retrieved from http://www.academyofct.org/page/OutcomeStudies
10. We make no claim that CBT is more effective for all psychological disorders, but because it is so easy to do and it is the most researched form of psychotherapy, it is often thought of as the gold standard to which other forms of treatment, including drugs, should be compared. See: Butler, Chapman, Forman, & Beck (2006).
11. Nine common cognitive distortions from the list in Robert L. Leahy, Stephen J. F. Holland, & Lata K. McGinn's book *Treatment Plans and Interventions for Depression and Anxiety Disorders*, 2nd ed. (New York, NY: Guilford Press, 2012).
12. For various definitions of "critical thinking," see: Defining critical thinking. (n.d.). *The Foundation for Critical Thinking*. Retrieved from https://www.criticalthinking.org/pages/defining-critical-thinking/766
13. Sue et al. (2007). The definition quoted is on p. 271. The term was first coined and discussed by Pierce (1970).
14. Unconscious or implicit associations are very real, although the relationships of such associations to discriminatory behavior are complex and are currently being debated by social psychologists. See: Rubinstein, Jussim, & Stevens (2018). For a defense of the role of implicit bias in causing discriminatory behavior, see: Greenwald, Banaji, & Nosek (2015).
15. Even when a person interacts with a bigot, CBT can help that person reduce the amount and likelihood of suffering.
16. Hamid, S. (2018, February 17). Bari Weiss, outrage mobs, and identity politics. *The Atlantic*. Retrieved from https://www.theatlantic.com/politics/archive/2018/02/bari-weiss-immigrants/553550
17. Miller, G. (2017, July 18). The neurodiversity case for free speech. *Quillette*. Retrieved from http://quillette.com/2017/07/18/neurodiversity-case-free-speech
18. FIRE. (2017). Bias Response Team Report. [Blog post]. Retrieved from https://www.thefire.org/first-amendment-library/special-collections/fire-guides/report-on-bias-reporting-systems-2017
19. For a review and critique of research on microaggressions, see Lilienfeld (2017).
20. For example, Heider (1958). One exception to this principle is very young children, who will often judge a well-intentioned act to be wrong if it accidentally causes harm. See: Piaget (1932/1965).
21. Utt, J. (2013, July 30). Intent vs. impact: Why your intentions don't really matter. *Everyday Feminism*. Retrieved from https://everydayfeminism.com/2013/07/intentions-dont-really-matter
22. Karith created and teaches the C.A.R.E. model (Conscious Empathy, Active Listening, Responsible Reaction, and Environmental Awareness) in her workshops and presentations.
23. K. Foster (personal communication, February 17, 2018).
24. Zimmerman, J. (2016, June 16). Two kinds of PC. *Inside Higher Ed.* Retrieved from https://www.inside-highered.com/views/2016/06/16/examination-two-kinds-political-correctness-essay

25. Rotter (1966).
26. For reviews, see Cobb-Clark (2015).
27. Buddelmeyer & Powdthavee (2015).
28. See, for example, the shout-downs of Charles Murray at Middlebury College and Heather Mac Donald at Claremont McKenna College, which we'll describe in chapter 4. FIRE maintains a database of disinvitation attempts: Disinvitation Database. (n.d.). Retrieved from https://www.thefire.org/resources/disinvitation-database
29. Bauer-Wolf, J. (2017, October 6). Free speech advocate silenced. *Inside Higher Ed.* Retrieved from https://www.insidehighered.com/news/2017/10/06/william-mary-students-who-shut-down-aclu-event-broke-conduct-code
30. About a third of the cases in which the push came from the right originated off campus, and half these cases involved religious organizations objecting to someone speaking about issues related to abortion and contraception. Of disinvitation efforts from the left, fewer than 5% were initiated from off-campus sources. To examine the data yourself, visit https://www.the fire.org/resources/disinvitation-database
31. Yiannopoulos, M. (2016, August 20). Trolls will save the world. *Breitbart.* Retrieved from http://www.breitbart.com/milo/2016/08/20/trolls-will-save-world
32. Stevens, S. (2017, February 7). Campus speaker disinvitations: Recent trends (Part 2 of 2) [Blog post]. Retrieved from https://heterodoxacademy.org/2017/02/07/campus-speaker-disinvitations-recent-trends-part-2-of-2
33. For more analysis of these trends, including a response to critics who claim that surveys show no recent changes in attitudes toward speech on campus, see Stevens, S., & Haidt, J. (2018, April 11). The skeptics are wrong part 2: Speech culture on campus is changing. Retrieved from https://heterodoxacademy.org/the-skeptics-are-wrong-part-2
34. Naughton, K. (2017, October). Speaking freely—What students think about expression at American colleges. *FIRE.* Retrieved from https://www.thefire.org/publications/student-attitudes-free-speech-survey
35. Socrates' fellow citizens ultimately accused him of impiety and of corrupting the youth of Athens. He was convicted by a jury and forced to drink poison. We'd like to think we are better able to tolerate "impiety" today.
36. Venker, S. (2015, October 20). Williams College's "Uncomfortable Learning" speaker series dropped me. Why? *FIRE.* Retrieved from http://www.foxnews.com/opinion/2015/10/20/williams-college-dropped-me-from-its-uncomfortable-learning-speaker-series-why.html
37. Paris, F. (2015, October 21). Organizers cancel Venker lecture. *The Williams Record.* Retrieved from http://williamsrecord.com/2015/10/21/organizers-cancel-venker-lecture
38. Wood, Z. (2015, October 18). Breaking through a ring of motivated ignorance. *Williams Alternative.* Retrieved from http://williamsalternative.com/2015/10/breaking-through-a-ring-of-motivated-ignorance-zach-wood. See also Wood's 2018 TED Talk: Why it's worth listening to people you disagree with. Retrieved from http://www.ted.com/talks/zachary_r_wood_why_it_s_worth_listening_to_people_we_disagree_with
39. Wood (2015); see n. 38.
40. Gray, (2012), p. 86.
41. Falk, A. (2016, February 18). John Derbyshire's scheduled appearance at Williams. *Williams College Office of the President.* Retrieved from https://president.williams.edu/letters-from-the-president/john-derbyshires-scheduled-appearance-at-williams

Chapter 3: The Untruth of Us Versus Them
Life Is a Battle Between Good People and Evil People

1. Sacks (2015), p. 51.
2. To protect her privacy, we have changed the student's name.
3. Adapted from the definition here: Cisnormativity. (2017). *The Queer Dictionary.* Retrieved from http://queerdictionary.blogspot.com/2014/09/definition-of-cisnormativity.html
4. Other than changing the name of the student and swapping in "[dean of students]" for the original "DOS," this was the exact text of the email.
5. You can see her explanation at minute 48 of this video: The CMC Forum (Producer). (2015, November 11). CMCers of color lead protest of lack of support from administration [Video file]. Retrieved from https://youtu.be/OlB7Vy-lZZ8?t=48m1s
6. Miller, S. (2015, November 18). VIDEO: CMCers of color lead protest of dean of students, administration. *The Forum.* Retrieved from http://cmcforum.com/news/11112015-video-cmcers-of-color-protest-dean-of-students-administration

7. Tidmarsh, K. (2015, November 11). CMC students of color protest for institutional support, call for dean of students to resign. *The Student Life.* Retrieved from http://tsl.news/news/5265

8. See the full video at: The CMC Forum (Producer). (2015, November 11). CMCers of color lead protest of lack of support from administration [Video file]. Retrieved from https://youtu.be/OlB7Vy-lZZ8?t=3s

9. Tidmarsh, K. (2015, November 11); see n. 7.

10. See that moment at time 41:33 of the video linked in n. 5.

11. We were not able to find any public statement of support, and when we emailed Spellman to ask if she knew of such a statement, she told us that she did not. Spellman, M. (personal communication, February 8, 2018).

12. Watanabe, T., & Rivera, C. (2015, November 13). Amid racial bias protests, Claremont McKenna dean resigns. *Los Angeles Times.* Retrieved from http://www.latimes.com/local/lanow/la-me-ln-claremont-marches-20151112-story.html

13. FIRE (2015, October 30). Email from Erika Christakis: "Dressing yourselves," email to Silliman College (Yale) students on Halloween costumes [Blog post]. Retrieved from https://www.thefire.org/email-from-erika-christakis-dressing-yourselves-email-to-silliman-college-yale-students-on-halloween-costumes

14. FIRE. (2015, October 27). Email from the Intercultural Affairs Committee [Blog post]. Retrieved from https://www.thefire.org/email-from-intercultural-affairs. Note that the Intercultural Affairs Committee is part of the dean's office.

15. Christakis, E. (2016, October 28). My Halloween email led to a campus firestorm—and a troubling lesson about self-censorship. *The Washington Post.* Retrieved from https://www.washingtonpost.com/opinions/my-halloween-email-led-to-a-campus-firestorm--and-a-troubling-lesson-about-self-censorship/2016/10/28/70e55 732-9b97-11e6-a0ed-ab0774c1eaa5_story.html. For the email from Erika Christakis, see n. 13.

16. Wilson, R. (2015, October 31). Open letter to Associate Master Christakis. *Down Magazine.* Retrieved from http://downatyale.com/post.php?id=430

17. By an extraordinary coincidence, Greg happened to be on the Yale campus that day and was present at the confrontation. To watch the videos that Greg took of the event, see: Shibley, R. (2015, September 13). New video of last year's Yale halloween costume confrontation emerges [Blog post]. Retrieved from https://www.thefire.org/new-video-of-last-years-yale-halloween-costume-confrontation-emerges

18. Kirchick, J. (2016, September 12). New videos show how Yale betrayed itself by favoring cry-bullies. *Tablet Magazine.* Retrieved from http://www.tabletmag.com/jewish-news-and-politics/213212/yale-favoring-cry-bullies

19. FIRE (Producer). (2015, November 7). Yale University students protest Halloween costume email (VIDEO 3). Retrieved from https://youtu.be/9IEFD_JVYd0?t=1m17s

20. On the question of whether the master creates an intellectual space or a home: the master plays a mixed role, partly residential and quasi-parental, partly intellectual. Jon graduated from Yale in 1985 and went to many academic events and talks in the home of the master of Davenport College.

21. President and Yale College dean underscore commitment to a "better Yale." (2015, November 6). *YaleNews.* Retrieved from https://news.yale.edu/2015/11/06/president-and-yale-college-dean-underscore-commitment-better-yale

22. Stanley-Becker, I. (2015, November 13). Minority students at Yale give list of demands to university president. *The Washington Post.* Retrieved from https://www.washingtonpost.com/news/grade-point/wp/2015/11/13/minority-students-at-yale-give-list-of-demands-to-university-president. See also: Next Yale. (2015, November 18). Next Yale demands for the Administration. Retrieved from https://www.thefire.org/next-yale-demands-for-the-administration

23. Schick, F. (2015, December 7). Erika Christakis leaves teaching role. *Yale Daily News.* Retrieved from https://yaledailynews.com/blog/2015/12/07/erika-christakis-to-end-teaching

24. Physics professor Douglas Stone spearheaded a public letter defending the Christakises that was signed over the course of many weeks by ninety professors, mostly in the sciences and the medical school. See also: Christakis, E. (2016, October 28). My Halloween email led to a campus firestorm—and a troubling lesson about self-censorship. *The Washington Post.* Retrieved from https://www.washingtonpost.com/opinions/my-halloween-email-led-to-a-campus-firestorm—and-a-troubling-lesson-about-self-censorship/2016/10/28/70e55732-9b97-11e6-a0ed-ab0774c1eaa5_story.html

25. For Claremont McKenna, see Watanabe, T., & Rivera, C. (2015, November 13). Amid racial protests, Claremont McKenna dean resigns. *Los Angeles Times.* Retrieved from http://www.latimes.com/local/lanow/la-me-ln-claremont-marches-20151112-story.html. For Yale, see Stanley-Becker, I. (2015, November 5). A confrontation over race at Yale: Hundreds of students demand answers from the school's first black dean. *The Washington Post.* Retrieved from https://www.washingtonpost.com/news/grade-point/wp/2015/11/05/a-confrontation-over-race-at-yale-hundreds-of-students-demand-answers-from-the-schools-first-black-dean

26. Tajfel (1970).

27. See overall review in Berreby (2005); see Hogg (2016) for a review of social identity theory; see Cikara & Van Bavel (2014) for a review of neuroscience work in this area.

28. Vaughn, Savjani, Cohen, & Eagleman (manuscript under review). For more on this study, see: iqsquared (Producer). (2012, June 22). David Eagleman: What makes us empathetic? IQ2 Talks [Video file]. Retrieved from https://youtu.be/TDjWryXdVd0?t=7m42s

29. For a review of this literature, including the debate over whether "group selection" played a role in the human story, over and above individual selection, see Haidt (2012), chapter 9. For a contrary view, see: Pinker, S. (2012, June 18). The false allure of group selection. *Edge*. Retrieved from https://www.edge.org/conversation/steven_pinker-the-false-allure-of-group-selection

30. Chapter 10 of *The Righteous Mind* (Haidt, 2012) describes the "hive switch," a psychological reflex in which self-interest is turned off and group interest becomes paramount; people lose themselves in the group. People can become tribal when the hive switch getting activated. The hive response is what happens when tribalism is activated intensely, particularly through highly engaging multisensory rituals.

31. This is the third of three basic principles in Jon's book *The Righteous Mind*.

32. We are using "tribalism" in a way that overstates the degree of closure and conflict of real tribes. For a description of how real tribes often draw from one another's practices and form alliances to reduce conflict, see Rosen, L. (2018, January 16). A liberal defense of tribalism. *Foreign Policy*. Retrieved from http://foreignpolicy.com/2018/01/16/a-liberal-defense-of-tribalism-american-politics

33. To learn more about how the campus trends described in this book are now influencing high schools, and to find resources for high school students who want to find a more open and intellectually diverse culture in college, please visit heterodoxacademy.org/highschool

34. Rauch, J. (2017, November 9). Speaking as a . . . *The New York Review of Books*. Retrieved from http://www.nybooks.com/articles/2017/11/09/mark-lilla-liberal-speaking

35. King (1963/1981), p. 52.

36. King (1963/1981), p. 51.

37. Mascaro (1995), p. 2.

38. Bellah (1967).

39. King, M. L. (1963, August 28). "I have a dream . . ." Retrieved from https://www.archives.gov/files/press/exhibits/dream-speech.pdf

40. King (1963); see n. 38. You can listen to an audio recording of the speech here: http://www.americanrhetoric.com/speeches/mlkihaveadream.htm

41. Most whites at the time did not see it this way. In a Harris poll a few months before he was assassinated, nearly 75% of Americans expressed disapproval of him, although he had been substantially more popular at the time of his 1963 *I Have a Dream* speech, and he is wildly popular now, with approval levels above 90%. It took time, but the ideas in his 1963 speech changed the country. See Cobb, J. C. (2018, April 4). When Martin Luther King Jr. was killed, he was less popular than Donald Trump is today. *USA Today*. Retrieved from https://www.usatoday.com/story/opinion/2018/04/04/martin-luther-king-jr-50-years-assassination-donald-trump-disapproval-column/482242002

42. Pauli Murray College. (n.d.). About Pauli Murray. Retrieved from https://paulimurray.yalecollege.yale.edu/subpage-2

43. Murray (1945), p. 24.

44. MainersUnited (Producer). (2012, November 2). Yes on 1: Mainers United for Marriage—Will & Arlene Brewster [Video file]. Retrieved from https://www.youtube.com/watch?v=rizfhtN6UVc

45. Chapters 2, 3, and 4 of *The Righteous Mind* (Haidt, 2012) provide a literature review in support of this claim.

46. We have quoted the version given in Haji (2011), p. 185.

47. The essay was removed, but screen shots of it can be found here: Coyne, J. (n.d.). Texas college newspaper publishes op-ed calling white DNA an "abomination" [Blog post]. Retrieved from https://whyevolutionistrue.wordpress.com/2017/11/30/texas-college-newspaper-publishes-op-ed-calling-white-dna-an-abomination. (The first line is actually a variant of a line from the Bhagavad Gita: "Now I am become white, destroyer of worlds.")

48. Cohn, A. (2017, December 13). Students, faculty, and administrators launch attack on Texas State University newspaper. *FIRE*. Retrieved from https://www.thefire.org/students-faculty-and-administrators-launch-attack-on-texas-state-university-newspaper

49. Defund the racist University Star. (2017, November 30). Retrieved from https://www.change.org/p/bobcat-liberty-council-defund-the-racist-star

50. Cervantes, D. (2017, November 28). Editor's note. *The University Star*. Retrieved from https://star.txstate.edu/2017/11/28/letter-from-the-editor-3

51. More details are found in Cohn (2017); see n. 48. See also: Trauth, D. (2017, November 28). Message from the president regarding University Star column. *Texas State University–Office of Media Relations*.

Retrieved from http://www.txstate.edu/news/news_releases/news_archive/2017/November-2017/Statement112917.html

52. As Marcuse explained in a postscript to the essay, added in 1968: "The Left has no equal voice, no equal access to the mass media and their public facilities—not because a conspiracy excludes it, but because, in good old capitalist fashion, it does not have the required purchasing power." Wolff, Moore, & Marcuse (1965/1969), p. 119.

53. Marcuse referred to "official tolerance granted to the Right as well as to the Left, to movements of aggression as well as to movements of peace, to the party of hate as well as to that of humanity." Wolff, Moore, & Marcuse (1965/1969), p. 85.

54. Wolff, Moore, & Marcuse (1965/1969), p. 109.

55. Wolff, Moore, & Marcuse (1965/1969), pp. 100–101.

56. Wolff, Moore, & Marcuse (1965/1969), p. 110.

57. Columbia Law School. (2011, October 12). Center for Intersectionality and Social Policy Studies established. Retrieved from http://www.law.columbia.edu/media_inquiries/news_events/2011/october2011/Intersectionality

58. Crenshaw (1989).

59. Degraffenreid v. General Motors Assembly Division, 413 F. Supp. 142 (E.D. Mo. 1976).

60. Collins & Bilge (2016), p. 7.

61. TED (Producer). (2016, October). The urgency of intersectionality [Video file]. Retrieved from https://www.ted.com/talks/kimberle_crenshaw_the_urgency_of_intersectionality

62. Morgan (1996), p. 107.

63. Morgan (1996), p. 106.

64. Morgan (1996), p. 106.

65. A video of the encounter is embedded in the documentary Silence U, which is available here (the scene begins at time 7:53): We the Internet (Producer). (2016, July 14). Silence U: Is the university killing free speech and open debate? We the Internet Documentary [Video file]. Retrieved from https://youtu.be/x5u aVFfX3AQ?t=7m55s

66. TED (2016); see n. 61.

67. For example, Creighton University posts on its website an exercise that is "designed to bring a group to certain conclusions regarding the concept of privilege and disadvantage." Based on various questions, people either step forward or step backward. It begins: "Few White people in the history of the U.S. have ever been convicted and executed for killing a person of color. All White persons take a step forward." Next: "The high school dropout rate for Latinos, Native Americans and African Americans is over 55%. Latinos, African Americans, and Native Americans take one step back." At the end of the exercise, whoever is at the front of the room has the most "privilege," and whoever is at the back has the least. The instructor then says, "Notice what groups of people are in the front and what groups of people are in the back." See: Privilege exercise (race focus). (n.d.). Retrieved from https://people.creighton.edu/~idc24708/Genes/Diversity/Privilege%20Exercise.htm

68. We do not know if ideas related to intersectionality were included in CMC's orientation process; the ideas may have come from their courses or from other students. But intersectional language is common in the video of the confrontation with Spellman: The CMC Forum (Producer) (2015, November 11). CMCers of color lead protest of lack of support from administration [Video file]. Retrieved from https://www.youtube.com/watch?v=OlB7Vy-lZZ8

69. Friedersdorf, C. (2017, May 8). The destructiveness of call-out culture on campus. The Atlantic. Retrieved from https://www.theatlantic.com/politics/archive/2017/05/call-out-culture-is-stressing-out-college-students/524679

70. Barrett, K. (2016, September 22). Walking on eggshells—How political correctness is changing the campus dynamic. The Sophian. Retrieved from http://www.thesmithsophian.com/walking-on-eggshells-how-political-correctness-is-changing-the-campus-dynamic

71. For extensive analyses of survey data showing that the campus dynamic related to speech has changed in the last few years, see Stevens, S., & Haidt, J. (2018, April 11), The skeptics are wrong part 2: Speech culture on campus is changing. Retrieved from https://heterodoxacademy.org/the-skeptics-are-wrong-part-2

72. Friedersdorf (2017); see n. 69.

73. Zimbardo (2007).

74. Eady, T. (2014, November 24). "Everything is problematic": My journey into the centre of a dark political world, and how I escaped. The McGill Daily. Retrieved from https://www.mcgilldaily.com/2014/11/everything-problematic

75. For an extended argument that political activity generally interferes with a scholar's ability to find the truth, see: Van der Vossen (2014).

76. Alexander (2010).
77. Balko (2013).
78. Silverglate (2009).
79. Right on Crime. (n.d.). The conservative case for reform. Retrieved from http://rightoncrime.com/the-conservative-case-for-reform
80. Hirsh, M. (2015, March/April). Charles Koch, liberal crusader? *Politico*. Retrieved from https://www.politico.com/magazine/story/2015/03/charles-koch-overcriminalization-115512
81. Lilla (2017), p. 9.
82. For an edited version of the interaction in an extraordinary video, see: Now This Politics (Producer). (2017, September 8). This unexpected moment happened when Black Lives Matter activists were invited on stage at a pro-Trump rally [Video file]. Retrieved from https://www.facebook.com/NowThisNews/videos/1709220972442719
83. Hains, T. (2017, September 20). "Black Lives Matter" leader wins over Trump supporters: "If we really want America great, we do it together." *Real Clear Politics*. Retrieved from https://www.realclearpolitics.com/video/2017/09/20/black_lives_matter_leader_wins_over_trump_supporters_if_we_really_want_america_great_we_do_it_together.html

Chapter 4: Intimidation and Violence

1. Mandela (2003), p. 545.
2. Warzel, C. (2016, July 19). Twitter permanently suspends Conservative writer Milo Yiannopoulos. *Buzz-Feed*. Retrieved from https://www.buzzfeed.com/charliewarzel/twitter-just-permanently-suspended-conservative-writer-milo
3. In the words of Milo Yiannopoulos, "Trolling is very important. . . . I like to think of myself as a virtuous troll, you know? I'm doing God's work." Moran, T., Taguchi, E., & Pedersen, C. (2016, September 1). Leslie Jones' Twitter Troll Has No Regrets Over Attacking the 'Ghostbusters' Actress. *ABC News*. Retrieved from https://abcnews.go.com/Entertainment/leslie-jones-twitter-troll-regrets-attacking-ghostbusters-actress/story?id=41808886. See also Yiannopoulos' statement: "A real troll, of course, does aim to provoke. They do aim to cause mild rage. They aim to prank, to goad, to wind people up. . . . So trolls, my message to you today is: once the election is over, get off your laptops and head down to your local campus." Yiannopoulos, M. (2016, August 20). Trolls will save the world. *Breitbart*. Retrieved from http://www.breitbart.com/milo/2016/08/20/trolls-will-save-world
4. Scott Crow, former Antifa organizer, explains: "The idea in Antifa is that we go where they [right-wingers] go. That hate speech is not free speech. That if you are endangering people with what you say and the actions that are behind them, then you do not have the right to do that. And so we go to cause conflict, to shut them down where they are." See Suerth, J. (2017, August 17). What is Antifa? *CNN*. Retrieved from https://www.cnn.com/2017/08/14/us/what-is-antifa-trnd/index.html
5. Kell, G. (2017, February 2). Campus investigates, assesses damage from Feb. 1 violence. *Berkeley News*. Retrieved from http://news.berkeley.edu/2017/02/02/campus-investigates-assesses-damage-from-feb-1-violence
6. Lochner, T. (2017, February 1). UC Berkeley: Protesters shut down Milo Yiannopoulos event, clash with police. *East Bay Times*. Retrieved from http://www.eastbaytimes.com/2017/02/01/uc-berkeley-cancels-breitbart-provocateur-milo-yiannopoulos-event
7. Park, M., & Lah, K. (2017, February 2). Berkeley protests of Yiannopoulos caused $100,000 in damage. *CNN*. Retrieved from http://www.cnn.com/2017/02/01/us/milo-yiannopoulos-berkeley/index.html
8. Riot forces cancellation of Yiannopoulos talk at UC Berkeley. (2017, February 1). *CBS SF Bay Area*. Retrieved from http://sanfrancisco.cbslocal.com/2017/02/01/berkeley-braces-for-protests-at-yiannopoulos-talk
9. Park & Lah (2017); see n. 7.
10. Arnold, C. (2017, February 1). Violence and chaos erupt at UC–Berkeley in protest against Milo Yiannopoulos. *USA Today College*. Retrieved from http://college.usatoday.com/2017/02/01/violence-and-chaos-erupt-at-uc-berkeley-in-protest-against-milo-yiannopoulos
11. Riot forces cancellation (2017); see n. 8.
12. Rioters break windows, set fire to force cancellation of Breitbart editor's UC–Berkeley talk. (2017, February 1). *Fox News*. Retrieved from http://www.foxnews.com/us/2017/02/01/rioters-break-windows-set-fire-to-force-cancellation-breitbart-editors-uc-berkeley-talk.html
13. RTQuestionsMore (Producer). (2017, February 1). Kiara Robles talks to RT International [Video file]. Retrieved from https://www.youtube.com/watch?v=SUQdlc8Gc-g&feature=youtu.be

14. Park & Lah (2017); see n. 7.
15. CNBC with Reuters and AP. (2017, February 1). Trump threatens UC Berkeley with funds cut after Breitbart editor's speech is canceled following riot. *CNBC.* Retrieved from https://www.cnbc.com/2017/02/01/uc-berkeley-on-lockdown-amid-protest-over-milo-yiannopoulos.html
16. "The demonstrators caused an estimated $100,000 in damage on campus, the university said, and an additional $400,000 to $500,000 elsewhere, according to Downtown Berkeley Association CEO John Caner." Kutner, M. (2017, February 1). Inside the black bloc protest strategy that shut down Berkeley. *Newsweek.* Retrieved from http://www.newsweek.com/2017/02/24/berkeley-protest-milo-yiannopoulos-black-bloc-556264.html
17. Freedman, W. (2017, February 1). VIDEO: Trump supporter pepper sprayed at Milo protest. *ABC 7 News.* Retrieved from http://abc7news.com/news/video-trump-supporter-pepper-sprayed-at-milo-protest/1733004
18. Mackey, R. (2017, February 4). Amid the chaos in Berkeley, a grinning face, covered in blood. *The Intercept.* Retrieved from https://theintercept.com/2017/02/04/amid-chaos-berkeley-grinning-face-covered-blood
19. Freedman (2017); see n. 17.
20. K. Redelsheimer & J. Jennings (personal communication, March 1, 2017). See also: Fabian, P. (Producer). (2017, February 2). Protestors beating people at Milo Yiannopoulos event @ U.C. Berkeley [Video file]. Retrieved from https://www.youtube.com/watch?v=GSMKGRyWKas
21. K. Redelsheimer (personal communication, March 1, 2017).
22. Gale, J. (2017, February). EXCLUSIVE FOOTAGE: Anarchists smash windows and riot at UC Berkeley after Milo Yiannopoulos's talk is canceled. *The Tab.* Retrieved from http://thetab.com/us/uc-berkeley/2017/02/02/exclusive-footage-anarchist-group-smashes-windows-sets-fire-sproul-riots-uc-berkeley-milo-yiannopouloss-talk-cancelled-3244
23. P. Jandhyala (personal communication, July 11, 2017).
24. UC Berkeley Campus Police tweeted: @UCBerkeley Milo event cancelled. Shelter in place if on campus. All campus buildings on lockdown. #miloatcal. Retrieved from https://twitter.com/ucpd_cal/status/826978649341440000?lang=en
25. Riot forces cancellation (2017); see n. 8.
26. Zoppo, A., Proença Santos, A., & Hudgins, J. (2017, February 14). Here's the full list of Donald Trump's executive orders. *NBC News.* Retrieved from https://www.nbcnews.com/politics/white-house/here-s-full-list-donald-trump-s-executive-orders-n720796
27. Helsel, P. (2017, February 2). Protests, violence prompt UC Berkeley to cancel Milo Yiannopoulos event. *NBC News.* Retrieved from https://www.nbcnews.com/news/us-news/protests-violence-prompts-uc-berkeley-cancel-milo-yiannopoulos-event-n715711
28. Lawrence, N. (2017, February 7). Black bloc did what campus should have. *The Daily Californian.* Retrieved from http://www.dailycal.org/2017/02/07/black-bloc-campus. See also a similar claim: Meagley, D. (2017, February 7). Condemning protesters same as condoning hate speech. *The Daily Californian.* Retrieved from http://www.dailycal.org/2017/02/07/condemning-protesters-condoning-hate-speech
29. When we contacted the UC Berkeley Office of Public Affairs, it refused to disclose whether any students had been disciplined by the university in connection with the protests, citing federal privacy laws. It later clarified that, in the month of February, two students were arrested: one for vandalism and one for failure to disperse. As far as we can tell, no students were punished by the university in any way, so there was no punishment that would act as a deterrent for future violent protests.
30. Bodley, M. (2017, February 2). At Berkeley Yiannopoulos protest, $100,000 in damage, 1 arrest. *SFGate.* Retrieved from http://www.sfgate.com/crime/article/At-Berkeley-Yiannopoulos-protest-100-000-in-1090 5217.php. See also: Berkeley free speech protests: Arrests, injuries, damages since February. (2017, April 25). *Fox News.* Retrieved from http://www.foxnews.com/politics/2017/04/25/berkeley-free-speech-protests-arrests-injuries-damages-since-february.html
31. In 2016, at California State University, Los Angeles, the university president canceled a speech about diversity by conservative Ben Shapiro, requiring that, instead, he "appear as part of a group of speakers with differing viewpoints on diversity" (something that had not been required of any other recent speakers). Eventually, the president relented, but at the event, students locked arms to prevent people from getting in. Some who tried to enter were pushed to the ground. After UC Berkeley failed to prevent violence on campus in February 2017, and Ben Shapiro was scheduled to speak there later in the year, threats of violence in response to his presence required approximately $600,000 of security. At least nine people were arrested, three of them reportedly for "banned weapons" (including an oversized cardboard sign), but otherwise Shapiro spoke without incident. (In 2016, Shapiro had spoken at Berkeley without significant protest.) See: Logue, J. (2016, February 24). Another Speaker Blocked. *Inside Higher Ed.* Retrieved from https://www.insidehighered.com/news/2016/02/24/cal-state-los-angeles-cancels-conservative-speakers-appearance.

See also: Steinbaugh, A. (2016, February 26). CSU Los Angeles President Fails to Prevent Shapiro Talk, But Protesters Try Their Hardest Anyway. *FIRE*. Retrieved from https://www.thefire.org/csu-los-angeles -president-fails-to-prevent-shapiro-talk-but-protesters-try-their-hardest-anyway. See also: Gomez, M. (2017, September 15). Nine people arrested at Ben Shapiro event at UC Berkeley. *The Mercury News*. Retrieved from https://www.mercurynews.com/2017/09/15/nine-people-arrested-at-ben-shapiro-event -at-uc-berkeley. See also: Alliance Defending Freedom. (2017, February 28). Cal State L.A. agrees to drop discriminatory speech policies, settles lawsuit. Retrieved from https://adflegal.org/detailspages/press -release-details/cal-state-l.a.-agrees-to-drop-discriminatory-speech-policies-settles-lawsuit. See also: UC Berkeley declares itself unsafe for Ann Coulter. (2017, April 20). *The Atlantic*. Retrieved from https://www .theatlantic.com/politics/archive/2017/04/uc-berkeley-declares-itself-unsafe-for-ann-coulter/523668. See also: Fehely, D. (2017, April 11). Conservative writer David Horowitz's talk at UC Berkeley cancelled. *CBS SF Bay Area*. Retrieved from http://sanfrancisco.cbslocal.com/2017/04/11/uc-berkeley-presses-campus -republicans-to-cancel-another-conservative-speaker. See also: McPhate, M. (2017, September 15). Califor- nia today: Price tag to protect speech at Berkeley: $600,000. *The New York Times*. Retrieved from https://www.nytimes.com/2017/09/15/us/california-today-price-tag-to-protect-speech-at-berkeley -600000.html

32. Cohen, R. (2017, February 7). What might Mario Savio have said about the Milo protest at Berkeley? *The Nation*. Retrieved from https://www.thenation.com/article/what-might-mario-savio-have-said-about -the-milo-protest-at-berkeley

33. Ashenmiller, J. (2013). Mario Savio. *Encyclopaedia Britannica Online*. Retrieved from https://www.britan nica.com/biography/Mario-Savio

34. Senju, H. (2017, February 7). Violence as self-defense. *The Daily Californian*. Retrieved from http://www .dailycal.org/2017/02/07/violence-self-defense

35. Meagley, D. (2017, February 7). Condemning protesters same as condoning hate speech. *The Daily Californian*. Retrieved from http://www.dailycal.org/2017/02/07/condemning-protesters-condoning -hate-speech

36. Dang, N. (2017, February 7). Check your privilege when speaking of protests. *The Daily Californian*. Re- trieved from http://www.dailycal.org/2017/02/07/check-privilege-speaking-protests

37. Overpass Light Brigade. (2016, December 14). Hate's insidious face: UW–Milwaukee and the "alt-right." Retrieved from http://overpasslightbrigade.org/hates-insidious-face-uw-milwaukee-and-the-alt-right

38. Lawrence (2017); see n. 28.

39. Villasenor, J. (2017, September 18). Views among college students regarding the First Amendment: Results from a new survey. Retrieved from https://www.brookings.edu/blog/fixgov/2017/09/18/views-among -college-students-regarding-the-first-amendment-results-from-a-new-survey. For criticism, see: Beckett, L. (2017, September 22). "Junk science": Experts cast doubt on widely cited college free speech survey. *The Guardian*. Retrieved from https://www.theguardian.com/us-news/2017/sep/22/college-free-speech-violence -survey-junk-science. For Villasenor's response, see: Volokh, E. (2017, October 23). Freedom of expression on campus: An overview of some recent surveys. *The Washington Post*. Retrieved from https://www.wash ingtonpost.com/news/volokh-conspiracy/wp/2017/10/23/freedom-of-expression-on-campus-an-overvie w-of-some-recent-surveys

40. McLaughlin, J., & Schmidt, R. (2017, September 28). National Undergraduate Study. *McLaughlin & Asso- ciates*. Retrieved from http://c8.nrostatic.com/sites/default/files/NATL%20Undergrad%209-27-17%20Pre sentation%20%281%29.pdf

41. McWhorter, J. (2017, June 30). A Columbia professor's critique of campus politics. *The Atlantic*. Retrieved from https://www.theatlantic.com/politics/archive/2017/06/a-columbia-professors-critique-of-campus-poli tics/532335

42. "The idea is that if you go against a certain orthodoxy, then it isn't only that you disagree, but that you also wish white people were still in charge, that you want people of color to sit down and shut up." See: McWhorter, J. (2016, November 29). The difference between racial bias and white supremacy. *Time*. Re- trieved from http://time.com/4584161/white-supremacy

43. Stack, L. (2017, January 21). Attack on alt-right leader has internet asking: Is it O.K. to punch a Nazi? *The New York Times*. Retrieved from https://www.nytimes.com/2017/01/21/us/politics/richard-spencer-punched -attack.html

44. In fact, we can make a prediction right now, while writing this book in 2017: Most of the negative reviews and responses to this book will at some point note our race and gender and then directly assert or vaguely hint that we are racists or sexists who are motivated primarily by the desire to preserve our privilege. We will then respond in the spirit of Mark Lilla, the author of a critique of identity politics titled *The Once and Future Liberal*. Lilla, an avowed liberal who wrote his book to help the Democrats start winning elections, responds to repeated name-calling by saying, essentially, "That is a slur, not an argument. Make an

argument and I'll respond to it." See, for example, Goldstein, E. R. (2016, December 15). Campus identity politics is dooming liberal causes, a professor charges. *Chronicle of Higher Education*. Retrieved from https://www.chronicle.com/article/Campus-Identity-Politics-Is/238694

45. See, for example, the extraordinary success of J. D. Vance's 2016 book *Hillbilly Elegy* and Arlie Russell Hochschild's 2016 book *Strangers in Their Own Land*, which covered some similar ground.

46. Goodnow, N., & Pethokoukis, J. (2014, October 16). "The Bell Curve" 20 years later: A Q&A with Charles Murray. *American Enterprise Institute*. Retrieved from http://www.aei.org/publication/bell-curve-20-years-later-qa-charles-murray

47. Stanger, A. (2017, March 13). Understanding the angry mob at Middlebury that gave me a concussion. *The New York Times*. Retrieved from https://www.nytimes.com/2017/03/13/opinion/understanding-the-angry-mob-that-gave-me-a-concussion.html

48. Independent, A. (2017, March 6). Middlebury College professor injured by protesters as she escorted controversial speaker. *Addison County Independent*. Retrieved from http://www.addisonindependent.com/201703middlebury-college-professor-injured-protesters-she-escorted-controversial-speaker

49. Seelye, K. (2017, March 3). Protesters disrupt speech by "Bell Curve" author at Vermont College. *The New York Times*. Retrieved from https://www.nytimes.com/2017/03/03/us/middlebury-college-charles-murray-bell-curve-protest.html

50. Independent (2017); see n. 48.

51. Murray, C. (2017, March 5). Reflections on the revolution in Middlebury. *American Enterprise Institute*. Retrieved from http://www.aei.org/publication/reflections-on-the-revolution-in-middlebury

52. A. Stanger (personal communication, January 5, 2018). Note that the mob at Middlebury appears to have been composed primarily of Middlebury students. In total, seventy-four students were disciplined: forty-eight were sanctioned for events during the lecture, and twenty-six received some form of punishment for their participation in the events after the main lecture disruption. See: Middlebury College completes sanctioning process for March 2 disruptions. (2017, May 23). Retrieved from http://www.middlebury.edu/newsroom/archive/2017-news/node/547896

53. Stanger (2017); see n. 47.

54. Blume, H. (2017, April 9). Protesters disrupt talk by pro-police author, sparking free-speech debate at Claremont McKenna College. *Los Angeles Times*. Retrieved from http://www.latimes.com/local/lanow/la-me-ln-macdonald-claremont-speech-disrupted-20170408-story.html

55. Wootson, C. R., Jr. (2017, April 10). She wanted to criticize Black Lives Matter in a college speech. A protest shuts her down. *The Washington Post*. Retrieved from https://www.washingtonpost.com/news/grade-point/wp/2017/04/10/she-wanted-to-criticize-black-lives-matter-in-a-college-speech-a-protest-shut-her-down

56. Gross, N. (2016, September 30). Is there a "Ferguson Effect"? *The New York Times*. Retrieved from https://www.nytimes.com/2016/10/02/opinion/sunday/is-there-a-ferguson-effect.html

57. ShutDown Anti-Black Fascists. (2017, April). SHUT DOWN anti-black fascist Heather Mac Donald [on *Facebook*] [via archive.is webpage capture]. Retrieved from http://archive.fo/qpbtW

58. When Jon visited Claremont McKenna College and gave a lecture in that same hall a year later, he learned from faculty members that most of the protesters were not students at Claremont McKenna. The protesters were mostly students at Pomona, Pitzer, and Scripps colleges, which are part of a consortium of five colleges whose students are free to take classes and attend events at all five schools.

59. We, Few of the Black Students Here at Pomona College and the Claremont Colleges. (n.d.). Response to Pomona College president David Oxtoby's "Academic freedom and free speech" email of April 7, 2017. Archive of Pomona Student Petition [Online document]. Retrieved from https://docs.google.com/document/d/1_y6NmxoIBLcZJxYkN9V1YfaPYzVSMKCA17PgBzz10wk/edit

60. Harris, S. (2017, November 17). The spurious move to stifle speech on campus because it is "dehumanizing." *Reason*. Retrieved from http://reason.com/archives/2017/11/17/the-move-to-stifle-speech-on-campus-beca

61. Linguist John McWhorter says that terms such as these are "tools for injury, not just dictionary terms." McWhorter, J. (2016, November 29). The difference between racial bias and white supremacy. *Time*. Retrieved from http://time.com/4584161/white-supremacy

62. Levenson, E., & Watts, A. (2017, October 13). Man beaten by white supremacists in Charlottesville is arrested. *CNN*. Retrieved from http://www.cnn.com/2017/10/12/us/charlottesville-deandre-harris-arrest/index.html

63. Jackman, T. (2017, August 27). Three men charged in Charlottesville attacks on counterprotesters. *The Washington Post*. Retrieved from https://www.washingtonpost.com/local/public-safety/three-men-charged-in-charlottesville-attacks-on-counterprotesters/2017/08/27/f08930a4-8b5a-11e7-84c0-02cc069f2c37_story.html

64. Raymond, A. K. (2017, December 15). Man who rammed crowd at Charlottesville rally charged with first-degree murder. *New York*. Retrieved from http://nymag.com/daily/intelligencer/2017/12/first-degree-murder-charge-for-man-who-killed-heather-heyer.html

65. Caron, C. (2017, August 13). Heather Heyer, Charlottesville victim, is recalled as "a strong woman." *The New York Times*. Retrieved from https://www.nytimes.com/2017/08/13/us/heather-heyer-charlottesville-victim.html

66. Buncombe, A. (2017, December 15). Heather Heyer was buried in secret grave to protect it from neo-Nazis after Charlottesville, reveals mother. *The Independent*. Retrieved from http://www.independent.co.uk/news/world/americas/heather-heyer-grave-secret-hide-nazis-charlottesville-attack-mother-reveals-a8113056.html

67. Nelson, L., & Swanson, K. (2017, August 15). Full transcript: Donald Trump's press conference defending the Charlottesville rally. *Vox*. Retrieved from https://www.vox.com/2017/8/15/16154028/trump-press-conference-transcript-charlottesville

68. See Jon's narration and interpretation of these events as an example of sacrilege and taboo violation: Haidt, J. (2017, August 21). Trump breaks a taboo—and pays the price. *The Atlantic*. Retrieved from https://www.theatlantic.com/politics/archive/2017/08/what-happens-when-the-president-commits-sacrilege/537519

69. See, for example, Phillip, A. (2017, August 17). Trump's isolation grows in the wake of Charlottesvile. *The Washington Post*. Retrieved from https://www.washingtonpost.com/politics/trumps-isolation-grows-in-the-wake-of-charlottesville/2017/08/17/5bf83952-81ec-11e7-82a4-920da1aeb507_story.html

70. Some religious groups did just this, beginning on the day of the Charlottesville march, when a large coalition of religious leaders locked arms, faced down the heavily armed racists, and sang about love. See: Jenkins, J. (2017, August 16). Meet the clergy who stared down white supremacists in Charlottesville. Retrieved from https://thinkprogress.org/clergy-in-charlottesville-e95752415c3e

71. Stevens, S. (2017, February 7). Campus speaker disinvitations: Recent trends (Part 2 of 2) [Blog post]. Retrieved from https://heterodoxacademy.org/2017/02/07/campus-speaker-disinvitations-recent-trends-part-2-of-2

72. Bauer-Wolf, J. (2017, October 5). ACLU speaker shouted down at William & Mary. *Inside Higher Ed*. Retrieved from https://www.insidehighered.com/quicktakes/2017/10/05/aclu-speaker-shouted-down-william-mary

73. Sullivan, S. (2017, October 19). Jane Doe wants an abortion but the government is hell bent on stopping her [Blog post]. Retrieved from https://www.aclu.org/blog/immigrants-rights/immigrants-rights-and-detention/jane-doe-wants-abortion-government-hell-bent

74. Stern, M. J. (2014, September 3). Translating terrorism: Is publishing radical Islamic texts on the internet a crime? *Slate*. Retrieved from http://www.slate.com/articles/technology/future_tense/2014/09/mehanna_at_the_supreme_court_is_translating_jihad_texts_a_crime.html

75. Glasser, I. (2017, August 22). Thinking constitutionally about Charlottesville. *HuffPost*. Retrieved from https://www.huffingtonpost.com/entry/aclu-charlottesville-free-speech_us_599c9bcae4b0d8dde9998c36

76. Truitt, F. (2017, October 2). Black Lives Matter protests American Civil Liberties Union. *The Flat Hat*. Retrieved from http://flathatnews.com/2017/10/02/black-lives-matter-protests-american-civil-liberties-union

77. Carey, E. (2017, October 6). President Schill speech suspended by protesting students. *Daily Emerald*. Retrieved from https://www.dailyemerald.com/2017/10/06/president-schill-speech-suspended-protesting-students

78. Schill, M. (2017, October 3). The misguided student crusade against "fascism." *The New York Times*. Retrieved from https://www.nytimes.com/2017/10/23/opinion/fascism-protest-university-oregon.html

79. Leou, R. (2017, October 17). Panelists discuss constitutional rights in first Free Speech 101 event. *Daily Bruin*. Retrieved from http://dailybruin.com/2017/10/17/panelists-discuss-constitutional-rights-in-first-free-speech-101-event

80. Kolman, J. (2017, October 13). Class struggle: How identity politics divided a campus. *Spiked*. Retrieved from http://www.spiked-online.com/newsite/article/how-identity-politics-divided-reed-college-black-lives-matter-free-speech/20417

81. Mendelsohn, D. (2015, March 16). Girl, interrupted: Who was Sappho? *The New Yorker*. Retrieved from https://www.newyorker.com/magazine/2015/03/16/girl-interrupted

82. Reedies Against Racism. (2016, November 2). An open letter to Lucia [on Facebook]. Retrieved from https://www.facebook.com/reediesagainstr4cism/posts/1186608438084694

83. Martínez Valdivia, L. (2017, October 27). Professors like me can't stay silent about this extremist moment on campuses. *The Washington Post*. Retrieved from https://www.washingtonpost.com/opinions/professors-like-me-cant-stay-silent-about-this-extremist-moment-on-campuses/2017/10/27/fd7aded2-b9b0-11e7-9e58-e6288544af98_story.html. For more on intimidation at Reed College, see Soave, R. (2016,

December 13). Reed College professor on social justice left: "I am a gay mixed-race woman. I am intimidated by these students" [Blog post]. Retrieved from http://reason.com/blog/2016/12/13/reed-college-professor-on-social-justice. And note this comment that Martínez Valdivia made on December 8, 2016, early in the protests: "I teach at Reed. I am intimidated by these students. I am scared to teach courses on race, gender, or sexuality, or even texts that bring these issues up in any way—and I am a gay mixed-race woman. There is a serious problem here and at other [liberal arts colleges], and I'm at a loss as to how to begin to address it, especially since many of these students don't believe in either historicity or objective facts. (They denounce the latter as being a tool of the white cisheteropatriarchy.)" Martínez Valdivia, L. [Blog comment, December 8, 2016] Re: Halberstam, J. (2016, December 7). Hiding the tears in my eyes—BOYS DON'T CRY—A legacy. [Blog post]. Retrieved from https://bullybloggers.wordpress.com/2016/12/07/hiding-the-tears-in-my-eyes-boys-dont-cry-a-legacy-by-jack-halberstam/#comment-13710

84. Kerr, E. (2018, February 1). "White supremacists are targeting college campuses like never before." *The Chronicle of Higher Education*. Retrieved from https://www.chronicle.com/article/White-Supremacists-Are/242403

85. Naughton, K. (2017, October). Speaking freely—What students think about expression at American colleges. *FIRE*. Retrieved from https://www.thefire.org/publications/student-attitudes-free-speech-survey/student-attitudes-free-speech-survey-full-text/#executiveSummary

86. De Botton, A. (n.d.). Political correctness vs. politeness. *The School of Life*. Retrieved from http://www.thebookoflife.org/political-correctness-vs-politeness

87. Barrett, L. (2017, July 14). When is speech violence? *The New York Times*. Retrieved from https://www.nytimes.com/2017/07/14/opinion/sunday/when-is-speech-violence.html

88. Haidt, J., & Lukianoff, G. (2017, July 18). Why it's a bad idea to tell students words are violence. *The Atlantic*. Retrieved from https://www.theatlantic.com/education/archive/2017/07/why-its-a-bad-idea-to-tell-students-words-are-violence/533970

89. Aurelius. *Meditations*, IV:7.

90. Haidt, J. (2017, March 2). Van Jones' excellent metaphors about the dangers of ideological safety [Blog post]. *Heterodox Academy*. Retrieved from https://heterodoxacademy.org/2017/03/02/van-jones-excellent-metaphors

Chapter 5: Witch Hunts

1. Hoffer (1951/2010), p. 19.
2. Pavlac (2009).
3. Pavlac (2009).
4. Norton (2007), Introduction.
5. Norton (2007), Introduction.
6. Durkheim (1915/1965). For an updated analysis of the joys of collective action and group ritual, see also: Ehrenreich (2006).
7. Bergesen (1978).
8. For an overview of the Cultural Revolution, see: MacFarquhar & Schoenhals (2006). See also this interview with a woman who joined the Red Guard at age thirteen: Xiangzhen, Y. (2016, May 15). Confessions of a Red Guard, 50 years after China's Cultural Revolution. Retrieved from http://www.cnn.com/2016/05/15/asia/china-cultural-revolution-red-guard-confession/index.html
9. Song, Y. (2011, August 25). Chronology of mass killings during the Chinese Cultural Revolution (1966–1976). *SciencesPo*. Retrieved from http://www.sciencespo.fr/mass-violence-war-massacre-resistance/en/document/chronology-mass-killings-during-chinese-cultural-revolution-1966-1976
10. Bergesen (1978), p. 20.
11. Bergesen (1978), p. 20.
12. Bergesen (1978), p. 21.
13. For example, see TheDemands.org, a site that arose within a few weeks of the 2015 Yale protests, at which students from eighty universities posted their demands.
14. See chapter 3. See also: Friedersdorf, C. (2016, May 26). The perils of writing a provocative email at Yale. *The Atlantic*. Retrieved from https://www.theatlantic.com/politics/archive/2016/05/the-peril-of-writing-a-provocative-email-at-yale/484418
15. See chapter 3. See also: Haidt, J. (2015, November 18). True diversity requires generosity of spirit [Blog post]. Retrieved from https://heterodoxacademy.org/2015/11/18/true-diversity-requires-generosity-of-spirit

16. DiGravio, W. (Publisher). (2017, March 2). Students protest lecture by Dr. Charles Murray at Middlebury College [Video file]. Retrieved from https://www.youtube.com/watch?v=a6EASuhefeI

17. Wiltermuth & Heath (2009). See also: Cohen, Ejsmond-Frey, Knight, & Dunbar (2009).

18. See Woodard (2011). The culture of safetyism and the most vigorous protests and shout-downs seem to occur mostly in just two of the eleven "nations" that Woodard identifies: Yankeedom (from New England to the upper Midwest) and The Left Coast (the coastal strip of the three West Coast states).

19. Tuvel (2017).

20. Johnson, K., Pérez-Peña, R., & Eligon, J. (2015, June 16). Rachel Dolezal, in center of storm, is defiant: "I identify as black." *The New York Times.* Retrieved from https://www.nytimes.com/2015/06/17/us/rachel-dolezal-nbc-today-show.html

21. See https://www.rhodes.edu/bio/tuvelr

22. Open letter to Hypatia. (n.d.). Retrieved from https://archive.is/lUeR4#selection-71.0-71.22

23. Note: A new paragraph with the sentence "The statement is not an exhaustive summary of the many harms caused by this article" was added to the open letter at approximately the 520th signature, on 5/1/2017. See: Open letter to Hypatia. (n.d.). Retrieved from https://docs.google.com/forms/d/1efp9C0MHch_6Kf gtlm0PZ76nirWtcEsqWHcvgidl2mU/viewform?ts=59066d20&edit_requested=true

24. Tuvel referred to Caitlyn Jenner as "Caitlyn (formerly Bruce) Jenner." "Deadnaming" is a term used to deride the practice of referring to transgender people by their former, "dead" names. The online version of the article was edited after publication, on May 4, 2017, and the correction reads in part: "[A]t the author's request, a parenthetical reference to Jenner's birth name was removed." See: Tuvel (2017). It's worth noting, though, that even Caitlyn Jenner herself insists, "I will refer to the name Bruce when I think it appropriate." See: Oliver, K. (2017, May 8). If this is feminism . . . *The Philosophical Salon.* Retrieved from http://thephilosophicalsalon.com/if-this-is-feminism-its-been-hijacked-by-the-thought-police. See also: Berenstain, N. (2017, April 29). Nora Berenstain on Rebecca Tuvel and Hypatia. *GenderTrender.* Retrieved from https://gendertrender.wordpress.com/nora-berenstain-on-rebecca-tuvel-and-hypatia

25. Bergesen (1978), p. 21.

26. Singal, J. (2017, May 2). This is what a modern-day witch hunt looks like. *New York.* Retrieved from http://nymag.com/daily/intelligencer/2017/05/transracialism-article-controversy.html

27. Sally Scholz, the editor to whom the open letter was addressed, issued this powerful statement in defense of the publication of Tuvel's article: "I firmly believe, and this belief will not waver, that it is utterly inappropriate for editors to repudiate an article they have accepted for publication (barring issues of plagiarism or falsification of data). In this respect, editors must stand behind the authors of accepted papers. That is where I stand. Professor Tuvel's paper went through the peer review process and was accepted by the reviewers and by me." See: Weinberg, J. (2017, May 6). Hypatia's editor and its board president defend publication of Tuvel article. *Daily Nous.* Retrieved from http://dailynous.com/2017/05/06/hypatias-editor-board-president-defend-publication-tuvel-article

28. Oliver (2017); see n. 24.

29. Outside of feminist philosophy, in the broader philosophical community, many professors did stand up for Tuvel and against the efforts to have her work retracted. The relevant community, from a Durkheimian perspective, was a subset of feminist philosophers.

30. Another open letter of condemnation and demand for retraction was aimed at Bruce Gilley, a political scientist at Portland State University in Oregon, for writing an essay arguing that colonialism conferred some benefits on colonized countries. The article was retracted after the journal editor received death threats. See Patel, V. (2018, March 21). Last fall, this scholar defended colonialism. Now he's defending himself. *The Chronicle of Higher Education.* Retrieved from https://www.chronicle.com/article/Last-Fall-This-Scholar/242880

31. Wax, A., & Alexander, L. (2017, August 9). Paying the price for breakdown of the country's bourgeois culture. *The Inquirer.* Retrieved from http://www.philly.com/philly/opinion/commentary/paying-the-price-for-breakdown-of-the-countrys-bourgeois-culture-20170809.html

32. Shweder (1996).

33. The letter said that all those who are against hateful ideas about racial superiority "must denounce faculty members that are complicit in and uphold white supremacy" by treating ideas like Wax's as "the very basis for white supremacy." See: Guest column by 54 Penn students & alumni—Statement on Amy Wax and Charlottesville. (2017, August 21). *The Daily Pennsylvanian.* Retrieved from http://www.thedp.com/article/2017/08/guest-column-amy-wax-charlottesville

34. Jon wrote a summary of the case and a defense of Wax. See: Haidt, J. (2017, September 2). In defense of Amy Wax's defense of bourgeois values [Blog post]. *Heterodox Academy.* Retrieved from https://heterodoxacademy.org/2017/09/02/in-defense-of-amy-waxs-defense-of-bourgeois-values. A few weeks later, the leader of the faculty letter of condemnation, Jonah Gelbach, wrote a long essay responding to the details of the Wax

& Alexander essay. See: Haidt, J. (2017, September 21). Jonah Gelbach responds to Amy Wax & Jon Haidt [Blog post]. *Heterodox Academy*. Retrieved from https://heterodoxacademy.org/2017/09/21/jonah-gelbach -responds-to-wax-and-haidt

35. Thucydides (431 BCE/1972). Book III, chapter 82, section 4.

36. See: Haidt (2012), chapters 2 and 4.

37. Eggertson (2010).

38. One of the best experiences of Jon's academic career was moderating a bipartisan working group of poverty experts who worked together to strip away partisanship from a complicated research literature and identify the programs that truly work. See: American Enterprise Institute/Brookings Working Group on Poverty and Opportunity. (2015, December 3). Opportunity, Responsibility, and Security. Retrieved from http://www.aei.org/publication/opportunity-responsibility-and-security. Chapter 5 evaluates early childhood interventions.

39. Duarte et al. (2015). See especially: Abramowitz, Gomes, & Abramowitz (1975). See also: Crawford & Jussim (2018).

40. On the personality, political, and behavioral correlates of openness, see: McCrae (1996). See also: Carney, Jost, Gosling, & Potter (2008).

41. Gosling (2008).

42. McClintock, Spaulding, & Turner (1965).

43. For more about the HERI survey, visit https://heri.ucla.edu

44. See analysis of all relevant studies prior to 2014 in Duarte et al. (2015). For the most recent data point, seventeen to one, see Langbert, Quain, & Klein (2016).

45. Langbert et al. (2016).

46. According to Langbert et al. (2016), which confirmed an earlier finding about New England using HERI data by Samuel Abrams, see: Abrams, S. J. (2016, July 1). There are conservative professors, just not in these states. *The New York Times*. Retrieved from https://www.nytimes.com/2016/07/03/opinion/sunday/there -are-conservative-professors-just-not-in-these-states.html

47. Duarte et al. (2015).

48. Of course, a progressive professor could still present conservative ideas. But as John Stuart Mill wrote, "Nor is it enough that he should hear the opinions of adversaries from his own teachers, presented as they state them, and accompanied by what they offer as refutations. He must be able to hear them from persons who actually believe them . . . he must know them in their most plausible and persuasive form." See: Mill (1859/2003), chapter 2, p. 72.

49. The Crimson Editorial Board. (2016, November 11). Elephant and man at Harvard. *The Harvard Crimson*. Retrieved from http://www.thecrimson.com/article/2016/11/11/ideological-diversity

50. Eagen, K., Stolzenberg, E. B., Zimmerman, H. B., Aragon, M. C., Sayson, H. W., & Rios-Aguilar, C. (2018, February 15). The American freshman: National norms fall 2016. *Higher Education Research Institute*. Retrieved from https://www.heri.ucla.edu/monographs/TheAmericanFreshman2016.pdf

51. Interestingly, this shift since 2012 is due entirely to a change among women. Male college students have not shifted to the left. Rather, the gender gap, in which women are more left-leaning than men, has widened from roughly 6 points in 2011 to roughly 12 points in 2016. Rempel, C. (2017, May 2). Political polarization among college freshmen is at a record high, as is the share identifying as "far left." *The Washington Post*. Retrieved from https://www.washingtonpost.com/news/rampage/wp/2017/05/02/political-polarization -among-college-freshmen-is-at-a-record-high-as-is-the-share-identifying-as-far-left

52. A wave of essays published in March 2018 claimed that nothing on campus had changed with regard to free speech. See, for example: Yglesias, M. (2018, March 12). Everything we think about the political correctness debate is wrong. *Vox*. Retrieved from https://www.vox.com/policy-and-politics/2018/3/12/17100496/ political-correctness-data. But on closer inspection of the data, Jon and his colleagues at Heterodox Academy showed that there had been many changes in average attitudes toward controversial speech and toward a greater willingness to use illiberal methods to prevent such speech. See: Stevens, S., & Haidt, J. (2018, March 19). The skeptics are wrong: Attitudes about free speech on campus are changing. *Heterodox Academy*. Retrieved from https://heterodoxacademy.org/skeptics-are-wrong-about-campus-speech

53. Bestcolleges.com. (n.d.). The 10 most liberal colleges in America. Retrieved from http://www.bestcolleges .com/features/most-liberal-colleges

54. Paros, M. (2018, February 22). The Evergreen Meltdown. *Quillette*. Retrieved from http://quillette.com/ 2018/02/22/the-evergreen-meltdown. See Evergreen's mission here: http://www.evergreen.edu/about/mis sion

55. Weiss, B. (2017, June 1). When the left turns on its own. *The New York Times*. Retrieved from https://www .nytimes.com/2017/06/01/opinion/when-the-left-turns-on-its-own.html

56. The Evergreen State College. (n.d.). Day of Absence & Day of Presence. Retrieved January 24, 2018, from https://evergreen.edu/multicultural/day-of-absence-day-of-presence
57. Ward (1994). An online version is available here: Ward, D. T. (1965). Day of absence—A satirical fantasy. *National Humanities Center*. Retrieved from http://nationalhumanitiescenter.org/pds/maai3/protest /text12/warddayofabsence.pdf
58. Weiss (2017); see n. 55.
59. Jaschik, S. (2017, May 30). Who defines what is racist? *Inside Higher Ed*. Retrieved from https://www .insidehighered.com/news/2017/05/30/escalating-debate-race-evergreen-state-students-demand-firing -professor
60. Volokh, E. (2017, May 26). "Professor told he's not safe on campus after college protests" at Evergreen State College (Washington). *The Washington Post*. Retrieved from https://www.washingtonpost.com/news/ volokh-conspiracy/wp/2017/05/26/professor-told-hes-not-safe-on-campus-after-college-protests -at-evergreen-state-university-washington
61. Long, K. (2017, June 10). Long-simmering discord led to The Evergreen State College's viral moment. *The Seattle Times*. Retrieved from https://www.seattletimes.com/seattle-news/education/discord-at-evergreen -state-simmered-for-a-year-before-it-boiled-over
62. Our source for the events of the prior year is Paros, M. (personal communication, January 10, 2018.) You can watch a video of the imaginary canoe scene, beginning at 1:06, here: The Evergreen State College Productions (Producer). (2016, November 18). Equity and inclusion council community report back [Video file]. Retrieved from https://youtube.com/watch?v-wPZT7CASvCs&feature-youtu.be&
63. Weinstein, B. (2017, May 30). The campus mob came for me—and you, professor, could be next. *The Wall Street Journal*. Retrieved from https://www.wsj.com/articles/the-campus-mob-came-for-me-and-you -professor-could-be-next-1496187482
64. Haidt, J. (2017, May 27). The blasphemy case against Bret Weinstein, and its four lessons for professors [Blog post]. Retrieved from https://heterodoxacademy.org/2017/05/27/this-weeks-witch-hunt
65. Caruso, J., & Gockowski, A. (2017, May 25). VIDEO: White prof harassed for questioning diversity event. *Campus Reform*. Retrieved from https://www.campusreform.org/?ID=9233
66. Kaufman, E. (2017, May 26). Another professor, another mob. *National Review*. Retrieved from http:// www.nationalreview.com/article/448034/evergreen-state-pc-mob-accosts-liberal-professor
67. In an Orwellian example of safetyism combined with the Untruth of Us Versus Them, protesters later de-scribed it as forming a "protective ring around the students of color conversing with Weinstein." Kozak-Gilroy, J. (2017, May 31). A year of events, a time line of protests. *Cooper Point Journal*. Retrieved from http://www.cooperpointjournal.com/2017/05/31/a-year-of-events-a-time-line-of-protests. For a civil con-versation between Weinstein and protesters after the confrontation, see Lavelle, C. (2017, May 23). This is what a discussion looks like [on *Facebook*]. Retrieved from https://www.facebook.com/celeste.lavelle/vid eos/10203256021397424
68. Anonymous (personal communication, August 23, 2017).
69. Andy Archive (Producer). (2017, May 28). Black Power activist students demand white professor resigns over "racism" [Video file]. Retrieved from https://youtu.be/ERd-2HvCOHI?t=4m2s
70. Boyce, B. (Producer). (2017, June 20). Is Evergreen a cult? [Video file]. Retrieved from https://youtu.be/ VfVRaExw1lI?t=4m24s. See also: Heying, H. (2017, October 2). First, they came for the biologists. *The Wall Street Journal*. Retrieved from https://www.wsj.com/articles/first-they-came-for-the-biologists-1506984033
71. Anonymous (personal communication, August 23, 2017).
72. Loury, G., & Weinstein, B. (Producer). (2017, June 30). Glenn Loury & Bret Weinstein—Bloggingheads.tv. [Video file]. Retrieved from https://bloggingheads.tv/videos/46681
73. "The protesters did let Bret leave, but they assigned 'handlers' to him and his students." Heying & Wein-stein (2017, December 12). Bonfire of the academies: Two professors on how leftist intolerance is killing higher education. *Washington Examiner*. Retrieved from https://www.washingtonexaminer.com/bonfire -of-the-academies-two-professors-on-how-leftist-intolerance-is-killing-higher-education
74. li5up6 (Producer). (2017, May 31). [MIRROR] Student takeover of Evergreen State College. [Video file]. Retrieved from https://www.youtube.com/watch?v=ynnNArPi8GM
75. VICE (Producer). (2017, June 16). Evergreen State College controversy (HBO) [Video file]. Retrieved from https://youtu.be/2cMYfxOFBBM?t=2m19s
76. Heying & Weinstein (2017, December 12); see n. 78. S See also Boyce, B.A. (2017, July 29). Social Network Justice at Evergreen [Video File]. Retrieved from https://youtu.be/Jye2C5r-QA0?t=8m23s
77. Sexton, J. (Publisher). (2017, July 13). Evergreen student: "I've been told several times that I'm not allowed to speak because I'm white" [Video file]. Retrieved from https://www.youtube.com/watch?v=OQ8WQ nsm14Y

78. best of evergreen (Publisher). (2017, May 27). Student takeover of Evergreen State College [Video file]. Retrieved from https://youtu.be/bO1agIlLlhg?t=6m14s

79. When asked, they said they were looking for "an individual" but refused to say whom. Campus police concluded they were looking for Bret Weinstein. Anonymous (personal communication, August 23, 2017).

80. Heying & Weinstein (2017, December 12); see n. 73.

81. Kozak-Gilroy (2017); see n. 67.

82. Kozak-Gilroy (2017); see n. 67.

83. I Hypocrite Too (Producer). (2017, May 29). Ableist students demand no homework Evergreen College [Video file]. Retrieved from https://www.youtube.com/watch?v=nh1wGFFsIts

84. CampusReform (Producer). (2017, June 1). Student protesters at Evergreen hold administrators hostage over demands [Video file]. Retrieved from https://youtu.be/Msfsp5Ofz4g

85. In a later VICE News documentary, interviewer Michael Moynihan tells Bridges, "A student told me that you're a white supremacist." Bridges replies, "I don't *believe* I am." The astonished Moynihan asks, "You don't *believe* you are but you accept that you *might* be?" Bridges replies, "No . . . well, it depends on what you mean by a white supremacist. What does that mean? I'm a white person in a position of privilege." VICE (2017); see n. 75.

86. The Liberty Hound (Producer). (2017, May 26). "All white people leave campus OR ELSE!!" Tucker covers INSANE Evergreen State College story [Video file]. Retrieved from https://youtu.be/n3SdJhJ2lps?t=4m10s. The police chief told Weinstein that "he needed to get off campus immediately, and off his bike, too, indefinitely. He was too easy a target on his bike, and the police couldn't protect him, as they had been ordered to stand down." Heying & Weinstein (2017, December 12).

87. Anonymous (personal communication, August 23, 2017).

88. Loury & Weinstein (2017); see n. 72. See also: Zimmerman, M. (2017, July 10). The Evergreen State College: Is speaking with Tucker Carlson a punishable offense? *HuffPost*. Retrieved from https://www.huffingtonpost.com/entry/the-evergreen-state-college-is-speaking-with-tucker_us_596318a5e4b0cf3c8e8d59fc. See also: Heying & Weinstein (2017); see n. 73. See also: Kanzenkankaku. (2017, June 1). Protesters lockdown Evergreen State College, situation spirals out of control [Online forum comment]. Retrieved from http://forums.fstdt.net/index.php?topic=7607.0. See also: Jaschik (2017); see n. 58.

89. The Liberty Hound (Producer). (2017, June 12). "It's not safe to go back": Tucker follows up with Evergreen prof Bret Weinstein [Video file]. Retrieved from https://www.youtube.com/watch?v=SNdNF93H3OU

90. Not including faculty emeritus.

91. Haidt, J. (2017, June 7). A second Evergreen professor speaks out [Blog post]. Retrieved from https://heterodoxacademy.org/2017/06/07/a-second-evergreen-professor-speaks-out

92. "Many members of the faculty were privately supportive, but too scared to speak up, and even too scared to vote their conscience in faculty meetings." Weinstein, B. (personal communication, February 19, 2018).

93. The Liberty Hound (Producer). (2017, May 26). "All white people leave campus OR ELSE!!" Tucker covers INSANE Evergreen State College story [Video file]. Retrieved from https://www.youtube.com/watch?v=n3SdJhJ2lps

94. Jennings, R. (2017, July 6). N.J. man accused of threat to "execute" college students out of jail. *NJ.com*. Retrieved from http://www.nj.com/morris/index.ssf/2017/07/morris_man_accused_of_threatening_college_3000_mil.html

95. Svrluga, S., & Heim, J. (2017, June 1). Threat shuts down college embroiled in racial dispute. *The Washington Post*. Retrieved from https://www.washingtonpost.com/news/grade-point/wp/2017/06/01/threats-shut-down-college-embroiled-in-racial-dispute. See also: Svrluga, S. (2017, June 5). Evergreen State College closes again after threat and protests over race. *The Washington Post*. Retrieved from https://www.washingtonpost.com/news/grade-point/wp/2017/06/05/college-closed-for-third-day-concerned-about-threat-after-protests-over-race. See also: Jennings (2017); see n. 94.

96. An Evergreen student emailed a professor, "Because I had shown some criticism to the protest that was occurring on campus in earlier weeks I have become targeted and harassed by a wide number of students on campus. Recently there have been a number of students who patrol lower campus with weapons like baseball bats and tasers who claim to be making the campus safer but in reality are making campus more hostile." Kabbany, J. (2017, June 5). Evergreen official asks student vigilantes to stop patrolling campus with bats, batons. *The College Fix*. Retrieved from https://www.thecollegefix.com/post/33027

97. The College Fix Staff. (2017, June 2). Evergreen State faculty demand punishment of white professor who refused to leave on anti-white day. *The College Fix*. Retrieved from https://www.thecollegefix.com/post/32946. See also: The Liberty Hound (2017, June 12); see n. 89.

98. Thomason, A. (2017, September 16). Evergreen State will pay $500,000 to settle with professor who criticized handling of protests. *The Chronicle of Higher Education*. Retrieved from http://www.chronicle

.com/blogs/ticker/evergreen-state-will-pay-500000-to-settle-with-professor-who-criticized
-handling-of-protests/120110
99. (2018, March 7). Former Evergreen chief of police alleges hostile work environment. *The Cooper Point Journal*. Retrieved from http://www.cooperpointjournal.com/2018/03/07/former-evergreen-chief-of-police
-alleges-hostile-work-environment-stacy-brown-makes-moves-towards-a-legal-claim-of-discrimination
-based-on-race-and-gender
100. Chasmar, J. (2016, September 2). Evergreen State College president slams Chicago's "tone deaf" approach to safe spaces. *The Washington Times*. Retrieved from http://www.washingtontimes.com/news/2016/sep/2/george-bridges-wash-college-president-slams-chicag
101. Jaschik (2017); see n. 59.
102. Richardson, B. (2017, May 29). Evergreen State College president expresses "gratitude" for students who took over campus. *The Washington Times*. Retrieved from http://www.washingtontimes.com/news/2017/may/29/evergreen-state-college-president-expresses-gratit
103. Zimmerman, M. (2017, July 25). A "Through the Looking Glass" perspective on The Evergreen State College. *HuffPost*. Retrieved from http://www.huffingtonpost.com/entry/a-through-the-looking-glass
-perspective-on-the-evergreen_us_5971bd7ae4b06b511b02c271
104. Parke, C. (2017, December 14). Evergreen professor who made anti-white comments resigns, gets $240G settlement. *Fox News*. Retrieved from http://www.foxnews.com/us/2017/12/14/evergreen-professor-who
-made-anti-white-comments-resigns-gets-240g-settlement.html
105. best of evergreen (Publisher) (2017, May 27). Student takeover of Evergreen State College [Video file]. Retrieved from https://youtu.be/bO1agIlLlhg?t=53s
106. Badger Pundit (Producer). (2017, July 12). Evergreen student: Campus unsafe for white students who want to focus on education [Video file]. *Fox News*. Retrieved from https://www.youtube.com/watch?v=pNwVWq8EjSs

Chapter 6: The Polarization Cycle

1. Reeves, R.V., & Joo, N. (2017, October 4). White, still: The American upper middle class. *Brookings*. Retrieved from https://www.brookings.edu/blog/social-mobility-memos/2017/10/04/white-still-the
-american-upper-middle-class
2. For evidence of this shift, with a growing preference for inclusion when it is presented as conflicting with freedom of speech, see: Stevens, S., & Haidt, J (2018, March 19). The skeptics are wrong: Attitudes about free speech are changing on campus. *Heterodox Academy*. Retrieved from https://heterodoxacademy.org/skeptics-are-wrong-about-campus-speech
3. Stanger, A. (2017, March 13). Understanding the angry mob at Middlebury that gave me a concussion. *The New York Times*. Retrieved from https://www.nytimes.com/2017/03/13/opinion/understanding-the
-angry-mob-that-gave-me-a-concussion.html
4. Pew Research Center. (2017, October 5). The partisan divide on political values grows even wider. Retrieved from http://www.people-press.org/2017/10/05/1-partisan-divides-over-political-values-widen
5. With the exception that Republicans' ratings of their own party dipped in 2016.
6. You can download the data yourself at http://www.electionstudies.org.
7. There were plenty of cultural conflicts, particularly in the 1960s and 1970s, but measures of political polarization in Congress were low; cross-partisan cooperation was high. Hare & Poole (2014).
8. See Putnam (2000) on social capital.
9. Greenblatt, A. (2016, November 18). Political segregation is growing and "We're living with the consequences." *Governing*. Retrieved from http://www.governing.com/topics/politics/gov-bill-bishop-interview
.html
10. For example, in a September 2017 survey of adults aged eighteen to thirty-four, only 11% of African Americans, 18% of Asian Americans, and 20% of Latino Americans had very or somewhat favorable views of the Republican Party. By contrast, those groups had a favorable view of the Democratic Party: 61%, 68%, and 52%, respectively. See: NBC News & GenForward Survey: September 2017 Toplines, p.4. Retrieved from http://genforwardsurvey.com/assets/uploads/2017/09/NBC-GenForward-Toplines-September-2017
-Final.pdf
11. Iyengar & Krupenkin (2018).
12. Pariser (2011). A "filter bubble" is what happens when the algorithms that websites use to predict your interests based on your reading/viewing habits work to avoid showing you alternative viewpoints. See:

El-Bermawy, M. (2016, November 18). Your filter bubble is destroying democracy. *Wired*. Retrieved from https://www.wired.com/2016/11/filter-bubble-destroying-democracy

13. Mann & Ornstein (2012).

14. Levitsky, S., & Ziblatt, D. (2018, January 27). How wobbly is our democracy? *The New York Times*. Retrieved from https://www.nytimes.com/2018/01/27/opinion/sunday/democracy-polarization.html

15. Others include increasing education (educated people are more partisan), increasing immigration and diversity, and the increasing importance of money in campaigns. See a list at Haidt, J., & Abrams, S. (2015, January 7). The top 10 reasons American politics are so broken. *The Washington Post*. Retrieved from https://www.washingtonpost.com/news/wonk/wp/2015/01/07/the-top-10-reasons-american-politics-are-worse-than-ever

16. Iyengar & Krupenkin (2018), p. 202.

17. Berry & Sobieraj (2014).

18. Cillizza, C. (2014, May 14). Just 7 percent of journalists are Republicans. That's far fewer than even a decade ago. *The Washington Post*. Retrieved from https://www.washingtonpost.com/news/the-fix/wp/2014/05/06/just-7-percent-of-journalists-are-republicans-thats-far-less-than-even-a-decade-ago

19. Littleton, J. (2017, May 29). The truth about the Evergreen protests. *Medium*. Retrieved from https://medium.com/@princessofthefaeries666/the-truth-about-the-evergreen-protests-444c86ee6307

20. Littleton, J. (2017, June 16). The media brought the alt-right to my campus. *The New York Times*. Retrieved from https://www.nytimes.com/2017/06/16/opinion/media-alt-right-evergreen-college.html?_r=0. See also: Pemberton, L. (2017, July 13). Evergreen students, faculty, and alumni hold discussion after unrest. *The Chronicle*. Retrieved from http://www.chronline.com/news/evergreen-students-faculty-and-alumni-hold-discussion-after-unrest/article_c9d9f5f8-67ef-11e7-8b53-5ff0ef03700b.html

21. Long, K. (2017, June 5). Evergreen State College reopens; threat deemed not credible. *The Seattle Times*. Retrieved from https://www.seattletimes.com/seattle-news/education/no-imminent-threat-at-evergreen-state-college-after-classes-canceled-for-third-day

22. Atomwaffen division visits Evergreen State College. (n.d.). Retrieved from https://www.bitchute.com/video/bZMiTj2TC5bf

23. TheFIREorg [Producer]. (2018, February 8). Lisa Durden on her famous Fox News interview [Video file]. Retrieved from https://www.youtube.com/watch?time_continue=310&v=PfmdlqdC3mE

24. L. Durden (personal communication, March 24, 2018).

25. In his statement, the newly appointed college president claimed that the college had been "immediately inundated with feedback from students, faculty and prospective students and their families expressing frustration, concern and even fear" about "the views expressed by a College employee," and said the college had a "responsibility to investigate those concerns." The president declared that the college "supports and affirms the right of free speech and independent views and expressions of those views for our faculty and staff" and that his "administration has a duty to set a strong example of tolerance." Statement from Essex County College president Anthony E. Munroe. (2017, June 23). Retrieved from http://www.essex.edu/pr/2017/06/23/statement-from-essex-county-college-president-anthony-e-munroe-3

26. What about the feedback that the college was "inundated" with? Public records indicate that for the first thirteen days after Durden's television appearance, only one person contacted the college to complain about Durden—and even before that person contacted the college, administrators had already started the process that led to her suspension. Two weeks after her appearance, the website NJ.com announced that Durden had been suspended. Shortly thereafter, administrators received twenty-nine emails, two Facebook messages, an unknown number of phone calls, and a single voicemail supporting the college for suspending "a teacher who wants to spew hate speech covered up by free speech." You can listen to the entire voicemail here: TheFIREorg [Producer]. (2017, January 21). Essex County College voicemail about Lisa Durden [Audio file]. Retrieved from https://youtu.be/pTYM30Q4NsE. See: Steinbaugh, A. (2018, January 23). After FIRE lawsuit, Essex County College finally turns over documents about firing of Black Lives Matter advocate. *FIRE*. Retrieved from https://www.thefire.org/after-fire-lawsuit-essex-county-college-finally-turns-over-documents-about-firing-of-black-lives-matter-advocate. See also: Carter, B. (2017, June 20). Going on Fox News cost me my job, professor claims. *NJ.com*. Retrieved from http://www.nj.com/essex/index.ssf/2017/06/essex_county_college_professor_suspended_after_fox.html

27. Flaherty, C. (2017, June 21). Suspended for standing up to Fox News? *Inside Higher Ed*. Retrieved from https://www.insidehighered.com/news/2017/06/21/college-allegedly-suspends-communications-adjunct-comments-about-race-fox-news. See also: Adely, H. (2017, October 27). For speaking out, N.J. professors are punished. *North Jersey*. Retrieved from https://www.northjersey.com/story/news/2017/10/27/professors-punished-for-speaking-out/777819001. See also: Steinbaugh, A. (2018, January 23). After FIRE lawsuit, Essex County College finally turns over documents about firing of Black Lives Matter

advocate. *FIRE*. Retrieved from https://www.thefire.org/after-fire-lawsuit-essex-county-college-finally-turns-over-documents-about-firing-of-black-lives-matter-advocate

28. Steinbaugh, A. (2017, October 20). Russia-linked Twitter account helped Drexel professor's "White Genocide" tweet go viral, prompting university investigation. *FIRE*. Retrieved from https://www.thefire.org/russia-linked-twitter-account-helped-drexel-professors-white-genocide-tweet-go-viral-prompting-university-investigation

29. Saffron, I. (2017, December 27). How a Drexel prof's Christmas "wish" stirred a Twitter tempest. *Philly.com*. Retrieved from http://www.philly.com/philly/news/20161227_How_a_Drexel_prof_s_Christmas_wish_stirred_a_Twitter_tempest.html

30. McLaughlin, S. (2017, December 29). Drexel professor resigns after months-long investigation, exile from campus. *FIRE*. Retrieved from https://www.thefire.org/drexel-professor-resigns-after-months-long-investigation-exile-from-campus

31. Thomason, A. (2017, December 28). Drexel professor whose charged tweets drew fire from the right will leave the university. *The Chronicle of Higher Education*. Retrieved from https://www.chronicle.com/article/Drexel-Professor-Whose-Charged/242124

32. Cornwell, P. (2017, June 1). Princeton professor cancels Seattle talk after Fox News segment, death threats. *The Seattle Times*. (Updated June 2, 2017). Retrieved from https://www.seattletimes.com/seattle-news/princeton-professor-cancels-seattle-talk-after-fox-news-segment-death-threats. See also: Trump a "racist, sexist megalomaniac," Princeton prof says in commencement speech. (2017, May 28). *Fox News*. Retrieved from http://www.foxnews.com/us/2017/05/28/trump-racist-sexist-megalomaniac-princeton-prof-says-in-commencement-speech.html

33. Haymarket Books. (2017, May 31). A statement from Keeanga-Yamahtta Taylor [Facebook post]. Retrieved from https://www.facebook.com/haymarketbooks/posts/1494045207312386

34. Bond, S.E. (2017, June 7). Why we need to start seeing the classical world in color. *Hyperallergic*. Retrieved from https://hyperallergic.com/383776/why-we-need-to-start-seeing-the-classical-world-in-color

35. Gurewitsch, M. (2008, July). True colors: Archaeologist Vinzenz Brinkmann insists his eye-popping reproductions of ancient Greek sculptures are right on target. *Smithsonian Magazine*. Retrieved from https://www.smithsonianmag.com/arts-culture/true-colors-17888

36. For example, American white supremacist group Identity Evropa tweeted a poster of a marble statue with the caption "PROTECT YOUR HERITAGE." @IdentityEvropa. (2016, November 3). Seattle has never looked better. #FashTheCity [Tweet]. Retrieved from http://web.archive.org/web/20171115062648/https://twitter.com/IdentityEvropa/status/794368750346588160. Cited in Bond (2017); see n. 34.

37. Of course, Bond said neither of these things. Hoft, J. (2017, July 18). University prof: Using white marble in sculptures is racist and creates "white supremacy." *Gateway Pundit*. Retrieved from http://www.thegatewaypundit.com/2017/07/university-prof-using-white-marble-sculptures-racist-creates-white-supremacy. See also: Jackson, D. (2017, June 8). Prof: "White marble" in artwork contributes to white supremacy. *Campus Reform*. Retrieved from https://www.campusreform.org/?ID=9285. See also: Krayden, D. (2017, June 10). Professor equates white marble statues with white supremacy. *The Daily Caller*. Retrieved from http://dailycaller.com/2017/06/10/professor-equates-white-marble-statues-with-white-supremacy

38. Mikelionis, L. (2017, June 9). Iowa university professor says "white marble" actually influences "white supremacist" ideas. *Education News*. Retrieved from http://www.educationviews.org/iowa-university-professor-white-marble-influences-white-supremacist-ideas

39. Osgerby, P. (2017, June 19). UI professor receives death threats over article on classical art. *Little Village*. Retrieved from http://littlevillagemag.com/ui-professor-receives-death-threats-over-article-on-classical-art

40. Charis-Carlson, J. (2017, June 19). UI prof's post on ancient statues, white supremacists elicits death threats. *Iowa City Press-Citizen*. Retrieved from https://www.press-citizen.com/story/news/2017/06/16/ui-classics-professor-receives-threats-after-online-essay-statuary-race/403275001. See also: Quintana, C. (2017, June 16). For one scholar, an online stoning tests the limits of public scholarship. *The Chronicle of Higher Education*. Retrieved from https://www.chronicle.com/article/For-One-Scholar-an-Online/240384

41. Allen, C. (2017, June 26). Liberal professors say bizarre things—and then blame the conservative media for reporting on them. *Independent Women's Forum*. Retrieved from http://iwf.org/blog/2804174/Liberal-Professors-Say-Bizarre-Things--and-Then-Blame-the-Conservative-Media-for-Reporting-on-Them

42. See Haidt. J. (2017, June 28). Professors must now fear intimidation from both sides. *Heterodox Academy*. Retrieved from https://heterodoxacademy.org/professors-must-now-fear-intimidation-from-both-sides

43. Schmidt, P. (2017, June 22). Professors' growing risk: Harassment for things they never really said. *The Chronicle of Higher Education*. Retrieved from https://www.chronicle.com/article/Professors-Growing-Risk-/240424?cid=rclink

44. Haidt, J. (2017, April 26). Intimidation is the new normal on campus. *The Chronicle of Higher Education*. Retrieved from https://www.chronicle.com/article/Intimidation-Is-the-New-Normal/239890

45. Flaherty, C. (2016, November 22). Being watched. *Inside Higher Ed.* Retrieved from https://www.inside highered.com/news/2016/11/22/new-website-seeks-register-professors-accused-liberal-bias-and-anti -american-values

46. Heterodox Academy condemned the Professor Watchlist. See: HxA Executive Team. (2016, November 24). Heterodox Academy condemns Professor Watchlist. Retrieved from https://heterodoxacademy.org/het erodox-academy-condemns-professor-watchlist

47. Middlebrook, H. (2017, November 14). The fascinating, if unreliable, history of hate crime tracking in the US. *CNN.* Retrieved from https://www.cnn.com/2017/01/05/health/hate-crimes-tracking-history-fbi/index .html. Middlebrook correctly notes that hate crimes are historically underreported; still, years of decline, followed by a sudden surge in 2015, may not be strictly attributable to changes in accounting methods.

48. FBI: US hate crimes rise for second straight year. (2017, November 13). *BBC News.* Retrieved from http:// www.bbc.com/news/world-us-canada-41975573

49. Farivar, M. (2017, September 19). Hate crimes rise in major US cities in 2017. *Voice of America.* Retrieved from https://www.voanews.com/a/hate-crimes-rising-in-us/4034719.html

50. Alfonseca, K. (2017, August 21). When hate meets hoax. *ProPublica.* Retrieved from https: //www.pro publica.org/arti cle/when-hate-meets-hoax. See also: Soave, R. (2018, January 19). Another hate crime at the University of Maryland turns out to be a hoax. *Reason.* Retrieved from http://reason.com/blog/2018 /01/19/a-second-hate-crime-at-the-university-of. See also: Gose, B. (1999, January 8). Hate-crime hoaxes unsettle campuses. *The Chronicle of Higher Education.* Retrieved from https://www.chronicle.com/article /Hate-Crime-Hoaxes-Unsettle/2836

51. Suspect in Mizzou threats identified as Lake St. Louis teen. (2015, November 11). *NBC12.* Retrieved from http://www.nbc12.com/story/30489913/um-police-arrest-suspect-who-made-racist-threats-on-social -media

52. Bui, L. (2017, October 17). U-Md. student to face hate-crime charge in fatal stabbing on campus. *The Washington Post.* Retrieved from https://www.washingtonpost.com/local/public-safety/u-md-student-to-face -hate-crime-charge-in-fatal-stabbing-on-campus/2017/10/17/a17bfa1c-b35c-11e7-be94-fabb0f1e9ffb _story.html

53. One charge was later reduced to accessory after the fact. See: Smithson, D. (2017, November 9). Cases continue in shooting after Spencer protest. *Ocala Star-Banner.* Retrieved from http://www.ocala.com/ news/20171109/cases-continue-in-shooting-after-spencer-protest. See also: Rozsa, L., & Svrluga, S. (2017, October 20). 3 men charged in shooting after white nationalist Richard Spencer's speech in Florida. *Chicago Tribune.* Retrieved from http://www.chicagotribune.com/news/nationworld/ct-shooting-richard -spencer-speech-20171020-story.html

54. Student in Trump shirt detained after brandishing knife, saying "Kill all illegals." (2018, February 16). *The Daily Beast.* Retrieved from https://www.thedailybeast.com/student-in-trump-shirt-who-brandished -knife-and-said-kill-all-illegals-detained

55. McWhorter, J. (2008, December 30). Racism in America is over. *Forbes.* Retrieved from https://www .forbes.com/2008/12/30/end-of-racism-oped-cx_jm_1230mcwhorter.html

56. On the sharp drop in Republican trust in universities since 2015, see Pew Research Center (2017, July 10). Sharp partisan divisions in views of national institutions. Retrieved from http://www.people-press .org/2017/07/10/sharp-partisan-divisions-in-views-of-national-institutions

Chapter 7: Anxiety and Depression

1. Solomon (2014), p. 110.

2. Novotney (2014).

3. By 2015, 22% of college students were seeking mental health services (10% on some campuses, up to 50% on others). And "54 percent of all college students report[ed] feeling overwhelming anxiety, up from 46.4 percent in 2010." See Estroff Marano, H. (2015, September 1). Crisis U. *Psychology Today.* Retrieved from https://www.psychologytoday.com/articles/201509/crisis-u

4. Levinson-King, R. (2017, March 13). Teen suicide on the rise among Canadian girls.*BBC News.* Retrieved from http://www.bbc.com/news/world-us-canada-39210463. See also: Canadian Institute for Health Information. (n.d.). Intentional self-harm among youth in Canada. Retrieved from https://www.cihi.ca/ sites/default/files/info_child_harm_en.pdf

5. Sanghani, R. (2017, March 16). Why are so many of Britain's teen girls struggling with mental health problems? *The Telegraph.* Retrieved from http://www.telegraph.co.uk/health-fitness/body/why-are-so-many -of-britains-teen-girls-struggling-with-mental-he. That article refers to a large longitudinal UK study,

which can be retrieved here: https://www.gov.uk/government/uploads/system/uploads/attachment_data/ file/599871/LSYPE2_w2-research_report.pdf. See also: Pells, R. (2017, July 9). Number of university students claiming special circumstances for mental health problems "soars." *The Independent*. Retrieved from http://www.independent.co.uk/news/education/education-news/number-of-university-students-men tal-health-problems-illness-claiming-special-circumstances-a7831791.html

6. Data on trends in the UK and Canada collected in 2018 and 2019 will be crucial for determining whether or not they have the same problem as the USA.

7. Allen, M. (2017, November 9). Sean Parker unloads on Facebook: "God only knows what it's doing to our children's brains." *Axios*. Retrieved from https://www.axios.com/sean-parker-unloads-on-facebook-god -only-knows-what-its-doing-to-our-childrens-brains-1513306792-f855e7b4-4e99-4d60-8d51 -2775559c2671.html

8. Twenge (2017), chapter 2.

9. Twenge (2017), p. 3

10. See Twenge (2017), Appendix B, Figures B1 and B2. The appendix is online; it can be retrieved at http:// www.jeantwenge.com/wp-content/uploads/2017/08/igen-appendix.pdf

11. Twenge (2017), chapter 4. See also: Twenge, Joiner, Rogers, & Martin (2017).

12. In 1994, Nolen-Hoeksema & Girgus (1994) found "no gender differences in depression rates in prepubescent children, but, after the age of 15, girls and women [were] about twice as likely to be depressed as boys and men." In a 2017 paper, Salk, Hyde, & Abramson (2017) found that gender differences emerged at twelve years old, which was earlier than had been previously thought.

13. The criteria are that a person reports having at least five out of nine symptoms nearly every day for a two-week period, as described in Hunter & Tice (2016). Retrieved from https://www.samhsa.gov/data/sites/ default/files/NSDUH-MethodSummDefsHTML-2015/NSDUH-MethodSummDefsHTML-2015/NS DUH-MethodSummDefs-2015.htm#b4-8

14. Hacking (1991), as described in Haslam (2016).

15. You can download the date and report at https://www.CDC.gov/injury/wisqars/fatal.html

16. Levinson-King, R. (2017, March 13). Teen suicide on the rise among Canadian girls. Retrieved from http:// www.bbc.com/news/world-us-canada-39210463

17. Office for National Statistics (UK). (2017, December 18). Suicides in the UK: 2016 registrations (point 6: Suicides in the UK by age). Retrieved from https://www.ons.gov.uk/peoplepopulationandcommunity/ birthsdeathsandmarriages/deaths/bulletins/suicidesintheunitedkingdom/2016registrations#sui cides-in-the-uk-by-age

18. Mercado, Holland, Leemis, Stone, & Wang (2017).

19. Twenge, Joiner, Rogers, & Martin (2018).

20. Vigen, T. (n.d.). Spurious correlations. Retrieved from http://www.tylervigen.com/spurious-correlations

21. If children have papers to write, or other homework that requires the use of a computer, that time does not appear to be correlated with depression.

22. Twenge (2017), pp. 82 and 84. For more in-depth analysis, see: Twenge et al. (2018).

23. Twenge discusses the issue of reverse correlation (that is, that depression causes teens to spend more time on screens) and links to studies suggesting that it is not the cause of the association. One of the studies she discusses was a true experiment using random assignment. People who were randomly assigned to give up Facebook for a week reported feeling less depressed at the end of the study. See: Twenge, J. (2017, November 14). With teen mental health deteriorating over five years, there's a likely culprit. Retrieved from https:// theconversation.com/with-teen-mental-health-deteriorating-over-five-years-theres-a-likely-culprit -86996

24. See discussion of eusociality and ultrasociality in Haidt (2012), chapter 9.

25. Twenge, Joiner, Rogers, & Martin (2018), p. 4.

26. Twenge (2017).

27. Twenge (2017).

28. Maccoby (1998).

29. Wood Rudulph, H. (2017, October 11). How women talk: Heather Wood Rudulph interviews Deborah Tannen. *Los Angeles Review of Books*. Retrieved from https://lareviewofbooks.org/article/how-women -talk-heather-wood-rudulph-interviews-deborah-tannen. Twenge echoes Tannen's concern when she says, "Girls use social media more often, giving them additional opportunities to feel excluded and lonely when they see their friends or classmates getting together without them," in Twenge (2017, September). Have smartphones destroyed a generation? *The Atlantic*. Retrieved from https:// www.theatlantic.com/ magazine/ archive/2017/09/has-the-smartphone-destroyed-a-generation/534198

30. Twenge (2017), Appendix F, figure F1. Online appendix can be retrieved from http://www.jeantwenge .com/wp-content/uploads/2017/08/igen-appendix.pdf

31. Arata, E. (2016, August 1). The unexpected reason Snapchat's "pretty" filters hurt your self-esteem. *Elite Daily*. Retrieved from https://www.elitedaily.com/wellness/snapchat-filters-self-esteem/1570236

32. Jowett, V. (2017, July 10). Inside the Snapchat filter surgery boom. *Cosmopolitan*. Retrieved from http://www.cosmopolitan.com/uk/beauty-hair/a9617028/celebrity-cosmetic-surgery-snapchat-filter-boom

33. Crick & Grotpeter (1995).

34. For example: Thielking, M. (2017, February 8). Surging demand for mental health care jams college services. *Scientific American*. Retrieved from https://www.scientificamerican.com/article/surging-demand-for-mental-health-care-jams-college-services. See also: Peterson, A. (2016, October 10). Students flood college mental-health centers. *The Wall Street Journal*. Retrieved from http://www.wsj.com/articles/students-flood-college-mental-health-centers-1476160902. See also: Tugend, A. (2017, June 7). Colleges get proactive in addressing depression on campus. *The New York Times*. Retrieved from https://www.nytimes.com/2017/06/07/education/colleges-get-proactive-in-addressing-depression-on-campus.html

35. Center for Collegiate Mental Health, Pennsylvania State University. (2016). 2016 annual report. Retrieved from https://sites.psu.edu/ccmh/files/2017/01/2016-Annual-Report-FINAL_2016_01_09-1gc2hj6.pdf

36. Higher Education Institute (HERI). The question was only added in 2010, and is asked only every other year. The exact question wording is: "Do you have any of the following disabilities or medical conditions? (Mark Yes or No for each item.)" The survey then lists seven different types of disabilities and conditions, including "Psychological disorder (depression, etc.)" with the option to select "Yes" or "No" for each. Survey instruments and data can be accessed at https://heri.ucla.edu/heri-data-archive

37. Reetz, D. R., Bershad, C., LeViness, P., & Whitlock, M. (2017). The Association for University and College Counseling Center Directors annual survey. Retrieved from https://www.aucccd.org/assets/documents/aucccd%202016%20monograph%20-%20public.pdf. See also summary and graph in: Tate, E. (2017, March 29). Anxiety on the rise. *Inside Higher Ed*. Retrieved from https://www.insidehighered.com/news/2017/03/29/anxiety-and-depression-are-primary-concerns-students-seeking-counseling-services

38. One study at a diverse, urban university found that 38% of the students in the study reported a history of deliberately self-harming at least once, 18% reported having intentionally self-harmed at least ten times, and 10% reported having deliberately self-harmed more than 100 times. Gratz, Conrad, & Roeter (2002). See also appendix F in the online appendices for Twenge (2017); Twenge offers additional graphs showing mental health outcomes from the American College Health Association Survey and the Youth Risk Behavior Surveillance System. The appendices can be retrieved from http://www.jeantwenge.com/wp-content/uploads/2017/08/igen-appendix.pdf

39. Zhiguo & Fang (2014).

40. Shin & Liberzon (2010).

41. Gotlib & Joormann (2010).

42. Prociuk, Breen, & Lussier. (1976). See also: Costello (1982).

43. Peterson, Maier, & Seligman (1993). See also: Seligman (1990).

44. Chen, Coccaro, & Jacobson (2012).

45. Clark, Algoe, & Green (2018).

Chapter 8: Paranoid Parenting

1. Denizet-Lewis, B. (2017, October 11). Why are more American teenagers than ever suffering from severe anxiety? *The New York Times*. Retrieved from https://www.nytimes.com/2017/10/11/magazine/why-are-more-american-teenagers-than-ever-suffering-from-severe-anxiety.html

2. Skenazy, L. (2008, April 1). Why I let my 9-year-old ride the subway alone. *The New York Sun*. Retrieved from http://www.nysun.com/opinion/why-i-let-my-9-year-old-ride-subway-alone/73976

3. Skenazy, L. (2015, January 16). I let my 9-year-old ride the subway alone. I got labeled the "World's Worst Mom." *The Washington Post*. Retrieved from https://www.washingtonpost.com/posteverything/wp/2015/01/16/i-let-my-9-year-old-ride-the-subway-alone-i-got-labeled-the-worlds-worst-mom/?utm_term=.7cbce60ca0e0

4. The main suspect in the case was not convicted until 2017. For a summary, see: McKinley, J. C. (2017, April 18). Pedro Hernandez gets 25 years to life in murder of Etan Patz. *The New York Times*. Retrieved from https://www.nytimes.com/2017/04/18/nyregion/pedro-hernandez-etan-patz-sentencing.html

5. Lafrance, A. (2017, February 14). When bad news was printed on milk cartons. *The Atlantic*. Retrieved from https://www.theatlantic.com/technology/archive/2017/02/when-bad-news-was-printed-on-milk-cartons/516675

6. National Crime Information Center. (n.d.) 2016 NCIC missing person and unidentified person statistics. Retrieved from https://www.fbi.gov/file-repository/2016-ncic-missing-person-and-unidentified-person -statistics.pdf/view

7. Polly Klaas Foundation. (n.d.). National child kidnapping facts. Retrieved from http://www.pollyklaas .org/about/national-child-kidnapping.html

8. ChildStats.gov. (n.d.). POP1 Child population: Number of children (in millions) ages 0–17 in the United States by age, 1950–2016 and projected 2017–2050. Retrieved from https://www.childstats.gov/ameri caschildren/tables/pop1.asp

9. Simpson, K. (2010, November 27). Dispelled kidnap myths do little to allay parents' fears. *The Denver Post.* Retrieved from http://www.denverpost.com/2010/11/27/dispelled-kidnap-myths-do-little-to-allay-parents -fears

10. For more on kidnapping trends, see: U.S. Department of Justice. (2016, June 14). Number of child abductions by strangers unchanged over past decade and a half; Fewer end in homicide. Retrieved from http:// www.unh.edu/ccrc/Presspacket/Stereotypical%20Kidnapping%20.pdf. Three interesting points: (1) Ninety-two percent of kidnapped children were returned safely to their families in 2011, compared with just 57% in 1997. (Technology, such as cell phone tracking, has been a big help to law enforcement.) (2) Four out of five children abducted by a stranger in 2011 did not live in a home with two parents (biological or adoptive). (3) One third of the children abducted were never reported missing. No adult was taking responsibility for them; they were kids who fell through the cracks. See: Flores, J. R. (2002, October). Nonfamily abducted children: National estimates and characteristics. Retrieved from http://www.pollyklaas .org/media/pdf/NISMARTIInonfamily.pdf

11. FBI Criminal Justice Information Services Division. (n.d.). Preliminary semiannual uniform crime report, January–June, 2015. Retrieved from https://ucr.fbi.gov/crime-in-the-u.s/2015/preliminary-semiannual -uniform-crime-report-januaryjune-2015

12. Kurutz, S. (2004, October 24). The age of the mugger. *The New York Times.* Retrieved from http://www .nytimes.com/2004/10/24/nyregion/thecity/the-age-of-the-mugger.html

13. At least, of missing white children. From 1979 to 1981, there was a horrific cluster of more than twenty-five fatal kidnappings of black children in Atlanta that became known as the Atlanta Child Murders. This killing spree garnered less national attention than the murders of Patz and Walsh, which occurred during those years.

14. There is no consensus among criminologists as to why crime went down so quickly all across America. Jon believes that the phaseout of leaded gasoline in the late 1970s and early 1980s is one major factor. See: Drum, K. (2016, February 11). Lead: America's real criminal element. *Mother Jones.* Retrieved from http:// www.motherjones.com/environment/2016/02/lead-exposure-gasoline-crime-increase-children-health

15. Infoplease. (n.d.) Homicide rate per 100,000, 1950–2015. Retrieved from https://www.infoplease.com/us/ crime/homicide-rate-1950-2014

16. Stapleton, A. C. (2015, February 6). Police: 6-year-old boy "kidnapped" for being too nice to strangers. *CNN.* Retrieved from http://www.cnn.com/2015/02/05/us/missouri-fake-kidnapping/index.html

17. Berchelmann, K. (2017, May 4). When can my child use the public restroom alone? *HealthyChildren.org.* Retrieved from https://www.healthychildren.org/English/tips-tools/ask-the-pediatrician/Pages/When- can-my-child-use-the-public-restroom-alone.aspx

18. Lowbrow, Y. (2014, June 9). 8 reasons children of the 1970s should all be dead. Retrieved from https:// flashbak.com/8-reasons-children-of-the-1970s-should-all-be-dead-323

19. YOURS News. (2012, February 20). Seatbelts—Saving thousands of lives around the world everyday . . . [Blog post]. Retrieved from http://www.youthforroadsafety.org/news-blog/news-blog-item/t/seatbelts_ saving_thousands_of_lives_around_the_world_everyday

20. Ganti et al. (2013).

21. DeNoon, D. J. (2003, May 13). Quit smoking so your kids won't start. *Web MD.* Retrieved from https:// www.webmd.com/smoking-cessation/news/20030513/quit-smoking-so-your-kids-wont-start

22. National Institute for Occupational Safety and Health. (n.d.). LEAD: Information for workers—Health problems caused by lead. Retrieved from https://www.cdc.gov/niosh/topics/lead/health.html

23. Christakis (2016), p. 131.

24. Taleb (2007).

25. For more on these backfire effects, see Greg Ip's perfectly titled book *Foolproof: Why Safety Can Be Dangerous and How Danger Makes Us Safe.* Ip (2015).

26. Skenazy (2008); see n. 2.

27. J. Lythcott-Haims (personal communication May 26, 2017).

28. Estroff Marano, H. (2004, November 1). A nation of wimps. *Psychology Today.* Retrieved from https:// www.psychologytoday.com/articles/200411/nation-wimps

29. J. Lythcott-Haims (personal communication May 26, 2017).
30. This is called the demographic transition. See: Grover, D. (2014, October 13). What is the Demographic Transition Model? *PopEd Blog*. Retrieved from https://www.populationeducation.org/content/what -demographic-transition-model
31. Parker, K., & Wang, W. (2013, March 14). Modern parenthood: Roles of moms and dads converge as they balance work and family. *Pew Research Center*. Retrieved from http://www.pewsocialtrends.org/2013/03/ 14/modern-parenthood-roles-of-moms-and-dads-converge-as-they-balance-work-and-family
32. L. Skenazy (personal communication, May 4, 2017).
33. Skenazy, L. (2015, June 11). 11-year-old boy played in his yard. CPS took him, felony charge for parents. *Reason*. Retrieved from http://reason.com/blog/2015/06/11/11-year-old-boy-played-in-his-yard-cps-t
34. WFSB Staff. (2014, July 9). Bristol mother charged with leaving child unattended in car. *Eyewitness News 3*. Retrieved from http://wfsb.com/story/25982048/bristol-mother-charged-with-leaving-child-unattend ed-in-car. (For more stories like this, visit https://letgrow.org/blog)
35. Skenazy, L. (2016, June 17) "16 is the appropriate age to allow children to be outside by themselves"—New Albany, Ohio, police chief. *Free-Range Kids*. Retrieved from http://www.freerangekids.com/16-is-the -appropriate-age-to-allow-children-to-be-outside-by-themselves-new-albany-ohio-police-chief
36. Lareau (2011), p. 3.
37. Putnam (2015), p. 117.
38. Putnam (2015), p. 117.
39. DeLoache et al. (2010).
40. The website for the research project is hosted by the Centers for Disease Control, at http://www.cdc.gov/ violenceprevention/acestudy
41. Putnam (2015), p.112.
42. Chetty, Friedman, Saez, Turner, & Yagen (2017). See a summary of that paper in this infographic: Some colleges have more students from the top 1 percent than the bottom 60. Find yours. (2017, January 18). *The New York Times*. Retrieved from https://www.nytimes.com/interactive/2017/01/18/upshot/some-colleges -have-more-students-from-the-top-1-percent-than-the-bottom-60.html
43. L. Skenazy (personal communication, May 4, 2017).

Chapter 9: The Decline of Play

1. LaFreniere (2011).
2. LaFreniere (2011), p. 479, asserts that "[i]n games involving chasing, children seem to prefer the fleeing position (e.g., in the game of tag and in all games modeled after tag, the preferred position is to be chased), which suggests that such play has more to do with our legacy as prey than our legacy as hunters."
3. LaFreniere (2011), p. 465. See also: Sandseter & Kennair (2011). See also: Gray, P. (2014, April 7). Risky play: Why children love it and need it. *Psychology Today*. Retrieved from https://www.psychologytoday.com/ blog/freedom-learn/201404/risky-play-why-children-love-it-and-need-it
4. Einon, Morgan, & Kibbler (1978). See also: Hol, Berg, Ree, & Spruijt (1999) for another experimental study with rat pups, and see Mustoe, Taylor, Birnie, Huffman, & French (2014) for a correlational study with marmosets. See a review of this literature in Gray (in press).
5. Black, Jones, Nelson, & Greenough (1998).
6. Johnson & Newport (1989). For a review of the famous case of the feral child "Genie," see Curtiss (1977). For deaf children things work the same way, with signs. Spoken words are not essential, but communication with others is.
7. This, at least, is the argument made by many researchers who study play, including Gray (in press), LaFreniere (2011), and Sandseter & Kennair (2011). We note that there is no direct experimental proof of this strong version of the claim—that play deprivation in childhood will alter adult personality. Controlled experiments such as the ones we described with rat pups can never be done with humans. In the rest of this chapter, we show why we think the claim is plausible and likely to be true.
8. Gray (2011). See also: Gray (in press).
9. Sandseter & Kennair (2011), p. 275.
10. Gray (2011), p. 444.
11. Singer, Singer, D'Agostino, & DeLong (2009), cited in Gray (2011).
12. Hirsh-Pasek, Golinkoff, Berk, & Singer (2009).
13. Gray (2011), p. 456.
14. Hofferth & Sandberg (2001), cited in Gray (2011).

15. As shown by mediation analyses in Twenge et al. (2018), which found that all forms of screen time are associated with negative mental health outcomes. Peter Gray, however, takes a more positive view of social interaction mediated by screens. He believes that it is real social interaction, and that multiplayer video games are a form of play. He also notes that online social interaction has the advantage of occurring, typically, without any adult supervision. He agrees, however, that online interaction lacks the benefits of vigorous physical play and that some forms of online interaction may turn out to be harmful to mental health. P. Gray (personal communication, February 8, 2018).

16. Hofferth & Sandberg (2001).

17. See review in Shumaker, H. (2016, March 5). Homework is wrecking our kids: The research is clear, let's ban elementary homework. *Salon*. Retrieved from https://www.salon.com/2016/03/05/homework_is_wrecking_our_kids_the_research_is_clear_lets_ban_elementary_homework. See also: Marzano, R., & Pickering, D. (2007, March). Special topic: The case for and against homework. *Educational Leadership, 64(6)*, 74–79. Retrieved from https://www.lincnet.org/cms/lib05/MA01001239/Centricity/Domain/108/Homework.pdf. See also: Cooper, Lindsay, Nye, & Greathouse (1998). See also: Cooper, Civey Robinson, & Patall (2006). See also: Cooper, Steenbergen-Hu, & Dent (2012).

18. "In the last 20 years, homework has increased only in the lower grade levels, and this increase is associated with neutral (and sometimes negative) effects on student achievement." National Education Association. (n.d.). Research spotlight on homework. Retrieved from http://www.nea.org/tools/16938.htm

19. L. Skenazy (personal communication, January 23, 2018).

20. Clements (2004), cited in Gray (2011).

21. Whitley, C. (2011, August 1). Is your child ready for first grade: 1979 edition. *ChicagoNow*. Retrieved from http://www.chicagonow.com/little-kids-big-city/2011/08/is-your-child-ready-for-first-grade-1979-edition. (We thank Erika Chistakis for pointing it out to us.)

22. Whitley (2011); see n. 21.

23. St. Theresa's Catholic School (Austin, TX). (2012, January). Expectations for incoming first graders. Retrieved from https://www.st-theresa.org/wp-content/uploads/2012/02/1st_Expectations.pdf

24. E. Christakis (personal communication, October 21, 2017).

25. Christakis (2016).

26. Gopnik, A. (2011, March 16). Why preschool shouldn't be like school: New research shows that teaching kids more and more, at ever-younger ages, may backfire. *Slate*. Retrieved from http://www.slate.com/articles/double_x/doublex/2011/03/why_preschool_shouldnt_be_like_school.html. See also: Gray, P. (2015, May 5). Early academic training produces long-term harm. *Psychology Today*. Retrieved from https://www.psychologytoday.com/blog/freedom-learn/201505/early-academic-training-produces-long-term-harm

27. Bassok, Latham, & Rorem (2016).

28. Common Core State Standards Initiative. (n.d.). Introduction to Common Core. Retrieved from http://www.corestandards.org/Math/Content/introduction

29. Common Core State Standards Initiative. (n.d.). English language arts standards » Reading: Foundational skills » Kindergarten. Retrieved from http://www.corestandards.org/ELA-Literacy/RF/K

30. E. Christakis (personal communication, June 2, 2017).

31. "Ironically, when today's kindergarten and first-grade teachers are asked to name the school-readiness skills most important for preschoolers to master, they invariably still rank social and emotional skills, such as being able to take turns or listen to a friend, above pre-academic skills, such as number and letter identification. But parents often see things very differently." Christakis (2016), p. 7.

32. Pew Research Center. (2015, December 17). Parenting in America: Children's extracurricular activities. Retrieved from http://www.pewsocialtrends.org/2015/12/17/5-childrens-extracurricular-activities

33. Mose (2016).

34. Scholarship America. (2011, August 25). Make your extracurricular activities pay off. *U.S. News & World Report*. Retrieved from https://www.usnews.com/education/blogs/the-scholarship-coach/2011/08/25/make-your-extracurricular-activities-pay-off

35. *Princeton Review*. (n.d.). 14 summer activities to boost your college application. Retrieved from https://www.princetonreview.com/college-advice/summer-activities-for-college-applications

36. Yale University Office of Institutional Research. (2016, November 30). Summary of Yale College admissions class of 1986 to class of 2020. Retrieved from https://oir.yale.edu/sites/default/files/w033_fresh_admissions.pdf

37. Deresiewicz (2015), p. 39.

38. J. Lythcott-Haims (personal communication, May 26, 2017). As Lenore Skenazy put it, these parents "are stalked by the twin fears that their children will be kidnapped . . . or not get into Harvard." L. Skenazy (personal communication, January 23, 2018).

39. Morrison, P. (2015, October 28). How "helicopter parenting" is ruining America's children. *Los Angeles Times*. Retrieved from http://www.latimes.com/opinion/op-ed/la-oe-morrison-lythcott-haims-20151028 -column.html

40. A. Duckworth (personal communication, March 19, 2018).

41. Bruni, F. (2016, January 19). Rethinking college admissions. *The New York Times*. Retrieved from https:// www.nytimes.com/2016/01/20/opinion/rethinking-college-admissions.html

42. Rosin, H. (2015, November 20). The Silicon Valley suicides. *The Atlantic*. Retrieved from https://www .theatlantic.com/magazine/archive/2015/12/the-silicon-valley-suicides/413140

43. Spencer, K. (2017, April 5). It takes a suburb: A town struggles to ease student stress. *The New York Times*. Retrieved from https://www.nytimes.com/2017/04/05/education/edlife/overachievers-student-stress-in -high-school-.html?_r=0

44. Farrell, A., McDevitt, J., & Austin, R. (2015). Youth risk behavior survey Lexington High School—2015 results: Executive summary. Retrieved from https://lps.lexingtonma.org/cms/lib2/MA01001631/Centric ity/Domain/547/YRBSLHSExecSummary08Mar16.pdf. See also: Luthar & Latendresse (2005). See also: Chawla, I., & Njoo, L. (2016, July 21). CDC releases preliminary findings on Palo Alto suicide clusters. *The Stanford Daily*. Retrieved from https://www.stanforddaily.com/2016/07/21/cdc-releases-preliminary-find ings-on-palo-alto-suicide-clusters

45. Chetty, Friedman, Saez, Turner, & Yagen (2017). See a summary of that paper in this infographic: Some colleges have more students from the top 1 percent than the bottom 60. Find yours. (2017, January 18). *The New York Times*. Retrieved from https://www.nytimes.com/interactive/2017/01/18/upshot/some-colleges -have-more-students-from-the-top-1-percent-than-the-bottom-60.html

46. Quoted in Brody, J. E. (2015, January 19). Parenting advice from "America's worst mom." *The New York Times*. Retrieved from https://well.blogs.nytimes.com/2015/01/19/advice-from-americas-worst-mom

47. Horwitz (2015).

48. Ostrom, E. (1990).

49. Ostrom, V. (1997).

50. Horwitz (2015), p. 10.

51. Iyengar & Krupenkin (2018).

52. Ortiz-Ospina, E., & Roser, M. (2017). Trust. Retrieved from https://ourworldindata.org/trust

53. Horwitz (2015), p. 3.

54. We note that this advice is less needed for students from less privileged backgrounds, who are more likely to experience unfairness and "bad luck" as a normal part of life.

55. Reilly, K. (2017, July 5). "I wish you bad luck." Read Supreme Court Justice John Roberts's unconventional speech to his son's graduating class. *Time*. Retrieved from http://time.com/4845150/chief-justice-john -roberts-commencement-speech-transcript

Chapter 10: The Bureaucracy of Safetyism

1. De Tocqueville (1839/2012), book 4, chapter 6.

2. FIRE letter to Northern Michigan University, August 25, 2016. (2016, September 19). Retrieved from https://www.thefire.org/fire-letter-to-northern-michigan-university-august-25-2016

3. THE "I CARE PROJECT": Revise NMU Student Self-Destructive Behavior Policy. (n.d.). *Change.org* [Petition]. Retrieved from https://www.change.org/p/northern-michigan-university-the-i-care-project-revise -nmu-student-self-destructive-behavior-policy

4. Singal, J. (2016, September 22). A university threatened to punish students who discussed their suicidal thoughts with friends (Updated). *The Cut*. Retrieved from https://www.thecut.com/2016/09/a-school-is -threatening-to-punish-its-suicidal-students.html

   Northern Michigan has since revised its policy; it no longer sends that letter, and by January 2016, it stopped prohibiting students from discussing self-harm with peers. See: Northern Michigan University. (2016). Northern Michigan University practice concerning self-destructive students changed January 2016. Retrieved from http://www.nmu.edu/mc/current-mental-health-communication

5. National Center for Educational Statistics (1993), p. 64.

6. Fast Facts: Back to School Statistics. (n.d.). National Center for Education Statistics. Retrieved from https://nces.ed.gov/fastfacts/display.asp?id=372

7. Digest of Education Statistics. (2016). Tables 333.10 (Revenues of public institutions) and (333.40) (Revenues of private institutions). National Center for Education Statistics. Retrieved from https://nces.ed.gov/ programs/digest/current_tables.asp

8. Gross Domestic Product 2016. (2017, December 15). World Bank Development Indicators Database. Retrieved from https://databank.worldbank.org/data/download/GDP.pdf

9. Digest of Education Statistics. (2016). Table 333.90 (Endowments). National Center for Education Statistics. Retrieved from https://nces.ed.gov/programs/digest/d16/tables/dt16_333.90.asp?current=yes

10. Of the top twenty-five universities as listed by *Times Higher Education*, the percentage of international students ranges from 16% at the University of Michigan to 45% at Carnegie Mellon. World University Rankings 2018. *Times Higher Education*. Retrieved from https://www.timeshighereducation.com/world -university-rankings/2018/world-ranking#!/page/0/length/25/sort_by/rank/sort_order/asc/cols/stats

11. World University Rankings 2018; see n. 10. Or perhaps it is nineteen of the top twenty-five. See also: Best Global Universities Rankings. (2018). *U.S. News & World Report*. Retrieved from https://www.usnews .com/education/best-global-universities/rankings

12. Kerr (1963).

13. "Universities' executive, administrative, and managerial offices grew 15 percent during the recession, even as budgets were cut and tuition was increased." Marcus, J. (2016, October 6). The reason behind colleges' ballooning bureaucracies. *The Atlantic*. Retrieved from https://www.theatlantic.com/education/archive/ 2016/10/ballooning-bureaucracies-shrinking-checkbooks/503066

14. See, for example, Catropa, D., & Andrews, M. (2013, February 8). Bemoaning the corporatization of higher education. *Inside Higher Ed*. Retrieved from https://www.insidehighered.com/blogs/strat edgy/bemoan ing-corporatization-higher-education

15. "Since 1975, according to a 2014 report from the American Association of University Professors, full-time administrative positions grew by 369 percent, whereas full-time tenure-track faculty grew by 23 percent and part-time faculty by 286 percent." Braswell, S. (2016, April 24). The fightin' administrators: The birth of a college bureaucracy. *Point Taken*. Retrieved from http://www.pbs.org/wgbh/point-taken/blog/ozy -fightin-administrators-birth-college-bureaucracy. See also: Christensen, K. (2015, October 17). Is UC spending too little on teaching, too much on administration? *Los Angeles Times*. Retrieved from http:// www.latimes.com/local/education/la-me-uc-spending-20151011-story.html

16. Campos, P. F. (2015, April 4). The real reason college tuition costs so much. *The New York Times*. Retrieved from https://www.nytimes.com/2015/04/05/opinion/sunday/the-real-reason-college-tuition-costs-so-much .html

17. Catropa & Andrews (2013); see n. 15. See also: Lewis (2007), pp. 4–5. See also: McArdle, M. (2015, August 13). Sheltered students go to college, avoid education. *Bloomberg View*. Retrieved from https://www .bloomberg.com/view/articles/2015-08-13/sheltered-students-go-to-college-avoid-education

18. Ginsberg (2011). Chapter 1, section "Shared Governance?" paragraphs 2–6.

19. Ginsberg (2011). Chapter 1, section "Professors and Administrators?" paragraph 16.

20. In one of the very few exceptions we know of, Oberlin president Marvin Krislov refused to accept a list of "non negotiable" demands. See Jaschik, S. (2016, January 21). Oberlin's president says no. *Inside Higher Ed*. Retrieved from https://www.insidehighered.com/news/2016/01/21/oberlins-president-refuses-negotiate -student-list-demands

21. Adler, E. (2018, March 15). Students think they can suppress speech because colleges treat them like customers. *The Washington Post*. Retrieved from http://wapo.st/2phMwCB?tid=ss_tw&utm_term=.75b5e 44fa1d0

22. See figure 5 on page 11 of Desrochers, D. M., & Hurlburt, S. (2016, January). Trends in college spending: 2003–2013. American Institutes for Research. *Delta Cost Project*. Retrieved from https://www.deltacost project.org/sites/default/files/products/15-4626%20Final01%20Delta%20Cost%20Project%20College% 20Spending%2011131.406.P0.02.001%20....pdf

23. Carlson, S. (2013, January 28). What's the payoff for the "country club" college? *The Chronicle of Higher Education*. Retrieved from https://www.chronicle.com/blogs/buildings/whats-the-payoff-for-the-country -club-college/32477. See also: College Ranker. (n.d.). Colleges as country clubs: Today's pampered college students. Retrieved from http://www.collegeranker.com/features/colleges-as-country-clubs. See also: Jacob, B., McCall, B. & Stange, K. M. (2013, January). College as country club: Do colleges cater to students' preferences for consumption? National Bureau of Economic Research. Retrieved from http://www.nber .org/papers/w18745.pdf. *Forbes* poked fun at the practice by comparing colleges and country clubs to "Club Fed" minimum-security correctional facilities. Pierce, K. (2014, July 29). College, country club or prison? *Forbes*. Retrieved from https://www.forbes.com/special-report/2014/country-college-prion.html

24. A 2013 survey by NIRSA (formerly the National Intramural-Recreational Sports Association) found ninety-two schools with pending recreation center projects totaling $1.7 billion. Cited in Rubin, C. (2014, September 19). Making a splash: College recreation now includes pool parties and river rides. *The New York Times*. Retrieved from https://www.nytimes.com/2014/09/21/fashion/college-recreation-now -includes-pool-parties-and-river-rides.html. See also: Koch, J. V. (2018, January 9). Opinion: No college kid

needs a water park to study. *The New York Times*. Retrieved from https://www.nytimes.com/2018/01/09/opinion/trustees-tuition-lazy-rivers.html

25. Stripling, J. (2017, October 15). The lure of the lazy river. *The Chronicle of Higher Education*. Retrieved from https://www.chronicle.com/article/The-Lure-of-the-Lazy-River/241434

26. Papish v. Bd. of Curators of the Univ. of Missouri et al., 410 U.S. 667 (1973) (reinstating a student expelled for distributing an underground student newspaper with an offensive cartoon and headline); Texas v. Johnson, 491 U.S. 397 (1989) (flag burning).

27. For simplicity, we'll use the term "administrators" to include those who run the university, and all the deans and offices that have anything to do with student life. This includes much (but not all of) the professional staff on campus other than the faculty—generally the people *students* mean when they talk about "the administration" of a university.

28. Greg's first book, *Unlearning Liberty* (Lukianoff 2014), covering campuses from around 2001 to 2012, presents dozens of examples of administrators overreacting.

29. After placing the professor on leave and forcing him to undergo a psychiatric evaluation, the college eventually rescinded its punishment. See: Victory: College backtracks after punishing professor for "Game of Thrones" picture. (2014, October 28). *FIRE*. Retrieved from https://www.thefire.org/victory-college-backtracks-punishing-professor-game-thrones-picture

30. College declares Haymarket Riot reference a violent threat to college president. (2015, June 8). *FIRE*. Retrieved from https://www.thefire.org/college-declares-haymarket-riot-reference-a-violent-threat-to-college-president. FIRE sent two letters to Oakton, but nothing further occurred in this case; the school didn't retract its cease-and-desist letter, but no formal action was taken against the professor.

31. Harris, S. (2016, September 1). Speech code of the month: Drexel University. *FIRE*. Retrieved from https://www.thefire.org/speech-code-of-the-month-drexel-university

32. FIRE rates colleges' speech codes as "red light," "yellow light," or "green light." (FIRE's speech code ratings are explained in full at https://www.thefire.org/spotlight/using-the-spotlight-database.) The University of West Alabama's "red light" policies are still in effect, including the ban on harsh text messages or insults. Jacksonville State's speech codes have changed over the years; most recently in 2017. It now has an overall yellow light rating. You can see which colleges are rated as red, yellow, or green at https://www.thefire.org/spotlight. See also: (n.d.). Spotlight: Jacksonville State University. Retrieved from https://www.thefire.org/schools/jacksonville-state-university. See also: (n.d.). Spotlight: University of West Alabama. Retrieved from https://www.thefire.org/schools/university-of-west-alabama

33. Harris, S. (2009, May 29). McNeese State revises "public forum" policy but still prohibits "derogatory" speech. *FIRE*. Retrieved from https://www.thefire.org/mcneese-state-revises-public-forum-policy-but-still-prohibits-derogatory-speech

34. Univ. of Cincinnati Chapter of Young Americans for Liberty v. Williams, 2012 U.S. Dist. LEXIS 80967 (S.D. Ohio June 12, 2012).

35. You can see a wide variety of campus codes at: Spotlight Database and Activism Portal. (2018). *FIRE*. Retrieved from https://www.thefire.org/spotlight

36. In the fifteen years between September 12, 2001, and December 31, 2016, there were eighty-five "violent extremist" attacks in the United States, an average of less than half a dozen per year. Valverde, M. (2017, August 16). A look at the data on domestic terrorism and who's behind it. *PolitiFact*. Retrieved from http://www.politifact.com/truth-o-meter/article/2017/aug/16/look-data-domestic-terrorism-and-whos-behind-it

37. The webpage listed on the signs explains: "The New York University Bias Response Line provides a mechanism through which members of our community can share or report experiences and concerns of bias, discrimination, or harassing behavior that may occur within our community." NYU Bias Response Line. (n.d.). Retrieved from http://www.nyu.edu/about/policies-guidelines-compliance/equal-opportunity/bias-response.html

38. FIRE. (2017). 2017 Report on Bias Reporting Systems. *[Blog post]*. Retrieved from https://www.thefire.org/first-amendment-library/special-collections/fire-guides/report-on-bias-reporting-systems-2017

39. See a review of such biases in Haidt (2006), chapter 2.

40. See Pappano, L. (2017, October 31). In a volatile climate on campus, professors teach on tenterhooks. *The New York Times*. Retrieved from https://www.nytimes.com/2017/10/31/education/edlife/liberal-teaching-amid-partisan-divide.html. See also: Belkin, D. (2017, February 27). College faculty's new focus: Don't offend. *The Wall Street Journal*. Retrieved from https://www.wsj.com/articles/college-facultys-new-focus-dont-offend-1488200404

41. Suk Gersen, J. (2014, December 15). The trouble with teaching rape law. *The New Yorker*. Retrieved from https://www.newyorker.com/news/news-desk/trouble-teaching-rape-law

42. Steinbaugh, A. (2016, July 7). University of Northern Colorado defends, modifies "Bias Response Team" as criticism mounts and recording emerges. Retrieved from https://www.thefire.org/university-of-northern -colorado-bias-response-team-recording-emerges

43. Melchior, J.K. (2016, July 5). Exclusive: Transcript of bias response team conversation with censored professor. *Heat Street* (via Archive.org). Retrieved from https://web.archive.org/web/20160805130848/https:// heatst.com/culture-wars/exclusive-transcript-of-bias-response-team-conversation-with -censored-professor

44. Note that this is very similar to the case of Lindsay Shepherd at Wilfrid Laurier University in Canada. Shepherd showed a clip from a televised debate without condemning, in advance, one of the sides of the debate. It can be risky to stage a debate in class if any student feels strongly that one side is correct. See: Grinberg, R. (2017, November 23). Lindsay Shepherd and the potential for heterodoxy at Wilfrid Laurier University. *Heterodox Academy*. Retrieved from https://heterodoxacademy.org/lindsay-shepherd-and -the-potential-for-heterodoxy-at-wilfrid-laurier-university

45. As FIRE's Adam Steinbaugh notes, "academic freedom chilled politely is still academic freedom chilled." See: Steinbaugh, A. (2016, July 7); see note 2.

46. Or sometimes not well intended. Given the political dynamics of many campuses, which we described in chapters 4 and 5, bias response tools can easily be used in malicious ways. In the early days of these systems, in 2009, one of the students who worked on the Bias Response Team at California Polytechnic State University admitted in an interview that one target of the system would be the "teacher who isn't politically correct or is hurtful in their actions or words." In a case at John Carroll University, several students used the school's bias response apparatus to target one student in what appeared to be a prank. See: Cal Poly suspends reporting on "politically incorrect" faculty and students. (2009, June 1). *FIRE*. Retrieved from https://www.thefire.org/cal-poly-suspends-reporting-on-politically-incorrect-faculty-and-students-2. See also: John Carroll University. (2015, December). Bias reports 2014–2015. Retrieved from http://webme dia.jcu.edu/diversity/files/2015/12/2014-2015-Bias-Report-web-version.pdf

47. 20 U.S.C. § 1681 et seq. (1972).

48. See Davis v. Monroe County Board of Education, 526 U.S. 629, 633 (1999); Bryant v. Indep. Sch. Dist. No. I-38, 334 F.3d 928, 934 (10th Cir. 2003).

49. Civil Rights Act of 1964 § 7, 42 U.S.C. § 2000e-2 (a)(1) & (2) (1964) (prohibiting discrimination in hiring or workplace on the basis of "race, color, religion, sex, or national origin"); Education Amendments of 1972 § 9, 20 U.S.C. § 1681(a) (1972) (prohibiting discrimination in education "on the basis of sex").

50. Student wins Facebook.com case at University of Central Florida. (2006, March 6). *FIRE*. Retrieved from https://www.thefire.org/student-wins-facebookcom-case-at-university-of-central-florida

51. Note that a school can and should use a very low threshold for making support or counseling services available for anyone who *feels* harassed. The bar for *punishing speakers* accused of saying something harassing should be higher. Under Title IX, for example, a reported victim is entitled to ameliorative steps before, and even without, a determination of wrongdoing by the accused. The mistake, we believe, is to conflate the two, such that if one person *feels* offended by a one-off speech act, another person should generally be *charged* with harassment. A school that makes such a conflation is codifying and teaching the Untruth of Emotional Reasoning and encouraging moral dependence.

52. Janitor/student Keith John Sampson received a letter informing him that he had been found guilty of racial harassment for "openly reading the book related to a historically and racially abhorrent subject." Lukianoff, G. (2008, May 2). Judging a book by its cover—literally. Retrieved from https://www.thefire .org/judging-a-book-by-its-cover-literally-3

53. For examples, see Gluckman, N., Read B., Mangan, K. & Qulantan, B. (2017, November 3). Sexual harassment and assault in higher ed: What's happened since Weinstein. *The Chronicle of Higher Education*. Retrieved from https://www.chronicle.com/article/Sexual-HarassmentAssault/241757; Anderson, M.D. (2017, October 19). How campus racism could affect black students' college enrollment. *The Atlantic*. Retrieved from https://www.theatlantic.com/education/archive/2017/10/how-racism-could-affect-black -students-college-enrollment/543360/; Berteaux, A. (2016, September 15). In the safe spaces on campus, no Jews allowed. *The Washington Post*. Retrieved from https://www.washingtonpost.com/news/ acts-of-faith/wp/2016/09/15/in-the-safe-spaces-on-campus-no-jews-allowed/?utm_term=.2bb76389a248

54. Silverglate, H. A. (1999, January 26). Memorandum to free speech advocates, University of Wisconsin. Retrieved from https://www.thefire.org/memorandum-to-free-speech-advocates-university-of-wisconsin

55. Doe v. University of Michigan, 721 F.Supp. 852, 865 (E.D. Mich. 1989).

56. Corry v. Leland Stanford Junior University, No. 740309 (Cal. Super. Ct. Feb. 27, 1995) (slip op.).

57. Bhargava, A., & Jackson, G. (2013, May 9). Letter to President Royce Engstrom and University Counsel Lucy France, Esq., University of Montana. U.S. Department of Justice, Civil Rights Division, & U.S.

Department of Education, Office for Civil Rights. Retrieved from https://www.justice.gov/sites/default/files/opa/legacy/2013/05/09/um-ltr-findings.pdf

58. Kipnis, L. (2015, February 27). Sexual paranoia strikes academe. *The Chronicle of Higher Education*. Retrieved from https://www.chronicle.com/article/Sexual-Paranoia-Strikes/190351

59. During the investigation, Kipnis was told she could not involve a lawyer; she could not record her meetings with investigators; and, initially, she was told she would not even be informed of the charges against her until she attended the meetings. Cooke, R. (2017, April 2). Sexual paranoia on campus—and the professor at the eye of the storm. *The Guardian*. Retrieved from https://www.theguardian.com/world/2017/apr/02/unwanted-advances-on-campus-us-university-professor-laura-kipnis-interview

60. Title IX Coordinating Committee response to online petition and ASG resolution. (2014, March 4). *Northwestern Now*. Retrieved from https://news.northwestern.edu/stories/2014/03/title-ix-coordinating-committee-response-to-online-petition-and-asg-resolution

61. Suk Gersen, J. (2017, September 20). Laura Kipnis's endless trial by Title IX. *The New Yorker*. Retrieved from https://www.newyorker.com/news/news-desk/laura-kipniss-endless-trial-by-title-ix

62. A defamation suit filed against Kipnis by a student continues. Meisel, H. (2018, March 7). HarperCollins can't escape suit over prof's assault book. *Law360*. Retrieved from https://www.law360.com/articles/1019571/harpercollins-can-t-escape-suit-over-prof-s-assault-book

63. FIRE (Producer). (2016, April 6). In her own words: Laura Kipnis's "Title IX inquisition" at Northwestern [Video file]. Retrieved from https://youtu.be/vVGOp0IffOQ?t=8m58s

64. Campbell & Manning (2014). See also their expansion of this work in Campbell & Manning (2018).

65. Campbell & Manning (2014), p. 695.

66. Campbell & Manning (2014), p. 697.

67. Read the email from Erika Christakis here: FIRE (2015, October 30). Email from Erika Christakis: "Dressing Yourselves," email to Silliman College (Yale) students on Halloween costumes. *FIRE*. Retrieved from https://www.thefire.org/email-from-erika-christakis-dressing-yourselves-email-to-silliman-college-yale-students-on-halloween-costumes

Chapter 11: The Quest for Justice

1. Rawls (1971), p. 3. Rawls was one of the leading political philosophers of the twentieth century, famous for asking what kind of society we would design if we had to do it from behind a "veil of ignorance" as to what role we would occupy in the society.

2. Data from Ghitza & Gelman (2014) is made interactive in Cox, A. (2014, July 7). How birth year influences political views. *The New York Times*. Retrieved from https://www.nytimes.com/interactive/2014/07/08/upshot/how-the-year-you-were-born-influences-your-politics.html?_r=0

3. The year 1965 saw the passage of the Voting Rights Act, the Watts riot, the march on Selma, and an increase in protests of the Vietnam War as America's involvement intensified; 1972 saw the reelection of Richard Nixon over the "peace candidate," George McGovern, in a landslide—a crushing blow to many in the counterculture. Most Americans born in 1954 could vote in that election; nobody born in 1955 was eligible.

4. Ghitza & Gelman (2014). The paper uses presidential approval ratings as an easily available proxy for the political events occurring in each year—if the president is wildly popular during your late teens (and you're white), you're more likely to vote for that party for the rest of your life. But the authors acknowledge that a variety of "political shocks" are likely to have effects; for example, assassinations, riots, and so on. The model is more descriptive of white voters than it is of black or Hispanic voters.

5. Pyramid Film Producers (Producer). (1969). The World of '68 [Video file]. Retrieved from https://archive.org/details/worldof68

6. Sloane, Baillargeon, and Premack (2012) found that twenty-one-month-old infants looked longer at these violations of proportionality than at scenes where only the person who worked was rewarded. See review of the literature on the early emergence of fairness in Bloom (2014).

7. Damon (1979); Kanngiesser & Warneken (2012).

8. Almas, Cappelen, Sorensen, & Tungodden (2010).

9. Starmans, Sheskin, & Bloom (2017).

10. See Adams (1963); Adams (1965); Huseman, Hatfield & Miles (1987); Walster, Walster, & Berscheid (1978).

11. Walster, Walster, & Berscheid (1978).

12. Ross & Sicoly (1979). See Fiske (1992) for discussion of how concerns about equality and proportionality vary across relationships and contexts.

13. Adams & Rosenbaum (1962).

14. Lind & Tyler (1988). See also: Tyler & Blader (2014). See also: earlier work by Thibaut and Walker (1975).
15. Tyler & Huo (2002).
16. There is a line of research arguing that causality sometimes runs the other way: many people want to justify the status quo, and this desire motivates them to rationalize existing injustices. See this accessible and recent overview: Jost, J. T. (2017). A theory of system justification. *American Psychological Association.* Retrieved from http://www.apa.org/science/about/psa/2017/06/system-justification.aspx
17. Hayek (1976); Nozick (1974).
18. This definition can no longer be found on the website of the National Association of Social Workers, but it was in use until at least August 11, 2017. It can be accessed at: NASW. (2017, August 11). Social justice [via web.archive.org]. Retrieved from https://web.archive.org/web/20170811231830/https://www.socialwork ers.org/pressroom/features/issue/peace.asp
19. Putnam (2015), pp. 31–32, notes that "if forced to choose, Americans at all income levels say by nearly three to one that it is 'more important for this country . . . to ensure everyone has a fair chance of improving their economic standing [than] to reduce inequality in America.'" The survey questions he cites come from a survey conducted in 2011 by the Pew Economic Mobility Project.
20. See research on System Justification Theory, for example, Jost, Banaji, & Nosek (2004).
21. See discussion in chapter 3, and see Crenshaw's TED talk: TED (Producer). (2016, October). Kimberlé Crenshaw at TEDWomen 2016—The urgency of intersectionality [Video file]. Retrieved from https:// www.ted.com/talks/kimberle_crenshaw_the_urgency_of_intersectionality
22. Sometimes members of the minority group are motivated to deny these injustices as well; see research on System Justification Theory, for example, Jost, Banaji, & Nosek (2004).
23. Guinier (1994).
24. Bolick, C. (1993, April 30). Clinton's quota queens. *The Wall Street Journal.*
25. Lewis, N. A. (1993, June 4). Clinton abandons his nominee for rights post amid opposition. *The New York Times.* Retrieved from http://www.nytimes.com/1993/06/04/us/clinton-abandons-his-nominee-for-rights -post-amid-opposition.html
26. See U.S. Dept. of Education, Office for Civil Rights. (1979, December 11). A policy interpretation: Title IX and intercollegiate athletics. Retrieved from https://www2.ed.gov/about/offices/list/ocr/docs/t9interp.html
27. A 1993 federal appellate decision, *Cohen v. Brown Univ.*, would foreshadow what became the official position of the Department of Education three years later. In *Cohen*, members of the women's gymnastics and volleyball teams sued Brown after their teams were cut, allegedly for financial reasons. The court held that Brown had violated Title IX, because the percentage of varsity opportunities for women was lower than the percentage of female enrollment; that there was substantial unsatisfied interest from women to play sports; and that, to comply with Title IX, Brown must either fully accommodate the underrepresented sex or provide opportunities equal to the proportions in its enrollment. See: 991 F.2d 888, 899 (1st Cir. 1993). In other words, if the interest of the underrepresented sex cannot be fully accommodated, the overrepresented sex's opportunities must be reduced until the proportions match.
28. Effectively all but five colleges in the country. For more on "Dear Colleague" letters, see: Admin. (2013, May 28). Frequently asked questions regarding the federal "blueprint" for sexual harassment policies on campus. *FIRE.* Retrieved from https://www.thefire.org/frequently-asked-questions-regarding-the-federal -blueprint-for-sexual-harassment-policies-on-campus/#whatisdcl
29. Cantú, N. V. (1996, January 16). Clarification of intercollegiate athletics policy guidance: The three-part test [Dear Colleague letters]. U.S. Department of Education. Retrieved from https://www2.ed.gov/about/of fices/list/ocr/docs/clarific.html
30. A second way to achieve compliance was to show that the school had "made progress" toward reaching the first standard. A third way was to show that the interest of the underrepresented gender had been "fully and effectively accommodated"—to show that, in practice, there weren't enough women left wanting to play a sport to field a team. These two options would seem to let schools off the hook for achieving equal outcomes, but, in practice, the only ways to satisfy these standards invited close scrutiny by the Office for Civil Rights, and one of the top goals of any compliance professional is to avoid an investigation by a government agency. The only way to definitively stave off an investigation is to satisfy the first certification method, which is what nearly all schools have chosen to do.
31. For evidence that schools were being held to the highest standard, see Thomas, K. (2011, April 25). College teams, relying on deception, undermine gender equity. *The New York Times.* Retrieved from http://www .nytimes.com/2011/04/26/sports/26titleix.html
32. Thomas, K. (2011, May 1). Colleges cut men's programs to satisfy Title IX. *The New York Times.* Retrieved from http://www.nytimes.com/2011/05/02/sports/02gender.html
33. Deaner, Balish & Lombardo (2016). They also report a variety of evidence that prenatal exposure to testosterone for girls correlates with later interest in sports, particularly more typically masculine sports.

34. Deaner et al. (2012).
35. Of course, a skeptic could argue that these differences were caused by differences in early-childhood so-cialization—for example, the fact that in toy stores, the aisles of toys for girls and boys are so different, with much less sporting equipment offered for girls. Perhaps, but efforts to change children's gendered play behavior by treating them in a gender-neutral or gender-reversed way have a poor history of success; see the sad case of David Reimer, for example, in Burkeman, O., & Younge, G. (2004, May 12). Being Brenda. *The Guardian*. Retrieved from https://www.theguardian.com/books/2004/may/12/scienceandnature .gender. Toy stores seem to be responding to gendered preferences rather than causing them. And even if gendered sports preferences were caused entirely by early socialization rather than by prenatal hormones, that would not justify requiring universities to insist on equal outcomes, although it would have implications for elementary schools.
36. Thomas (2011, April 25); see n. 31.
37. Chang (2018).
38. Rivlin-Nadler, M. (2013, August 17). More buck for your bang: People who have more sex make the most money. *Gawker*. Retrieved from http://gawker.com/more-bang-for-your-buck-people-who-have-more -sex-make-1159315115
39. The actual study indicates that because "sexual activity is considered to be a barometer for health, quality of life, well-being and happiness," and "health, cognitive and non-cognitive skills and personality are important factors that affect the wage level," "it is unclear whether this correlation represents a causal relationship." Drydakis, N. (2013). The effect of sexual activity on wages. *IZA Discussion Paper No. 7529*. Retrieved from http://ftp.iza.org/dp7529.pdf
40. Sue et al. (2007), p. 274, define microinvalidations as "communications that exclude, negate, or nullify the psychological thoughts, feelings, or experiential reality of a person of color."
41. Gender differences in cognitive abilities are generally small or nonexistent. Gender differences in what people find interesting and enjoyable are often large, consistent across cultures, and related to exposure to prenatal hormones. For a summary of research on gender differences related to occupational choice, see Stevens, S., & Haidt, J. (2017). The Google memo: What does the research say about gender differences? *Heterodox Academy*. Retrieved from https://heterodoxacademy.org/the-google-memo-what-does-the -research-say-about-gender-differences
42. Tetlock, Kristel, Elson, Green, & Lerner (2000).
43. See Nordhaus, T., & Shellenberger, M. (2013, Winter). Wicked polarization: How prosperity, democracy, and experts divided America. *The Breakthrough Institute*. Retrieved from https://thebreakthrough.org/ index.php/journal/past-issues/issue-3/wicked-polarization

Chapter 12: Wiser Kids

1. Stevens, S., & Haidt, J. (2018, March 19). The skeptics are wrong: Attitudes about free speech are changing on campus. *Heterodox Academy*. Retrieved from https://heterodoxacademy.org/skeptics-are-wrong -about-campus-speech
2. Diamond, A. (2016, November 17). South Korea's testing fixation. *The Atlantic*. Retrieved from https:// www.theatlantic.com/education/archive/2016/11/south-korean-seniors-have-been-preparing-for-today -since-kindergarten/508031
3. Diebelius, G. (2018, February 27). Head teacher bans children from touching snow for "health and safety" reasons. *Metro News*. Retrieved from http://metro.co.uk/2018/02/27/head-teacher-bans-children-touching -snow-health-safety-reasons-7345840
4. We recognize that some children are targets of true bullying, and adults should neither ignore nor minimize behavior that falls under the definition of bullying. "The widely accepted definition of bullying involves three criteria: 1) Repetition: a child is the target of a pattern of aggressive behavior, or a child engages in a pattern of aggressive behaviors against others. 2) A power imbalance exists between the children involved (the child with more power is aggressive against the child with less power). 3) The aggressive child intends to do the other child or children harm." Paresky, P. (2016). We're giving bullying a bad name. *Psychology Today*. Retrieved from https://www.psychologytoday.com/blog/happiness-and-the-pursuit -leadership/201604/we-re-giving-bullying-bad-name
5. Play:groundNYC: built for children, by children. (n.d.). Retrieved from https://play-ground.nyc. For a brief history of adventure playgrounds, visit https://play-ground.nyc/history. To see a video about this kind of playground, visit https://www.youtube.com/watch?time_continue=1&v=74vOpkEin_A
6. Daniel Shuchman is also the chairman of the board of FIRE.

7. "Let Grow License." Available at www.LetGrow.org/LetGrowLicense

8. Of course, the nature of an "abuse of authority" is that it exceeds what is legally allowed; accordingly, we cannot guarantee that someone won't detain your child. Forming an advocacy group of like-minded parents, and approching local law enforcement to educate them before there's a dispute may help avoid conflict. Additionally, this is not legal advice; it's parenting advice. You should consult a licensed attorney in your state/province/country for legal advice.

9. E. Christakis (personal communication, February 18, 2018).

10. Grant, A. (2017, November 4). Kids, would you please start fighting? *The New York Times*. Retrieved from https://www.nytimes.com/2017/11/04/opinion/sunday/kids-would-you-please-start-fighting.html

11. The American Institute for Cognitive Therapy: https://www.cognitivetherapynyc.com

12. R. Leahy (personal communication, January 23, 2017).

13. Chansky (2004).

14. Beck Institute: https://beckinstitute.org. Other CBT resources include David Burns's classic books *Feeling Good: The New Mood Therapy* (1980) and *The Feeling Good Handbook* (1999).

15. Leahy, R. (n.d.). Anxiety files. *Psychology Today*. Retrieved from https://www.psychologytoday.com/blog/anxiety-files

16. PTSD: National Center for PTSD. (n.d.). U.S. Department of Veterans Affairs. Retrieved from https://www.ptsd.va.gov/public/materials/apps/cpt_mobileapp_public.asp

17. AnxietyCoach. (n.d.). *Mayo Clinic*. Retrieved from https://itunes.apple.com/us/app/anxietycoach/id56594 3257?mt=8. For more information on CBT apps, see ADAA-reviewed mental health apps at https://adaa .org/finding-help/mobile-apps

18. Mindful Staff (2017, January 11). Jon Kabat-Zinn: Defining mindfulness. *Mindful*. Retrieved from https://www.mindful.org/jon-kabat-zinn-defining-mindfulness

19. Mindful Schools. (n.d.). Research on mindfulness. Retrieved from https://www.mindfulschools.org/about -mindfulness/research. School-based mindfulness programs are also beneficial. See: Ohio Mental Health Network, Project Aware Information Brief. (n.d.). School-based mindfulness interventions. Retrieved from http://resources.oberlinkconsulting.com/uploads/infobriefs/Final_Mindfulness_Brief_No_3.pdf

20. Rempel, K. (2012).

21. Gelles, D. (n.d.). Mindfulness for children. *The New York Times*. Retrieved from https://www.nytimes .com/guides/well/mindfulness-for-children

22. Emory-Tibet Partnership (n.d.). CBCT. Retrieved from https://tibet.emory.edu/cognitively-based-compas sion-training. And for a program at the University of Massachusetts Medical School that combines CBT with mindfulness (Mindfulness-Based Cognitive Therapy), see: Center for Mindfulness. (n.d.). A mindful way through depression. MBCT: Mindfulness-based cognitive therapy. Retrieved from https://www.um assmed.edu/cfm/mindfulness-based-programs/mbct-courses

23. Solzhenitsyn (1975).

24. TED (Producer). (2011, April 26). On being wrong—Kathryn Schulz [Video file]. Retrieved from https://www.youtube.com/watch?v=QIeRgTBMX88

25. We expect that we will have gotten some things wrong in this book, and we will maintain a page of corrections at TheCoddling.com, where we will thank critics for pointing out our mistakes.

26. H. Cooper (personal communication, February 27, 2018). Also see: Cooper, Civey Robinson, & Patall (2006).

27. SBS Dateline (Producer). (2014, October 21). No rules school [Video File]. Retrieved from https://www .youtube.com/watch?v=r1Y0cuufVGI

28. This can work before school begins in the morning, too. For more information, see Let Grow. (2017, March 4). Let Grow Play Club Final [Video file]. Retrieved from https://youtu.be/JX2ZG0b9I-U. The seven schools in the Patchogue-Medford school district on Long Island, NY, have been piloting the Let Grow Play Club, which involves almost no adult interference. Lori Koerner, principal at the Tremont Elementary School there, says, "This may have been one of the most amazing experiences in my 28 years in education." She adds that she saw "No bullying . . . It's almost like they don't argue, because they know there's nobody that's gonna jump in and help them solve the problem, so they have to just get along." See: News Desk. (2018, January 25). Pat-Med debuts before school play program. *Patchogue Patch*. Retrieved from https:// patch.com/new-york/patchogue/pat-med-debuts-school-play-program

29. One option is to have kids keep their phones zipped in a lockable cell phone pouch, which performing artists like comedian Dave Chappelle are beginning to require at their shows. The pouches are distributed upon entry, phones are locked inside, and while everyone still has his or her phone, they are unusable until tapped on an unlocking device and retrieved from the pouch. See, for example, Yondr. (n.d.). How it works. Retrieved from https://www.overyondr.com/howitworks

30. American Academy of Pediatrics Policy Statement. (2013). The crucial role of recess in school. Retrieved from http://pediatrics.aappublications.org/content/pediatrics/early/2012/12/25/peds.2012-2993.full.pdf

31. *Intellectual Virtues Academy:* http://www.ivalongbeach.org

32. You can read book reviews, articles, and chapters of Professor Baehr's books by going to his website: https://jasonbaehr.wordpress.com/research. There you can also download *Educating for Intellectual Virtues: An Introductory Guide for College and University Instructors*: https://jasonbaehr.files.wordpress.com/2013/12/e4iv_baehr.pdf

33. International Debate Education Association: https://idebate.org/start-debate-club

34. Intelligence Squared debates are found at https://www.intelligencesquaredus.org/debates

35. Reeves, Haidt, & Cicirelli (2018). The book is titled *All Minus One: John Stuart Mill's Ideas on Free Speech Illustrated.* A free version of the e-book can be downloaded from HeterodoxAcademy.org/mill

36. Available at OpenMindPlatform.org

37. Common Sense Media's research is available at https://www.commonsensemedia.org/research

38. Clark, Algoe, & Green (2018).

39. The nonprofit organizations Common Sense Media and the Center for Humane Technology are working together to shift how technology affects the mind. You can find suggestions for how to reduce the negative effects of smartphone use here: http://humanetech.com/take-control

40. In general, we oppose overmanaging and over-monitoring kids. But in this case, given the sophistication of the social media companies in manipulating users and given the high levels of self-reported device addiction among teens and the possible links to depression and suicide, we think that the use of external constraints and parental monitoring is appropriate.

41. People report lower levels of empathy toward conversation partners in the presence of a mobile device. See: Misra, Cheng, Genevie, & Yuan, M. (2014). See also: Nauert, R. (2017, May 25). Parents' digital distractions linked to kids' behavioral issues. *Psych Central.* Retrieved from https://psychcentral.com/news/2017/05/25/parents-digital-distractions-linked-to-kids-behavioral-issues/121061.html

42. "Regularly sleeping fewer than the number of recommended hours is associated with attention, behavior, and learning problems. Insufficient sleep also increases the risk of accidents, injuries, hypertension, obesity, diabetes, and depression. Insufficient sleep in teenagers is associated with increased risk of self-harm, suicidal thoughts, and suicide attempts." Paruthi, S., et al. (2016). Recommended amount of sleep for pediatric populations: A consensus statement of the American Academy of Sleep Medicine. *Journal of Clinical Sleep Medicine, 12*(6): 785–786. Retrieved from https://aasm.org/resources/pdf/pediatricsleepduration consensus.pdf

43. Stanford Medicine News Center. (2015, October 8). Among teens, sleep deprivation an epidemic. Retrieved from https://med.stanford.edu/news/all-news/2015/10/among-teens-sleep-deprivation-an-epidemic.html. See also: Twenge (2017), chapter 4.

44. Twenge (2017). Also, in *Reclaiming Conversation* (2015) by MIT professor Sherry Turkle, Turkle reports that one middle school dean told her, "Twelve-year-olds play on the playground like eight-year-olds," (p. 3). Turkle notes that children are delayed in their ability to read others' emotions, their friendships are superficial, and there has been a general decline in empathy among college students. See also: Turkle, S. (2015, September 26). Stop Googling. Let's talk. *The New York Times.* Retrieved from https://www.nytimes.com/2015/09/27/opinion/sunday/stop-googling-lets-talk.html

45. Arnett (2004) wrote about "emerging adulthood" as a new phase of life in the late teens and early twenties, as marriage and parenthood started to arrive later and later in the postwar decades.

46. Dunn, L. (2017, April 24). Why your brain would love it if you took a gap year. *Forbes.* Retrieved from https://www.forbes.com/sites/noodleeducation/2017/04/24/why-your-brain-would-love-it-if-you-took-a-gap-year/#7d59496e41e2. See also: Southwick, N. (2014, December 2). What do college admissions really think of your gap year? Retrieved from https://www.gooverseas.com/blog/what-do-college-admissions-really-think-of-your-gap-year

47. Aspen Ideas. (n.d.). A civic rite of passage: The case for national service. Retrieved from https://www.aspenideas.org/session/civic-rite-passage-case-national-service

48. Service Year Alliance. (n.d.). What we do. Retrieved from http://about.serviceyear.org/what_we_do

49. McChrystal, S. (2014, November 14). How a national service year can repair America. *The Washington Post.* Retrieved from https://www.washingtonpost.com/opinions/mcchrystal-americans-face-a-gap-of-shared-experience-and-common-purpose/2014/11/14/a51ad4fa-6b6a-11e4-a31c-77759fc1eacc_story.html

50. Learn more about gap years at https://www.GapYearAssociation.org

51. Varadarajan, T. (2018, February 16). The free-speech university. *The Wall Street Journal.* Retrieved from https://www.wsj.com/articles/the-free-speech-university-1518824261

Chapter 13: Wiser Universities

1. To list just a few others, giving only the English translations: Brandeis University: "Truth, even unto its innermost parts"; California Institute of Technology and Johns Hopkins University: "The truth shall make you free"; Colgate University: "For God and Truth"; Howard University: "Truth and Service"; Northwestern University: "Whatsoever things are true"; University of Michigan: "Art, Science, Truth."

2. Pew Research Center. (2017, July 10). Sharp partisan divisions in views of national institutions: Republicans increasingly say colleges have negative impact on U.S. *U.S. Politics and Policy*. Retrieved from http://www.people-press.org/2017/07/10/sharp-partisan-divisions-in-views-of-national-institutions

3. Marx wrote this line in 1845, in his *Theses on Feuerbach*, which was published as an appendix to Engels (1888/1976). The quoted line is on p. 65. It is also engraved in English on his tomb, in London.

4. As we showed in chapter 5, The Evergreen State College changed its mission statement in 2011 to include the phrase "Evergreen supports and benefits from a local and global commitment to social justice . . ." Brown University has considered a similar move, as can be seen in this documentary: Montz, R. (2016). Silence U: Is the university killing free speech and open debate? We the internet documentary. Retrieved from https://www.youtube.com/watch?v=x5uaVFfX3AQ. After the president spoke of Brown's "bedrock commitment to social justice and equity," a group of faculty members wrote, "We applaud and are hopeful about the call of the president and provost to unite around a University agenda of social justice." Brown Faculty Members (2015, November 13). Brown faculty members: Supporting students of color in changing Brown. *The Brown Daily Herald*. Retrieved from http://www.browndailyherald.com/2015/11/13/brown-faculty-members-supporting-students-of-color-in-changing-brown

5. Dreger (2015), p. 262.

6. Dreger (2015), p. 262.

7. A good deal of this language often comes from the American Association of University Professors (AAUP), which was founded in 1915 to fight for academic freedom on campus. The AAUP's statements from 1915 and 1940 are well thought out and inspirational commitments to academic freedom and free inquiry, and later statements by the AAUP on student speech and "extramural" speech (when a professor speaks off campus) also do an excellent job. AAUP. (1940). Statement of principles on academic freedom and tenure. Retrieved from https://www.aaup.org/report/1940-statement-principles-academic-freedom-and-tenure. See also: AAUP. (1915). Declaration of principles on academic freedom and tenure. Retrieved from https://www.aaup.org/NR/rdonlyres/A6520A9D-0A9A-47B3-B550-C006B5B224E7/0/1915Declaration.pdf

8. FIRE. (n.d.). Adopting the Chicago Statement. Retrieved from https://www.thefire.org/student-network/take-action/adopting-the-chicago-statement

9. You can find the policies of more than 450 colleges and universities at www.thefire.org. Universities can join the growing number of colleges whose policies earn a "green light" rating from FIRE, which usually produces positive publicity for a university. As of the final draft of this manuscript, forty colleges and universities have received a green light rating. You can see which colleges are rated as red, yellow, or green at https://www.thefire.org/spotlight/using-the-spotlight-database

10. You can find some information on each school's openness to viewpoint diversity, including its response to recent speech disruptions, by consulting the Heterodox Academy Guide to Colleges, available at http://heterodoxacademy.org/guide-to-colleges

11. Arnett, J. J. (2004).

12. Professors and deans can use the Campus Expression Survey, a free tool created by Heterodox Academy, to measure the speech climate on campus. Available at http://heterodoxacademy.org/campus-expression-survey

13. Simmons, R. J. (2014, May 18). Commencement address, Smith College. Retrieved from https://www.smith.edu/about-smith/smith-history/commencement-speakers/2014. Simmons was chosen as the substitute commencement speaker after Christine Lagarde, former managing director of the International Monetary Fund, withdrew in response to student protests.

14. This distinction could have been made clearer in the much-discussed 2016 letter sent to University of Chicago incoming freshmen by Dean of Students Jay Ellison. It read in part, "[W]e do not condone the creation of intellectual 'safe spaces' where individuals can retreat from ideas and perspectives at odds with their own." You can read the dean's entire letter here: https://news.uchicago.edu/sites/default/files/attachments/Dear_Class_of_2020_Students.pdf

15. Haidt, J. (2017, March 2). Van Jones' excellent metaphors about the dangers of ideological safety [Blog post]. *Heterodox Academy*. Retrieved from https://heterodoxacademy.org/2017/03/02/van-jones-excellent-metaphors

16. See, for example, Sidanius, Van Laar, Levin, & Sinclair (2004), which found a variety of negative effects (including decreased feeling of common identity and increased feelings of ethnic victimization) from participation in "ethnic enclaves" in college. Effects were similar for minority students, and for white students in fraternities.

17. Murray, P. (1945). An American Credo. *CommonGround, 5* no.2 (1945): 24. Retrieved from http://www .unz2.com/print/Common Ground-1945q4-00022

18. See BridgeUSA.org, and see a profile of the group in: Khadaroo, S. T. (2017, October 26). The anti-Washington: College group offers a model for debating politely. *The Christian Science Monitor.* Retrieved from https://www.csmonitor.com/EqualEd/2017/1026/The-anti-Washington-College-group-offers-a-model -for-debating-politely

Conclusion: Wiser Societies

1. Thomas Babington Macauley. From his book review on *Southey's Colloquies on Society,* published in the *Edinburgh Review* in January 1830. Retrieved from http://www.econlib.org/library/Essays/macS1.html

2. Facebook says it is now trying to foster more "meaningful interactions"; see Vogelstein, F. (2018, January 11). Facebook Tweaks Newsfeed to Favor Content From Friends, Family. *Wired.* Retrieved from https:// www.wired.com/story/facebook-tweaks-newsfeed-to-favor-content-from-friends-family

3. Tsukayama, H. (2018, March 1). Twitter's asking for help on how to be less toxic. *The Washington Post.* Retrieved from https://www.washingtonpost.com/news/the-switch/wp/2018/03/01/twitters-asking-for -help-on-how-to-be-less-toxic/?utm_term=.4b28ef8a631b. See especially this post by researchers working with Twitter: Measuring the health of our public conversations. (2018, March 1). *Cortico.* Retrieved from https://www.cortico.ai/blog/2018/2/29/public-sphere-health-indicators

4. Common Sense Media. (2018, February 5). Common Sense partners with the Center for Humane Technology; Announces "Truth About Tech" Campaign in response to escalating concerns about digital addiction. Retrieved from https://www.commonsensemedia.org/about-us/news/press-releases/common-sense-partners -with-the-center-for-humane-technology-announces

5. De la Cruz, D. (2018, March 29). Utah passes "free-range" parenting law. *The New York Times.* Retrieved from https://www.nytimes.com/2018/03/29/well/family/utah-passes-free-range-parenting-law.html

6. See: Illing, S. (2017, December 19). Reciprocal rage: Why Islamist extremists and the far right. *Vox.* Retrieved from https://www.vox.com/world/2017/12/19/16764046/islam-terrorism-far-right-extremism-isis

7. See: Illing, S. (2017, October 13). 20 of America's top political scientists gathered to discuss our democracy. They're scared. Retrieved from https://www.vox.com/2017/10/13/16431502/america-democracy-decline -liberalism

8. See: Chua (2018).

9. See: Rauch, J. (2017, November 9). Speaking as a . . . *The New York Review of Books.* Retrieved from http:// www.nybooks.com/articles/2017/11/09/mark-lilla-liberal-speaking

10. Rauch, J. (2018, February 16). Have our tribes become more important than our country? *The Washington Post.* Retrieved from https://www.washingtonpost.com/outlook/have-our-tribes-become-more-important -than-our-country/2018/02/16/2f8ef9b2-083a-11e8-b48c-b07fea957bd5_story.html

11. @DalaiLama. (2018, May 21). [Tweet]. Retrieved from https://twitter.com/DalaiLama/status/9984974101 99437312

12. Klein, A. (2010, April 26). Not cool: The U of C tops HuffPo's anti-party list. *The Chicago Maroon.* Retrieved from https://www.chicagomaroon.com/2010/04/26/not-cool-the-u-of-c-tops-huffpo-s-anti-party-list

13. Franklin, B. (1750). Available at https://founders.archives.gov/documents/Franklin/01-04-02-0009

Appendix 1: How to Do CBT

1. For a review of self-help books for depression, see Anderson et al. (2005).

Appendix 2: The Chicago Statement on Principles of Free Expression

1. You can read the committee's report here: https://freeexpression.uchicago.edu/sites/freeexpression.uchi cago.edu/files/FOECommitteeReport.pdf

REFERENCES

This section contains all books and academic articles referred to in the text or in the endnotes. Citations for newspaper and magazine articles, reports, blog posts, and online videos are given in the endnotes.

Abramowitz, S. I., Gomes, B., & Abramowitz, C. V. (1975). Publish or politic: Referee bias in manuscript review. *Journal of Applied Social Psychology, 5*(3), 187–200.

Adams, J. S. (1963). Towards an understanding of inequity. *The Journal of Abnormal and Social Psychology, 67*(5), 422–436.

Adams, J. S. (1965). Inequity in social exchange. In L. Berkowitz (Ed.), *Advances in experimental social psychology* (Vol. 2, pp. 267–299). New York, NY: Academic Press.

Adams, J. S., & Rosenbaum, W. B. (1962). The relationship of worker productivity to cognitive dissonance about wage inequities. *Journal of Applied Psychology, 69,* 161–164.

Alexander, M. (2010). *The new Jim Crow: Mass incarceration in the age of colorblindness.* New York, NY: The New Press.

Almas, I., Cappelen, A. W., Sorensen, E. O., & Tungodden, B. (2010). Fairness and the development of inequality acceptance. *Science, 328,* 1176–1178.

Anderson, L., Lewis, G., Araya, R., Elgie, R., Harrison, G., Proudfoot, J., ... Williams, C. (2005). Self-help books for depression: How can practitioners and patients make the right choice? *British Journal of General Practice, 55*(514), 387–392.

Aristotle. (1941). *Nichomachean ethics* (W. D. Ross, Trans.). New York, NY: Random House.

Arnett, J. J. (2004). *Emerging adulthood: The winding road from the late teens through the twenties.* New York, NY: Oxford University Press.

Aurelius, M. (2nd century CE/1964). *Meditations* (M. Staniforth, Trans.). London: Penguin Books.

Balko, R. (2013). *Rise of the warrior cop: The militarization of America's police forces.* New York, NY: Public Affairs.

Bassok, D., Latham, S., & Rorem, A. (2016). Is kindergarten the new first grade? *AERA Open, 1*(4), 1–31.

Bellah, R. N. (1967). Civil religion in America. *Journal of the American Academy of Arts and Sciences, 96*(1), 1–21.

Bergesen, A. J. (1978). A Durkheimian theory of "witch-hunts" with the Chinese Cultural Revolution of 1966–1969 as an example. *Journal for the Scientific Study of Religion, 17*(1), 19.

Berreby, D. (2005). *Us and them: Understanding your tribal mind.* New York, NY: Little, Brown.

Berry, J. M., & Sobieraj, S. (2014). *The outrage industry: Public opinion media and the new incivility.* New York, NY: Oxford University Press.

Bishop, B. (2008). *The big sort: Why the clustering of like-minded America is tearing us apart.* Boston, MA: Houghton Mifflin Harcourt.

Black, J. E., Jones, T. A., Nelson, C. A., & Greenough, W. T. (1998). Neuronal plasticity and the developing brain. In N. E. Alessi, J. T. Coyle, S. I. Harrison, & S. Eth (Eds.), *Handbook of child and adolescent psychiatry* (Vol. 6, pp. 31–53). New York, NY: John Wiley & Sons.

Bloom, P. (2014). *Just babies: The origins of good and evil.* New York, NY: Penguin Random House.

Boethius. (ca. 524 CE/2011). *The consolation of philosophy* (R. H. Green, Trans.). Mansfield Centre, CT: Martino.

Bonanno, G. A., Westphal, M., & Mancini, A. D. (2011). Resilience to loss and potential trauma. *Annual Review of Clinical Psychology, 7,* 511–535.

Buddelmeyer, H., & Powdthavee, N. (2015). Can having internal locus of control insure against negative shocks? Psychological evidence from panel data. *Journal of Economic Behavior and Organization, 122*, 88–109.

Burns, D. D. (1980). *Feeling good: The new mood therapy.* New York, NY: Avon Books.

Burns, D. D. (1999). *The feeling good handbook.* New York, NY: Plume.

Butler, A. C., Chapman, J. E., Forman, E. M., & Beck, A. T. (2006). The empirical status of cognitive-behavioral therapy: A review of meta-analyses. *Clinical Psychology Review, 26*(1), 17–31.

Byrom, T. (Ed. and Trans.). (1993). *Dhammapada: The sayings of the Buddha.* Boston, MA: Shambhala.

Campbell, B., & Manning, J. (2014). Microaggression and moral cultures. *Comparative sociology, 13*, 692–726.

Campbell, B., & Manning, J. (2018). *The rise of victimhood culture: Microaggressions, safe spaces, and the new culture wars.* [No city]: Palgrave Macmillan.

Carney, D. R., Jost, J. T., Gosling, S. D., & Potter, J. (2008). The secret lives of liberals and conservatives: Personality profiles, interaction styles, and the things they leave behind. *Political Psychology, 29*(6), 807–840.

Chan, W. T. (Ed. and Trans.). (1963). *A source book in Chinese philosophy.* Princeton, NJ: Princeton University Press.

Chang, E. (2018). *Brotopia: Breaking up the boys' club of Silicon Valley.* New York, NY: Portfolio/Penguin.

Chansky T. (2004). *Freeing your child from anxiety: Powerful, practical solutions to overcome your child's fears, worries, and phobias.* New York, NY: Random House.

Chen, P., Coccaro, E. F., & Jacobson, K. C. (2012). Hostile attributional bias, negative emotional responding, and aggression in adults: Moderating effects of gender and impulsivity. *Aggressive Behavior, 38*(1), 47–63.

Chetty, R., Friedman, J. N., Saez, E., Turner, N., & Yagen, D. (2017). Mobility report cards: The role of colleges in intergenerational mobility. Unpublished manuscript, retrieved from: http://www.equality-of-opportunity.org/papers/coll_mrc_paper.pdf

Christakis, E. (2016). *The importance of being little: What young children really need from grownups.* New York, NY: Viking.

Christakis, N. A. (2008, December 10). This allergies hysteria is just nuts. *BMJ, 337.*

Chua, A. (2018). *Political tribes: Group instinct and the fate of nations.* New York, NY: Penguin Press.

Cikara, M., & Van Bavel, J. J. (2014). The neuroscience of intergroup relations: An integrative review. *Perspectives on Psychological Science, 9*(245).

Clark, J. L., Algoe, S. B., & Green, M. C. (2018). Social network sites and well-being: The role of social connection. *Current Directions in Psychological Science, 27*(1), 32–37.

Clements, R. (2004). An investigation of the status of outdoor play. *Contemporary Issues in Early Childhood, 5*(1), 68–80.

Cohen, E. E., Ejsmond-Frey, R., Knight, N., & Dunbar, R. I. (2009). Rowers high: Behavioural synchrony is correlated with elevated pain thresholds. *Biology Letters, 6*(1), 106–108.

Collier, L. (2016). Growth after trauma. *APA Monitor, 47,* 48.

Collins, P. H., & Bilge, S. (2016). *Intersectionality.* Cambridge, UK: Polity Press.

Cooper, H., Civey Robinson, J., & Patall, E. (2006). Does homework improve academic achievement? A synthesis of research, 1987–2003. *Review of Educational Research, Spring 2006, 76*(1), 1–62.

Cooper, H., Lindsay, J. J., Nye, B., & Greathouse, S. (1998). Relationships among attitudes about homework, amount of homework assigned and completed, and student achievement. *Journal of Educational Psychology, 90*(1), 70–83.

Cooper, H., Steenbergen-Hu, S., & Dent, A. (2012). Homework. In K. R. Harris, S. Graham, T. Urdan, A. G. Bus, S. Major, & H. L. Swanson (Eds.), *APA educational psychology handbook, Vol. 3. Application to learning and teaching* (pp. 475–495). Washington, DC: American Psychological Association.

Costello, E. J. (1982). Locus of control and depression in students and psychiatric outpatients. *Journal of Clinical Psychology 38*(2), 340–343.

Crawford, J. T., & Jussim, L. J. (2018). *The politics of social psychology.* New York, NY: Routledge.

Crenshaw, K. M. (1989). Demarginalizing the intersection of race and sex: A black feminist critique of antidiscrimination doctrine, feminist theory and antiracist politics. *University of Chicago Legal Forum, 1989*(1).

Crick, N. R., & Grotpeter, J. K. (1995). Relational aggression, gender, and social-psychological adjustment. *Child Development, 66*(3), 710–722.

Curtiss, S. (1977). *Genie: A psycholinguistic study of a modern-day "wild child."* Boston, MA: Academic Press.

Damon, W. (1979). *The social world of the child.* San Francisco, CA: Jossey-Bass.

de Tocqueville, A. (1839/2012). *Democracy in America* (E. Nolla, Ed.; J. T. Schleifer, Trans.) Indianapolis: Liberty Fund.

Deaner, R. O., Balish, S. M., & Lombardo, M. P. (2016). Sex differences in sports interest and motivation: An evolutionary perspective. *Evolutionary Behavioral Sciences, 10*(2), 73–97.

Deaner, R. O., Geary, D. C., Puts, D. A., Ham, S. A., Kruger, J., Fles, E., . . . Grandis, T. (2012). A sex difference in the predisposition for physical competition: Males play sports much more than females even in the contemporary U.S. *PLoS ONE, 7,* e49168.

DeLoache, J. S., Chiong, C., Sherman, K., Islam, N., Vanderborght, M., Troseth, G. L., Strouse, G. A., & O'Doherty, K. (2010). Do babies learn from baby media? *Psychological Science, 21*(11), 1570–1574.

Deresiewicz, W. (2015). *Excellent sheep: The miseducation of the American elite and the way to a meaningful life.* New York, NY: Free Press.

Dreger, A. (2015). *Galileo's middle finger: Heretics, activists, and one scholar's search for justice.* New York, NY: Penguin Books.

Duarte, J. L., Crawford, J. T., Stern, C., Haidt, J., Jussim, L., & Tetlock, P. E. (2015). Political diversity will improve social psychological science. *Behavioral and Brain Sciences, 38,* 1–13.

Durkheim, E. (1915/1965). *The elementary forms of the religious life* (J. W. Swain, Trans.). New York, NY: Free Press.

Du Toit, G. D., Katz, Y., Sasieni, P., Mesher, D., Maleki, S. J., Fisher, H. R., . . . Lack, G. (2008). Early consumption of peanuts in infancy is associated with a low prevalence of peanut allergy. *Journal of Allergy and Clinical Immunology, 122*(5), 984–991.

Du Toit, G. D., Roberts, G., Sayre, P. H., Bahnson, H. T., Radulovic, S., Santos, A. F., . . . Lack, G. (2015). Randomized trial of peanut consumption in infants at risk for peanut allergy. *New England Journal of Medicine, 372*(9), 803–813.

Ebner, J. (2017). *The rage: The vicious circle of Islamist and far right extremism.* New York, NY: Tauris.

Eggertson, L. (2010, March 9). Lancet retracts 12-year-old article linking autism to MMR vaccines. *CMAJ: Canadian Medical Association Journal, 182*(4), E199–E200. http://doi.org/10.1503/cmaj.109-3179

Ehrenreich, B. (2006). *Dancing in the streets: A history of collective joy.* New York, NY: Metropolitan Books.

Einon, D., Morgan, M. J., & Kibbler, C. C. (1978). Brief periods of socialization and later behavior in the rat. *Developmental Psychobiology, 11,* 213–225.

Engels, F. (1888/1976). *Ludwig Feuerbach and the end of classical German philosophy.* Peking: Foreign Languages Press.

Epictetus & Lebell, S. (1st–2nd century/1995). *Art of living: The classical manual on virtue, happiness, and effectiveness.* New York, NY: HarperOne.

Fiske, A. P. (1992). The four elementary forms of sociality: Framework for a unified theory of social relations. *Psychological Review, 99*(4), 689–723.

Foa, E. B., & Kozak, M. J. (1986). Emotional processing of fear: Exposure to corrective information. *Psychological Bulletin, 99,* 20–35.

Frankl, E. (1959/2006). *Man's search for meaning.* Boston, MA: Beacon Press.

Ganti, L., Bodhit, A. N., Daneshvar, Y., Patel, P. S., Pulvino, C., Hatchitt, K., . . . Tyndall, J. A. (2013). Impact of helmet use in traumatic brain injuries associated with recreational vehicles. *Advances in Preventive Medicine, 2013,* 1–6.

Ghitza, Y., & Gelman, A. (2014, July 7). The Great Society, Reagan's revolution, and generations of presidential voting. Working paper. Retrieved from https://static01.nyt.com/newsgraphics/2014/07/06/generations2/assets/cohort_voting_20140707.pdf

Ginsberg, B. (2011). *The fall of the faculty: The rise of the all-administrative university and why it matters.* New York, NY: Oxford University Press.

Gosling, S. (2008). *Snoop: What your stuff says about you.* New York, NY: Basic Books.

Gotlib, I. H., & Joormann, J. (2010). Cognition and depression: Current status and future directions. *Annual Review of Clinical Psychology, 6,* 285–312.

Gratz, K. L., Conrad, S. D., & Roemer, L. (2002). Risk factors for deliberate self-harm among college students. *American Journal of Orthopsychiatry 1,* 128–140.

Gray, H. H. (2012). *Searching for utopia: Universities and their histories.* Berkeley: University of California Press.

Gray, P. (2011). The decline of play and the rise of psychopathology in children and adolescents. *American Journal of Play, 3*(4), 443–463.

Gray, P. (In press). Evolutionary functions of play: Practice, resilience, innovation, and cooperation. In P. Smith & J. Roopnarine (Eds.), *The Cambridge handbook of play: Developmental and disciplinary perspectives.* New York, NY: Cambridge University Press.

Greenwald, A. G., Banaji, M. R., & Nosek, B. A. (2015). Statistically small effects of the Implicit Association Test can have societally large effects. *Journal of Personality and Social Psychology, 108*(4), 553–561.

Guinier, L. (1994). *The tyranny of the majority: Fundamental fairness in representative democracy.* New York, NY: Free Press.

Hacking, I. (1991). The making and molding of child abuse. *Critical Inquiry, 17,* 253–288.

Haidt, J. (2006). *The happiness hypothesis: Finding modern truth in ancient wisdom.* New York, NY: Basic Books.

Haidt, J. (2012). *The righteous mind: Why good people are divided by politics and religion.* New York, NY: Pantheon Books.

Haji, N. (2011). *The sweetness of tears.* New York, NY: William Morrow.

Hare, C., & Poole, K. T. (2014). The polarization of contemporary American politics. *Polity, 46,* 411–429.

Haslam, N. (2016). Concept creep: Psychology's expanding concepts of harm and pathology. *Psychological Inquiry, 27*(1), 1–17.

Hayek, F. A. (1976). *The mirage of social justice,* Vol. 2 of *Law, legislation, and liberty.* Chicago, IL: University of Chicago Press.

Heider, F. (1958). *The psychology of interpersonal relationships.* New York, NY: John Wiley & Sons.

Hirsh-Pasek, K. Golinkoff, R. M., Berk, L. E., & Singer. D. G. (2009). *A mandate for playful learning in preschool: Presenting the evidence.* New York, NY: Oxford University Press.

Hoffer, E. (1951/2010). *The true believer: Thoughts on the nature of mass movements.* New York, NY: Harper Perennial Modern Classics.

Hofferth, S. L., & Sandberg, J. F. (2001). Changes in American children's time, 1981–1997. In S. L. Hofferth & T. J. Owens (Eds.), *Children at the millennium: Where have we come from? Where are we going?* (pp. 193–229). Amsterdam: Elsevier.

Hogg, M. A. (2016). Social identity theory. *Encyclopedia of Identity,* 3–17.

Hol, T., Berg, C. V., Ree, J. V., & Spruijt, B. (1999). Isolation during the play period in infancy decreases adult social interactions in rats. *Behavioural Brain Research, 100*(1–2), 91–97.

Holland, J. H. (1992). Complex adaptive systems. *Daedalus, 121,* 17–30.

Hollon, S. D., & DeRubeis, R. J. (In press). Outcome studies in cognitive therapy. In R. L. Leahy (Ed.), *Contemporary cognitive therapy: Theory, research, and practice* (2nd ed.). New York, NY: Guilford Press.

Horwitz, S. (2015). Cooperation over coercion: The importance of unsupervised childhood play for democracy and liberalism. *Cosmos+Taxis,* 3–16.

Hunter, D., & Tice, P. (2016, September). 2015 national survey on drug use and health: Methodological summary and definitions: B.4.8 Major depressive episode (depression). Rockville, MD: Substance Abuse and Mental Health Services Administration.

Huseman, R. C., Hatfield, J. D., & Miles, E. W. (1987). A new perspective on equity theory: The equity sensitivity construct. *Academy of Management Review, 12,* 222–234.

Ip, G. (2015). *Foolproof: Why safety can be dangerous and how danger makes us safe.* New York, NY: Little, Brown.

Iyengar, S., & Krupenkin, M. (2018). The strengthening of partisan affect. *Advances in Political Psychology, 39,* Suppl. 1, 2018, 201–218.

Johnson, J. S., & Newport, E. L. (1989). Critical period effects in second language learning: The influence of maturational state on the acquisition of English as a second language. *Cognitive Psychology, 21*(1), 60–99.

Jost, J. T., Banaji, M. R., & Nosek, B. A. (2004). A decade of system justification theory: Accumulated evidence of conscious and unconscious bolstering of the status quo. *Political Psychology, 25*(6), 881–919.

Kahneman, D. (2011). *Thinking fast and slow.* New York, NY: Farrar, Straus and Giroux.

Kanngiesser, P., & Warneken, F. (2012). Young children consider merit when sharing resources with others. *PLOS ONE 7,* e43979. https://doi.org/10.1371/journal.pone.0043979

Kerr, C. (1963). *The uses of the university.* Cambridge, MA: Harvard University Press.

King, M. L. (1963/1981). *Strength to love*. Philadelphia, PA: Fortress Press.

LaFreniere, P. (2011). Evolutionary functions of social play: Life histories, sex differences, and emotion regulation. *American Journal of Play, 3*(4), 464–488.

Langbert, M., Quain, A. J., & Klein, D. B. (2016). Faculty voter registration in economics, history, journalism, law, and psychology. *Econ Journal Watch, 13*(3), 422–451.

Lareau, A. (2011). *Unequal childhoods: Class, race, and family life*. 2nd edition. Berkeley: University of California Press.

Leahy, R. L., Holland, S. F. J., & McGuinn, L. K. (2011). *Treatment plans and interventions for depression and anxiety disorders*. 2nd edition. New York, NY: Guilford Press.

Lewis, H. R. (2007). *Excellence without a soul: Does liberal education have a future?* New York, NY: PublicAffairs.

Lilienfeld, S. O. (2017). Microaggressions. *Perspectives on Psychological Science, 12*(1), 138–169.

Lilla, M. (2017). *The once and future liberal: After identity politics*. New York, NY: Harper.

Lind, E. A., & Tyler, T. R. (1988). *The social psychology of procedural justice*. New York, NY: Plenum Press.

Lukianoff, G. (2014). *Unlearning liberty: Campus censorship and the end of American debate*. New York, NY: Encounter Books.

Luthar, S., & Latendresse, S. (2005). Children of the affluent: Challenges to well-being. *Current Directions in Psychological Science, 14*, 49–53.

Maccoby, E. E. (1998). *The two sexes: Growing up apart, coming together*. Cambridge, MA: Harvard University Press.

MacFarquhar, R., & Schoenhals, M. (2006). *Mao's last revolution*. Cambridge, MA: Harvard University Press.

Mandela, N. (2003). *In his own words*. New York, NY: Little, Brown.

Mann, T. E., & Ornstein, N. J. (2012). *It's even worse than it looks: How the American constitutional system collided with the new politics of extremism*. New York, NY: Basic Books.

Marano, H. E. (2008). *A nation of wimps*. New York, NY: Crown Archetype.

Mascaro, J. (Ed. and Trans.). (1995). *Buddha's teachings*. New York, NY: Penguin Classics.

McClintock, C. G., Spaulding, C. B., & Turner, H. A. (1965). Political orientations of academically affiliated psychologists. *American Psychologist, 20*(3), 211–221.

McCrae, R. R. (1996). Social consequences of experiential openness. *Psychological Bulletin, 120*(3), 323–337.

Mercado, M. C., Holland, K., Leemis, R. W., Stone, D. M., & Wang, J. (2017). Trends in emergency department visits for nonfatal self-inflicted injuries among youth aged 10 to 24 years in the United States, 2001–2015. *JAMA, 318*(19), 1931.

Mill, J. S. (1859/2003). *On liberty*. New Haven, CT: Yale University Press.

Milton, J., & Blake, W. (2017). *Paradise lost*. London: Sirius Publishing.

Misra, S., Cheng, L., Genevie, J., & Yuan, M. (2014). The iPhone effect: The quality of in-person social interactions in the presence of mobile devices. *Environment and Behavior, 48*(2), 275–298.

Morgan, K. P. (1996). Describing the emperor's new clothes: Three myths of educational (in-)equity. In A. Diller et al., *The gender question in education: Theory, pedagogy, and politics* (pp. 105–122). Boulder, CO: Westview Press.

Mose, T. R. (2016). *The playdate: Parents, children, and the new expectations of play*. New York, NY: New York University Press.

Murray, P. (1945). An American credo. *Common Ground, 1945*(4), 22–24.

Mustoe, A. C., Taylor, J. H., Birnie, A. K., Huffman, M. C., & French, J. A. (2014). Gestational cortisol and social play shapes development of marmosets' HPA functioning and behavioral responses to stressors. *Developmental Psychobiology, 56*, 1229–1243.

National Center for Education Statistics. (1993, January). 120 years of American education: A statistical portrait. Retrieved from https://nces.ed.gov/pubs93/93442.pdf

Nietzsche, F. W. (1889/1997). *Twilight of the idols* (R. Polt, Trans.). Indianapolis, IN: Hackett Publishing.

Nolen-Hoeksema, S., & Girgus, J. S. (1994, May). The emergence of gender differences in depression during adolescence. *Psychological Bulletin, 115*(3), 424–443.

Norton, M. B. (2007). *In the devil's snare: The Salem witchcraft crisis of 1693*. New York, NY: Random House.

Novotney, A. (2014). Students under pressure: College and university counseling centers are examining how best to serve the growing number of students seeking their services. *Monitor on Psychology, 45*, 36.

Nozick, R. (1974). *Anarchy, state, and utopia.* New York, NY: Basic Books.

Okada, H., Kuhn, C., Feillet, H., & Bach, J. (2010). The "hygiene hypothesis" for autoimmune and allergic diseases: An update. *Clinical & Experimental Immunology, 160,* 1–9.

Ostrom, E. (1990). *Governing the commons: The evolution of institutions for collective action.* New York, NY: Cambridge University Press.

Ostrom, V. (1997). *The meaning of democracy and the vulnerability of democracies.* Ann Arbor: University of Michigan Press.

Pariser, E. (2011). *The filter bubble: How the new personalized web is changing what we read and how we think.* New York, NY: Penguin Press.

Pavlac, B. A. (2009). *Witch hunts in the Western world: Persecution and punishment from the Inquisition through the Salem trials.* Westport, CT: Greenwood Press.

Peterson, C., Maier, S. F., & Seligman, M. E. P. (1993). *Learned helplessness: A theory for the age of personal control.* New York, NY: Oxford University Press.

Piaget, J. (1932/1965). *The moral judgement of the child* (M. Gabain, Trans.). New York, NY: Macmillan.

Pierce, C. M. (1970). Offensive mechanisms. In F. B. Barbour (Ed.), *The black seventies* (pp. 265–282). Boston, MA: Porter Sargent.

Pinker, S. (2016). *The blank slate: The modern denial of human nature.* New York, NY: Penguin Books.

Pinker, S. (2017). *Enlightenment now: The case for reason, science, humanism,* and progress. New York, NY: Viking.

Prociuk, T. J., Breen, L. J., & Lussier, R. J. (1976). Hopelessness, internal-external locus of control, and depression. *Journal of Clinical Psychology 32*(2), 299–300.

Putnam, R. D. (2000). *Bowling alone: The collapse and revival of American community.* New York, NY: Simon & Schuster.

Putnam, R. D. (2015). *Our kids: The American dream in crisis.* New York, NY: Simon & Schuster.

Rawls, J. (1971). *A theory of justice.* Cambridge, MA: Harvard University Press.

Reeves, R. V., Haidt, J., & Cicirelli, D. (2018). *All minus one: John Stuart Mill's ideas on free speech illustrated.* New York, NY: Heterodox Academy.

Rempel K. (2012). Mindfulness for children and youth: A review of the literature with an argument for school-based implementation. *Canadian Journal of Counselling and Psychotherapy, 46*(3), 201–220.

Ridley, M. (2010). *The rational optimist: How prosperity evolves.* New York, NY: Harper.

Ross, M., & Sicoly, F. (1979). Egocentric biases in availability and attribution. *Journal of Personality & Social Psychology, 37,* 322–336.

Rubinstein, R., Jussim, L., Stevens, S. (2018). Reliance on individuating information and stereotypes in implicit and explicit person perception. *Journal of Experimental Social Psychology, 75,* 54–70.

Sacks, J. (2015). *Not in God's name.* New York, NY: Random House.

Salk, R., Hyde, J., Abramson, L. (2017). Gender differences in depression in representative national samples: Meta-analyses of diagnoses and symptoms. *Psychological Bulletin, 143*(8), r783–822.

Sandseter, E., & Kennair, L. (2011). Children's risky play from an evolutionary perspective: The anti-phobic effects of thrilling experiences. *Evolutionary Psychology, 9,* 257–284.

Seligman, M. (1990). *Learned optimism: How to change your mind and your life.* New York, NY: Vintage Books.

Shakespeare, W. (ca. 1600/2008). *Hamlet* (G. R. Hibbard, Ed.). Oxford, UK: Oxford University Press.

Shin, L. M., & Liberzon, I. (2010). The neurocircuitry of fear, stress, and anxiety disorders. *Neuropsychopharmacology, 35*(1), 169–191.

Shweder, R. A. (1996). True ethnography: The lore, the law, and the lure. In R. Jessor, A. Colby, & R. A. Shweder (Eds.), *Ethnography and human development* (pp. 15–52). Chicago, IL: University of Chicago Press.

Sidanius, J., Van Laar, C., Levin, S., & Sinclair, S. (2004). Ethnic enclaves and the dynamics of social identity on the college campus: The good, the bad, and the ugly. *Journal of Personality and Social Psychology, 87,* 96–110.

Silverglate, H. A. (2009). *Three felonies a day: How the Feds target the innocent.* New York, NY: Encounter Books.

Singer, D. G., Singer, J. L., D'Agostino, H., & DeLong, R. (2009). Children's pastimes and play in sixteen nations: Is free-play declining? *American Journal of Play, 1*(3), 283–312.

Sloane, S., Baillargeon, R., & Premack, D. (2012). Do infants have a sense of fairness? *Psychological Science, 23*(2), 196–204.

Solomon, A. (2014). *The noonday demon: An atlas of depression.* New York, NY: Scribner Classics.

Solzhenitsyn, A. I. (1975). *The Gulag Archipelago, 1918–1956: An experiment in literary investigation* (Vol. 2) (T. P. Whitney, Trans.) New York, NY: Harper Perennial.

Starmans, C., Sheskin, M., & Bloom, P. (2017). Why people prefer unequal societies. *Nature Human Behaviour, 1*(4), 0082.

Sue, D. W., Capodilupo, C. M., Torino, G. C., Bucceri, J. M., Holder, A. M., Nadal, K. L., & Esquilin, M. (2007). Racial microaggressions in everyday life: Implications for clinical practice. *American Psychologist, 62*(4), 271–286.

Tajfel, H. (1970). Experiments in intergroup discrimination. *Scientific American, 223*(5), 96–102.

Taleb, N. N. (2007). *The black swan: The impact of the highly improbable.* New York, NY: Random House.

Taleb, N. N. (2012). *Antifragile: Things that gain from disorder.* New York, NY: Random House.

Tetlock, P. E., Kristel, O. V., Elson, B., Green, M., & Lerner, J. (2000). The psychology of the unthinkable: Taboo trade-offs, forbidden base rates, and heretical counterfactuals. *Journal of Personality and Social Psychology, 78*, 853–870.

Thibaut, J. W., & Walker, L. (1975). *Procedural justice: A psychological analysis.* Hillsdale, NJ: L. Erlbaum Associates.

Thucydides (1972). *History of the Peloponnesian War.* (R. Warner, Trans.). London: Penguin Classics.

Tuvel, R. (2017). In defense of transracialism. *Hypatia, 32*(2), 263–278.

Twenge, J. M. (2017). *iGen: Why today's super-connected kids are growing up less rebellious, more tolerant, less happy—and completely unprepared for adulthood—and what that means for the rest of us.* New York, NY: Atria Books.

Twenge, J. M., Joiner, T. E., Rogers, M. L., & Martin, G. N. (2018). Increases in depressive symptoms, suicide-related outcomes, and suicide rates among U.S. adolescents after 2010 and links to increased new media screen time. *Clinical Psychological Science, 6*(1), 3–17.

Tyler, T. R., & Blader, S. L. (2014). *Cooperation in groups: Procedural justice, social identity, and behavioral engagement.* New York, NY: Psychology Press.

Tyler, T. R., & Huo, Y. J. (2002). *Trust in the law: Encouraging public cooperation with the police and courts.* New York, NY: Russell Sage Foundation.

van der Vossen, B. (2014). In defense of the ivory tower: Why philosophers should stay out of politics. *Philosophical Psychology, 28*(7), 1045–1063. doi: 10.1080/09515089.2014.972353

Vaughn, D., Savjani, R. R., Cohen, M., & Eagleman, D. M. (under review). Empathy is modulated by religious affiliation of the other.

Walster, E. H., Walster, G. W., & Berscheid, E. (1978). *Equity: Theory and research.* Boston, MA: Allyn & Bacon.

Ward, D. T. (1994). *Happy ending and day of absence: Two plays.* New York, NY: Dramatists Play Service.

Wiltermuth, S. S., & Heath, C. (2009). Synchrony and cooperation. *Psychological Science, 20*(1), 1–5.

Wolff, R. P., Moore, B., & Marcuse, H. (1965/1969). *A critique of pure tolerance.* Boston, MA: Beacon Press.

Woodard, C. (2011). *American nations: A history of the eleven rival regional cultures of North America.* New York, NY: Viking.

Zhiguo, W., & Fang, Y. (2014). Comorbidity of depressive and anxiety disorders: Challenges in diagnosis and assessment. *Shanghai Archives of Psychiatry, 26*(4), 227–231.

Zimbardo, P. G. (2007). *The Lucifer effect: Understanding how good people turn evil.* New York, NY: Random House.

INDEX

abuse, 25, 26, 175
Adam, 166
Adam Walsh Child Resource Center, 166
Adler, Eric, 198–99
adulthood, 148, 250, 257
Adverse Childhood Experiences (ACE), 175, 176
aggression, 40, 71
   in girls versus boys, 155, 161
   microaggressions, 40–46, 51, 71, 77, 145, 205,
     210, 260
Albright, Madeleine, 48
Alexander, Larry, 107–8
Alexander, Michelle, 74
Algoe, Sara, 159
allergies, 21–22
   peanut, 19–21, 23–24, 30, 164, 236, 237
American Academy of Pediatrics, 247
American Civil Liberties Union (ACLU), 92, 216
American Enterprise Institute, 87
American National Election Study, 129
America's Most Wanted, 166
Antifa, 81, 83, 91
Antifragile (Taleb), 22–23, 164, 170
antifragility, 22–24, 28, 31, 146, 164, 176, 178,
    193, 206, 237, 246
anxiety, 5, 12, 24, 30, 33–34, 125, 126, 157, 164
   cognitive behavioral therapy and, 7–8, 29
   cognitive distortions and, 7–8, 10, 158–59, 161
   depression and, 158
   in girls versus boys, 149–51, 160
   overprotection and, 183
   play deprivation and, 183
   rates of, 149–51, 157–58, 160, 183, 185
   safetyism and, 158
Aristotle, 253
art of association, 191–92, 194, 211
Ashworth, Kevin, 163
Atlantic, 42, 72, 95, 190
   "The Coddling of the American Mind"
     (Lukianoff and Haidt), 10–12, 31, 37, 121,
     145, 156, 205
Atomwaffen Division, 133
Axelrod, David, 96

Baby Boom generation, 110, 111, 167, 174
Baehr, Jason, 247–48

Balko, Radley, 74
Barrett, Lisa Feldman, 95
Beck, Aaron, 36–37
Beck, Glenn, 132
Bell Curve, The (Herrnstein and Murray), 87
Berenstain, Nora, 105
Bergen Community College, 201
Bergesen, Albert, 100–103, 105–7, 119
Berkeley, University of California at, 12, 81–87,
    90, 94, 120
bias reporting systems, 204–6, 212
*Big Sort, The: Why the Clustering of Like-Minded
    America Is Tearing Us Apart* (Bishop), 130
Bilge, Sirma, 68
Bill of Rights, 222–23
Bishop, Bill, 130
Black Lives Matter (BLM), 75, 88,
    133, 134
Black Swan, The (Taleb), 22
blaming, 38, 39, 278
Bloom, Paul, 218
Boethius, 34, 35
Bond, Sarah, 136–37
brain, 153, 181–84, 193, 194
Breitbart News, 81
Bridges, George, 115–17, 119, 198
Brookings Institution, 86
Brown, Stacy, 116, 118–19
Brown University, 26–28, 70, 259
Bruni, Frank, 190
Buddha, ix, 34, 35, 60, 95, 241
bullying, 25, 26, 246

call-out culture, 5, 10, 71–73, 77, 86, 158
Cambridge Analytica, 265
Campbell, Bradley, 209, 210
Carlson, Tucker, 118, 133, 134
Carter, Jimmy, 224
catastrophizing, 38, 50, 84–85, 89, 145, 190, 201,
    212, 277
Center for Collegiate Mental Health, 156
Centers for Disease Control, 190
charitable interpretations, *see* principle
    of charity
Charleston church shooting, 139
Charlottesville rally, 90–92, 94, 97, 139

Chicago Statement on Principles of Free Expression, 255–56, 268, 279–81
Chinese Cultural Revolution, 100–102
children
  academic and career pressures on, 174, 235, 236
  adversity and, 175–76
  books for, 172
  cognitive behavioral techniques for, 241–42
  community of, 239–40
  conflict resolution and disagreement skills in, 191–92, 194, 211, 212, 240, 248, 258–60
  democracy and, 191–94
  and fear of strangers and abduction, 165–67, 178, 186, 194, 235, 238
  mindfulness and, 242
  phones and, see phones
  play and, see play
  school and, see school
  sleep and, 250
  structured lives of, 188–89, 246
  suggestions for, 235–51
  summer camps for, 240
  wisdom and, 235–51
  year of service or work after high school, 250–51, 257
  see also parenting
Christakis, Erika, 56–57, 71, 102–3, 127, 165, 187, 188, 210–11, 240
Christakis, Nicholas, 56–57, 127
Chronicle of Higher Education, 208
Chua, Amy, 267
Ciccariello-Maher, George, 135
civil rights laws, 206, 207
civil rights movement, 60–61, 65, 67, 84, 216, 221, 222, 230
Claremont McKenna College (CMC), 53–55, 88–90, 102–3, 120, 134, 175
Clark, Jenna, 159
Clinton, Bill, 222, 224
coddling, use of word, 13–14
cognitive behavioral therapy (CBT), 3, 7–9, 14, 29, 51, 95, 144–45, 196, 259
  Boethius and, 34–36
  children and, 241–42
  effectiveness of, 37
  how to do, 275–78
  as microaggression, 42
cognitive distortions, 7–10, 14, 36–40, 50, 84–85, 89, 144–45, 196–97, 212, 259
  anxiety and, 7–8, 10, 158–59, 161
  categories of, 37–38, 277–78
  depression and, 7–8, 10, 36–37, 150, 158–59, 161
  parenting and, 177–78

safetyism and, 177–78
  see also emotional reasoning
college campuses, see universities
Collins, Patricia Hill, 68
Collins, Richard, III, 139
Columbia University, 6, 7, 40, 255
Coming Apart (Murray), 87
Common Core, 188
common-enemy identity politics, 62–67, 71–73, 76, 77, 89–90, 119–20, 244
common-humanity identity politics, 60–62, 74–76, 221, 244
Common Sense Media, 249
concept creep, 24–27, 31–32, 105, 150, 205
  harassment and, 206–9
  safety and, 24–25, 27, 259
  trauma and, 25–26
  violence and, 85–86
confirmation bias, 109, 131, 258, 259
conflict resolution and disagreement skills, 191–92, 194, 211, 212, 240, 248, 258–60
Congress, 131
Consolation of Philosophy, The (Boethius), 34, 35
Constitution, U.S., 222–23
Cooper, Harris, 185, 245
correlation:
  causation and, 227–29, 231–32
  spurious, 152, 228
Coulter, Ann, 83
Crenshaw, Kimberlé Williams, 67–68, 71, 221
Crick, Nicki, 155
crime, 167, 186, 238, 266
criminal justice system, 74
critical thinking, 39, 113, 259
CYA (Cover Your Ass), 203, 211, 212

Daily Californian, 84
Dalai Lama, 267
Day of Absence, 114–15
Deaner, Robert, 225
debate clubs, 248
democracy, 66, 191–94, 222–23, 254
Democracy in America (Tocqueville), 195
Democrats, 129–31, 213, 216
  see also politics
Department of Education, 207
Department of Justice, 207
depression, 5, 12, 24, 30, 125, 126, 143, 157, 164, 250
  activities correlated with, 152–53
  anxiety and, 158

cognitive behavioral therapy and, 7–8
cognitive distortions and, 7–8, 10, 36–37, 150, 158–59, 161
first-person account of, 143–44
in girls versus boys, 149–51, 160
play deprivation and, 183
rates of, 149–50, 157–58, 160, 183, 185
safetyism and, 158
see also suicide
Depression, Great, 130
Deresiewicz, William, 189
Diagnostic and Statistical Manual of Mental Disorders (DSM), 25
dichotomous thinking, 38, 39, 50, 85, 89, 145, 177, 277
dignity culture, 209–10
disconfirm, inability to, 278
disconfirmation, institutionalized, 109, 110, 229
discounting positives, 38, 177, 277
distributive justice, 217–21, 227, 230, 231
Dolezal, Rachel, 104
Dreger, Alice, 254–55
Drexel University, 135, 202
Duckworth, Angela, 190
Duke, Annie, 248–49
Durden, Lisa, 134–35
Durkheim, Emile, 100, 102, 103, 106–8, 113–15, 120

Eady, Trent, 73
Eagleman, David, 58
Ebner, Julia, 266–67
economy, 13, 152
education:
    purpose of, 254
    see also school; universities
emotional reactivity, 95–96
emotional reasoning, 3, 4, 33–51, 119, 177, 202, 208, 212, 241, 247, 259, 278
disinvitations of speakers and, 47–51
microaggressions and, 40–46
"see something, say something" and, 203–4
subjective standards and, 25–26
Enlightenment Now (Pinker), 264
Epictetus, 33, 34, 50
equality:
    absolute, 65
    distributive justice and, 218
    fairness and, 218
equal-outcomes social justice, 223–27, 230, 231
equity theory, 218–20, 226, 227, 231
Essex County College, 134–35
Evergreen State College, 114–21, 133, 198
EverydayFeminism.com, 44

Excellent Sheep (Deresiewicz), 189
exclusion, 246–47
experience-expectant development, 182–84

fairness, 217–18, 222
    equity theory and, 218–20, 226, 227, 231
    procedural justice and, 219
    see also justice
Fall of the Faculty, The: The Rise of the All-Administrative University and Why It Matters (Ginsberg), 198
Facebook, 49, 55, 105, 107, 130, 146–47, 207, 265
fascism, 86, 89, 92
FBI, 138, 166, 261
feminism, 49, 94, 104, 105, 107, 208
filter bubble, 130–31
First Amendment, 5, 64, 82, 116, 138, 200–201, 256
forbidden base rates, 229
fortune-telling, 89, 277
Foster, Karith, 44–45, 51, 55
Foucault, Michel, 69
Foundation for Individual Rights in Education (FIRE), 5, 47, 64, 74, 94, 135, 145, 200, 202, 204, 216, 255
Fox News, 118, 133–35
fragility, 2–4, 9, 14, 19–32, 119, 170, 171, 177, 196, 202, 212, 236, 258–59
    antifragility, 22–24, 28, 31, 146, 164, 176, 178, 193, 206, 237, 246
    see also safetyism
Franklin, Benjamin, 269
Free-Range Kids movement, 164, 211, 238
free-range parenting bill, 266
free speech, 5–6, 31, 65, 84, 138, 200–203, 207, 212, 251
    Chicago Statement on Principles of Free Expression, 255–56, 268, 279–81
    First Amendment and, 5, 64, 82, 116, 138, 200–201, 256
    free speech zones, 202–3
    and responding to pressure campaigns and outrage, 256–57
    speech codes, 207, 256
Friedersdorf, Conor, 72
From #BlackLivesMatter to Black Liberation (Taylor), 135

Galileo's Middle Finger (Dreger), 254–55
Game of Thrones, 201
Gandhi, Mahatma, 98
gap year, 250–51, 257
Gastañaga, Claire Guthrie, 92
Gawker, 228
Gelman, Andrew, 213, 214
gender pronouns, 24–25

General Motors (GM), 67
Generation X, 167, 174, 184–85
Generation Z, *see* iGen
genes, 182
Ghitza, Yair, 213, 214
Gibson, William, 9–10
Gingrich, Newt, 131
Ginsberg, Benjamin, 198
good people versus evil; us versus them, 3–4,
    14, 53–77, 85, 90, 92, 119–20, 132, 177, 206,
    243–44, 247, 259–60
    see also groups
Gopnik, Alison, 21, 24
Grant, Adam, 240
Gray, Hanna Holborn, 50, 51
Gray, Peter, 183–85, 190–91, 193–94, 238
Greatest Generation, 110
Greek statues, 136–37
Green, Melanie, 159
grit, 190
Grit (Duckworth), 190
Gross, Neil, 88
groups, 44, 57–59, 68, 70–71, 76, 100, 120
    collective effervescence in, 100, 103
    minimal group paradigm, 57–58
    moral matrices and, 9, 10
    self-segregation in, 130
    solidarity in, 108–9
    tribalism and, 57–59, 76, 130, 131, 153, 267
    us versus them and good people versus evil,
        3–4, 14, 53–77, 85, 90, 92, 119–20, 132, 177,
        206, 243–44, 247, 259–60
    see also identity politics
groupthink, 73, 106, 108, 113, 131
Guinier, Lani, 222
Gulag Archipelago, The (Solzhenitsyn), ix, 243
Gunn, Tommy, 75

Haidt, Max, 19–20
Halloween costumes, 56, 102, 165
Hamid, Shadi, 42–43
Hampshire College, 135
Hannity, Sean, 132
Happiness Hypothesis, The (Haidt), 2, 35
harassment, concept creep and, 206–9
Harvard Law School, 205
Harvard University, 112, 253
Haslam, Nick, 25–26
hate crimes and speech, 86, 94, 126, 138–39
Haymarket riot, 201
Hennessy, Matthew, 49
Heterodox Academy, 248
Heyer, Heather, 91, 139
Heying, Heather, 116, 118
Higher Education Research Institute, 113
Hitler, Adolf, 63, 91

Hoffer, Eric, 99
Holder, Eric, 48
Holland, Stephen, 37
homework, 185–86, 245
honor cultures, 209
Horowitz, David, 83
Horwitz, Steven, 191–92, 211
How to Raise an Adult (Lythcott-Haims), 165
Huo, Yuen, 220
hygiene hypothesis, 21–22
Hypatia: A Journal of Feminist Philosophy,
    104–5
Hyperallergic, 136

Identity Evropa, 136
identity politics, 59–67, 76, 259
    common-enemy, 62–67, 71–73, 76, 77, 89–90,
        119–20, 244
    common-humanity, 60–62, 74–76,
        221, 244
    positive trends in, 266–67
    schools and, 244
iGen, 146–51, 174–75, 178
    anxiety and depression in, *see* anxiety;
        depression
    college and, 31, 145, 148, 156–59, 174–75, 185
    play and, 185
    politics and, 213, 214
    safetyism and, 30–31, 156, 158, 161
iGen (Twenge), 30–31, 146–49, 152–54, 159
immune system, 21–22, 164
Importance of Being Little, The (Christakis), 165
"In Defense of Transracialism" (Tuvel),
    104–7, 121
institutionalized disconfirmation, 109, 110, 229
intellectual humility, 244, 247
intellectual virtues, 247, 258
Intellectual Virtues Academy, 247–48
intent, 51, 86, 104–5
    charitability in interpreting, 42, 51, 55,
        243–44, 260
    impact versus, 43–44, 46
    microaggression theory and, 40–46, 51, 71, 77
internet, 237, 241
    see also social media
intersectionality, 67–69, 71, 76–77, 90
intimidation, 14, 81–98
intuitive justice, 217–21
    distributive, 217–21, 227, 230, 231
    procedural, 217, 219–22, 227, 230, 231
Islamist extremists, 266–67
Iyengar, Shanto, 130–32

Jacksonville State University, 202
Jandhyala, Pranav, 82
Jenner, Caitlyn, 104, 105, 205–6

Jennings, John, 82
Jensen, Mike, 205–6
Jews, 63, 90, 126
Jim Crow laws, 221
Johnson, Samuel, 269
Jones, Van, 96–98, 192, 259
judgment focus, 278
justice, 217–21, 223, 254
    distributive, 217–21, 227, 230, 231
    intuitive, 217–21
    procedural, 217, 219–22, 227, 230, 231
    see also social justice

Kabat-Zinn, Jon, 242
Kaiser, Sandra, 133
Kerr, Clark, 197
kindergarten, 185, 187–88
King, Martin Luther, Jr., 60–62, 75, 76, 98
Kipnis, Laura, 208–10
Krupenkin, Masha, 130–32
Ku Klux Klan, 12, 90, 91, 207
Kuran, Timur, 267

labeling, 38, 39, 50, 89, 145, 150, 277
LaFreniere, Peter, 181
Lagarde, Christine, 48
language development, 182
Lareau, Annette, 173–75, 179, 235
Las Vegas shooting, 12
law education, 205
Leahy, Robert, 37, 241–42
LEAP (Learning Early About Peanut Allergy),
    20–21
learned helplessness, 158
Let Grow 164, 238–39
    Licence, 238–39
Levitsky, Steven, 131
Lexington High School, 190
Lilla, Mark, 74–75
Limbaugh, Rush, 132
locus of control, 46, 70, 158
Louisiana State University (LSU), 199
Lythcott-Haims, Julie, 165, 169–70, 190

Macaulay, Thomas Babington, 265
Mac Donald, Heather, 88–89, 126
Maher, Bill, 48
Mandela, Nelson, 81, 98
Manning, Jason, 209, 210
Mao Zedong, 100–101
Marano, Hara Estroff, 170
Marcus Aurelius, 95
Marcuse, Herbert, 64–71
marriage equality, 61–62
Martínez Valdivia, Lucía, 93
Marx, Karl, 64, 254

Marxism, 64, 65
matrix, matrices, 9–10
May Day, 201
McChrystal, Stanley, 251
McElroy, Wendy, 26–28
McGinn, Lata, 37
McLaughlin and Associates, 86
McNally, Richard, 29
McNeese State University, 203
McWhorter, John, 86
media, 130–32, 137
Meng Tzu (Mencius), 19
mental health, 26, 140, 143–61, 266
    of college students, 156–59
    in girls versus boys, 149–51, 154–56,
        160, 161
    self-harming and, 151, 195–96
    and social media and phones, 146–47, 152–56,
        159–61, 265
    see also anxiety; depression
#MeToo Movement, 12, 27
microaggressions, 40–46, 51, 71, 77, 145, 205,
    210, 260
Middlebury College, 12, 87–88, 90, 103, 127
Mill, John Stuart, 248
Millennials, 30, 31, 156, 160, 175, 178, 184–85,
    188, 213
Milton, John, 34
mindfulness, 242
mind reading, 38, 41, 212, 277
Misoponos, 1–4, 14, 34, 50
moral dependency, 209–12
moral judgments, intent versus impact in,
    43–44, 46
moral matrices, 9, 10, 58
moral values, 61–62
Morgan, Kathryn Pauly, 68–69
Murray, Charles, 87–88, 103, 127
Murray, Pauli, 61, 62, 75–76, 260

Nader, Ralph, 24
National Association of Social Workers, 220
National Center for Missing & Exploited
    Children, 166, 168
Nazis and neo-Nazis, 12, 63, 64, 90–92, 133,
    139, 140
negative filtering, 38, 177, 277
negative partisanship, 131–32, 140
Neuromancer (Gibson), 9–10
New Jersey Transit, 203–4
*New Jim Crow, The: Mass Incarceration in the Age
    of Colorblindness* (Alexander), 74
New Left, 65, 67
New Republic, 6
Newsome, Hawk, 75–76
Newton, Isaac, 125

New York, 106
New Yorker, 205
New York Sun, 163
New York Times, 6, 26, 88, 92, 95, 127, 133,
    190, 226
New York University (NYU), 204–5
Nietzsche, Friedrich, 2, 22
1960s, 213–14, 216, 230
No Child Left Behind, 188
Noonday Demon, The: An Atlas of Depression
    (Solomon), 143
Northern Michigan University, 200, 211
Northwestern University, 208
Notre Dame vs. the Klan: How the Fighting Irish
    Defeated the Ku Klux Klan (Tucker), 207
NW Anxiety Institute, 163

Oakton Community College, 201
Obama, Barack, 11, 96, 140, 214
Obama, Malia, 250
Oberlin College, 24–25
Occupy Wall Street, 129
Oliver, Kelly, 106–7
Olivia (Claremont student), 53–55, 175
Once and Future Liberal, The: After Identity
    Politics (Lilla), 74–75
On Liberty (Mill), 248
oppression, 6, 44, 46, 57, 64, 65, 68–71
Orlando nightclub shooting, 12
Ostrom, Elinor, 191
Ostrom, Vincent, 191, 192
Our Kids: The American Dream in Crisis
    (Putnam), 173–76
overgeneralizing, 38, 39, 50, 277
overprotection, 13
    in parenting, 126, 148, 164, 165, 167–72, 183,
        201–2, 235, 236, 266
    see also fragility; parenting; safetyism
overreaction, 201, 203
overregulation, 201–3

parenting, 125, 126, 163–79, 192
    and actual versus imagined risk,
        167–68
    and arrest for neglect, 171–72, 266
    and assuming capability in children, 237
    and child's walking to places alone, 169–70,
        237–39
    cognitive distortions and, 177–78
    concerted cultivation style of, 173, 174, 176,
        179, 235–36
    free-range, 164, 211, 238, 266, 268
    Let Grow License and, 238–39
    natural growth style of, 174, 179
    overprotective (helicopter), 126, 148, 164, 165,
        167–72, 183, 201–2, 235, 236, 266

prepare the child for the road, not the road for
    the child, 23, 237–40
    risk taking and, 238
    school policies and, 245–49
    social class and, 173–76, 179
    societal pressures and, 171
    suggestions for, 235–51
Parker, Sean, 147
Paros, Mike, 118
Patz, Etan, 165, 166
Paxson, Christina, 27
"Paying the Price for Breakdown of the Country's
    Bourgeois Culture" (Wax and Alexander),
    107–8, 121
peanut allergies, 19–21, 23–24, 30, 164,
    236, 237
Peck, Don, 10
personalizing, 277
Pew Research Center, 128
phones, 30, 146, 147, 152–54, 159–61, 194, 214
    and limiting device time, 249–50
    school and, 247
    see also social media
Pinker, Steven, 264, 265
play, 125, 126, 178, 181–94
    brain and, 181–84, 193
    free, 183–86, 188, 189, 191, 193–94, 235–37,
        245–46, 266
    importance of, 181–83, 193–94
    outdoor, 184, 186, 266
    playgrounds, 183, 238
    risk and, 183–85, 236, 238, 246
polarization, 121, 125–41, 251, 265
    affective, 129, 131–32, 141
    outrage and, 133–38, 261
police, attitudes toward, 219–20
political correctness, 46, 94–95, 202
Political Tribes: Group Instinct and the Fate of
    Nations (Chua), 267
politics, 213–14
    alt-right, 81, 84, 118, 139, 266
    bipartisanship in, 131
    birth year and, 213–14
    filter bubble and, 130–31
    left-wing, 5, 110–13, 126–27, 132–38, 141, 199
    negative partisanship in, 131–32
    from 1940s to 1980, 130
    right-wing, 5, 63, 110–13, 118, 126, 127,
        132–38, 141
    universities and, 110–13, 121, 126–27, 132–38,
        141, 199, 258
    see also polarization
Pomona College, 89–90
positives, discounting, 38, 177, 277
post-traumatic stress disorder (PTSD), 25,
    28–29

power, 53, 66
    intersectionality and, 68
prejudice, 25, 40–44, 46
    see also racism
Princeton Review, 189
principle of charity, 42, 51, 55, 243–44, 260
privilege, 68–71
problems of progress, 13–14, 170, 264
procedural justice, 217, 219–22, 227, 230, 231
professors:
    political perspectives of, 110–13,
        121, 258
    retraction demands and, 103–4, 107–8, 121
    social media and, 137, 141, 201
    trust between students and, 205–6, 212
    viewpoint solidarity and diversity among,
        108–13, 121, 258
proportionality, 217–19, 224, 227
proportional-procedural social justice,
    220–23, 231
Putnam, Robert, 173–76, 236

racism, 6, 42, 44–45, 64, 71, 140
    civil rights movement and, 60–61
    Halloween costumes and, 56,
        102, 165
    intimidation and threats, 138–40
    Jim Crow laws, 221
    white supremacists, 12, 86, 87, 89–91, 94
Rage, The: The Vicious Circle of Islamist and Far
    Right Extremism (Ebner), 266–67
rape culture, 26–28
rape law, teaching of, 205
Rational Optimist, The (Ridley), 264–65
Rauch, Jonathan, 59, 267
Rawls, John, 213
Redelsheimer, Katrina, 82
Reed College, 93, 127
regret orientation, 278
religion:
    American civil, 60–61
    rituals in, 100
Renaissance, 136
"Repressive Tolerance" (Marcuse),
    65–67
Republicans, 129–31, 213, 216
    see also politics
rider-and-elephant metaphor, 35, 36, 51, 62
Ridley, Matt, 264–65
Righteous Mind, The: Why Good People Are
    Divided by Politics and Religion (Haidt), 9
Right on Crime, 74
Rise of the Warrior Cop: The Militarization of
    America's Police Forces (Balko), 74
risk, 185, 237
    actual versus imagined, 167–68

play and, 183–85, 236, 238, 246
    see also safety
rituals, 100
Roberts, John, 192–93
Roman statues, 136–37
Roof, Dylann, 139
Roosevelt, Franklin D., 74

Sacks, Jonathan, 53, 64
safety, 6–7, 9, 14, 24–25, 29–30, 96, 148
    and actual versus imagined risk, 167–68
    crime and, 167, 186, 238, 266
    improvements in child safety, 168–69
    meaning of, and concept creep, 24–25, 27,
        246–47, 259
    threats and, 138–40, 260–61
safetyism, 29–30, 85, 104, 121, 125, 164, 165, 194,
    203, 246–47
    on campus, 12, 24–26, 96–97, 125, 145–46, 148,
        195–212, 268
    cognitive distortions and, 177–78
    dangers of, 168–71
    exclusion and, 246–47
    iGen and, 30–31, 156, 158, 161
    overprotective parenting, 126, 148, 164, 165,
        167–72
    rise of, 24–26, 121
    safe spaces, 26–31, 96, 145, 210, 259
    school and, 236
    trigger warnings, 6–7, 24, 28, 29, 31,
        145, 210
Salem witch hunts, 99–100
San Bernardino attack, 12
Sanders, Bernie, 213
Savio, Mario, 84
schemas, 36–38, 57, 150, 177
Schill, Michael, 92
school (K–12), 59, 185–89, 194
    college admissions and, 189–91, 194, 235, 236,
        257–58, 268
    debate teaching in, 248
    discussions on coursework in, 248
    first-grade readiness checklists, 186–87, 238
    grades in, 190
    homework, 185–86, 245
    ideas for elementary schools, 245–47
    ideas for middle schools and high schools,
        247–49
    identity politics and, 244
    influencing policies at, 245–49
    kindergarten, 185, 187–88
    phones at, 247
    recess at, 245–47
    safetyism and, 236
    year of service or work between high school
        and college, 250–51, 257

Schulz, Kathryn, 244
"see something, say something," 203–4
Seligman, Martin, 158
September 11, 2001, attacks, 200, 203
Service Year Alliance, 251
sexism, 6, 44, 71
sexual misconduct and assault, 27
  law education and, 205
  #MeToo Movement and, 12, 27
Shakespeare, William, 34
Shapiro, Ben, 83
Sheskin, Mark, 218
shoulds, 277
Shuchman, Daniel, 238
Shulevitz, Judith, 26–28
Silverglate, Harvey, 74
Simmons, Ruth, 259
Singal, Jesse, 106
Skenazy, Lenore, 163–65, 169, 171, 172, 177, 185,
    211, 238
sleep, 250
smartphones, see phones
Smith College, 72
snowballs, and danger, 236
social class:
  parenting and, 173–76, 179
  universities and, 174, 176
social justice, 111, 125, 126, 213–32
  and correlation as causation, 227–29, 231–32
  definition and use of term, 217, 220–21, 223
  equal-outcomes, 223–27, 230, 231
  major news stories related to, 214–16
  proportional-procedural, 220–23, 231
social media, 5, 10, 30, 130, 133, 139, 145, 194,
    203, 259
  call-out culture and, 71–73
  curation and comparisons in, 154–55, 161
  Facebook, 49, 55, 105, 107, 130, 146–47,
    207, 265
  impact on girls, 154–56
  and limiting device time, 249–50
  mental health and, 146–47, 152–56,
    159–61, 265
  positive trends in, 265–66
  professors and, 137, 141, 201
  Twitter, 81, 130, 135–37, 147, 265
  virtue signaling and, 73
Socrates, 49, 50
Solomon, Andrew, 143
Solzhenitsyn, Aleksandr, ix, 243
Soviet Union, 130, 243
Spellman, Mary, 54–55, 57, 71, 102–3, 105–6, 134
Spencer, Richard, 139
Spock, Benjamin, 174
sports, 152, 189, 225–26
  Title IX and, 224–25

spurious correlations, 152, 228
Stalin, Joseph, 243
Stanger, Allison, 87–88, 103, 127, 140
Starmans, Christina, 218
statues, Greco-Roman, 136–37
"sticks and stones" saying, 210
Stoicism, 95–96, 98
Stone, Geoffrey, 255, 279
Student Nonviolent Coordinating Committee, 84
Sue, Derald Wing, 40–42
suicide, 5, 24, 30, 143–44, 152
  academic competition and, 190
  rates of, 150–51, 160, 183, 190
  sharing thoughts of, 195–96
Suk Gersen, Jeannie, 205
summer camps, 240
Supreme Court, 61

Tajfel, Henri, 57–58, 76
Taleb, Nassim Nicholas, 22–23, 28, 164, 170
Tannen, Deborah, 154
Taylor, Keeanga-Yamahtta, 135–36
Tea Party, 129
telos, 253–55
Tenbrink, Tyler, 139
terrorism, 11–12, 204
  September 11, 2001, attacks, 200, 203
Tetlock, Phil, 229
Texas State University, 63–64, 67
Theodoric, 34
Theory of Justice, A (Rawls), 213
Thinking in Bets: Making Smarter Decisions
    When You Don't Have All the Facts (Duke),
    248–49
threats, 138–40, 260–61
Three Felonies a Day: How the Feds Target the
    Innocent (Silverglate), 74
Thucydides, 108–9
Title IX, 206–8, 223–25
Tocqueville, Alexis de, 191, 195
tolerance, 65–66
transgenderism, 104–5, 205–6
transracialism, 104
trauma, 25–26, 28–29, 31–32, 33
  PTSD, 25, 28–29
Treatment Plans and Interventions for Depression
    and Anxiety Disorders (Leahy, Holland, and
    McGinn), 37
tribalism, 57–59, 76, 130, 131, 153, 267
  see also groups
trigger warnings, 6–7, 24, 28, 29, 31, 145, 210
Trump, Donald, 12, 82–83, 87, 96, 112, 114, 127,
    135, 139, 140
  Charlottesville and, 91, 94
  supporters of, 75–76, 81, 83
truth, 253–55, 268

Tucker Carlson Tonight, 118, 133, 134
Turning Point USA (TPUSA), 138
Tuvel, Rebecca, 104–7, 121, 127
Twenge, Jean, 30–31, 146–49, 152–54, 159, 160, 164, 185
Twitter, 81, 130, 135–37, 147, 265
Tyler, Tom, 219–20
Tyranny of the Majority, The (Guinier), 222

UCLA, 92
Unequal Childhoods: Class, Race, and Family Life (Lareau), 173–75
unfair comparisons, 278
universities, 5, 8, 10, 11, 59, 125–26, 214
  admissions to, 189–91, 194, 235, 236, 257–58, 268
  amenities at, 199, 211
  bureaucracy at, 125, 126, 192, 194, 195–212
  canon wars at, 7
  Chicago Statement and, 255–56, 268, 279–81
  consumerist mentality at, 198–200, 211
  corporatization of, 197–98, 211
  cross-partisan events at, 261
  distorted thinking modeled by administrators at, 200–203
  diversity among professors in, 108–13, 121, 258
  diversity among students in, 43, 258, 260
  expansion of, 197–98
  freedom of inquiry at, 255–57
  free speech at, 5–6, 31, 65, 84, 200–203
  heckler's veto and, 257
  iGen and, 31, 145, 148, 156–59, 174–75, 185
  intellectual virtues and, 258
  intimidation and violence at, 81–98
  mental health and, 156–59
  as multiversities, 197, 253
  political orientation and, 110–13, 121, 126–27, 132–38, 141, 199, 258
  preparation for life following, 8–9
  productive disagreement in, 258–60
  regulations at, 192, 200–203, 211–12
  and responding to pressure campaigns and outrage, 256–57
  retraction demands at, 103–4, 107–8, 121
  safe spaces and, 26–31, 96, 145, 210, 259
  safetyism at, 12, 24–26, 96–97, 125, 145–46, 148, 195–212, 268; *see also* safetyism
  school spirit at, 260
  social class and, 174, 176
  speakers at, 6, 27, 47–51, 87, 199
  suggestions for, 253–62
  trigger warnings and, 6–7, 24, 28, 29, 31, 145, 210
  trust between professors and students at, 205–6, 212

  truth and, 253–55, 268
  wisdom and, 253–62
University of California, 197
  Berkeley, 12, 81–87, 90, 94, 120
  Los Angeles, 92
University of Central Florida, 207
University of Chicago, 119, 251, 253, 268
  Chicago Statement on Principles of Free Expression, 255–56, 268, 279–81
University of Cincinnati, 203
University of Connecticut, 202
University of Iowa, 136–37
University of Michigan, 184, 207
University of Missouri, 11
University of Northern Colorado, 205–6
University of Oregon, 92
University of Pennsylvania, 107, 108
University of Virginia, 12, 188, 223–27
University of West Alabama, 202
Unsafe at Any Speed (Nader), 24
us versus them; good people versus evil, 3–4, 14, 53–77, 85, 90, 92, 119–20, 132, 177, 206, 243–44, 247, 259–60
  see also groups

vaccination, 21
Valenti, Jessica, 26–27
Venker, Suzanne, 49
victimhood culture, 209–10
victimization, 41–42, 46, 57, 126
viewpoint diversity, 11, 109, 112–13, 121, 248, 258
vindictive protectiveness, 10, 235
violence, 81–98
  definition of, 85–86
  words as, 84–86, 89, 94–98, 145, 158
Virginia Rowing Association, 223
virtue signaling, 73
vulnerability, culture of, 209, 210
  see also fragility

Wall Street Journal, 222
Walsh, Adam, 165–66
Walsh, John, 166
Ward, Douglas Turner, 114
War on Cops, The (Mac Donald), 88
Washington Post, 93, 199
Wax, Amy, 107–8, 121, 126
Weinstein, Bret, 114–19, 127, 133
"what if" questions, 278
Where You Go Is Not Who You Will Be: An Antidote to the College Admissions Mania (Bruni), 190
white genocide, 135, 136
white nationalists and white supremacists, 12, 86, 87, 89–91, 94, 135, 136, 139, 140, 266
Will, George, 48

William & Mary, 92
Williams College, 49–50
Wilson, E. O., 7
wisdom, 1–15
  children and, 235–51
  societies and, 263–69
  universities and, 253–62
witch hunts, 99–121
  crimes against collective in, 101, 119
  fear of defending the accused in, 102, 106–7, 119
  four properties of, 101–2, 119, 120
  retraction demands and, 103–4, 107–8, 121
  in Salem, 99–100
  as sudden outbursts, 110, 119
  trivial or fabricated charges in, 102, 106, 119

Wood, Zachary, 49, 50
words:
  choice of, 54–55, 102–3, 105–6
  as violence, 84–86, 89, 94–98, 145, 158
World War II, 57, 92, 110, 130

Yale University, 11, 55–57, 61, 102, 120, 165, 189, 253
Yiannopoulos, Milo, 48, 50, 81–85, 95, 97, 120
YouTube, 55, 130

Ziblatt, Daniel, 131
Zimmer, Robert, 251